MASS POLITICS AND CULTURE IN DEMOCRATIZING KOREA

How has Korea achieved one of the most successful transitions to democracy during the past decade? This pioneering book offers a dynamic and global account of Korea's place in the current third wave of democratization. Drawing on a unique sample of six national sample surveys conducted in Korea since 1988, the book carefully examines the evolution, contours and consequences of Korean democratization from the perspective of Korean people themselves and their experiences throughout the entire course of democratic change. Richly comparative, the book considers emerging democracies in East Asia, and in Europe and Latin America, in light of the Korean experience. Notably, it presents non-Western alternatives to institutional and cultural democratization, characterizing and distinguishing Korea as a non-Western and Confucian model of democratization.

Doh C. Shin is Professor of Political Science at the University of Illinois at Springfield. He has taught widely in the United States and Korea in the areas of comparative politics, and Asian culture and politics. He is the co-author of *Korean Democracy and its Future* (1990); *Korea in the Global Wave of Democratization* (1994); *The Cultural Dynamics of Democratization in Spain* (1998); *and Institutional Reform and Democratic Consolidation in Korea* (1999).

CAMBRIDGE ASIA-PACIFIC STUDIES

Cambridge Asia-Pacific Studies aims to provide a focus and forum for scholarly work on the Asia-Pacific region as a whole, and its component sub-regions, namely Northeast Asia, Southeast Asia and the Pacific Islands. The series is produced in association with the Research School of Pacific and Asian Studies at the Australian National University and the Australian Institute of International Affairs.

Editor: John Ravenhill

Editorial Board: James Cotton, Donald Denoon, Mark Elvin, David Goodman, Stephen Henningham, Hal Hill, David Lim, Ron May, Anthony Milner, Tessa Morris-Suzuki

MASS POLITICS AND CULTURE IN DEMOCRATIZING KOREA

DOH C. SHIN
University of Illinois, Springfield

CAMBRIDGE
UNIVERSITY PRESS

PUBLISHED BY THE PRESS SYNDICATE OF THE UNIVERSITY OF CAMBRIDGE
The Pitt Building, Trumpington Street, Cambridge, United Kingdom

CAMBRIDGE UNIVERSITY PRESS
The Edinburgh Building, Cambridge CB2 2RU, UK   http://www.cup.cam.ac.uk
40 West 20th Street, New York, NY 10011–4211, USA   http://www.cup.org
10 Stamford Road, Oakleigh, Melbourne 3166, Australia

First published 1999

Printed in Singapore by Kin Keong Printing Co.

Typeface New Baskerville (Adobe) 10/12pt. System QuarkXPress® [PH]

A catalogue record for this book is available from the British Library

National Library of Australia Cataloguing in Publication data

Shin, To-chŏl.
Mass politics and culture in democratizing Korea.

Bibliography.
Includes index.
ISBN 0 521 65146 8.
ISBN 0 521 65823 3 (pbk.)

1. Democracy – Korea (South). 2. Democracy. 3. Korea
(South) – Politics and government – 1988– . 4. Korea
(South) – Civilization. I. Title. (Series: Cambridge
Asia-Pacific studies).

320.95195

Library of Congress Cataloging-in-Publication Data

Shin, To-chŏl.
Mass politics and culture in democratizing Korea.
p. cm. – (Cambridge Asia–Pacific studies)
Includes bibliographical references and index.
ISBN 0 521 65146 8 (alk. paper).– ISBN 0 521 65823 3 (alk.
paper)
1. Democracy – Korea (South) 2. Democratization – Korea (South)
3. Korea (South) – Politics and government – 1988– I. Title.
II. Series
JQ1729. A15S55   1999
320.95195 – dc21   98-49357

ISBN 0 521 65146 8 hardback
ISBN 0 521 67823 3 paperback

Contents

Part II Average Citizens

Part III Representative Institutions

List of Figures and Tables

Figures

Tables

Acknowledgments

A study that tries to monitor and compare the cultural and institutional dynamics of democratization is, by nature, a collaborative enterprise requiring a great deal of hard work and generous support from many institutions and people in many different countries. This particular study of Korean democratization was undertaken in 1988 when the Republic of Korea formally began its transition to democracy. The study was completed in 1998 when Korea became the first new democracy in Asia where the leader of an opposition party assumed the presidency through the electoral process. Over these ten years, I have benefited greatly from the financial support of a large number of organizations, and the advice, encouragement, and professional assistance of many people here in the United States and elsewhere.

Institutionally, private and public organizations in the United States, Korea, Great Britain, and Japan provided financial support for the administration of six national sample surveys in Korea. The Asia Foundation, the Aspen Institute, the British Social and Economic Research Council, Foundation for the Advanced Study of International Development, the Korea Foundation, the Korea Legislative Development Institute, the National Science Foundation, and the Social Science Research Council provided the funding of one or more of these costly national surveys. The Seoul National University Institute of Social Sciences and Gallup-Korea undertook the necessary fieldwork for these surveys. The Institute for Public Affairs and the Illinois Legislative Studies Center at the University of Illinois at Springfield granted me release time from my teaching obligations and provided for the other necessary resources for the analysis of these surveys and the preparation of the manuscript itself. Final work on the book was facilitated by the invitation to be Visiting Professor at the Korea Advanced Institute of

Science and Technology in Taejon, Korea. I would like to thank each of these institutions for their special contribution which made this book possible.

Intellectually, many scholars in several different countries helped me to expand my own horizons with their ideas, develop further my own ideas, and graciously permitted me to compare my survey findings with theirs. Chey Myung and Kim Kwang Woong of Seoul National University warmly welcomed me to their institution on two occasions and helped me, both intellectually and financially, to initiate and pursue an ongoing survey research project in Korea. Years of close collaboration with Kim Kwang Woong enriched my work especially in Chapters 5 and 7. Peter McDonough of Arizona State University initiated me into the study of Korean democratization in a comparative perspective and co-authored Chapter 8 of this volume. Jack Van Der Slik of the University of Illinois at Springfield unceasingly encouraged and helped me to work on the manuscript and co-authored Chapter 5 of the book. Richard Rose of the Center for the Study of Public Policy at the University of Strathclyde initiated me into the arts and sciences of collaborative survey research and directly helped me to design and analyze the 1997 Korean survey which subsequently led to a comparison of the data thus obtained with similar data culled from Central and Eastern Europe. Samuel Barnes of Georgetown University kindly translated Spanish-language question- naires which permitted my use of the data obtained from his surveys which had been conducted in Spain. Larry Diamond of Stanford University helped me to situate my study of Korean democratization in a global context. More than anyone else, it was Conrad Rutkowski of the Institute for Applied Phenomenology who carefully read and re-read all the different versions of the entire manuscript for years and contributed a great deal to the improvement of its overall quality.

Special thanks go to the three scholars who reviewed the manuscript for Cambridge University Press. They are: Bruce Cumings of the University of Chicago, James Cotton of the Australian Defence Force Academy, University of New South Wales, and Sunhyuk Kim of the University of Southern California. These three reviewers corrected numerous factual and other oversights, and provided helpful sug- gestions for the expansion and timely revision of the manuscript particularly in view of the economic and political changes that have recently taken place in Korea.

In writing this book, I have drawn on the survey research that a number of my colleagues conducted in other countries. I am delighted to name these colleagues here. They are: Laszlo Bruszt and Janos Simon, Russell Dalton, Dieter Fuchs, Giovanna Guidorossi, and Palle Svensson, Geoffrey Evans and Stephen Whitefield, James Gibson and Raymond

Duch, Han Bae Ho and Auh Soo Young, Max Kaase, Marta Lagos, Peter McDonough, Samuel Barnes, and Antonio Lopez Pina, Mary McIntosh and Martha Abele, Arthur Miller, William Reisinger, and Vicki Hesli, Leonardo Morlino and Jose Montero, Park Dong Suh and Kim Kwang Woong, Richard Rose, William Mishler, and Christian Haerpfer, Shin Myungsoon, Shyu Huoyan, Sidney Verba, Kay Schlozman, and Henry Brady, and Frederick Weil. Findings from their national and cross-national surveys made it possible to identify and examine Korea's place in the current wave of global democratization.

In several places in the book, I have drawn on two previous articles published in *Korea Journal* and *Democratization*, and the papers presented at a number of international conferences and professional meetings. These include the international conferences on democratization organized by the Japanese Political Science Association, the University of Sao Paulo, and Seoul National University, and the meetings of the American Politican Science Association, the International Political Science Association, the International Society of Political Psychology, the International Sociological Association, the Korean Association of International Studies, the Korean Political Science Association, and the Midwest Political Science Association.

Professionally, this book owes a great deal to the gracious and kind assistance of many individuals affiliated with various educational and research institutions. Park Moo Ik and Na Sun Mee of Gallup-Korea, offered very generous support for the conduct of the last three surveys reported in the book. At the University of Illinois, Karen Wyett helped me to prepare earlier versions of the manuscript and Brenda Suhling worked tirelessly for months to prepare more than 100 tables and figures reported in the book. Barbara Ferrara and Rob Raleigh were of invaluable assistance through all phases of this study, managing research grants from various sources. At Harvard–Yenching Library, Yoon Choong Nam assembled all the necessary materials for the interpretation of survey data. At Cambridge University Press, Phillipa McGuinness as its senior commissioning editor and John Ravenhill as its series editor were most generous in their praise of the manuscript and offered contract terms that were most agreeable. Paul Watt copy-edited the final manuscript carefully, promptly, and thoughtfully. Ray Kitson proved to be a tireless and vigilant proofreader. Alan Walker made his painstaking efforts in compiling the index to this volume. To all these professionals, I would like to express my profound gratitude.

And I am greatly indebted to my loving wife, Haelim, who has never failed to support my academic life and be there when I was in need. Dedicating this book to her, I hope and pray that she will continue to tolerate me for another five years so that I can complete another major book on the Korean economic crisis. Sueme and Eugene, my two children with inquisitive minds, I am sure, will continue to wonder why their father, unlike many other scholars, had to spend ten years on this book.

Note on Names, and Figures and Tables

In the text and notes, this book has followed both custom and tradition in the usage of personal names. In the case of Korean and Chinese names, family or surnames are presented first followed by their representive given names. In the case of American and European names, the order is reversed; given names are presented first followed by family or surnames. In the references, however, all the names mentioned, whether Asian or non-Asian, are presented exactly in the same order: the surname of every sole or first author is presented first and separated by a comma from his or her given name. In the case of other authors, given names are presented first followed by family or surnames.

This book contains an unusually large number of charts and tables. They were prepared especially for those citizens, community leaders, and public officials who are directly involved in the process of democratic reform with little or unavailing exposure to the scholarly literature on democratization. The charts and tables are also intended to provide benchmark data against which measurements and comparisons of democratic developments in Korea and other Asian democracies can be undertaken.

For permission to use quotations at the beginning of various chapters I would like to thank Cambridge University Press, Chatham House (for Giovanni Sartori), William C. Crotty, Bruce Cumings, Harry Eckstein, Sanford Lakoff, Juan J. Linz and Alfred Stepan, Seymour Martin Lipset, William Mishler, *New York Times*, Richard Rose, and Sidney Verba.

Every effort has been made to obtain permission to use copyright material reproduced in this book. The publishers would be pleased to hear from copyright holders they have not been able to contact.

N

Pyongyang

NORTH
KOREA

SOUTH
KOREA

KWANGWON DO

SEOUL

Inchon

KYONGGI DO

CHOONGCHUNG
PUKDO

CHOONGCHUNG
NAMDO

Taejon

KYONGSANG
PUKDO

Yellow
Sea

Chonju

Taegu

CHOLLA
PUKDO

KYONGSANG
NAMDO

Kwangju

Pusan

CHOLLA
NAMDO

0   50   100 km

Major cities and provinces in South Korea

Preface

"Today's inauguration of President Kim Dae Jung marks an
advance for South Korean democracy and a new chance for
reconciliation on the Korean Peninsula. It also starts a
widely watched test of whether economic openness and
political accountability can cure East Asia's financial ills."

New York Times, February 25, 1998: A22

"South Korea has made huge strides toward establishing a
democratic culture . . . When a nascent democracy, and
Asian power, makes the transfer of civil authority in this
manner, the people of the US and Western Europe should
take note."

Wall Street Journal, December 22, 1992: A12

As recently as a few years ago, the Republic of Korea (hereafter Korea)
was known merely as "an economically advanced but politically backward
nation" (Chu, Fu & Moon 1997: 277). For nearly three decades
(1961–88), without interruption, the military ruled the country with
iron-clad control over its political institutions as well as civil society in
general. Under the pretense of protecting the nation from communist
forces in the North and securing national prosperity, military leaders
prohibited all types of organizations as well as individual citizens from
engaging in any activities that challenged their repressive rule.[1] The
National Assembly and the courts were also forced to serve as institutional tools that merely approved and supported the policies formulated
in the executive branch, which was controlled by the military. As a result,
neither an independent judiciary nor an independent press existed.
Daily newspapers and other news media, for example, had to publish the
same stories by following the formal guidelines issued by government
security agencies.

Since the collapse of military rule in 1988, however, Korea has rapidly
become a politically new state. Over a relatively short period of time, the
country has successfully carried out a series of sweeping democratic
reforms (Seoul National University Institute of Social Development
1996; see also Kihl 1995; M. Kil 1994; Y. Lee 1997; Paik 1995). These
reforms have expanded civil liberties and political rights by downsizing
and overhauling the various security agencies, which meddled in every
important decision of both government and private organizations and
controlled the behavior of private citizens.[2] The reforms have also firmly

xxii

established civilian control over the military by purging military generals and disbanding secret societies within the military establishment (Moon & Kang 1995; Steinberg 1996).

Indeed, Korea has been more successful than many of its democratizing predecessors and contemporaries in transforming its authoritarian political institutions and culture (Diamond 1996; H. B. Im 1996). The country has also become the first new democracy in Asia that peacefully transferred power to an opposition party. Therefore, in the Western media and scholarly community today, Korea is mentioned increasingly as a possible model of democratization for the emerging post-authoritarian countries in the world (Gibney 1992; International Forum for Democratic Studies et al. 1996; *New York Times* 1992; Sigur 1993; *Wall Street Journal* 1992).

Nonetheless, Korea's remarkable success in democratization still remains largely unexplored using the theories and methods of comparative political inquiry. Unlike its counterparts in Europe and Latin America, Korea has received little attention in the large body of theoretical and empirical literature that is concerned with the world's current wave of democratization (Gunther, Diamandouros & Puhle 1995; Hadenius 1992, 1997; Higley & Gunther 1992; Linz & Stepan 1996a; Przeworski 1991; Rueschemeyer, Stephens & Stephens 1992). In all of this literature, not a single volume can be found to offer a comprehensive and balanced account of the Korean example, which "challenges directly the notion that Confucian societies don't really want democracy" (*Wall Street Journal* 1992) and offers "an East Asian model of prosperity and democracy" (*New York Times* 1995).

In the recent literature on Korean development, however, a limited number of individual volumes are currently available in English on the democratization of Korean politics and culture since 1988 when the democratic Sixth Republic of democratic Korea was founded (Bedeski 1994; S. Choi 1997; Clarke 1988; Cotton 1993, 1994, 1995a; Cumings 1997; Diamond, Henriksen & Shin 1999; Diamond & Kim 1998; Korean Political Science Association 1995; M. Lee 1990; Pae 1992; MacDonald 1990; Moon & Mo 1998; Shin, Zho & Chey 1994; Sigur 1993, 1994; Wells 1995; S. Yang, 1995).[3] Most of these case studies are edited volumes of articles written by individual scholars. Without exception, they are devoted to thick descriptions of the institutional and procedural aspects of democratic change. As a result, very little is known about the shifting role that the Korean mass public has played in the democratization process.[4] Much less has been learned about how the changing patterns of their attachment to, and involvement in, the process compare with what has been observed in other new and old democracies.

The Approaches of the Study

This book seeks to define and distinguish the Korean model of democratization in terms of what the Korean people themselves have actually experienced during the course of change. *Culturally*, the study examines how and why Koreans have oriented and reoriented themselves away from authoritarianism and toward democratic politics as well as to what extent they have engaged in the democratic process since the founding of the Sixth Republic of democratic Korea in 1988. *Structurally*, this book investigates how significant progress has been achieved in democratizing the various elements of the military dictatorship and its authoritarian political procedures. *Substantively*, it assesses how democratic reforms have affected the performance of principal representative institutions and the quality of life that the Korean people experience. *Methodologically*, this book unravels the direction and trajectories of institutional and cultural democratization through systematic analyses of their perceptions of those changes since 1988 when Korea began its transition to democracy.

Five perspectives – three conceptual, one theoretical, and one methodological – are central to this comparative inquiry investigating the cultural, structural, and substantive dynamics of Korean democratization. First, this study rejects what has been called "procedural minimum" definitions of democracy (Collier & Levitsky 1997: 434). In the tradition of Schumpeter (1976), Dahl (1971) and Huntington (1989), considerable efforts have been made recently by leading scholars to standardize the use of the term *democracy* by confining its defining attributes primarily to the electoral domain of political life (Diamond, Linz & Lipset 1990; Di Palma 1990a; O'Donnell & Schmitter 1986; Rose & Mishler 1996). As a result, there is a growing tendency among political scientists and development planners to equate democracy with the mass public's free, fair, and competitive elections of political leadership on a regular basis.

In the minds of ordinary citizens in new democracies, however, democracy is not equated merely with the political procedures featuring the periodic participation of the mass public in fully contested elections; this will be discussed in Chapter 2. Conceptually, for the masses who have suffered a great deal of political oppression, injustice, and poverty for all or most of their lives, democracy symbolizes much more than the abolition of repressive political institutions and the replacement of authoritarian political leaders (J. Choi 1993a; Drakulic 1993; Hahm & Rhyu 1997). Democracy represents opportunities and resources for a better quality of human life for "it never systematically adopts a line of conduct hostile to the majority" (de Tocqueville 1956: 101). It also represents "a more equitable and humane society" (Macpherson 1977: 94). As Hahm & Rhyu (1997: 48) aptly sum up, democracy is "an interacting, all encompassing system that is bigger than any one regime." In other words, democratization is a movement that enhances the human lot and constitutes a process of transformation taking place at the levels of individual citizens, political institutions, and the political regime itself. Therefore, all the significant changes taking place at the macro as well as micro levels are considered in this study to offer a comprehensive and balanced account of democratization.

Further, in this study democracy is not considered merely as a dichotomous phenomenon; instead, it is viewed as a continuum of variation (Bollen 1993; Diamond 1996; Vanhanen 1997). Seen as a movement toward democracy and away from non-democratic rule, democratization is viewed as a dynamic historical process consisting of several analytically distinct, but empirically overlapping, stages. In the logic of causal sequence, these stages may run from the decay and disintegration of authoritarian rule or totalitarianism through the emergence of a new democracy to consolidation of the democratic regime (Huntington 1991: chap. 3; Karl & Schmitter 1994: 52–4; O'Donnell & Schmitter 1986: 8–9; see also Rose & Shin 1997; D. Shin 1994). In reality, however, democratization has often failed to proceed sequentially, and as Diamond (1992) aptly sums up, some democracies abort as soon as they emerge while others erode as much as they consolidate. In short, democratization does not proceed in a smooth, linear fashion; it is often subject to a series of crises and reversals. The end product is not always a full or stable democracy (Munck 1994; Schmitter 1994).

As a country in the current wave of democratization, Korea has successfully completed the first two stages of democratization and is in the midst of the third and most difficult consolidation phase (Diamond, Henriksen and Shin 1999; Diamond & Kim 1998; H. B. Im 1996; B. Kim 1996; Steinberg 1996). During consolidation, new democracies, like the one in Korea, face more challenging tasks than they did during the earlier phases (Huntington 1996b; Schmitter 1995b; Schmitter & Santiso 1998). The earlier transition phase, for example, dealt with a well-defined series of tasks, such as the overthrow of an authoritarian regime, the passage of a new democratic constitution, and the installation of a new government through a free and fair election. In sharp contrast, the consolidation phase is confronted with a multitude of urgent challenges and problems, most of which cannot even be defined clearly (Linz & Stepan 1996b; O'Donnell 1996). Economic crises, "perverse" institutions, political corruption, and punishment of authoritarian crimes are among some of those problems.

Unlike the earlier stages in which the masses were neither greatly involved nor their attitudes directly relevant (Di Palma 1990a: 144–52; Przeworski 1991: 50–53), democratic consolidation involves a multitude of new and inexperienced political actors trying to secure their share of benefits from the new regime (Mo 1996; Tarrow 1994; Whitehead 1989). Therefore, consolidation cannot be achieved only by those elites who are "superficially" or "expediently" committed to democracy. For a transitional democracy to become a consolidated democracy, citizens must be convinced of the virtues of democracy and play active roles in the process (Diamond 1994a; Gibson, Duch & Tedin 1992; Rose & Mishler 1996; Sorensen 1993). "Without public involvement in the process, democracy lacks both its legitimacy and its guiding force" (Dalton 1998: 4). In other words, there can be no consolidated democracy without democrats both at the top and at the bottom of the ladder (Hermet 1991: 250).

There are several specific reasons why a new democracy becomes fully consolidated when ordinary citizens embrace it to the fullest extent. Democracy is government by *demos* (the people) and, thus, cannot be foisted upon the unwilling for any extended period of time. Among ordinary citizens, those who stop viewing democracy as the best form of government are likely to embrace anti-democratic movements and overthrow a newly installed democratic regime, especially during a serious crisis. When citizens begin to question the legitimacy of their regime, they should be unwilling to oppose any regression to authoritarian rule so that their incipient democratic regime weathers economic crises and other policy failures (Dalton 1997: 5; Inglehart 1990: 24). When they confer legitimacy on the regime, it can govern effectively by making decisions and committing resources without resort to coercion (Dalton 1996: 370; Mishler & Rose 1997: 2). When those citizens participate actively in the democratic political process, however, political leaders can be restrained and held accountable for their actions. Most importantly, citizen democrats can force, if they so choose, an unwilling leadership to expand democratic rights and opportunities to those excluded from the democratic process by the original pacts, which were negotiated with authoritarian elites during the transition phase. This, in turn, thaws frozen democracy and helps move it toward the full ideals of democracy (Diamond 1994a).

Korea and all other new democracies with long records of authoritarian rule, moreover, require periodic institutional renovation and renewal to respond effectively to newly emerging public preferences. Even after the transition to democracy, many of their key institutions refuse to serve the public and cling to the old practice of authoritarian rule.[5] Political corruption and repression continue to pose serious threats to the institutional foundation of new democracies (Fitzgibbon 1994; Fox 1994; Friedman 1994; Karl 1995; O'Donnell 1996; Steinberg 1995). To restrain such perverse institutions and to improve their practices, new democracies must rely on "the wings of an efficacious and mobilized citizenry" (Diamond 1994a: 246). For that reason, this study emphasizes the democratic transformation of mass culture and politics as a defining characteristic of democratic consolidation. As Linz & Stepan (1996b: 6) point out, "a democratic regime is consolidated when a strong majority of public opinion holds the belief that democratic procedures and institutions are the most appropriate way to govern collective life in a society such as theirs and when the support for anti-system alternatives is quite small or more or less isolated from the pro-democratic forces."

In studying the dynamics of mass public opinion and behavior, this inquiry emphasizes the importance of distinguishing between democracy as an ideal and democracy as a practice. It also stresses the need to distinguish between democratization as a normative phenomenon and democratization as an empirical phenomenon (Rose & Mishler 1996; Sartori 1987). A tremendous gap exists between a people's aspiration for democracy as a political ideal and their capacity to carry out democratic politics (Rose, Shin & Munro 1999). Also, a wide disparity exists between a people's desire for the expansion of limited democracy and their willingness to become involved in acts of reform. Popular judgments that democracy is preferable to authoritarian rule are not of much use if the disposition or willingness to engage in direct action does not exist (D. Shin 1995). Choosing or projecting democracy as a preferable alternative of rule by itself does not even guarantee the disintegration of an authoritarian regime, not to mention the construction or consolidation of a democratic state (Przeworski 1991). In the real world of democratization, political preferences matter only when they are translated into specific demands and action. Democratization can, therefore, be translated into a national development program of paramount importance and urgency only when there is a great deal of willingness to become involved in various acts of reform.

Finally, this study is grounded in the convention that the best way to understand the dynamics of democratic opinion and behavior is to engage in survey research asking people directly what they think and how they choose to act in the political process. Rigorously conducted sample surveys of the mass public can determine the breadth, depth, character, direction, and stability of its support for and involvement in democratic politics (Gibson 1996a; Rose & Haerpfer 1996). Those surveys can also offer empirical answers to fundamental questions about the extent to which differences between individuals within countries – young and old, educated and uneducated, or men and women – are as important or more important than differences between countries in institutions and history.

Databases

Ideally, the comparative study of cultural and political dynamics in democratizing Korea requires attitudinal and behavioral data from mass public surveys conducted in several other new democracies of Asia and other regions. In addition, it is highly desirable to obtain longitudinal survey data, which allows for the unraveling of such dynamics in each individual country and a comparison of those dynamics across countries and regions. Unfortunately, these types of desirable data – cross-national and longitudinal surveys – are not currently available for secondary analysis from any single source (Kaase 1994).

Therefore, to expand the availability of relevant data for this comparative inquiry, two separate strategies were employed. The first was to replicate in Korea some of the key items asked in several national and cross-national surveys conducted recently in other new democracies. The second strategy was to assemble, from a variety of published sources, the survey findings on those countries that can be considered functionally equivalent for our purpose. Undoubtedly each of these strategies is far from an ideal method of cross-national survey research, which requires close collaboration and co-operation among the groups of researchers working in their own countries. Nevertheless, the two strategies, when taken together, represent the optimal way to overcome a variety of real-world limitations in the comparative study of Korean democratization.

The main empirical base of the study consists of six parallel surveys of the Korean mass public conducted over the past nine years, beginning in 1988. The Institute of Social Sciences (ISS) at Seoul National University conducted the first two surveys during the first democratic government of President Roh Tae Woo: in October 1988 (N = 2007), in November 1991 (N = 1185), and the third one in the first year of the second democratic government of President Kim Young Sam: in November 1993 (N = 1198). The Korea-Gallup conducted the last three surveys during the Kim Young Sam government: in November 1994 (N = 1500), in January 1996 (N = 1000), and in May 1997 (N = 1117).

The ISS and Gallup Polls selected their samples to represent the population of the Republic of Korea aged twenty and over. The advance report of the Population and Housing Census of the National Statistical Office was used first to stratify the population by region (*Do*) and the eight large cities on the basis of their proportionate share of the national population. The island of Cheju-Do, with 1.2 percent of the total population, was excluded. Secondly, each region or large city was stratified by administrative subdivisions (*Dong, Eup, Myun*) on the basis of its proportion of the population. At the third stage, the primary sampling units (*ban* or *village*) were randomly selected, with six to eight households in a *ban* and twelve to fifteen in a *village*. At the household level, the interviewer was instructed to select for interview the person whose birthday came next. Respondents to the six surveys were all interviewed, face-to-face, at their residences. The average interviews lasted from thirty to sixty minutes. In the surveys conducted by Gallup, 10 percent of those interviews were verified on a random basis.[6]

The six parallel surveys assembled for this study constitute a much more discriminating tool than a variety of other sample surveys that individual scholars and various institutions have recently conducted in order to find out how Koreans are adapting to democratic change. With very few exceptions, other surveys are one-time surveys offering nothing more than snapshots of the continuously changing process of Korean politics; they cannot tell us about how Koreans have shifted in their opinions and behavior during the course of democratization. Moreover, the same surveys were designed primarily on the basis of a destination model measuring how near or far Korea is from ideal norms or principles of Western liberal democracy (see Rose & Haerpfer 1996). Implicit in this model is a teleological assumption that Koreans are becoming like citizens of Western democracies. This assumption runs directly counter to the indisputable reality that Koreans neither interpret nor value democracy in the same way as Westerners do (Hahm 1997; Kihl 1994; B. K. Kim & J. Y. Suh 1997).

The six national sample surveys of the Korean electorate were analyzed jointly in order to trace the trajectories, direction, and magnitude of institutional and cultural democratization for the Korean political system as a whole (Appendix A describes in detail the procedures of analyzing these surveys). Of these six surveys, three surveys were analyzed separately to investigate, in depth, the varying facets of democratization taking place at each of the three levels – individual, institutional, and systemic. Specifically, the 1993 survey by the ISS was analyzed to examine consequences of democratization for the quality of Korean life as well as the democratization of partisan politics. The 1994 survey by the Gallup Polls was analyzed to determine the competence and involvement of the Korean people in a democratic polity and the dynamics of their reactions to democratization. The 1996 survey served as a database for the assessment of President Kim Young Sam's democratic reforms and legislative democratization.

Results of these analyses are compared with those from similar surveys conducted recently in other countries during the current wave of democratization. In East Asia, for example, Korea is compared with Taiwan, another affluent dragon state that joined in the wave almost simultaneously with similar cultural and economic backgrounds. From a recent survey conducted in Taiwan by Fu Hu and Chu Yun-han (1996), five items were selected and replicated in the 1997 Korean survey. In addition, findings from the four parallel surveys conducted in Taiwan over the 1991–95 period are compared with those from the Korean surveys conducted over a similar period for the direction and trajectories of cultural democratization in the two East Asian states.

In this study, Korea is also compared with former military regimes in Latin America and Southern Europe as well as former communist countries in Eastern and Central Europe. Peter McDonough and his associates conducted, over the 1978–90 period, four waves of national sample surveys in Spain, which is one of the oldest in the current wave of democratization. In Eastern and Central Europe, the Lazarsfeld Society in Vienna and the Center for the Study of Public Policy at the University of Strathclyde in Glasgow, the Erasmus Foundation for Democracy in Budapest, and the United States Information Agency conducted multination surveys to compare popular support for democracy across new and old democracies there (McDonough, Barnes & Pina 1998; McIntosh et al. 1994; Rose & Haerpfer 1996; Bruszt & Simon 1990–91). Similar surveys were also conducted by teams of individual scholars in the United States and England in several new Eastern and Central European democracies (Gibson 1996a, 1996b; Gibson & Duch 1993; Miller, Hesli & Reisinger 1993, 1994; Evans & Whitefield 1995). In Latin America, Marta Lagos (1997) conducted multinational surveys called the Latino Barometer. Findings from these and other European and Latin American surveys served as benchmarks for our comparison.

Themes and Organization

The central finding of this study is that a large majority of Koreans have become favorably oriented toward the political ideals of democracy and the goals of building a democratic nation. In principle, they have increasingly joined the ranks of democrats for they have gained more knowledge and exposure to the mechanics of democratic politics. They have also experienced more positive than negative impacts from democratic change on the quality of their own personal lives as well as their nation's. They not only prefer to live in a democracy but also approve of the democratic transformation of authoritarian political institutions. In practice, however, most of these newly born democrats

are not yet fully committed to removing the residue of authoritarian rule
and to expanding the currently limited democracy. Nor are they always
willing to abide by the fundamental norms and rules of the democratic
political game, which are widely regarded in the literature as key factors
in the consolidation of new democracies (Gibson 1996a; Huntington
1996b; March & Olsen 1995; Miller, Reisinger & Hesli 1993; Linz &
Stepan 1996a).

[margin note: Masses support dem' in principle, not practice.]

To remould authoritarian cultural codes while fostering pro-
democratic behavior among the democratically inclined masses is the
most challenging and uncertain phase of Korean democratization. This
process of democratic cultural transformation is highly challenging
because the growth of pro-democratic dispositions does not necessarily
bring about corresponding changes in anti-authoritarian or communitarian dispositions. The process is extremely uncertain because of the
continuing presence of ideological and military threats from the
communist North.

The dynamics and consequences of democratization at the *political
system* level form the major organizing theme for the first part of this
book, and democratization among *average citizens* constitutes the guiding
theme of the second part. While the democratization of *political institutions* representing the mass public in the policy process constitutes the
main theme of the third part, the *exceptionalism* of Korean democratization at the systemic and individual levels serves as the theme for the
fourth part. The fifth part concludes this study.

The book begins with a prelude outlining an historical account of the
democracy movement in Korea over the past fifteen years. It treats a
number of basic questions including: What class of events led to the
downfall of the military dictatorship headed by former General Chun
Doo Whan? Why did the democratic transition in 1988 fail to make a
clean and/or radical break with the military authoritarian regimes that
existed for nearly three decades? What institutional reforms, political as
well as non-political, have been implemented thus far to consolidate
nascent democratic rule? What major political events occasioned public
approval of President Kim Young Sam, the first civilian president of the
democratic Sixth Republic, to fall from 90 percent to below 10 percent
and ended his 5-year tenure as the most "heroic failure" in the history of
Korean politics? What impact will the election of Kim Dae Jung, an
opposition party candidate and a native of the Cholla region, as the
second civilian president of the Sixth Republic have on Korea's journey
to full democracy and its Asian neighbors? These questions are initially
explored as a prelude to more in-depth analyses that immediately follow.

Chapter 1 "Uncertain Dynamics of Democratization" offers a dynamic
and holistic account of democratization in Korea at the system level.

How much progress has been achieved in democratizing the authoritarian system of governance and cultural values? How much progress has been achieved in empowering the Korean people and making their government respond to their demands and preferences? By aggregating results from six parallel surveys measuring both the experienced and desired level of democracy by the Korean people themselves, the chapter documents trends and the nature of the democratization that is taking place in the Korean political system as a whole.

Chapter 2 "The Human Meaning of Democratization" addresses three related questions. One question involves how democratization is understood among ordinary Koreans, who have little or no background in democratic political theory, and how their understanding of democratic change differs from that of peers in new and old democracies. Another question pertains to how democratization has actually affected the quality of life experienced by those Koreans in the private, as well as public spheres.

Chapter 3 "Commitment to Democratic Consolidation" begins to examine the several notable facets of democratization taking place at the individual level. How strongly are individual Koreans supportive of democracy as a regime in action? To what degree do they abide by procedural norms of democratic politics? How willing are they to remove the residue of authoritarian politics and expand the current practice of limited democracy? Who are "authentic" democrats? Who are "convenient" or "fair weather" democrats? Are Koreans more solid in their democratic commitment than citizens of other new democracies? These questions are addressed to identify and compare the levels, patterns, and sources of Korean commitment to the consolidation of democratic polity.

Chapter 4 "Citizen Competence and Participation" focuses on the capability and involvement of the Korean people in democratic politics and the community. Based on Sniderman's (1981) supposition that citizens of a democratic state should be cognitively open-minded, this chapter evaluates the cognitive competence of the Korean people in democratic politics. Utilizing Putnam's (1993) research finding that public propensity for civic association is the key to the consolidation of democracy, this chapter also examines the density of associational membership and changing trends in political participation. How much are the Korean people involved in voluntary associations and political activities? Are they involved more extensively than the citizens of Brazil, Spain, and other new democracies? Does greater civic and political engagement mean a stronger commitment to democratization and increasing dissociation from authoritarianism among the Korean masses? These questions allow us to explore and analyze the supply of social stock and political resources that can amplify the currently limited democracy.

Chapter 5 "Legislative Assemblies" takes up the democratization of legislative assemblies – the oldest and most prominent institutions of modern democracy. Assuming that the survival and growth of new democratic assemblies require growing popular support, this chapter examines the levels and patterns of support for the ideal and practice of representative democracy among the Korean people. The chapter also assumes that such support depends largely upon satisfactory legislative performance and examines the magnitude and trajectories of public approval for the performance of the National Assembly and its individual representatives.

Chapter 6 "Political Parties" deals with interactions between individual citizens and political parties, which constitute another integral channel of representing their preferences in the policy-making process. Are Koreans more strongly attached to political parties than their European and Latin American counterparts? Have years of democratic rule in Korea brought about a broader basis of popular support for its parties? Have those years of democratic rule also enhanced their capacity to respond to the interests and preferences of Korea's people? These questions are addressed in light of neo-corporatist and other theoretical models.

Chapter 7 "Consolidating a Nascent Democracy" documents that President Kim Young Sam's democratic reforms and campaigns, during the early years of his tenure, constitute a communitarian model of democratic consolidation. Emphasizing the importance of forming a democratic community instead of self-interested compliance among individual citizens, President Kim's model differs greatly from those based on the liberal and constitutional notions of democracy. Stressing the importance of purifying the authoritarian past and purging authoritarian elements from the democratic political process, Kim's model contrasts sharply, in both substance and style, with what has been observed in other new democracies.

Chapter 8 "Acquiring Democratic Orientations" asks, How have the Korean people oriented and reoriented to democratic regime change? Why have some Koreans continued or strengthened their support for democratization while others have failed to do so? These questions are explored using two pairs of contrasting theoretical perspectives concerning changes in Korea's economy, politics, and life quality. Retrospective versus prospective perspectives as well as egocentric versus sociotropic perspectives are considered in order to portray a more accurate account of why individual citizens transform their democratic temper in distinct ways. The central argument of this chapter is that

Koreans, unlike citizens of the former communist states in Eastern and Central Europe, acquired their support for democratization incrementally through experience with the consequences of regime change.

Chapter 9 "Korean Democracy: Problems and Prospects" rounds out the study by highlighting the notable features of democratization in Korea, determining its relevance as a Confucian model of democratization, and assessing its problems and prospects for becoming a fully consolidated democracy in the near future. The features that have shaped the direction and trajectory of Korean democracy during the past decade are highlighted and compared with those observed in Taiwan in order to determine whether the Korean experience of democratic change can legitimately be characterized as a Confucian model of democratization. This comparison reveals that the two dragon states involve, and are likely to involve, similar contours and trajectories of democratization. The legacies of Confucianism and developmental capitalism together with military threats from the communist rival regime are likely to keep Korea drifting along as a limited democracy, and they are likely to have the same effect on the Taiwanese democracy.

The Significance of the Study

This study represents significant departures from other studies of democratization in Korea. This book offers a more comprehensive and dynamic account of democratization in Korea than those currently available from the English and Korean literature on the subject. It also offers a comparative assessment of the place that Korean democracy occupies in the current wave of global democratization. Unlike other studies, this volume considers democratization as a multi-level phenomenon and examines the significant political changes that have taken place at three different levels – systemic, institutional, and individual. This study also compares and contrasts the democratization of mass politics and culture in Korea with other countries during the current wave of democratization – those in East Asia, Central and Eastern Europe, and in Latin America. In addition, it is the first volume assembling a very unique set of time–series data featuring six parallel surveys of the Korean mass public. These survey data, covering the entire first decade of Korean democratization, allow for a meaningful assessment of its past and future dynamics.

Theoretically, this book on Korean democratization tests in a Confucian country of East Asia a variety of Western hypotheses concerning the dynamics of attitudinal, behavioral, and institutional democratization, including those of cultural diffusion, economic rationality, mass communications, and political learning. Unlike existing survey-based studies of European and Latin American democracies (Dalton 1994; Gibson, Duch & Tedin 1992; Evans & Whitefield 1995; Lagos 1997; McDonough, Barnes & Pina 1998; Moises 1993; Morlino & Montero 1995; Rose 1992; Rose, Mishler & Haerpfer 1998; Weil 1994), this volume examines the consequences of democratization for the quality of human life from two contrasting theoretical perspectives; the one advocated by theorists of communitarian democracy and the other by those of participatory democracy. The impacts resulting from democratization on the public and private spheres of Korean life are assessed comparatively to test the validity of communitarian and participatory theories of democracy.

Finally, this book integrates the important concerns of two different disciplines: political science and quality of life. Since Angus Campbell and Philip E. Converse published *The Human Meaning of Social Change* in 1972, considerable advancements have been made in studying the quality of life. Undoubtedly, most of these conceptual and method-ological advancements can provide new concepts, insights, perspectives, and even tools for a more meaningful study of politics that reflects the sentiment Aristotle expressed 2500 years ago: "The end of the state is not mere life, rather, a good quality of life." With few exceptions (Barnes 1982; Barnes et al. 1979; Inglehart 1990), these developments in the study of life quality to date have rarely been adapted to the study of democratic politics. Unlike prior research on electoral behavior and democratic support (Duch 1995; Lewis-Beck 1988; MacKuen, Erikson & Stimson 1992), this study emphasizes the overall quality of life, not merely economic welfare, as the major driving force of democratic movements.

Introduction

"... democracy is not a gift or a political regime that one is born with but something that must be fought for every inch of the way, in every society. In this sense, the Korean struggle has been so enduring that there may be no country more deserving of democracy in our own time than the Republic of Korea."

Bruce Cumings (1997: 339)

In January 1981, General Chun Doo Whan, who had headed the Military Security Command under the Park Chung Hee government (1961–79), won the election for the President of the Fifth Republic of Korea and without an opposition candidate gained a 7-year term.[1] With the assumption of power by General Chun, Korea entered a new era of military dictatorship devoid of political rights and civil liberties. Under the pretext of national security and political stability, the Chun government disbanded all political parties, purged their leaders, and banned hundreds of other politicians, labor union leaders, and university students from engaging in any political activities. The military government also forced the news media to follow the strict guidelines issued by the Ministry of Information and Culture, including one to label anti-government protesters as pro-communist elements.

Like all other military dictatorships, the Chun government could not survive on such heavy-handed measures of repression alone. Even with its remarkable success in reviving the stagnant economy and expanding diplomatic relations with many countries, the Chun government won little support from the Korean people; it kept being challenged and haunted by the issues of political legitimacy and oppression. President Chun Doo Whan came to power through a military coup in 1979 after the brutal repression of opposition movements in Kwangju and other cities.[2] But in the eyes of Koreans, who were no longer living in dire poverty, they saw Chun's government as not only repressive but also illegitimate.

The collapse of military rule began in 1985 two years after its leaders attempted to boost its legitimacy through a series of liberalization measures, including the lifting of the ban on political activities by purged politicians. Leaders intended to make the ruling Democratic

1

Justice Party popular and electorally competitive through these liberalization measures (S. Kim 1998). Yet such measures did not help the
Chun government gain any greater support from the Korean electorate.
Instead, they helped political parties, churches, labor unions, and
student groups to form a united front against the repressive government. As a result, the government had to contend with unified forces of
opposition, which became increasingly popular among the middle class
and other segments of the Korean population (Hsiao & Koo 1997).

In the 1985 National Assembly election, the New Korea Democratic
Party (NKDP), formed just four weeks before the election, captured
seats in fifty out of ninety-two electoral districts and won 29 percent of
the total votes. Its popular support was only 6 percentage points lower
than the ruling Democratic Justice Party received. As the largest opposition bloc in the National Assembly, the NKDP together with other
opposition forces demanded that the authoritarian constitution of the
Fifth Republic be amended to provide for the direct election of the
president by the people (S. Kim 1996: 91). At the same time, there was a
growing awareness among the Korean electorate that the current
indirect method of electing the president should be modified to end
more than two decades of military rule.

In the face of large-scale anti-government demonstrations in all major
cities in February 1986, the Chun government agreed in principle to
the opposition's demand for public debate on constitutional revision.
The opposition under the leadership of Kim Young Sam and Kim Dae
Jung, however, broke with the NKDP led by moderate Lee Man Sup and
remained adamantly unwilling to retreat from its original proposal for a
popularly elected presidential system. In response, the government
unilaterally and imprudently suspended the debate in April 1987. Under
pressure, the government disclosed in May the death by torture of a
university student undergoing police interrogation, and admitted to
an attempted cover-up of the incident. In early June, the ruling
Democratic Justice Party nominated as its presidential candidate Roh
Tae Woo, a former general and a key participant in the 1979 coup, as
Chun's hand-picked successor through the existing unpopular method
of indirect election.

This sequence of events during the first half of 1987 not only under-
mined further the shaky moral foundation of the military government
but also alienated even the politically apathetic and conservative segments of the Korean population. As a result, the Korean mass public
politicized and mobilized against the immoral and repressive government at a level never before observed (S. Kim 1998). Church and civic
leaders, white- and blue-collar workers, and housewives volunteered to
join militant university students in street demonstrations. As the mass

movements to topple the government broadened and intensified during the first half of June 1987, street demonstrations became daily events.

From June 10 to June 29, the period often referred to as the "June Popular Uprising,"[3] street demonstrations drew increasingly larger crowds and became uncontrollable by the police forces acting alone (Korean Consortium of Academic Associations 1997). The Chun government was confronted with a painful choice between bringing in the army to quell those demonstrations just a few months before the scheduled Summer Olympics and making a wholesale concession to the demands of anti-government forces. Under intense pressure from the United States and many other international organizations including the International Olympic Committee, the military government was forced to choose the latter (Chu, Fu & Moon 1997: 37). After seventeen consecutive days of street demonstrations and the firing of 351,200 tear-gas canisters during the early month of June, the government agreed to popular demands for democratic reforms. To their total surprise, for the first time in twenty-six years, the Korean people were called "the masters of the country" and asked to produce a democratic political miracle, deserving enough to be recorded in world history (Haberman 1987).

Formally, Korea began its transition to democracy on June 29, 1987 when Roh Tae Woo, the presidential candidate of the ruling Democratic Justice Party, announced an 8-point pledge, which was subsequently dubbed the June 29 Declaration of Democratic Reform.[4] Shortly thereafter, the National Assembly adopted this Declaration, which marked the first threshold of Korea's democratic transition from a military dictatorship. It served as a blueprint for the amendment of the Fifth Republic's authoritarian constitution and paved the way for enacting a series of major institutional reforms. They included: (1) the amendment of the constitution for the direct election of the president, (2) the revision of the presidential election law to ensure the freedom of candidacy and fair competition in direct popular elections, (3) the granting of amnesty to Kim Dae Jung and other political prisoners and allowing them to resume political activities, (4) the protection of human dignity and promotion of basic rights, including an unprecedented extension of the Writ of Habeas Corpus, (5) restoring freedom of the press by abolishing the repressive Basic Press Law, (6) the institution of educational autonomy and local self-government through the popular election of local assemblies and executive heads of local governments, (7) the creation of a new political climate for dialogue and compromise especially among competing political parties, and (8) carrying out bold social reforms to build a clean, honest society and to promote a secure, happy life.

Building upon Roh's June 29 Declaration, the National Assembly drafted and approved the new constitutional framework for the democratic Sixth Republic on October 12, 1987. Sixteen days later, on October 28, the new democratic constitution was ratified by 93 percent of voters in a national referendum. This constitution was not based on the principles of parliamentary democracy, which many consolidologists believe contribute to the stability and accountability of democratic regimes (Linz 1990b; Stepan & Skach 1993). Instead, it was premised primarily on the principles of presidential democracy, namely, the separation of powers and checks and balances among the various branches of the government (Linz 1990a; Mainwaring & Shugart 1997). The constitution of the democratic Sixth Republic provides that the president be elected directly by a plurality of voters every five years for one 5-year term so that the president can have an independent and personal mandate directly from the electorate.

To initiate the democratic Sixth Republic, the first free presidential election was held on December 16, 1987. In this first election of a president by direct votes in twenty-six years, the opposition could not agree on a single candidate to challenge Roh Tae Woo, the candidate of the ruling Democratic Justice Party. The opposition was split among the three most prominent Kims in Korean politics: Kim Young Sam (Reunification Democratic Party), Kim Dae Jung (Peace and Democracy Party), and Kim Jong Pil (New Democratic Republican Party). In this 4-way race, Roh Tae Woo was elected with a mere plurality (37%) of the total votes cast while only two of the three Kims (Kim Young Sam and Kim Dae Jung) together garnered a majority (55%) of the votes. In this election, in which the divided opposition allowed the military to continue its rule in a democratic facade, regionalism emerged as the most powerful influence in Korea's electoral politics. Residents of the Yongnam, Honam, and Choongchung provinces overwhelmingly supported, respectively, Kim Young Sam, Kim Dae Jung, and Kim Jong Pil as the favorite sons of their regions.

On February 25, 1988, the Sixth Republic of Korea was born with the inauguration of President Roh Tae Woo, a former general who attended the Military Academy with his immediate predecessor, Chun Doo Whan. With his inauguration as the new president, Korea joined the third-wave family of new democracies (Diamond et al. 1997; Huntington 1991; D. Shin 1994). But due to his close association with Chun and direct involvement in the previous military dictatorship, the Roh government was widely regarded as a mixed government or a *dictablanda* (liberalized authoritarianism), a mere extension of authoritarian rule. As one of the key players and the greatest beneficiary of the authoritarian Fifth Republic President Roh was unable to dissociate himself from the legacies of the past military dictatorship, not to mention the removal of their leadership and institutional apparatus (S. Kim 1998: 12).

The Roh government failed to secure a majority of seats in the 13th National Assembly elected on April 26, 1988 and was further constrained in implementing democratic reforms. In this election, which adopted a mixed electoral system featuring single-member districts in place of two-member districts, the four parties led by the four major candidates of the 1987 presidential election solidified their standing as regional parties: Kim Dae Jung's Party for Peace and Democracy in Cholla, Roh Tae Woo's Democratic Justice Party in North Kyongsang, Kim Young Sam's Reunification Democratic Party in South Kyongsang, and Kim Jong Pil's New Democratic Republican Party in Choongchung (Bae & Cotton 1993: 177).

Most surprising was that the ruling Democratic Justice Party received 34 percent of the popular vote and won only 125 seats, twenty-five seats short of a majority in the 299-seat National Assembly. Three opposition parties (Party for Peace and Democracy with seventy seats, Reunification Democratic Party with fifty-nine seats, and New Democratic Republican Party with thirty-five seats) collectively held a substantial majority of 164 seats. For the first time in the history of Korean politics, the opposition controlled the majority of the National Assembly seats, creating what is frequently dubbed the *yeoso yadae* (small government party, big opposition) phenomenon. As a result of this phenomenon there were frequent legislative deadlocks and impasses.

In an attempt to reverse the *yeoso yadae* phenomenon in the National Assembly, the ruling Democratic Justice Party negotiated a merger with Kim Young Sam's Reunification Democratic Party and Kim Jong Pil's Democratic Republican Party. On January 23, 1990, the merger was announced after months of behind-the-scenes negotiations. It led to the creation of a grand "conservative party" called the Democratic Liberal Party, which was often compared with the Liberal Democratic Party in Japan. Enjoying over a two-thirds majority, this new ruling party was able to resort to the age-old authoritarian method of *blitzkrieg* tactics and enacted as many as twenty-three bills in the National Assembly without the participation of the opposition members (J. Y. Kim 1993: 46).

In March and June 1991, two rounds of local assembly elections took place. On the basis of the Local Autonomy Election Act which was enacted in April 1988, and the subsequently agreed 2-stage plan among four political parties, the first round of local assembly elections was held on March 26 in small cities, counties, and urban districts with a population of 300,000 and less. The second round was held on June 20 in six major cities and nine provinces. Voter turnout tended to be low with 55 percent for the first round and 59 percent for the second round of local assembly elections. The ruling Democratic Liberal Party won a landslide victory in the second round with two-thirds or 564 of 866 metropolitan and provincial assembly seats.

The Roh Tae Woo government (1988–92) carried out a variety of pro-democratic reforms to establish the institutional structure of liberal democracy that would safeguard political rights and civil liberties among individual citizens as well as their respective civic and political associations (Cotton 1993, 1994, 1995a). Laws of Assembly and Demonstration were enacted in March 1989, and a new Constitutional Court was created to protect the democratic constitution and human rights by preventing any branch of the national and local government from abusing its power. The laws governing judicial proceedings were also modified to make the judicial system more independent of executive control and less subject to political interference. The Basic Press Law, one of the most repressive legal tools of the authoritarian Fifth Republic, was formally repealed in November 1987 in order to ensure freedom of expression and association. The Roh government made freedom of the press *de facto* by abandoning the various extra-legal practices of controlling the news media, which involved issuing official guidelines and press cards. The government also liberalized restrictions on foreign travel and bans on the publication and possession of works on communism and North Korea. With these reforms, the Korean political system began to democratize substantively beyond the procedural realm of its electoral politics.

On March 24, 1992, the second round of quadrennial national legislative elections was held to establish the 14th National Assembly. The ruling Democratic Liberal Party, which had dominated the previous National Assembly with 216 of its 299 seats, took only 149 seats – one seat shy of even a simple majority. The Democratic Party, which was jointly led by Kim Dae Jung and Lee Ki Taek, Kim Young Sam's former deputy, increased its strength to ninety-seven seats while the newly founded Unification National Party by Chung Ju Yung, a business tycoon, won thirty-one seats. These results signified a stunning defeat for the ruling party although it managed to avoid the *yeoso yadae* problem with the absorption of nine of the twenty-one independent winners. The voter turnout was 72 percent, 4 percentage points lower than in the last parliamentary elections. As in all the previous elections, regionalism played a significant role, especially in the Honam and Yongnam provinces.

A significant step was taken to expand the limited practice of representative democracy in Korea during May 1992. The ruling party selected Kim Young Sam as its presidential candidate through an openly contested nomination process for the first time in the history of Korean political parties. Doing away with the authoritarian practice of having the current party president choose his successor and instituting a procedure promoting open competition among candidates marked the dawning of a new age of intra-party democracy.

On February 25, 1993, the ruling party's nominee Kim Young Sam assumed the second presidency of the Sixth Republic. By winning 42 percent of the popular vote, he became the first civilian president in more than three decades. Unlike Roh Tae Woo, the first president of the Sixth Republic, Kim Young Sam was a civilian dissident who fought for democracy for decades. Although marred by his association with former President Roh and the party formed by his military clique, Kim's presidency formally marked the end of military and quasi-military rule and represented a real opportunity to fulfil the Korean people's wishes for clean government and aspirations for a full democracy. As the first completely civilian president since 1962, Kim was also given a popular mandate to complete the final phase of democratic transition by fully restoring the principle of civilian supremacy over the military, which had ruled the country since 1960.

Upon his inauguration, President Kim Young Sam launched a series of broad-ranging and far-reaching reforms and received the overwhelming support of the Korean population. One of his first reforms was to swiftly dismantle the deeply entrenched power bases of the previous regimes, which a succession of military leaders had established. President Kim purged the generals and colonels who had been key players in those regimes. He disbanded the Hana Hoe Club, a secret clique in the Army whose members had served as pillars of the military for thirty years. By downsizing and restructuring the Agency for National Security Planning, the Military Security Command, and other security agencies, President Kim eliminated a reserved domain of their authority and decision-making, and restored the supremacy of civilian rule; this is an absolute prerequisite for the consolidation of nascent democratic rule.

On August 12, 1993, President Kim Young Sam issued an emergency decree banning anonymous bank accounts and requiring the mandatory use of real names in all financial transactions. The financial reform measure, which was subsequently approved by the National Assembly, aimed at dismantling the structure of political corruption by severing the collusive links between government and businesses. It also aimed at ensuring a rule of law by formally banning underground economic dealings that often involved tax evasions as well as illicit and speculative investments. The real-name accounting system sought to dismantle the economic foundation of corrupt authoritarian rule by enforcing the democratic principles of transparency and accountability in economic life in Korea.

Korea as a new democracy entered a new era of representative government on June 27, 1995 with the simultaneous elections of executive heads and legislators at both high and low tiers of local government. For the first time in thirty-four years, Koreans were given an opportunity to elect governors of provinces, mayors of cities, and heads of counties and urban wards. In the elections of local administrators, who previously had been appointed by the central government, the ruling party suffered a major defeat, losing in ten of the fifteen elections to choose governors and mayors of large metropolitan areas. Regardless of their consequences for political parties, these local elections held every four years would make local government officials accountable to their voters. Such elections would also allow individual voters to engage themselves in the democratic political practice of self-rule at the grass-roots level.

On December 19, 1995, the Kim Young Sam government enacted a special law under which two former presidents and other military leaders were brought to justice. By characterizing the May 18, 1980 mass uprising in Kwangju as a pro-democracy movement, the government supported the passage of the "May 18 Special Law", which authorized the prosecution of those who were responsible for the massacre of hundreds of protesters in Kwangju during May 1980. By defining the December 12, 1979 seizure of power as "a coup-like military revolt," the law also authorized the prosecution of those who destroyed constitutional order at that time by staging a coup d'etat.

In April 1997 the Supreme Court upheld lower court rulings sentencing former President Chun Doo Whan to life in prison and his successor, Roh Tae Woo, to seventeen years. The Court found Chun guilty of mutiny, treason, murder, and corruption and Roh guilty of mutiny, treason, and corruption. In addition, the two former presidents were convicted of bribery and fined heavily: Chun, US$276 million and Roh, US$350 million – the amounts they were found to have received while in office. Although they were pardoned and freed two years later, the imprisonment of two former presidents on charges of authoritarian crimes constitutes the most notable anti-authoritarian campaign ever imposed by any third-wave democracy (see Rosenberg 1995).

A third round of national legislative elections was held on April 11, 1996 to choose the entire membership of the 15th National Assembly. As in the first two rounds, the ruling party failed to win a clear majority. With 35 percent of the total vote, President Kim's New Korea Party won 139 of 299 seats – eleven seats shy of majority status. For the third time since the democratic regime change in 1988, the ruling party was outnumbered by the opposition and faced the *yeoso yadae* problem. As in the previous assembly, the government party "manufactured" a majority by inducing eight independents and three opposition Democratic Party members to join its camp.

As in the earlier parliamentary elections, regional ties served as the key to candidate selection in several parts of the country. In the Honam region, the National Congress for New Politics, Kim Dae Jung's new party, captured all but one of thirty-seven seats. In Kim Young Sam's Pusan and South Kyongsang, his New Korea Party won all but five of forty-four seats. In Kim Jong Pil's Choongchung provinces, his United Liberal Democrats captured seventeen of the twenty-one contested seats. There was no sign that regionalism was in retreat from Korean electoral politics, although an increasingly larger proportion of eligible voters became disillusioned and withdrew from the process. The turnout rate in this third quadrennial parliamentary election of the democratic Sixth Republic was 64 percent – 8 percentage points lower than in the 1992 elections, and 12 percentage points lower than in the 1988 election.

Despite all the electoral reforms implemented during the first half of his 5-year term, President Kim Young Sam made little headway in democratizing the electoral process by curtailing the pernicious roles of money and regionalism. At the same time, Kim began to lose control of his crucial campaign against the political corruption that he vowed to eradicate. After he took office in February 1993, President Kim refused to accept political donations from businesses and vowed to sever the ties between government and businesses that had been fostered by decades of military rule. To this end, he enacted and implemented a strict code of ethics and purged hundreds of public officials, including the Speaker of the National Assembly and the Chief Justice of the Supreme Court. Under the Public Officials' Ethics Act, thousands of high-ranking officials were required to register and reveal their assets on a yearly basis. But in the face of his promise to root out rampant corruption and despite the various steps taken to reduce graft and influence peddling, members of his own cabinet and his close associates became implicated in a series of political scandals which began to unfold, beginning in early 1996 (Koh 1997).

In March 1996 a member of the Blue House staff, who had worked for President Kim for nineteen years, was arrested on charges of accepting a bribe from a construction company in exchange for helping it to get a permit to build condominiums. In June, the head of the Security Oversight Commission was arrested on charges of accepting bribes. The Defense Minister was arrested in October for accepting a bribe from a defense contractor in return for helping win a contract to manufacture helicopters. The Health and Welfare Minister resigned in November on suspicion of accepting a bribe from an optometrist association. In that same month, the president of Seoul Bank was arrested on charges of accepting a bribe in return for arranging a loan. In January 1997, when

Hanbo Steel Company, Korea's second largest steel producer, collapsed under nearly US$6 billion in debt, President Kim's second son was known to play a key role in arranging the huge sums of bank loans for the ailing company in exchange for contributions to his own 1992 presidential campaign (Shim & Lee 1997). On February 19, prosecutors indicted nine people on charges of graft. Among them were President Kim's own fundraiser and his Interior Minister. A few months later, his second son was arrested and sentenced to a 3-year prison term for accepting bribes and tax evasion.

President Kim Young Sam apologized to the nation on February 25, saying, "I lower my head in shame for involvement of people close to me in the scandal (Hanbo). I feel appalled and sorry for the situation, and I am humbly ready to take any reproach and criticism for the state of affairs" (quoted in Shim 1997a: 16). Notwithstanding all these apologies, his failure to police corruption in his own inner circles made a mockery of his much trumpeted anti-corruption campaign. His own son's involvement in bribery, influence peddling, and political slush funds destroyed the moral legitimacy of his political leadership in the country where "the logic which undergirds the actual practice of politics derives from the traditional Confucian political discourse" (Hahm 1997: 66). Moreover, Kim's persistent refusal to reveal a detailed account of his 1992 campaign fundraising irreparably tarnished his image as "Mr Clean."

Finally, President Kim Young Sam's leadership as a democratic reformer suffered severe damage in December 1996 when he ordered the ruling party to railroad two important pieces of anti-democratic legislation through the National Assembly in a pre-dawn, secret meeting to which opposition lawmakers were not invited. The Law for the Agency for National Security Planning was revised to revive its domestic political role of spying on Korean citizens, which was outlawed in 1994. Specifically, the Agency was reauthorized to investigate, arrest, and interrogate people accused of making favorable comments about North Korea or not reporting memberships in groups considered sympathetic to the North. The second piece of legislation, the New Labor Law, made it easier for companies to dismiss workers, hire replacements for striking workers, and adjust working hours. In an attempt to "fight against communist forces" and "improve international competitiveness," the Kim Young Sam government fell back into the repressive measures of the authoritarian past. But intense pressure from labor unions, student groups, university professors, religious organizations, and the opposition parties forced the government to halt its reversal toward authoritarianism by annulling the December laws. Kim Young Sam, who came to power on an anti-authoritarian plank, was accused of being a civilian dictator harboring authoritarian ambitions (Shim 1997a: 17).

The spectacular bribes-for-loans scandals and humiliating anti-authoritarian legislative debacles seriously wounded the Kim Young Sam government and paralyzed its capacity to lead and govern the country. In the wake of these unforgivable misdeeds and inexcusable blunders, President Kim was stripped of all his authority; he became both morally and politically dead in the minds of the people (Shim 1997c). Koreans from all walks of life turned their backs on the president whom they once cheered enthusiastically as their national hero for purging the almighty military, humbling powerful business, and prosecuting the two untouchable former presidents. After weeks of labor strikes during the month of January 1997, President Kim's approval rating in the polls plunged to 18 percent; it had been over 90 percent in 1993 (*Economist* 1997b).[5] In December when Korea required to be rescued by the International Monetary Fund, his approval rating fell further – to below 10 percent. President Kim was blamed for betraying his nation and humiliating his people and all of his reforms were viewed as abject failures. Ironically, he began his presidency as the greatest national hero undertaking bold reforms for a new era of democratic politics, but he ended it as Korea's greatest political failure (Kristof 1997c).[6]

On December 18, 1997, Kim Dae Jung won the election. By 41 percent of the popular vote, he became the third president of the Sixth Republic during the most peaceful and most corruption-free presidential race Korea has ever experienced. It was also the country's least expensive presidential race in a long time (M. Shin 1998). Five years earlier when he was running against Kim Young Sam, the candidate of the ruling party, army generals openly warned that they would stage a coup rather than allow Kim Dae Jung to become the president. This time no such talk took place. Previously, the ruling party spent enormous sums of money during the presidential races in order to bribe voters. This did not occur. The ruling party distanced itself from the dirty-money politics of the past (Kristof 1997b).

Kim Dae Jung, who had run in the presidential races three times before (1971, 1987, and 1992), succeeded in his fourth attempt for a number of reasons.[7] First, he was elected in part because Korea was suffering from the worst economic crisis since the Korean War. Many Koreans blamed the ruling Grand National Party for economic mismanagement and sought to punish it by choosing the candidate who had never been associated with Korea's ruling establishments. The ruling party, on the other hand, failed to deliver a single candidate to its potential voters. In the July 21 nominating convention, the party chose Lee Hoi Chang in a runoff election against the second place finisher, Rhee In Je. Defying his own pledge to abide by the outcome of the nominating process, Rhee defected from the ruling party, ran for the presidency as the candidate of his New Party by the People, and received half as many votes (19%) as the votes that Lee managed to retain (39%). Kim Dae Jung was also elected partly because of the strategic coalition that his National Congress for New Politics negotiated with Kim Jong Pil's United Liberal Democrats.[8] As the favorite son of the Choongchung provinces, Kim Jong Pil could deliver the necessary minimum votes for Kim Dae Jung's victory – the only political dream that had never failed to captivate residents of Kim Dae Jung's Cholla region.

Kim Dae Jung's victory, which is often compared with the elections of South Africa's Nelson Mandela and Poland's Lech Walesa, represents the victory of political as well as social opposition because he came from Cholla, the region that has long been discriminated against both politically and socially. It also challenges the Western view of Asian democracy as one in which the peaceful transfer to the opposition is seen as hopeless. Upon his election, Kim Dae Jung quickly moved to support the passage of financial reform bills mandated by the IMF loan deal. He demanded the fundamental restructuring of governmental agencies and major conglomerates controlling over three-quarters of Korea's gross domestic product. At the same time, he began to tame the most militant and powerful labor unions in Asia, which had pushed wages up five-fold in the past decade.

Kim Dae Jung's endeavors to restructure crony capitalism and the old ways of running politics have begun to dispel the view that the democratically elected government is not capable of implementing the major reforms essential to democratic consolidation. The ultimate outcome of the Kim Dae Jung government, however, will be shaped and determined by its capacity to nurture the new politics of compromise and to overcome the political parameters set by the *yeoso yadae* problem that the new government faces as much as the Roh Tae Woo and Kim Young Sam governments did before.

PART I

The Political System

CHAPTER 1

Uncertain Dynamics
of Democratization

"History is as much or more of a story of backsliding than of progress."

Jean-François Revel (1993: 93)

"Yet democracies have always been, and still are, failure prone."

Giovanni Sartori (1987: xiii)

Many of the new democracies in today's world evolved out of military dictatorships; Korea is one of those countries where the military ruled for decades. In Korea, however, military rule lasted much longer than in many other countries. When the Korean military acceded to popular demands for a democratic regime change, it was more than a decade after the democratic transitions from military rule took place in Southern Europe during the mid-1970s.[1]

As discussed in the Introduction, the democratization of military rule in Korea officially began on June 29, 1987, when the government party candidate for the presidency, Roh Tae Woo, yielded to popular demands for a sweeping political liberalization, which included the direct election of the president, freedom of the press, and the easing of restrictions on human rights.[2] With the inauguration of former General Roh as the first president of the Sixth Republic of Korea on February 25, 1988, the country became an electoral democracy, which is often characterized as a hybrid regime combining elements of both military rule and democracy (see Karl 1995; Schmitter 1994). Five years later, on February 25, 1993, this regime was transformed into a civilian democracy when Kim Young Sam assumed the second presidency of the Republic.

Unlike new democracies in Latin America, Korea has fully restored civilian rule by extricating the military from power, and has also fully established the minimal architecture of procedural democracy (J. Choi 1993a; S. Kim 1994; Moon & Kim 1996a; C. W. Park 1997; Steinberg 1996; Wade & Kang 1993). Accordingly, Korean democracy today meets the criteria of procedural democracy or polyarchy specified by Dahl (1971) and many other scholars (Rose, Mishler & Haerpfer 1998; Schmitter & Karl 1991): a political regime characterized by free and fair elections, universal adult suffrage, multi-party competition, civil

Procedural democracy

15

liberties, and a free press. In the words of Kim Byung-Kook (1996: 1), "electoral politics has become the only possible game in town for resolving political conflicts."

As a result of democratizing political institutions and procedures, a number of notable advances have been achieved since Korea began its transition to democracy in 1987. Laws have been passed and enforced to promote fair and free elections at all government levels. Three rounds of free and competitive elections have been held to choose a new president, and three rounds of parliamentary elections have been held to choose district representatives to the National Assembly. In local communities, there are now governors and legislators popularly elected rather than appointed by the central government. In the wake of these democratic elections and reforms, political power has been redistributed not only among the three branches of the central government but also between central and local government agencies. Moreover, Korea has begun to establish a new tradition of peaceful succession of political leaders. Each time a new president was elected by popular election, for example, his predecessor peacefully surrendered office, and his challengers graciously accepted defeat.

The president and all ranking government officials are now legally required to disclose their family assets on an annual basis. No longer may anyone, either in politics or business, hide his or her illicit financial transactions in accounts under fictitious names. Also, the military and security establishments are prohibited from interfering in decisions of the judiciary and dictating what to print to the news media. Furthermore, military and security agencies possess no power of veto in the policy-making process (Cotton 1995a: 3). The signs are ubiquitous that the political process associated with democracy is firmly established in the Korean political landscape.

Research on these institutional reforms only, however, fails to offer a comprehensive and balanced picture of the democratic changes taking place in this country. Focusing solely on the formal procedures and rules of a new democratic political order ignores the equally important informal rules and cultural norms, which may be undermining the performance of democratic institutions as well as the substantive outcomes of formal reforms (Fuchs, Guidorossi & Svensson 1995; Hahm & Rhyu 1997; H. B. Im 1997c; O'Donnell 1996; Sanger 1997). If a few photographs of democratic institutions and rules were taken at certain points in time, the true dynamics of democratic change would be blurred (Steinberg 1996: 2).

The main objective of this first chapter is to provide a holistic and dynamic account of how both the military dictatorship and authoritarian political culture of Korea were transformed into a democracy. How can the process of Korean democratization be characterized to date? What forces have shaped its direction and trajectory? How much progress has been made in constructing democratic political institutions and transforming mass culture of the authoritarian past? How much progress has been made in the empowerment and representation of ordinary Koreans in the political process? How does Korean democratization to date compare with what has been noted in other newly democratizing countries? These questions are considered in the context of six parallel surveys conducted in Korea since 1988 as well as similar surveys conducted recently in other new democracies.

This chapter begins with the theory that democratization is a dynamic and complex phenomenon involving a political regime and its culture as well as their respective interactions. A brief discussion follows concerning the forces that have powerfully shaped the overall contours and dynamics of democratization. After discerning the trends in the democratic transformation of the authoritarian character of a political regime and its mass culture, the chapter investigates how democratic political institutions and culture have interacted with each other. Next, it assesses the impact of procedural democratization on the responsiveness of the Korean political system to ordinary citizens and their influence on policy-making. The chapter concludes with a comparative analysis of Korean democratization in progress and at repose.

The longitudinal and comparative analyses reported below are predicated on two simple premises derived from experiential and holistic perspectives. First, ordinary people, experiencing changes in the formal and informal rules of the political game on a daily basis, are the best judges of those changes (Fuchs, Guidorossi & Svensson 1995: 329). Second, these same people are intellectually capable of perceiving and considering all those changes together for a global assessment of the political regime and culture in which they live (Mishler & Rose 1996: 557; see also Andrews & Withey 1976).

Conceptualization

To investigate both the institutional dynamics and substantive outcomes of democratization in Korea, this study rejects the static, procedural notion of democratic politics.[3] This idea of the democratic political process as a stand-alone concept is too shallow to capture the true meaning of democratic change. Also, the present study rejects the conventional view of democratic change as a dichotomy, which Huntington (1989, 1991) has employed. If democratic change is perceived as occurring only in kind, not in phases and paces, its dynamics cannot be unraveled adequately.

Specifically, democratization involves much more than competitive elections on a regular basis and representative institutions at all levels of government. In the democratic process of electing political leaders and formulating legislation, average citizens should be able to exert some influence; hence the phrase "government by the people." Within Confucianism, this concept is expressed by the term *minbon*. When one considers the other side of the equation, however, and speaks of political leaders and governmental institutions as distinct from the citizen masses, these leaders and instruments of government should concern themselves with enacting legislation and implementing public policy in response to the changing preferences and demands of its citizens; hence, the phrase "government for the people." Within Confucianism, this concept is expressed by the term *wimin*.[4] Taken in this context, the process of empowering the once-powerless masses and restructuring recalcitrant institutions in the direction of greater accountability and responsiveness should be viewed as an integral facet of democratization (Dahl 1989; Linz & Stepan 1996a; Rose & Shin 1997; Sartori 1995). The gist of our conceptualization is that *popular empowerment* and *systemic responsiveness* are at the core of substantive democratization.[5]

The present study, therefore, considers both the procedural and substantive changes that have occurred as two different, but interconnected, spheres that affect the mass citizenry and the political regime itself. At the regime level, democratization refers to the extent to which authoritarian structures and procedures are transformed into democratic ones and, in the process, become more responsive to the mass citizenry (Dahl 1971, 1989; Huber, Rueschemeyer & Stephens 1997). At the citizenry level, democratic change refers to the extent to which average citizens reorient themselves to democracy from authoritarianism and become politically empowered (Fox 1994; Lakoff 1996; Macpherson 1977; Sartori 1995). Accordingly, this chapter explores how broadly such procedural and substantive changes have occurred at each level.

The scope of democratization in this study extends far beyond the input and output phases of the political process as they are constantly shaped by the interactions between citizens and their democratic regime. The dynamic interactions between political institutions and culture of a democratic political order are considered to be another integral part of procedural democratization (O'Donnell 1996). The more democratically congruent political institutions and cultural values are with each other, the greater the extent to which democratization is achieved at the systemic level. Conversely, the lower the level of democratic congruence between the two domains of a political system, the lesser the degree there is of democratic progress (Fuchs, Guidorossi & Svensson 1995).

The study, reported in this chapter, also regards democratization as a continuous process of change involving a complex system of factors and trajectories. Constantly evolving at phases and at paces over time, democratic change cannot be adequately captured in a few black-and-white snapshots, which are based on a dichotomous view of procedural democracy (Diamond 1996; Rose & Mishler 1994). A more accurate and meaningful account of Korean democratization requires a broader and dynamic notion of democratic change that continuously occurs in both procedural and substantive domains of political life (B. Kim 1996; Steinberg 1996). The proposed notion of democratic change allows for an accurate appraisal of the direction, trajectory, and consequences of Korean democratization.

Contours of Democratization

What factors have shaped the process of democratizing the Korean polity and culture and how have they contributed? Without doubt, democratization has not evolved by great leaps and bounds in Korea. Despite a few surprises, such as the merger between the ruling and opposition parties in January 1990, democratization has been mostly a conservative movement that falls short of major policy restructuring and ideological or partisan realignment.[6] The roots of this conservative democratization lie primarily in the dynamic interplay of three factors: (1) inhibitions imposed by military threats from the North, which is ruled by the leftist ideology of communism, (2) the economic legacies of authoritarian capitalism, which has moulded an ideology of obsessive pragmatism; and a parochial culture of regionalism, and (3) the "transplacement" mode of democratic transition featuring a series of binding agreements between authoritarian and democratic forces.

History shows that the superpowers have not been kind to Korea as far as democratization is concerned. After World War II, leaders of communist totalitarianism and capitalist democracy forcibly partitioned Korea, like Germany and Vietnam, into ideologically and militarily opposed states. Unlike Germany and Vietnam, however, Korea still remains divided as the last military frontier of the Cold War. Even today, the democratic South has to remain on guard – not only against military threats from the communist North but also against ideological challenges to its national ethos of liberal democracy. This continuing division of territory has been the most pernicious influence on the democratization of the authoritarian regime and culture in the South.

More than anything else, the 1950 military invasion fortified authoritarian rule in the South (Koo 1993: 240; H. C. Sohn 1995: chap. 5). To counter invading communist forces and their sympathizers, as well as to regain the lost territory, a right-wing military dictatorship was established indefinitely as the only viable regime for the people of the South. As Choi Jang Jip (1993b: 23) points out, "the war gave the state [right-wing dictatorship] an ideological base for building its legitimacy" and "anti-communism became the premier motif for the ideological legitimation of the South Korean state." Even after the end of the Korean War in 1953, unending threats from the communist North have served to justify the continuing use of oppressive measures on political dissidents and, thereby, this rationale prolonged the existence of such a dictatorship in the South.

Backed by Soviet communism, the Korean War also prevented liberal and democratic values from being transplanted in the South. The ideological tone of the war prohibited the mass media and intellectual circles from dissociating communism from other progressive movements promoting economic equality and social justice. "The crude anti-communist ideology or mentality, which emerged from the war," Kim Byung-Kook (1994: 27) points out, "reduced Korea's capacity to develop new democratic values and ideals." The inevitable outcome was that, for decades, the authoritarian values of law and order remained unchallenged as the ruling ideology underpinning the dictatorship.

In postwar Korea, no distinction could be made between the tenets of communism from the liberal, democratic principles and ideas of social democracies in Western Europe and Scandinavia. Such leftist and heterodoxical ideas were regarded as "impure," or "unclean," and officially declared subversive to the survival of an independent, "democratic" state in the South, and they were banned completely from public debate (H. Sohn 1995: chap. 5). In the Korean model of democracy, anti-communism became the most crucial of its defining characteristics. "Conformity to the national anti-communist ideology became the template against which all else was judged, and mechanisms were established to monitor variations from the official theme" (Steinberg 1997: 157). By equating democracy with anti-communism, ruling elites of both civilian and military dictatorships removed leftist and other ideologically progressive elements from the Korean political process (J. Choi 1993b: 23). The Korean masses, on the other hand, were so indoctrinated with the right-wing ideologies of authoritarian rule and state capitalism that they remained steadfastly hostile to all politicians and intellectuals who challenged the cultural foundation of the dictatorship. In short, the ideological polarization and military hostility between North and South Korea not only delayed but also confined democratic reforms in the latter, predominantly within the bounds of procedural minima.

In addition to ongoing military conflicts with the North and deeply ingrained public antipathy toward communism, growing economic prosperity under the military governments circumscribed both the meaning and strategy of Korean democratization. Authoritarianism-sponsored prosperity, unlike the military threats from the North, served to set the course of democratic reforms on a procedural path while strategically allowing those reforms to be implemented on a slow and gradual basis. With one of the fastest growing economies in the world, authoritarian Korea was not in urgent need of fixing what appeared to have worked economically well for decades. During the first decade of democratic rule, neither opposition parties nor the government has demanded the fundamental restructuring of developmental capitalism, such as breaking up the *chaebols*, which unfairly and inhumanely dominate the Korean economy.

Economically, democratization in Korea contrasts strikingly with what has been debated in Latin America and Eastern Europe (see Bunce 1995). In Latin America, the debate has concentrated on the fixing of its malfunctioning economic institutions (H. B. Im 1996; Moon & Kim 1996b; Haggard & Kaufman 1995). In Eastern Europe, it has involved much more than economic institutions; it has extended to the restructuring of a bankrupt economy as well as the building of a fragile civil society (Lagos 1997; Rose, Mishler & Haerpfer 1998). In Korea, especially during the first democratic government period (1988–92), conflict over the distribution of economic rewards was quite intense (McDonough & Shin 1995; Moon & Kim 1996b). But any restructuring of the age-old developmental capitalist system had never been a major issue until the International Monetary Fund demanded it as part of the US$58.5 billion rescue program in December 1997.[7]

Culturally or normatively, an ideological truncation on the left and the economic legacies of military rule have collaborated to keep many Koreans within the bounds of conservatism and pragmatism. For those Koreans who personally benefited from authoritarianism-fostered prosperity, developmental capitalism, although politically imperfect, was an economically workable and prudential settlement under the guidance of powerful politicians and technocrats. Democracy was, accordingly, viewed as a sort of political uncertainty that might heighten the sense of economic risk. For this reason, many Koreans may still feel highly ambivalent toward the furtherance of democracy as a form of government; they prefer to live in a pluralistic democracy while remaining attached to strong leadership for effective governance.

Under the Fourth and Fifth Republics of military dictatorship, ruling elites consistently favored the Kyongsang provinces, at the expense of

Cholla and other regions, in allocating development projects and recruiting government officials.[8] For decades, such acts of favoritism and discrimination have powerfully motivated individual Koreans to form the habit of defining their political identities and interests primarily in terms of the region in which they were born or residing (see Shin & Rose 1997: 37–8). Although the practices of past discrimination have virtually ended in the post-authoritarian era, regional ties continue to outweigh political ideology, party identification, and class interests as a defining characteristic of electoral politics (N. Lee 1993). In the parochial culture of regionalism, individual politicians and political parties are not strongly motivated to debate policy issues from a truly national perspective. As Steinberg (1996: 14) notes, their reliance on regionalism prolongs the process of democratic consolidation and undercuts the effectiveness of democratic governance.

The successful management of the national economy by the military also gave the ruling generals considerable leverage in dealing with democratic forces during the course of political transition; they were able to negotiate their gradual and slow retreat from power (H. B. Im 1994, 1995). Even in the face of mounting pressures from college students, churches, labor union members, and other anti-military forces, Korean generals did not surrender in order to immediately retreat to the barracks. Instead, they successfully negotiated a series of pacts and agreements with opposition leaders, which Huntington (1991) characterizes as a "transplacement" of authoritarian rule.

Those pacts allowed the Korean military to win the first democratic presidential election in 1987 and remain key players in the first democratic government under the leadership of former General Roh Tae Woo. In the second democratic government headed by the civilian president Kim Young Sam, the political party of former General Chun Doo Whan and his associates of the military dictatorship of the Fifth Republic remained in power following its merger with smaller conservative opposition parties in early 1990 and a change in name to the New Korea Party in 1995. Even President Kim Dae Jung of the current, third government of the Sixth Republic has formed a coalition with Kim Jong Pil who played a key role in the 1961 military coup and organized the Korean Central Intelligence Agency for the Park Chung Hee government. As a result, the institutional and legal apparatus of military rule has not been completely overhauled. Even in procedural terms, current Korean democratization represents no rupture with the authoritarian past (Hahm & Rhyu 1997: 40; see also H. B. Im 1996; S. J. Kim 1994).

At the core of authoritarian residue is the National Security Law that was promulgated in 1948. Under this law, it is still a crime to praise North Korea or visit its homepage on the Internet (*Economist* 1997a).

Even those who listen to its radio broadcasts continue to be imprisoned. According to Minkahyup, a human rights group in Korea quoted in a recent *New York Times* article (Kristof 1998), there are 478 political prisoners in Korean jails. Even under President Kim Dae Jung, a former dissident and inmate himself, the country is reported in the article to "imprison far more political offenders than many other countries in the region." Even under the democratic Sixth Republic, as in the authoritarian past, tolerance of communism remains "an unaffordable luxury."

In summary, the menace of communism in the North and the economic success of authoritarian capitalism have shaped the conservative contours of Korean democratization. Politically, rulers have changed hands from the military to the civilian. Nonetheless, they still remain in a conservative alliance without the beneficial effects of stable mass-based political parties or the pluralization of ruling ideology. Economically, *dirigiste* capitalism remains the hegemonic vision among the Korean people, including elites and masses. Ideologically, a new subculture of liberalism and pluralism has been merely grafted onto the dominant cultural values of authoritarian Confucianism and parochial regionalism. Conservatism, pragmatism, and gradualism have been the dominant characteristics of Korean democratization (H. C. Sohn 1993).

Transforming Authoritarian Rule
Instituting a Democratic Regime

To what degree has the Korean military regime democratized since the Sixth Republic was inaugurated with the free and direct election of its president in 1988? What has been the direction and trajectory of its democratization? Obviously, these questions prompted a series of surveys repeating the same questions for the entire period of Korean democratization. Beginning in 1988, we conducted six national sample surveys; respondents were asked in each survey to rate their current political system on a 10-point ladder scale (see Appendix B B1.3). A score of 1 on this scale indicates "complete dictatorship" while a score of 10 indicates "complete democracy."

For each of the six parallel surveys covering the 1988 to 1997 period, Figure 1.1 reports the average score on the 10-point scale. For each survey, Table 1.1 reports the percentage of respondents who rated their political system as authoritarian by selecting one of the bottom four steps (1 through 4) and as democratic by selecting one of the top four steps (7 through 10) on the ladder scale. The greater the mean in the figure is, the more democratized the Korean political system is perceived. The percentage on the table corresponds to the proportion of the Korean people who claim the experience of democratic politics.

Figure 1.1 Public Perceptions of the Sixth Republic of Korea on a 10-Point Democracy–Dictatorship Scale, 1988–97

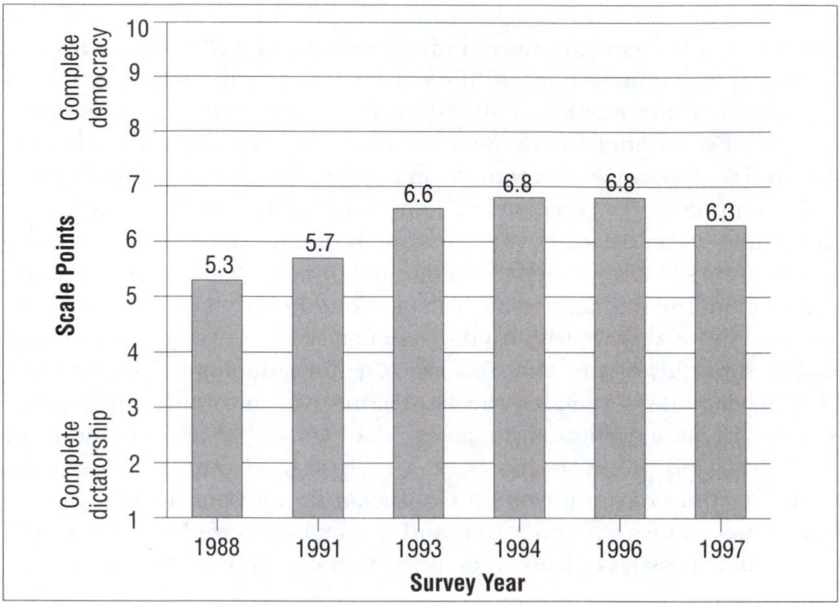

Source: Korean Democratization Surveys

According to the means reported in Figure 1.1, the structures and processes of the Korean political system democratized on a steady and incremental basis for the first six years of democratic rule. The average ratings on the 10-point scale rose steadily from 5.3 in 1988 to 5.7 in 1991 and 6.6 in 1993 to 6.8 in 1994. The percentages of Koreans rating the political system as democratic also rose similarly over the 6-year period. A comparison of these ratings makes it clear that Korea was moving successively from a hybrid type of political system to a limited democratic state during the first six years of its democratic rule.

In October 1988, when the first government of the Sixth Republic was less than a year old, a minority of 27 percent of the people replied that they were living in a democracy by placing it on one of the top four steps on the 10-point scale (see Table 1.1). This democratic rating was 5 percentage points smaller than the rating indicating that the new regime was not different from its authoritarian predecessor. Over the next six years, democratic perceptions of the regime steadily rose while authoritarian perceptions steadily declined. Beginning in 1993, when Kim Young Sam was elected to head the second democratic government as the first civilian president in three decades, a different pattern emerged: democratic perceptions grew into a majority, outnumbering authoritarian

Table 1.1 Perceptions of the Existing Political System, 1988–97 (percent)

| Survey Year | Types of Perceptions | | | |
	Democratic (A)	Authoritarian (B)	Difference (C = A–B)	(N)
1988	27.4	32.1	–4.7	(2007)
1991	34.3	23.5	+10.8	(1185)
1993	59.3	8.5	+50.8	(1198)
1994	61.6	7.5	+54.1	(1500)
1996	62.3	6.7	+55.6	(1000)
1997	46.2	8.2	+38.0	(1117)

Source: Korean Democratization Surveys

perceptions. As of November 1994, about three-fifths (62%) of the Korean population believed that Korea had become a democratic state.

Since 1994, positive change has no longer been observed in either the means or percentage ratings monitoring the democratization of the authoritarian rule, which was led by the military for three decades. For the 1994–96 period, very little change was observed in either of the measures, indicating that the upward trajectory of institutional democratization leveled off. In 1996, for example, the mean on the 10-point scale stood at the same step (6.8) as it had done two years before. The percentage of the Korean people rating their political system as democratic was also virtually identical with the figure (62%) reported in 1994. In 1997, however, both the mean and percentage ratings stood much lower than they were in 1996. On a 10-point scale, the mean now stands at 6.3, a score which is half a point lower than the 1996 figure. The percentage rating Korea as a democratic state is 16 percentage points lower than the figure one year before (46% to 62%). At present, it is a minority, not a majority, who judge the Korean political system to be a democracy. In the eyes of the Korean people, the democratization of their political system has stalled prematurely after six years of steady progression and reversed its path downward. The steadily upward trajectory of democratic consolidation, which is soon followed by the movement toward deconsolidation, is the pattern of procedural democratization in Korea thus far.

How did the democratic progress of the regime of President Kim Young Sam compare to the Fifth Republic headed by former general Chun Doo Whan? This question requires a comparison of popular assessments of the former with those of the latter. As an aid in the evaluation, respondents to the six surveys were asked to rate the Chun

Table 1.2   Assessments of the Chun Doo Whan Regime, 1988–97

Survey Year	Mean on 10-Point Scale	Percentages		
		Authoritarian (A)	Democratic (B)	Difference (C = A–B)
1988	3.1	80.8	3.2	+77.6
1991	4.0	60.0	10.6	+49.4
1993	3.6	70.3	7.1	+63.2
1994	4.1	61.6	5.4	+56.2
1996	3.4	72.3	5.7	+66.6
1997	3.9	62.4	7.3	+55.1

Source: Korean Democratization Surveys

regime on the same, 10-point ladder scale, as shown in Appendix B B1.1. Table 1.2 reports its mean scores on this scale together with the percentages of citizens who rated its character as authoritarian and democratic.

As expected, the Korean people are now much less critical of the Chun regime than they were immediately after it ended in disgrace ten years ago. Despite the likely fading memories of its repressive rule, the authoritarian character of the Chun regime remains remarkably stable in the minds of the people. For the past ten years, substantial majorities, (ranging from 60% to 81%) have consistently perceived Chun's regime as an authoritarian regime. More notable is the fact that nearly a third (29%) still remember the Chun regime as a complete, or nearly complete, dictatorship and place it at one of the two bottom steps (1st and 2nd) on the 10-point ladder scale.

To estimate the magnitude of progress in democratizing the military dictatorship, the ratings of the Chun regime from the earlier 1988 survey are used as a benchmark to compare the Kim Young Sam regime with those from the latest, 1997 survey. According to the means on the 10-point ladder scale, the Korean political system has advanced about one-third (3.2) of the way to a full democracy.

In terms of percentages, the people reporting democratic political experience have increased by 43 percentage points (3% under the Chun regime to 46% under the Kim Young Sam regime). Those experiencing authoritarian rule, on the other hand, have declined by a greater margin of 73 percentage points (81% to 8%). When 81 percent of the authoritarian rating for the Chun regime is compared with 46 percent of the democratic rating for the Kim regime, it is evident that the basic character of the Korean political system has been transformed from an overwhelmingly authoritarian to a partially democratic regime during the past decade of democratic rule.

Practising Democratic Politics

Political regimes, either authoritarian or democratic, are all collective undertakings and, thus, require satisfactory operation to justify their continuing existence. Like all other human institutions, a successful installation of new regimes does not necessarily guarantee their satisfactory operation. Of all regimes, moreover, democratic ones are more challenging and difficult to operate than their authoritarian or totalitarian counterparts mainly because more people take part in the process of the former than the latter.

How well has the democratic Sixth Republic of Korea been operating? To explore this question, four recent surveys (1991, 1993, 1996, and 1997) asked respondents to rate, on a 10-point scale, the way in which this democratic regime functions (Appendix B F2). A score of 1 represents "complete dissatisfaction" while a score of 10 "complete satisfaction." Table 1.3 reports means and percentages for those expressing dissatisfaction and satisfaction with the newly instituted democratic regime.

A comparison of means reveals considerable upward and downward shifts in the evaluation of the functioning of Korean democracy, indicating a high degree of uncertain dynamics. In November 1991, when the first democratic government led by former general Roh Tae Woo was three years old, the average on the 10-point scale was 4.8 – a score lower than its midpoint (5.5). Two years later, when Kim Young Sam assumed the presidency of the second democratic government as the first civilian president in three decades, it rose to 6.2, a score higher than the midpoint of the scale. In January 1996, when Kim's government was three years old, the ratings of Korean democracy in operation averaged 5.8 – slightly above the midpoint. In June 1997, when his government was engulfed in a series of corruption scandals, the average declined to

Table 1.3 Public Assessments of the Performance of the Sixth Republic (on a 10-Point Dissatisfaction–Satisfaction Scale)

Survey Year	Mean on 10-Point Scale	Percentages			
		Satisfied (A)	Dissatisfied (B)	Difference (A–B)	(N)
1991	4.8	19.6	42.9	–23.3	(1185)
1993	6.2	45.5	15.5	+30.0	(1198)
1996	5.8	35.6	19.0	+16.6	(1000)
1997	4.9	18.4	36.3	–17.9	(1117)

Source: Korean Democratization Surveys

4.9, which is virtually identical to the one six years ago. In short, the overall perceived quality of Korean democracy has failed to improve to any significant degree since 1991; also it has not established a clear pattern of movement, either upward or downward. To date, the quality of democratic performance in Korea, as perceived by the mass public, has been of a mixed nature and on a haphazard course.

This trend becomes more evident when percentage ratings in Table 1.3 are compared across the four survey periods. In any of the periods, a majority of the Korean people did not express dissatisfaction with the way their new democratic regime operated. They also did not express satisfaction with its operation under the Roh or Kim government. In the eyes of the people, many new institutions of a representative democracy have successfully been implanted on the Korean soil. These democratic institutions, nevertheless, have neither satisfied nor dissatisfied the majority of Koreans.

For a comprehensive portrayal of the dynamics of institutional democratization in Korea over the past five years, Table 1.4 considers the perceived character of the Sixth Republic together with the perceived quality of its operation. In 1991, about three-fifths (61%) judged their political regime as neither democratic nor functioning to their satisfaction. Since that time, the proportion of such completely negative ratings has fallen considerably – by 27 percentage points to one-third (34%) in 1993 and 11 percentage points to one-half (50%) in 1997. The proportion of fully positive ratings, on the other hand, has not been on the steady rise; it has been on a sharp rise/sharp fall trajectory. Consequently, a small minority (15%) still believe that their political system is a democracy and that it also functions well. To a large majority, the Korean political system today does not represent a well-functioning democracy.

Table 1.4   Character and Quality Assessments of the Sixth Republic of Korea, 1991–97

Regime	Change	Year			
Democratic character	Satisfying operation	1991	1993	1996	1997
NO	NO	61.4	33.6	33.4	50.2
NO	YES	4.5	8.5	6.0	3.4
YES	NO	19.1	20.9	31.0	31.4
YES	YES	15.1	37.0	29.6	15.0

Source: Korean Democratization Surveys

Transforming Authoritarian Culture
Pro-Democratic Dispositions

How much progress has been made by Koreans in their preference for democracy over authoritarian rule? The democratic transformation of authoritarian cultural values has been monitored with the last five of our six surveys by asking respondents to indicate, on a 10-point ladder scale, the extent to which they thought their country should be democratized (Appendix B C1.3). Figure 1.2 shows that the desire of the Korean people to live in a democracy increased for the 1991 to 1994 period and has varied little since then.

In 1991, when a question soliciting the desired level of democratization was asked for the first time, responses averaged 6.8 on the 10-point scale. In 1994, the mean jumped to 8.6 – indicating that, in a relatively short span of three years, the Korean people perceived themselves as advancing nearly one-fifth of the way toward becoming a fully democratic nation. For the 1994–96 period, however, their democratic desire remained unchanged. Since then, it has leveled off at 8.4.

A comparison of the percentage ratings of self-avowed democrats and authoritarians in Table 1.5 also reveals a similar pattern of change. The

Figure 1.2 Desired Levels of Democratization on a 10-Point, Democracy–Dictatorship Scale, 1991–97

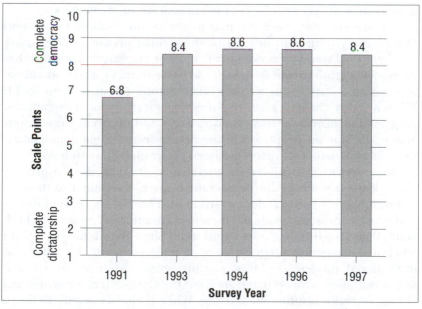

Source: Korean Democratization Surveys

Table 1.5   Percentages of Self-Avowed Democrats and Authoritarians

| Survey Year | Types of Political Preferences (%) | | | (N) |
	Democratic (A)	Authoritarian (B)	Difference (C = A–B)	
1991	60.3	13.5	+46.8	(1185)
1993	91.1	1.4	+89.7	(1198)
1994	93.6	1.5	+92.1	(1500)
1996	90.6	2.1	+88.5	(1000)
1997	91.5	1.6	+89.9	(1117)

Source: Korean Democratization Surveys

relative number of authoritarians among the Korean population dropped sharply from 14 percent to 2 percent while that of democrats soared from 60 percent to 94 percent for the 1991 to 1994 period. During that same time, more dramatic increases were found in those expressing the desire to live in a perfect, or nearly perfect, democracy by choosing one of the two top steps (9th and 10th) on the ladder scale. From 1991 to 1994, the percentage of strong democrats more than tripled (from 18 to 57). From the second half of the first democratic government headed by Roh Tae Woo to the first half of the second democratic government, one-third of the Korean population became democrats, and two-fifths joined the ranks of strong democrats.

In sharp contrast, from the first to the second half of the second democratic government headed by the civilian president Kim Young Sam, the total number of democrats has not increased; instead, it has decreased slightly (from 94% to 92%). The number of democrats of strong identification has also declined slightly (from 57% to 51%). These negative changes, taken together, suggest that no more significant progress has been made in democratizing authoritarian dispositions among the Korean people. As in the case of institutional democratization, cultural democratization has been prematurely put on hold.

The trajectories of cultural democratization to date, as measured by levels of the preference for democratic change, are similar to those of institutional or structural democratization. The first six years of democratic rule witnessed a steady and incremental pattern of progress in both cultural and institutional democratization. Since that initial period, no additional democratic progress has been achieved in either a cultural or institutional dimension. More notably, major advances in cultural democratization have occurred always in the aftermath of governmental change or major institutional reforms. When political institutions fail to democratize further, so does political culture. This suggests that culture may not be a cause of institutional democratization (Friedman 1994: 20).

Anti-Authoritarian Dispositions

Sharp increases in the preference for democracy over the past eight years, moreover, have not brought about parallel declines in authoritarian values or an outright rejection of those values. Specifically, the percentage of those voicing desires for more democratization has risen – in 1988 (78%), 1993 (79%), 1994 (84%), 1996 (91%), and 1997 (90%) (Appendix B E3.3). During that same period, however, there was no discernible decline in the percentage believing that authoritarian rule is more effective than democracy in tackling the serious problems facing the Korean nation.

In 1988, 16 percent of the national sample disagreed with the statement that "democracy will be able to solve all the serious problems facing the nation." In 1993, about the same percentage (17%) agreed with the statement that "dictatorship is more successful than a democratic government in solving the nation's serious problems." In 1994, over three times as many (61%) agreed, at least somewhat, with the statement that "The dictatorial rule led by a strong leader like Park Chung Hee is much better than a democracy to tackle the various problems facing our country." Again, in 1996, a majority (53%) were in agreement with the statement: "For our country these days, strong leadership is needed more than democracy." In 1997, a greater majority (67%) were clinging to the authoritarian political habit by agreeing with the statement: "The dictatorial rule led by a strong leader like Park Chung Hee is much better than a democracy to tackle the various problems facing our country."

Obviously, one decade of democratic rule has not helped the majority of Koreans to overcome the authoritarian political tendencies into which they had long been socialized. Consequently, they still live in a world of political ambivalence – desiring to be free from political oppression while simultaneously wanting to be led by a strong leader. As experienced in West Germany decades ago, their political ambivalence reflects "the juxtaposition of two valued goals: order and democracy" (Dalton 1994: 477).

Regional Rivalry

Unlike many other new democracies, Korea is fortunate to be an ethnically, as well as linguistically, homogeneous society. Yet, Korea has been highly polarized by a long history of regional rivalries – especially between the Cholla (Honam) and Kyongsang (Yongnam) provinces (Park & Jang 1998; see also Bae & Cotton 1993; J. Choi 1993b; Dong 1997; H. Lee 1995). As in post-Franco Spain, these rivalries must be eased to build a democratic political system in which "bargaining and

Figure 1.3   Changing Magnitude of Correlation Between Region and
Authoritarian Preference, 1988–97

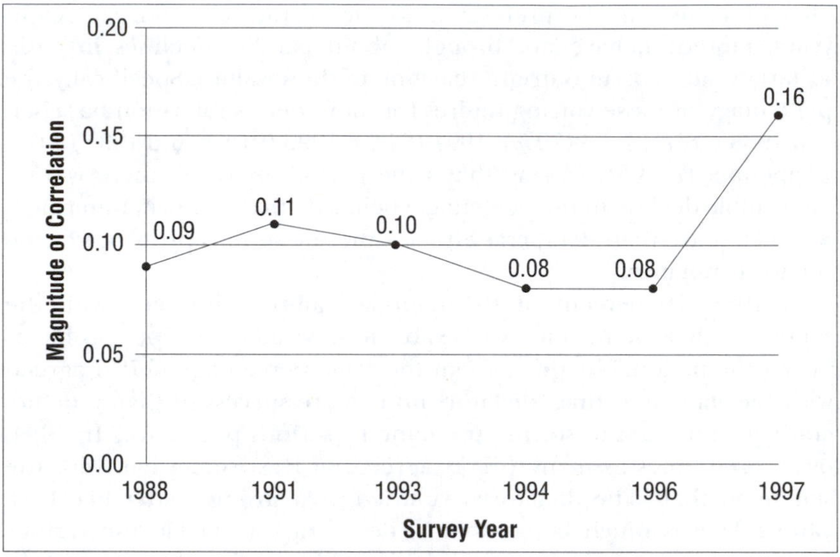

Source: Korean Democratization Surveys

compromise have become commonplace" (McDonough, Barnes & Pina
1994: 351).

In an attempt to monitor any slackening of political conflicts resulting
from a parochial culture of regionalism, we calculated the correlations
(*eta*) between the region of residence and preference for dictatorship
over democracy as a means of handling a variety of national problems.
Figure 1.3 displays changes in the magnitude of these correlation
coefficients over the past ten years of democratic rule. The higher the
correlations, the greater the level of political disagreements among
residents of different regions and the lower their chance for political
compromises. Conversely, lower correlations represent the lower the
level of their political polarization, the greater the chance for their
political co-operation.

Judging from the absence of any significant downward trend in the
magnitude of its correlation coefficients, each region has changed little
as a force contributing to political divisions among the Korean population. More alarming is its rising influence during the past year, as
indicated by a significant increase in the coefficient. The *eta* coefficient
declined slightly to 0.08 in 1994 from 0.09 in 1988 but has doubled to
0.16 in 1997 from 0.08 in 1996. A similar trend is also observed in
the percentage difference between residents of the Cholla and
Kyongsang regions in support of authoritarianism. The percentage

differential index rose from four in 1988, through five in 1991, to an all-time high of twenty-eight points in 1997. Obviously, a parochial culture of regionalism still remains undiminished as a force polarizing the Korean political process.

Democratic Congruence Between Regime and Culture

Overall progress in a country's democratization involves more than the democratization of the political regime and its cultural values on their own. The country becomes more democratic in relation to the extent to which its institutions and values become democratically congruent with each other (Fuchs, Guidorossi & Svensson 1995: 327). This dimension of Korea's democratic progress is estimated in terms of the percent of respondents who not only desired but also affirmed the democratization of their political system. Figure 1.4 shows upward and downward fluctuations in the expressed degree to which the public's desire to live in a democracy is realized.

In 1988, the year when the first democratic government of the Sixth Republic was inaugurated, only one-fifth (20%) found this regime congruent with their democratic desire. With the inauguration of the

Figure 1.4   Changing Levels of Democratic Congruence Between Institutions and Values, 1988–97

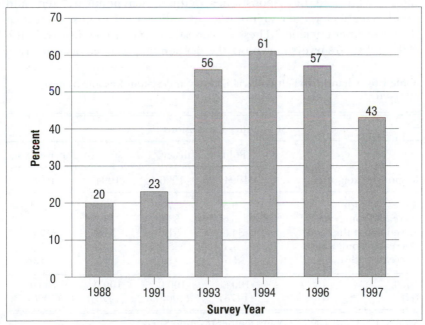

Source: Korean Democratization Surveys

second democratic government, more than one-half (56%) of the
Korean population found congruence between their democratic affinity
and regime character. A year later when President Kim carried out a
series of bold reform measures such as the real-name accounting system,
about three-fifths (61%) found their political system commensurate with
their desire for democracy. With no more reforms of any substantive
significance taking place in 1995 and 1996, the percentage of those
Koreans has declined to 43, which is 18 percentage points lower than
what it was in 1994. Nonetheless, when this latest rating is compared with
the one for 1988, it is apparent that the overall level of democratization
in Korea has increased two-fold since it formally began its democratic
transition in 1988.

Substantive Democratization

For human existence to become truly meaningful, democratization has
to bring about significant improvements to the extent that a political
system responds to the preferences of the mass public with "a rich
bundle of substantive goods" (Dahl 1989: 175). In addition, it should
bring about similar changes to enable the masses, who were oppressed
for long periods by heavy-handed authoritarian rulers, to influence the
making of public policies (Dahl 1992; Sartori 1995). How has democratization affected the responsiveness of the Korean political system, and
how has it affected the real influence its ordinary citizens exert on what
the government decides? These two questions were asked directly in the
1994 and 1996 surveys to explore the deepening presence of democracy

Table 1.6   Changes in Felt Political Efficacy and System Responsiveness,
1994–96

| | Substantive Dimensions (%) | | | |
| | Political efficacy | | System responsiveness | |
Response Categories	1994	1996	1994	1996
Increased a lot	9.5	7.2	10.5	6.4
Increased somewhat	46.6	33.6	43.2	38.5
Stayed about the same	34.5	51.6	34.7	47.8
Decreased somewhat	7.7	5.7	10.4	5.4
Decreased a lot	1.7	1.9	1.2	1.9
Total	100.0	100.0	100.0	100.0
(N)	(1475)	(1000)	(1475)	(1000)

Sources: 1994 and 1996 Korean Democratization Surveys

in the policy-making process (Appendix B B3 and B5). For each survey, Table 1.6 reports the distribution of the responses to these questions across four categories extending from "increased a great deal" to "decreased a great deal."

In 1994, a slim majority (54%) replied that the current democratic political system was *very much* or *somewhat more* responsive to their preferences than the old authoritarian political system. A slightly greater proportion (56%) reported feeling a greater sense of influence under the new democratic government than the old military regime. When the percentage ratings for both the input and output phases of the democratic political process are considered together, about two-thirds (64%) experienced at least some degree of substantive improvements in political life. Those experiencing significant improvements in *both* phases of the process, however, comprised only a small percentage (5%) of the Korean population.

In the 1996 survey, majorities reported no substantive improvements in either the input or the output phases of the policy-making process. In responding to public preferences, considerably less than half (45%) of the Korean population judged the current regime to be more responsive than its authoritarian predecessor that was dominated by the military. In their attempts to exert political influence, a smaller minority (41%) said they were feeling a greater sense of influence under the current democratic regime. Although a small majority (54%) still feel that they benefited, at least somewhat, from that change, a minuscule proportion (2%) now claims that the eight years of democratic rule has brought about significant progress toward empowering and representing the mass citizenry in the political process.

A comparison of these 1994 and 1996 ratings reveals that the past two years have represented significant declines in the view that the democratic Sixth Republic does a better job of running the government for and by the people than that of the authoritarian Fifth Republic. It appears likely that the longer the Korean people wait for the democratic government to tackle the age-old problems of redistributing wealth and providing protection against discrimination, the more they become impatient and disenchanted with democratic governance itself. For that reason, an increasing number of ordinary Koreans are now refusing to draw a distinction between the two republics in heeding and transforming their substantive concerns into tangible governmental actions.

While about seven-tenths (73%) agree that the institutional apparatus of the military regime was dismantled, only a small minority (27%) experience greater degrees of political influence and representation in the wake of such regime transformation. To a majority of the Korean people, it is evident that the democratization of authoritarian political institutions has failed to bring about a profound shift in the way policies are formulated and implemented.[9] In their eyes, the evolution in substantive democratization is a much slower and more unsteady process than it was in procedural democratization.

Cross-National Comparisons
Institutional Democratization

How does democratization in Korea compare with what has occurred in other new democracies? To date, none of the other national and cross-national surveys conducted elsewhere has sought to monitor progress in institutional or cultural democratization on the 10-point numeric scales that have been used in the Korean surveys. To assess the actual practice of new democracies in Europe and Latin America, however, surveys often asked a question which reads: "How much are you satisfied with the way democracy works in your country – very satisfied, fairly satisfied, not very satisfied, or not at all satisfied?" Positive responses to this question, asked in 1996 Latino Barometer surveys of eighteen countries, are selected to compare with similar responses from the 1997 Korean survey that replicated the question. Figure 1.5 reports the percentages of those expressing satisfaction with the functioning of Korean and eighteen other new democracies, including that of Spain, which is one of the oldest in the current wave of global democratization.

As the figure illustrates, Korea ranks fourth in the extent of satisfaction with the actual practice of democracy, and it is one of the four countries where half or more of the populations expressed satisfaction with democratic practice. As one of the oldest and consolidated third-wave democracies, Spain (57%) stands out as the democratically most satisfied of the nineteen countries compared in Figure 1.5. Not much behind this Southern European democracy are the two oldest Latin American democracies – Uruguay (52%) and Costa Rica (51%) – and Korea (50%). Korea leads the rest of fifteen new democracies by substantial margins (ranging from 16% to 39%).

How does the current practice of Korean democracy compare with those of Spain and older democracies when they were at a comparable stage of democratic consolidation? To explore this question, the 1996 Korean survey replicated an item that Morlino & Montero (1995) asked in their 1985 surveys of four countries in Southern Europe: "With which of the following statements do you agree?: (1) Our democracy works well, (2) Our democracy has many defects, but it works, and (3) Our democracy is getting worse, and soon it will not work at all." Table 1.7 presents results of three European surveys alongside those of the 1996 Korean survey. In 1985, when the European surveys were conducted, the

Figure 1.5   Comparing the Satisfied with the Practice of Democracy

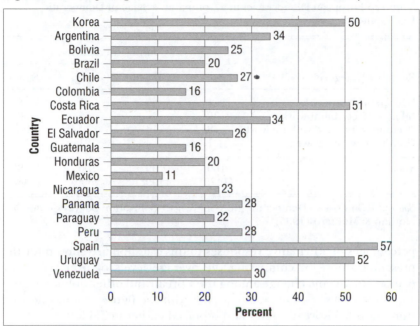

Sources: 1997 Korean Democratization Survey; 1996 Latino Barometer quoted in Lagos (1997)

Greek, Portuguese, and Spanish democracies were slightly older than is the Korean democracy now. Of the four countries listed in Table 1.7, however, Korea (81%) and Greece (81%) are the two countries where about four-fifths viewed the practice of their democracy in a positive light. In both Portugal (68%) and Spain (68%), about seven-tenths gave positive ratings. The overall conclusion we derived from comparisons with countries in Latin America and Southern Europe is that Korea, as a new democracy, tends to perform better than most of its predecessors in those regions.

Cultural Democratization

Do Koreans also tend to favor the idea of democracy to a greater extent than citizens of other new democracies? This question is explored with national random sample surveys of the adult populations of Bulgaria, Estonia, Hungary, Lithuania, Poland, Romania, Russia, and Ukraine (Evans & Whitefield 1995). In these 1993 surveys, the following question was asked: "How do you feel about the aim of introducing democracy in your country in which parties compete for government?" National

Table 1.7 Comparing Evaluations of Korean Democracy with those of Southern European Democracies at a Comparable Stage of Democratic Development

Response Categories	Country (percent)			
	Korea	Greece	Portugal	Spain
"Our democracy works well"	11	35	5	8
"Many defects, but it works"	70	46	63	60
"Getting worse, and will not work"	18	14	11	20
"Don't know/no answer"	1	4	21	11
Total	100	99	100	99
(N)	(1475)	(1998)	(2000)	(2488)

Sources: 1996 Korean Democratization Survey; 1985 4-Nation Survey quoted in Morlino & Montero (1995)

percentages of affirmative responses to this question are chosen for the present purpose of comparing the average levels of preference for democratic regime change among the Korean and other publics. Figure 1.6 reports these percentages together with the figure that was derived from the 1993 Korean survey and reported earlier in Table 1.5.

The wording of the question asked in the European surveys is different from the one in the Korean survey, which asked respondents to express, on a 10-point scale spanning from a low of 1 (complete dictatorship) to a high of 10 (complete democracy), their preference for democratic regime change. However, both questions could be considered functionally equivalent, intending to tap idealistic attachment to democracy. Figure 1.6 reveals that supporters of democratic regimes involve a significantly larger percentage in Korea than in any of the eight European countries surveyed. Korea leads all of these countries with the exception of Romania by as much as 30 percentage points or more and it leads Romania by 10 percentage points. It also leads four European new democracies (Estonia, Poland, Russia, and Ukraine) by 40 percentage points or more. These findings indicate that Koreans are more in favor of democratic transition from authoritarian rule than their Eastern European contemporaries are.

How does the Koreans' attachment to the idea of democracy compare to what has been noted in old consolidated democracies? To explore this question, the 1997 Korean survey replicated an item recently asked in old democracies of Europe and Scandinavia. Table 1.8 presents results from the Korean survey and the 1992 Eurobarometer survey, which asked respondents whether they were in favor of or against the idea of democracy "in principle." From the table, we see that in all of the European countries, about 90 percent are in favor of the idea of democracy.

Figure 1.6   Cross-National Differences in Support for the Idea of Democratization

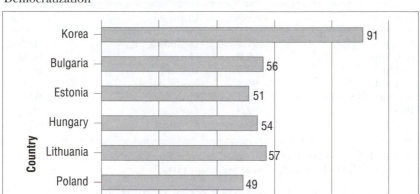

Sources: 1993 Korean Democratization Survey; 1993–94; 7-Nation Surveys quoted in Evans & Whitefield (1995)

In Korea, also, about 90 percent favor the idea. To be more precise, 92 percent of the Korean people prefer to live in a democracy. This figure is very close to those for Belgium (93%), Ireland (93%), and Italy (93%). When compared to the general level of public attachment to the idea of democracy, Korea appears to resemble many consolidated democracies in Europe.

Summary and Conclusions

Democratization in Korea during the past decade has not been a revolutionary process; instead, it has been an evolutionary process unfolding at unsteady and uneven paces. Furthermore, Korean democratization has not been a unidirectional process of progress; it has been a multi-directional movement, which can be characterized by two steps forward and one step backward. Although new democratic institutions and procedures have been implanted, the old values and practices of authoritarian politics have not been supplanted by the new values and practices of democratic politics. Consequently, the Korean polity today appears to resemble a mixed system combining the elements of democ-

Table 1.8 Comparison of Support for the Idea of Democracy

Country	Percent	Country	Percent
Korea	91.7	Denmark	97.5
Belgium	92.9	Germany	95.9
Britain	95.3	Ireland	93.3
Luxembourg	98.2	Netherlands	97.5
Northern Ireland	95.4	France	94.8
Italy	92.9	Greece	98.7
Spain	95.5	Portugal	95.5

Sources: 1997 Korean Democratization Survey; The Eurobarometer Survey No. 31 quoted in Fuchs, Guidorossi & Svensson (1995)

racy with those of authoritarianism (H. B. Im 1997a). Nonetheless, it is more accurate to characterize the current political system as a democracy rather than an authoritarian regime as Choi Jang Jip's (1996) balanced analysis suggests.

As a democracy, however, Korea today merely meets the minimalist or Schumpeterian requirement of electoral competition. Even as an electoral or procedural democracy, Korean democracy is limited because little competition exists among alternative ideas and rival organizations (B. Kim 1996: 2). In addition, it is restricted because it still excludes the labor force from the political process (Y. T. Jung 1997: 16; H. C. Sohn 1995: 267). Restricted participation and limited competition in the political process alone clearly signify that Korea has not made much progress in consolidating incipient democratic rule during the first decade of its democratization.

Structurally, all the basic institutions of representative democracy have been installed on a widespread basis; however, they have not been advancing at a steady pace toward higher levels of democracy. In addition, the progress of institutional democratization, to date, has been confined to the procedural aspects of democratic politics. As Jung Young-Tai (1997: 16) points out, political institutions, whether democratically elected or not, are still dominated by the *chaebol* conglomerates as they were under the authoritarian government. This has left the interests of the masses largely under-represented in formulating and implementing public policy. Consequently, in the eyes of its masses, the Korean political system is government elected *by* the people, but it is not government *for* the people. As a democracy, therefore, it has yet to improve much – especially in its ability to respond to the preferences of a majority of its citizenry.

Culturally, Korean democratization has also been of a limited nature. It has not been accompanied by a necessary transformation from authoritarian political customs to democratic practices. There have been no significant declines in the authoritarian political orientations into which Koreans have long been socialized. Therefore, a majority of the people still believe that authoritarian solutions are more instrumental than democratic ones in dealing with the nation's most serious problems. Also, elements of Korean political culture remain fragmented and polarized, mostly due to rivalries in the country's southern regions. While generational and ideological differences are no longer very influential in reorienting the Korean people toward democracy and away from authoritarianism, regional differences still remain a considerable force that reshapes their democratic and authoritarian dispositions. The presence of significantly different regional cultures especially in the Cholla and Kyongsang regions, for example, makes it difficult to establish the necessary groundwork for political bargaining.

These and other problems surrounding political institutions and cultural values make it clear that Korea is still far from being a consolidated democracy. For all the problems, however, its people as a whole remain attracted to the idea of democracy as much as citizens of other new and old consolidated democracies. At the same time, Koreans tend to perceive the practice of their new democratic regime in a more positive light than their peers elsewhere view theirs. Based on these findings, one may be tempted to conclude that Korea is better poised to prevent any reversal to authoritarian rule and become a fully consolidated democracy than other new democracies. In order for Korean democracy to consolidate fully, however, it requires much more than popular preference for and satisfaction with democracy.

CHAPTER 2

The Human Meaning of Democratization

"The care of human life and happiness, not their destruction, is the first and only legitimate end of good government."

Thomas Jefferson (1809: 16:359)

"A good democratic government not only considers the demands of its citizenry (that is, responsive), but also acts efficaciously upon those demands (that is, effective)."

Robert D. Putnam (1993: 63)

Many years have passed since the massive and powerful wave of democratization was celebrated with Beethoven's "Ode to Joy" in reunited Berlin. After the celebration, the democratic euphoria following the demise of oppressive authoritarian rule has faded in virtually every region of the world. Today, from Central Europe to South America and from East Asia to the Middle East, the somber tones of Wagner's *Götterdämmerung* are more often than not heard, echoing the struggling fate of democratization (Schlesinger 1997; Zakaria 1997). In Russia, for example, an increasing number of citizens are now expressing the view that only a dictatorship can save their country from a further decline in its quality of life.[1]

In many other new democracies as well, a growing number of ordinary citizens are questioning the real value of democratic transitions from authoritarian rule (Auchincloss 1992; Dalton 1996: 281; Jowitt 1992; S. W. Kim 1997). They appear to be asking themselves: "What have all the democratic reforms that have been implemented so far accomplished?" "What type of political reform is needed in order to bring about significant improvements in the quality of our lives and our country's?" "Is a democratic expansion or an authoritarian reversal required?" Undoubtedly these are not the questions concerning the changing institutional context or cultural environment with which ordinary citizens of new democracies have to deal. Instead, citizens focus on the human dimension of democratic reform involving its true meaning and real consequences, which they experience on a daily basis.[2]

As I will illustrate in Chapter 8, the perceived impact of democratic reform on humans shapes the dynamics of popular support for a newly instituted democratic regime itself. As Weil (1989) suggests, new democratic regimes are supported for what they are believed to be as well as for how they are perceived to perform. Mishler & Rose (1996: 563) point out that popular support for those regimes depends, also, upon how they are expected to perform in the future. Therefore, continuing support for new democracies, like the one in Korea, requires more than positive evaluations of democracy-in-principle; it also relies on favorable evaluations and expectations of democracy-in-action.

.The objective of this chapter is to explore the human consequences of democratization regarding the quality of Korean life. Specifically, consequences of past and future democratic change for the quality of life among the Korean people are evaluated from a global, or holistic, perspective, i.e. their life quality as a whole rather than by its constituent domains. In addition, those consequences are evaluated from a relative perspective by comparing their new democratic regime with the past authoritarian and *potential* future democratic ones. Combining these two perspectives, this chapter addresses a number of questions that have been largely ignored in prior research on democratization.

How has the advent of democracy in Korea affected the quality of life that its citizens experience in their daily lives? Do the Korean people expect any more gains or losses from the further expansion of their limited democracy? How have all the democratic reforms implemented to date affected Korea as a place for ordinary Koreans in which to live? Have those reforms enhanced the quality of Korean life on a broad basis? Which sphere of Korean life, public or private, has benefited and will benefit more from democratization? This chapter addresses these questions by means of analyzing the national sample survey conducted in November 1993.

Premises

Four premises underlie the analysis of the 1993 survey, which is reported below. First, democratization is a dynamic and multifaceted phenomenon involving the transformation of the very essence of human existence and its meaning. Unlike other types of political change, democratic regime transition brings about a fundamental shift in the nature of the relationships between fellow human beings and their basic orientation toward life itself (Drakulic 1993; Rosenberg 1995; de Tocqueville 1956; Wong 1996).

Second, the real meaning of democratic change, like beauty, can be understood only by those who directly experience it on a daily basis (B. K. Kim 1997; Thompson 1970). The best judges of Korean democratization as a human phenomenon are, therefore, neither political scientists, trained in democratic theory, nor political leaders chosen to represent the Korean electorate. Ordinary Koreans, who demanded democratic change even at the risk of their own lives, are best qualified to judge its consequences for their own lives and their country's.

The third premise is that ordinary Koreans, like their counterparts in other democratizing countries, react either positively or negatively to a broad range of the specific measures adopted to democratize authoritarian rule. With the accumulation of these reactions, citizens are capable of making global reports on democratic regime change as a whole or in general. In addition, they are able to make such global assessments of democratic political life from a variety of absolute and relative perspectives (Andrews & Withey 1976; Campbell, Converse & Rodgers 1976).

Finally, a global assessment of a new democratic regime from a *relative* perspective is assumed to matter a great deal more to its survival and functioning than that of an *absolute* perspective. In this regard, Mishler & Rose (1996) point out that a new democracy does not have to be valued in itself; it suffices to be preferred as the least evil of the regimes in which people have lived all or most of their lives. In their words, fear of the past and hope for the future make support for democracy buoyant.

Prior Research

To date, the human consequences of democratization have been explored exclusively through the comparison of different types of political systems in terms of availability of, or access to, the resources necessary for satisfying human needs. Some scholars, for example, have sought to determine whether or not democracies are more successful in achieving economic development and equality while avoiding famine and other human disasters (Burkhart & Lewis-Beck 1994; Barrow 1994; Cheng & Krause 1991; Feng 1997; Inkeles 1991; Leblang 1997; Nelson 1994; Przeworski & Limongi 1997; Remmer 1993). Others have sought to determine whether or not democracies are more peace-loving and less murderous than non-democracies (Rummel 1995; Russett 1993). Still others have sought to determine whether democracies contribute to health, literacy, and other physical qualities of human life (Ersson & Lane 1996; B. Moon 1991; Sen 1993; D. Shin 1989).

In short, previous studies have focused on cross-regime comparisons of economic and other tangible resources for human life instead of directly examining changes in these resources in the wake of democratization. With few exceptions these analyses of aggregate data have been concerned merely with the physical environment or objective conditions of life attributable to democratic rule (Leftwich 1996; see also Haggard & Kaufman 1995; Hadenius 1992). National and cross-national sample surveys, on the other hand, have focused exclusively on economic life (Clarke, Dutt & Kornberg 1993; Duch 1993, 1995; Gibson 1996b; Finifter & Mickiewicz 1992; McIntosh & Mac Iver 1992; McIntosh et al. 1994; Miller, Hesli & Reisinger 1994; Rose & Haerpfer 1994, 1996).[3]

More access to and improvements in economic and other objective life conditions, however, do not necessarily mean an experience of greater well-being, i.e. greater happiness among a larger proportion of the citizenry. As recent research on the quality of life indicates (Andrews 1986; Andrews & Withey 1976; Campbell 1981; Campbell, Converse & Rodgers 1976), rising affluence and improvements in other life conditions do not necessarily bring about a greater sense of well-being. For these reasons, much of the empirical research to date, whether based on public opinion surveys or aggregate data, has failed to determine whether or not democratic transition and consolidation actually enhance the quality of life as perceived and envisioned by the people themselves.

Theoretical Considerations

Democratic theorists of various persuasions have long argued that a democratic political system contributes to a greater quality of life among its citizens (Dahl 1989; Gastil 1992; Warren 1992).[4] According to Powell (1982), who summarizes this literature, the citizens of democracies, unlike those of non-democracies, are free to pursue what they privately cherish in their own lives. Moreover, in the public sphere of their lives, competitive and periodic elections provide ordinary citizens with opportunities to take part in the political process and also allow them the opportunity to express a variety of their needs and preferences. The democratic mechanism of mass participation and competition also encourages political leaders to be responsive to those public interests – especially to those of a majority rather than a small minority.

What specific needs and desires of the citizenry can be fulfilled by the transformation of authoritarian rule into a democracy? Democracy has been recommended as an instrument for the fulfilment of various human needs and desires, which include a desire for self-enhancement (Lane 1962; Macpherson 1977; Pateman 1970; Sniderman 1975), altruism (Lasswell 1951; McClosky & Zaller 1984; Schwartz 1987), moral virtue (Dahl 1989), self-interest (Schumpeter 1976), and social recognition (Fukuyama 1992). In other words, advocates of democracy argue that democratization can serve both personal and social utility functions. On a personal level, democracy can contribute to the interest and welfare of individual citizens. Socially, democracy can promote the welfare of the community in which citizens live. These ideas pose several questions. Does democratization actually serve the personal utility function of all citizens? Does it serve the social utility function of every national or local community? Which utility function does it serve more effectively, and why? These and other important questions, concerning the real meaning of democratization for citizens, have not been systematically addressed in the large body of the existing scholarly literature.

Up to this point, considerable disagreement exists in the literature over the specific roles that democratization would play in the private and public spheres of human life. Jean-Jacques Rousseau, James Madison, de Tocqueville, Max Weber, and other theorists of communitarian democracy have argued that democracy maximizes the public good by aggregating and reconciling conflicting interests among divergent groups of the citizenry. Conversely, John Stuart Mill, John Dewey, Carole Pateman, and other theorists of participatory democracy have emphasized that democracy maximizes opportunities for self-growth and self-governance. Adding to the confusion, these two contrasting democratic theories of human development have not been subjected to empirical testing by political scientists or other social scientists.

Key Concepts

In the minds of ordinary people, democratization involves much more than the transformation of repressive political institutions and the replacement of political leaders – a dimension of regime change that can be relatively easily and quickly accomplished (Rose & Mishler 1994). Having lived all or most of their lives in political repression and economic poverty, the mass publics of nascent democracies bring many expectations to the process of democratic change and view it as "a means to effectuate improvement in the overall quality of human life" (Sklar 1996: 40). Also, the meaning of democratization varies a great deal from one segment of the public to another within the same country (Miller, Hesli & Reisinger 1995, 1997; Simon 1994). During the peak of the 1987 pro-democracy movement in Korea, for example, its supporters were divided into two opposing camps, one concerned mostly with electoral politics and the other with political freedom as well as economic equality or social justice (S. Kim 1997: 1138). Even to the same citizenry, moreover, the meaning of democratization can change over time with perceived successes or failures in the actual practice of democratic politics.[5]

In view of the fact that democratization is really an ongoing process, one which lends itself to varying definitions, this study allowed ordinary citizens themselves to characterize what it actually meant to them. Naturally, the categories, arising from their own construction of the reality of democratization, would reflect the true meanings, which individual citizens attach to the very process, more accurately than the ones preconceived by those engaged in the research (Dryzek & Berejikian 1993).

Quality of life, like democratization, means different things to different people. To some, for example, it means more income and a bigger house; to others, it signifies more leisure time or cleaner air. Thus, equating quality of life with any particular type of a valued resource for human life does not permit a comprehensive and accurate assessment of the impact of democratization (see Campbell 1981; Glazer & Mohr 1987; Szalai & Andrews 1980). Therefore, in an attempt to make such an assessment, this study encouraged respondents in the 1993 survey to define and assess quality of life both as they perceived it and as they envisioned it.

Popular Conceptions of Democratization

How do the Korean people conceptualize democratization? Do they tend to agree with the notion that democratization is merely a process of political change involving the removal of tyranny and the establishment of representative institutions (Huntington 1989, 1996b; see also Dahl 1971; Rose, Mishler & Haerpfer 1998; Schmitter & Karl 1991)? Or, do Koreans tend to agree with the idea that embraces democratization as central to the solution to human dilemmas and suffering? According to de Tocqueville (1956: 136), "the gradual growth of democratic manners and institutions should be regarded, not as the best, but the only means of preserving freedom; and it . . . might be adopted as the most applicable and the fairest remedy for the present ills of society." Likewise, Friedman (1994: 35) contends that democratic change is "humanly and universally attractive" mainly because "beyond safeguarding against the general and extreme evils of chaos, plunder, alienation, fallibility, and ultimate disasters, democracy decreases the likelihood of painful daily indignities."

Conceptions of democratization among the Korean people were explored in the 1993 survey with a card containing several statements they might associate with democracy. The question, as shown in *Expectation* Appendix B A1, was phrased as follows: "People expect different things *from* from democratic change. Please look over the statements listed on this *democracy* card and identify all those you personally consider important to democratic political development in our country."

1 Expansion of political freedom
2 Participation of the mass public in politics
3 Economic development in the country
4 Guarantees for people's economic livelihood
5 Free competition among political parties

Figure 2.1   "Important" Features of Democratization

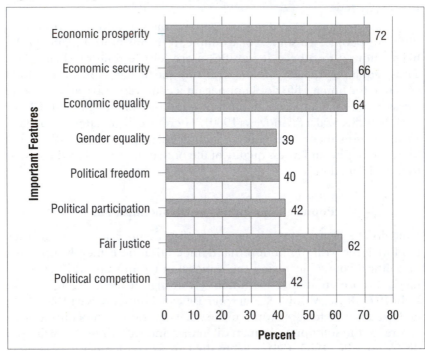

Source: 1993 Korean Democratization Survey

    6 A system of justice that treats everyone fairly
    7 Reducing the gap between the rich and the poor
    8 Achieving equality between the genders.

Four of these statements (1, 2, 5, and 6) focus on the political rights typically associated with the procedural or minimal notion of democracy, and the other four (3, 4, 7, and 8) correspond to the social and economic rights often associated with the substantive or maximal notion. For each statement, Figure 2.1 reports the percent who responded that it would be important to Korean democratization.

The Korean people are far from being united over what they consider the important components of democratization. Of the eight characteristics they were asked to evaluate, for example, none was cited by an overwhelming majority, i.e. two-thirds or more. Only four – national economic development, economic security, fair justice system, and economic equality – were cited as important components by majorities ranging from 62 percent to 72 percent. Among these four components of democratization, only one – a system of equal justice – is of a political nature, and the other three concern economic or social rights. The component that Koreans most frequently cited is national economic development (72%); this was followed by economic security (66%), economic inequality (64%), and fair justice (62%).

Of the three political characteristics that have been discussed most frequently in the literature as truly defining democracy, even a simple majority did not endorse them as important. The two procedural norms featuring public participation in the political process and free competition among political parties were each endorsed by a little over two-fifths (42%). More surprising is that an even smaller minority (40%) cited the expansion of political freedom as important to the process of Korean democratization. Taken together, these findings make it clear that Koreans, as a whole, are not inclined to equate democratization merely with political reforms – a minimalist definition advocated by scholars of liberal democracy.

Do Koreans tend to subscribe to a maximalist definition that emphasizes not only the expansion of political rights but also the improvement of socioeconomic life? A large majority (63%) associated democratization with four or more of the eight characteristics they were asked to choose. Moreover, a larger majority (78%) chose both political and socioeconomic rights as important to democratization. Only a small minority expressed concern solely with either socioeconomic rights (17%) or political rights (4%). In the minds of ordinary Koreans, democracy tends to be seen as "a quality pervading the whole life" (Macpherson 1977: 5). Based on this evidence, it is reasonable to conclude that Koreans tend to appreciate democratization as a movement to improve their human lot rather than merely as a governmental reform that seeks to improve their prospects in the political marketplace.

Retrospective Evaluations

The consequences of past and future democratic change for the quality of life were explored by means of Hadley Cantril's (1965) "self-anchoring striving scale," which has been widely used in studying life quality around the world (Andrews & Withey 1976; Campbell, Converse & Rodgers 1976; Gallup International Institute 1976). This instrument asks individuals to imagine "the best life" and "the worst life" and to indicate their past, present, and future locations on a 10-step life-ladder scale spanning the two extremes. By comparing the numeric ratings across different points in time, researchers have frequently measured experienced and expected changes in the quality of life (Andrews 1986; Barnes 1982; Gallup International Institute 1976; Szalai & Andrews 1980).

Figure 2.2 The Experienced Quality of Personal and National Life in Authoritarian and Democratic Eras on a 10-Point Scale

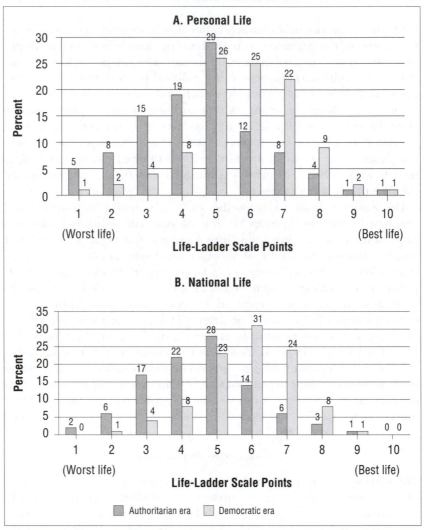

Source: 1993 Korean Democratization Survey

Specifically, the 1993 survey asked two sets of three questions in order to assess how past democratization has affected the quality of private and public life in Korea. The first set concerns the private sphere of life, which ordinary Koreans experience on an individual basis (Appendix J1(1)–J1(3)). The second set deals with the public sphere in which Koreans are involved as members of the national community (Appendix

I1(1)–I1(3)). On the 10-point scale, respondents were asked to assess their own and their country's lives at three different points in time or circumstance: (1) when they were living under the old Chun Doo Whan government, (2) at the present time under the Kim Young Sam government, and (3) at the present time if the authoritarian regime had to continue. The responses to both sets of questions were considered together to accurately ascertain the human consequences of past democratic change in terms of their magnitude, direction, and depth.

On what step of the ladder scale did Koreans mark what they had experienced during the period of authoritarian rule headed by President Chun Doo Whan (1980–88)? Where did they place themselves nearly six years later (November 1993) as citizens of the democratic regime under the leadership of President Kim Young Sam? Figure 2.2 displays the distribution of their responses to each of these questions across ten steps on the ladder scale.

When Koreans were asked to evaluate living under the harsh and repressive authoritarian regime of President Chun Doo Whan, a large majority responded negatively in regard to themselves and their country. On the 10-step life-ladder, three-quarters chose the bottom five steps in order to indicate the quality of private and public lives. These life-ladder steps chosen by a vast majority indicate varying degrees of ill-being rather than well-being. In the minds of Koreans in the surveys, authoritarian Korea was predominantly a nation of ill-being.

With the collapse of the military dictatorship and the restoration of civilian rule, Korea is becoming a nation of well-being. In striking contrast to the authoritarian period, a majority of Koreans chose the top five steps rather than bottom five of the life-ladder; they are now giving positive ratings to themselves as well as their country. As shown in Figure 2.2, positive ratings for democratic Korea are even higher than the negative ones, which represent its authoritarian past. It is evident that the quality of Korean life has been transformed from the negative to the positive with the establishment of a democratic regime.

In an attempt to determine the exact nature of this change in life quality, we calculated and compared average ladder scale ratings for the two spheres of life quality. According to the means, the quality of personal life has changed for the better by 1.3 steps of the ladder (from 4.5 to 5.8). The quality of national life has also improved by 1.3 steps (from 4.6 to 5.9). Such upward shifts represent considerable progress in building a nation of well-being, which indicates that Korea is a new democratizing country where the quality of its citizens' lives has been improving.

Significant improvements in the quality of Korean life in recent years, nonetheless, cannot be attributed solely to democratic regime change.

To deal with this concern, we asked respondents to locate on the same ladder scale the steps on which the quality of their personal and national lives would have been experienced today if the authoritarian rule of President Chun Doo Whan had been allowed to continue in their country (Appendix B I1.3 and J1.3) Their responses to the questions were taken into account to more accurately estimate the impact of democratic regime change on the quality of their private and public lives.

If the authoritarian rule had continued until the time of the survey, the mean rating for private life would have remained at the same level (4.5) while the same rating for public life would have shifted upward by 0.1 step (from 4.6 to 4.7). These findings confirm the popular view that the authoritarian regime would have brought about little improvement in the overall quality of Korean life. Under the military government, the Korean people as a whole would have remained as personally discontented as they were prior to the installation of a democratic regime six years ago, and their country would have remained as nearly undesirable a place to live as it had been before.

An index was constructed to measure the net impacts of democratization on the quality of Korean life. Scores were calculated by subtracting individual respondents' ladder ratings, indicating the quality of life they would have experienced without the democratic transition, from their ratings for what they were actually experiencing with the democratic change. The index scores run from a low of –9 to a high of +9. The lowest score (–9) signifies that democratization was perceived as having transformed the best quality of life into the worst one. The highest score (+9), on the other hand, shows the opposite pattern of having transformed the worst into the best quality of life. Positive scores indicate that democratization has contributed to the quality of life, and negative scores indicate that democratization has detracted from it. Whether positive or negative, the higher the scores, the greater the extent of democratic impact on the quality of life.

According to this index measuring democratic impact, democratization itself has affected the quality of life among a large majority of the Korean population – over two-thirds (69%) in their private lives and three-quarters (75%) in their public lives. Yet it has rarely brought about the complete transformation of life quality from the worst to the best or, conversely, from the best to the worst. A small minority (3%) believed that the democratic political change moved their life-quality ratings either upward or downward by five steps or more on the 10-step ladder scale. Of those affected by democratic change, over two-thirds reported a movement of only one or two steps on the scale; this is only a modest change.

Being a multi-dimensional movement, the advent of democracy cannot be expected to bring about greater well-being for everyone. This was
confirmed. Nevertheless, democratic reforms in Korea for the 1988–93
period were far more conducive than detrimental to the quality of life.
With respect to personal life, 67 percent gained from those reforms
while 14 percent lost. In national life, 65 percent gained, while 14 percent lost during the same democratic reforms. While 38 percent
experienced net improvements in private as well as public lives, only
10 percent have experienced net declines in both. This is the most
significant evidence to support the participatory and pluralist theories
of democracy, which hold that democratization, if managed well,
continues to improve the human condition.

Another significant finding shows that democratic regime change
does not affect the two spheres of citizens' lives equally. However, when
comparing the two different spheres of Korean life, it has been more
effective in improving public life. Of those who have gained only in one
sphere, for example, gainers in public life lead those in private life (by a
margin of 13% to 8%). This evidence, together with what will be presented in Chapter 8, supports Jean-Jacques Rousseau and other theorists
of communitarian democracy who claim that democratization, at least
in its initial phase, contributes more to public life than to private life.

Table 2.1 reports a 5-point index summarizing the overall impacts of
democratic regime change on the perceived quality of life that Koreans
attribute to it. It scores a low of −2 when the private and public spheres
of Korean life were perceived as being affected negatively, and it scores
a high of +2 when both spheres were perceived as being affected
positively. According to the percentage figures reported in the table,
gainers from democratic reform outnumber losers by a large margin
(71% to 13%). For every Korean who has experienced a decline in the
overall quality of his or her life, more than five have experienced an
improvement. Moreover, of the majority who have gained, over three
times as many are absolute gainers, i.e. those who have gained in their
private as well as public lives. Of the minority who have lost, on the other
hand, there is little difference between absolute and relative losers.
Between absolute gainers and absolute losers from democratization
during its initial period, however, the former surpass the latter by a
margin of 54 to 8 percent.

On the basis of these findings, what can be said about democratization
concerning its disparate impact on the human lot? First, it can be argued
that the current wave of democratization, although massive and
powerful, is unlikely to affect all members of the society. It does not
uniformly affect every sphere of the human lot nor does it necessarily
enhance life. As a human phenomenon, democratization affects people

Table 2.1 Overall Depth of Democratic Impact on Quality of Life as Perceived by Korean Citizens

	Distribution	
Index Values	Percentage	(N)
-2	7.6	(87)
-1 .	5.6	(64)
0	16.2	(186)
+1	16.6	(191)
+2	54.0	(622)
Total	100.0	(1150)

Source: 1993 Korean Democratization Survey

differently, and it affects the various spheres of their lives differently. All in all, however, democratization is a movement that mitigates human suffering and produces greater well-being, as de Tocqueville declared more than 150 years ago.

Prospective Evaluations

What political changes do the Koreans prefer as the means to enhance *their* well-being as well as that of their country? Is it the full consolidation of the existing limited democracy or a reversal to the military rule in which they lived in the past? To explore questions regarding the preferred type of political change, the 1993 survey first asked respondents to indicate on the 10-step ladder scale where they thought they and their country would stand five years in the future if President Kim Young Sam ended his tenure with complete success in all his efforts to further democratize Korean politics (Appendix B I1.4 and J1.4). The survey next asked them where, on the same scale, they and their country would stand five years in the future if those democratic reforms efforts fail completely and the military returns to rule the country again as it did before (Appendix B I1.5 and J1.5).

Figure 2.3 illustrates two contrasting patterns of response distribution: one for the alternative of a fully democratic state and the other for that of an authoritarian political system ruled by the military. In the first pattern, most respondents are clustered around the steps on the top one-fourth of the ladder; this indicates considerable degrees of well-being. In the second pattern, however, most of those same respondents are clustered around the steps on the bottom one-fourth of the ladder, which indicates considerable degrees of ill-being. These two patterns contrast sharply also with the one shown in Figure 2.2 for the

Figure 2.3   Expected Quality of Personal and National Life Under Full
Democracy and Military Rule on a 10-Point Scale

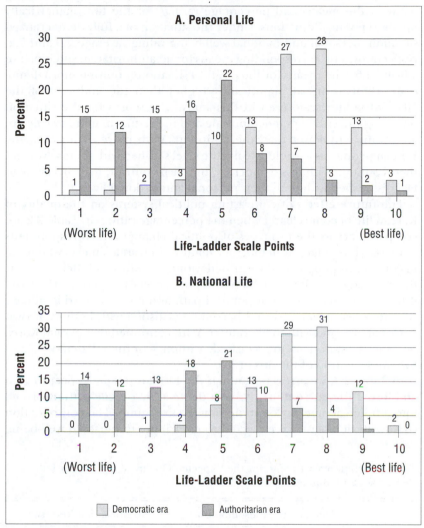

Source: 1993 Korean Democratization Survey

current limited democratic system in which most respondents are
clustered around the steps in the middle part of the life-ladder. Thus, to
most Koreans, democratic consolidation means a life of considerable
well-being; authoritarian reversal, a life of considerable ill-being; and the
status quo of limited democracy, a life mixed with well-being and
ill-being.

Table 2.2 summarizes the data presented in Figure 2.3. The most striking feature of the data in this table concerns the gaps existing between the means and percentage ratings for the two diametrically opposed political situations. Under the situation of a fully democratized situation, personal and national well-being ratings average 7.0 and 7.2, respectively. The corresponding means for an authoritarian situation are 4.0 and 4.0. The means for the political situation requiring more democratic reforms are all significantly higher than the midpoint of the 10-point ladder scale used in this study. The scores for the situation requiring the end of democratic rule and the return of military rule are all significantly lower than the midpoint. With more democracy, the Korean people, as a whole, are likely to feel satisfied with themselves and their country. With less democracy, in sharp contrast, they are likely to feel dissatisfied with both their personal and national lives.

The future effects of contrasting political systems on the quality of Korean life become clearer when the percentage ratings in Table 2.2 are compared across the two types of political change, which respondents were asked to judge. As democracy matures in Korea, an overwhelming majority of its people will be satisfied with themselves and their country; the satisfied would be more than four out of every five people. However, if Korea reverses its current political path and moves toward a military regime nearly as many would become dissatisfied with both their own personal lives and with their country. With continued democracy, Korea becomes a nation of the satisfied; without continued democracy, it becomes a nation of the dissatisfied.

In Table 2.3, we assess how much the Korean people expect to gain and lose if the current, newly born democratic regime is transformed into a fuller democracy or an authoritarian regime. The consolidation of Korean democracy is expected to contribute to personal well-being

Table 2.2 Summary Ratings for the Expected Quality of Life Under Full Democracy and Military Rule

| | Democratic Consolidation | | | | Authoritarian Reversal | | | |
| | Mean on ladder scale | Percentages | | | Mean on ladder scale | Percentages | | |
		pos.	neg.	dif.		pos.	neg.	dif.
Personal life	7.0	84	17	+67	4.0	20	80	−60
National life	7.2	89	11	+78	4.0	22	79	−57

Keys   pos: = positive   neg. = negative   dif. = difference
Source: 1993 Korean Democratization Survey

Table 2.3 Expected Impact of Democratic Consolidation and Authoritarian Reversal on the Quality of Personal and National Life

	Mean Ratings		Percentage Ratings					
	Authori-tarian reversal	Demo-cratic advance	Authoritarian reversal			Democratic advance		
			gain	loss	dif.	gain	loss	dif.
Personal life	−1.8	+1.2	11	72	−61	75	4	+71
National life	−1.9	+1.3	10	77	−67	83	3	+80

Source: 1993 Korean Democratization Survey

among 75 percent of the population and to detract from it among only 4 percent. The same change is expected to contribute to national well-being among 83 percent of the people while detracting from it among 3 percent. These statistics show that gainers lead losers by 71 percentage points in personal well-being and by 80 percentage points in national well-being. Indeed, a vast majority of the Koreans equate more democratization with greater well-being. Such an overwhelming sense of optimism about democratic consolidation appears to suggest that Koreans are convinced of the virtues of democratic politics.

From the data in Table 2.3, it is also clear that the Korean population, as a whole, rejects the restoration of a military dictatorship in their country. This type of regime change would detract from personal well-being among 72 percent of the people and from national well-being among 77 percent of the population. This reversal is expected to contribute to the quality of personal life among 11 percent of the population and to that of national life among 10 percent. Losers from the authoritarian political change lead gainers by 61 percent in personal well-being and 67 percent in national well-being. Clearly, the Korean population is strongly convinced that there are vices in authoritarian politics.

Table 2.4 provides a comparison of the overall expected consequences of democratic consolidation and a return to military rule by considering together the ratings of both personal and national well-being for each type of political change. The table shows that almost nine out of ten Koreans are likely to gain from the blossoming of democracy in at least one of the two life spheres surveyed. This proportion (87%) is almost nine times greater than those who are likely to gain from the restoration of authoritarian rule (10%). In terms of those who are likely to gain in both spheres of life quality, those gaining from the democratic expansion lead those gaining from the authoritarian reversal by an even greater margin (66% to 5%). As for those who are likely to lose in one or

Table 2.4 Expected Impact of Authoritarian Reversal and Democratic Consolidation on the Overall Quality of Korean Life

Values of the Overall Index of Life Quality	Types of Regime Change (percent)	
	Authoritarian reversal	Democratic advance
−2	64	1
−1	14	1
0	12	11
+1	5	21
+2	5	66
Total	100	100
(N)	(1156)	(1156)

Source: 1993 Korean Democratization Survey

both spheres, losers from the authoritarian change outnumber those from the democratic change by a large margin (78% to 2%). In terms of those who lose in both spheres, authoritarian losers lead democratic losers by the highest margin (64% to 1%).

For every person in Korea who is likely to gain from the authoritarian transformation of the current political system, nine Koreans are likely to do so from the further democratic transformation of the system. For every Korean who is likely to lose from the democratic change, as many as thirty-five Koreans are apt to lose from the authoritarian change. The rejection of authoritarian reversal is over three times stronger than the acceptance of democratic expansion.

On the basis of these findings, what can be said about the types of political change that are viewed as most and least conducive to the well-being of the Korean population? The findings, when considered together, make it clear that further advancement of democratization is the political change the Korean people want for themselves and their country. They believe that this type of regime change would contribute most to their well-being and least to their ill-being. The least desired type of political change is the movement away from democracy toward authoritarian rule. This is seen as contributing most to their ill-being and least to their well-being. This is compelling evidence that Koreans fear the authoritarian past and hope for the democratic future.

Patterns of Human Meaning

What kind of human phenomenon does the ongoing process of democratization represent to the Korean people? Does it represent an evolutionary process of human development? Or, does it represent a retrogressive process of the human lot? These questions are central to

Table 2.5 Patterns of Impact from Democratization on Korean Life

Patterns of Impact		Distribution	
Experienced	Expected	Percentage	(N)
Negative	Negative	0.5	(6)
Negative	Neutral	1.5	(17)
Negative	Positive	8.9	(102)
Neutral	Negative	0.5	(6)
Neutral	Neutral	2.5	(29)
Neutral	Positive	10.6	(122)
Positive	Negative	1.0	(12)
Positive	Neutral	7.3	(86)
Positive	Positive	67.2	(776)
Total		100.0	(1156)

Source: 1993 Korean Democratization Survey

an adequate understanding of the place that democratization occupies in Korean life, and they are explored in Table 2.5 by jointly considering retrospective and prospective views of the democratization process. The table lists nine distinctive patterns of the meaning that the Korean people attach to the ongoing process of democratization. The patterns were ascertained by cross-tabulating three categories of retrospective views – negative, neutral, and positive – with three identical categories of prospective views.

In Table 2.5, we see that Koreans are not concentrated in a few patterns; instead, they are spread across all nine patterns, including the two extreme ones of the consistently positive and consistently negative. This attests to the fact that there is no consensus on the human meaning of democratization among average Koreans, although it is identified in some scholarly circles with a progressive movement, which not only ended the long history of human misery and suffering but also embarked on a new era of greater human happiness (Fukuyama 1992).

Of the nine different patterns in the way that Koreans appreciate democratization, the prevailing pattern is a consistently steady progression. Two-thirds (67%) fall into this pattern of equating past, as well as future, democratic expansion with greater well-being. This is followed by two other patterns that also feature the progressive nature of democratization as a human phenomenon, i.e. the retrospectively negative–prospectively positive and the retrospectively neutral–prospectively positive. Slightly less than one-tenth (9%) fall in the former and slightly more than one-tenth (11%) in the latter. All in all, nearly nine out of ten Koreans (87%) believe in the progressive nature of democratic consolidation.

Among the least popular are three patterns, all of which relate democratic advances in the future to greater ill-being. These include: (1) the retrospectively negative–prospectively negative, (2) the retrospectively neutral–prospectively negative, and (3) the retrospectively positive–prospectively negative. All these three patterns together represent a minuscule 2 percent, indicating that a very small minority reject democratic consolidation as a retrogressive human movement.

In this regard, it should be noted that negative or neutral experiences of the past democratic change have not necessarily encouraged Koreans to project future democratic expansion in a negative light. Among those who attribute the decline in quality of their lives to the past democratization, for example, a vast majority (82%) still refuse to regard further democratization as a retrogressive movement; instead, they welcome it as an avenue toward their greater well-being in the future.[6] To a large majority of the Korean population, democratization in the past means a better life; to a larger majority, democratization in the future means genuine hope.

Cross-National Comparisons

Prior research has revealed notable differences in the way the publics of new and old democratic states appreciate democracy. While the publics of consolidated democracies in Western Europe tend to emphasize political rights, those of new Eastern European democracies tend to equate it more with economic prosperity and social rights than with political rights (McIntosh & Mac Iver 1993). Do the Korean people, as citizens of a new democracy, also emphasize socioeconomic rights over political rights?

This question, regarding the priority of democratic values, was examined by repeating in the 1993 survey an item asked in earlier European surveys. The item, as shown in Appendix B A2, asked Korean respondents to weigh six values – three political and three socio-economic – and choose the only value which they would consider most important to their country's democratic political development. As shown in Table 2.6, their choices were spread across all six categories: national economic development (23%), economic equality (16%), economic security (25%), fair justice (21%), free competition among political parties (5%), and political freedom (10%). None of these six categories, moreover, contains more than one-third of total responses; nor does any combination of two categories account for a majority. Undoubtedly, there is a great deal of disagreement among the Korean people over the priority of specific democratic values to be emphasized as a democratic developmental policy.

Table 2.6 "Most Important" Features of Democratization in Korea and Other Democracies

"Most Important" Features	New Democracies (%)						Old Democracies (%)		
	Korea	Bulgaria	Czechs	Hungary	Poland	Slovaks	Britain	France	West Germany
Economic Values									
Economic Prosperity	23	19	22	35	41	17	9	11	5
Economic Equality	16	12	17	10	11	24	10	16	4
Economic Security	25	16	22	26	18	26	14	17	14
TOTAL	(64)	(47)	(61)	(71)	(70)	(67)	(33)	(44)	(23)
Political Values									
Fair Justice System	21	32	24	20	12	15	34	40	50
Party Competition	5	11	12	4	7	12	13	10	18
Political Freedom	10	3	2	2	2	2	7	4	8
TOTAL	(36)	(46)	(38)	(26)	(21)	(29)	(54)	(54)	(76)

Note: Missing data are included
Sources: 1993 Korean Democratization Survey; McIntosh & Abele (1993)

Nonetheless, a general pattern of agreement emerges when the six categories are collapsed into two broader categories: political and socioeconomic. As Table 2.6 illustrates, Koreans choosing socioeconomic values over political values lead those emphasizing political values by a margin of nearly two to one (64% versus 36%). This pattern, featuring the preponderance of socioeconomic democrats over political democrats, closely resembles what has been noted for five other new democracies listed in the table – Bulgaria, the Czech Republic, Hungary, Poland, and the Slovak Republic. The Korean pattern together with those of the five other new democracies, however, contrasts sharply with what has been found in Great Britain, France, Italy, and West Germany. In these traditional democracies, political democrats outnumber socioeconomic democrats. The longer people live in a democracy, the more they are likely to become minimalist democrats emphasizing political rights over socioeconomic values. The greater the hardship the people experience, the more they are likely to become maximalist democrats emphasizing socioeconomic values.

How does democratization in Korea and Eastern Europe compare in its consequences for the quality of citizens' private and public lives? As in the 1993 Korean survey, the 1991 *Times–Mirror* Survey of six new democracies in Eastern Europe asked respondents to assess, on Cantril's "self-anchoring striving scale," their own lives and their country's from three points in time, including: (1) five years ago when they were living under the communist government, (2) the present time under the democratic government, and (3) five years from now. Progress or decline in each life sphere is estimated by subtracting its past ratings from its present ratings. Table 2.7 compares Korea and its six European

Table 2.7 Cross-National Differences in Shifts in the Perceived Quality of Life After Democratic Transition

	Private (%)			Public Life (%)		
	Progress	Decline	Balance	Progress	Decline	Balance
Korea	69	14	+55	76	12	+64
East Germany	34	33	+1	45	30	+15
Bulgaria	16	60	−44	8	79	−71
Czechoslovakia	29	49	−20	29	51	−22
Hungary	18	57	−39	11	68	−57
Poland	27	52	−25	44	37	+7
European Russia	21	57	−36	4	86	−82

Sources: 1993 Korean Democratization Survey; *Times–Mirror* Survey quoted in Kaase (1994)

peers in terms of those who have experienced positive and negative changes in life quality.

Of the seven democracies in the table, five register net declines rather than improvements in at least one of the two life spheres. They are: Bulgaria, Czechoslovakia, Hungary, Poland, and European Russia. Korea is one of only two countries (the other being East Germany) that have achieved net gains in private as well as public life spheres. The margins of such gains, however, are significantly larger for Korea than East Germany. While those margins for East Germany range from 1 percent in private life to 15 percent, the margins for Korea vary from 55 percent in private life to 64 percent in public life. This attests to the fact that democratization, to date, has been many times more conducive to the human lot in Korea than in Eastern Europe.

Summary and Conclusions

Empirical studies of democratization have been concerned primarily with questions concerning institutional and cultural dimensions. As a result, very little is known about the consequences of democratization – especially for the quality of life among members of the mass public who have demanded it. The purpose of this chapter has been to show the relevance of the historic phrase, "government for the people," to the study of democratizing countries and to illustrate that steady improvements in the quality of citizens' lives are absolutely necessary for their transformation into full democracies.

For a large majority of the Korean people, democratization means more than a political movement featuring an easy or swift trans-formation of an authoritarian political regime into "government by the people." It is embraced as an evolutionary process, which is premised and fueled on the universal principle of human enlightenment. Thus, instead of focusing on the building of electoral and representative political institutions, democratization is understood as a communal project that reduces human suffering and enhances human happiness.

On the whole, democratization in Korea, to date, has brought about significant improvements in the perceived well-being among the citizenry. In fact, the improvements are much more than have been noted in Eastern Europe. In addition, the full consolidation of limited democracy in Korea is widely expected to add more to what has already been achieved. A return to the old military regime, on the other hand, is more widely viewed as detracting from it. An absolute majority of Koreans are convinced of the virtues of democracy. The next chapter will examine how strongly committed Koreans are to consolidating their limited democracy.

PART II

Average Citizens

CHAPTER 3

Commitment to
Democratic Consolidation

"All democracy needs, aside from its basic institutions, are
democratic subjects: men and women who have internalized
the values of freedom, solidarity, tolerance, public
commitment and justice, and who will not break the rules to
gain their ends."

Raul Alfonsin (1992: 4)

"A stable democratic political future is the responsibility
and possibility of citizens enjoying their rights and
responsibilities under a democratic government."

Juan Linz (1990a: 160)

More than a decade after military rule was formally ended, Korea is still at
the crossroads of democracy and authoritarianism. Kristof (1996b: A3)
observes, "In many ways it [Korea] is a democratic society, and it yearns
for international recognition as an open and advanced country. Yet the
democratic filaments are intertwined with autocratic ones to make a
social fabric that is sometimes baffling to outsiders." Steinberg (1996: 1)
also observes, "Korea is a democratization anomaly. It now conforms to
the institutional requirements of a democratic state as usually defined by
Western political scientists, and has done so since 1987, but its attitudes
toward those institutions that comprise democracy are singularly circumscribed by traditional social and cultural norms and mores."[1] As these
and many other astute observers of Korean politics point out, age-old
authoritarian cultural values and behavioral norms pose the most serious
challenge to the further advancement of Korean democracy.[2]

In Korea, as in all other new democracies, newly installed representative institutions and procedures can crystalize into a truly democratic
pattern of political competition and co-operation only when ordinary
citizens become fully willing (Schmitter 1994). How strongly are Koreans
committed to the various tasks of consolidating their limited democratic
system into a mature and enduring democracy? How broadly based is
their commitment to democratic consolidation? Which segments of the
population are most and least strongly committed to it? How do they
differ in their commitment to those tasks? Why are some segments more
committed to democratic progression than others? This chapter will
focus on these questions dealing with the depth, breadth, types, and

sources of democratic commitment among the Korean masses. In addition, it attempts to comparatively assess Korea's current problems with, and future prospects for, democratic consolidation at the micro level of individual citizens.

Prior Survey Research on New Democracies

Ever since the current wave of democratization began to spread from Southern Europe into other regions in the late 1970s, teams of individual scholars and research institutions have conducted numerous surveys to monitor and compare political orientations and behavior among the mass publics of these new democracies and determine their sources and dynamics (e.g. Gibson 1996a, 1996b; Hahn 1991; Bruszt & Simon 1992; McDonough, Barnes & Pina 1986; Miller, Hesli & Reisinger 1994; Moises 1993; Rohrschneider 1994; Rose & Mishler 1994). Studies based on these surveys have, by and large, failed to address adequately the unique problems and dangers involved in the consolidation stage of democratization for conceptual, theoretical, and methodological reasons.[3]

Many of these survey-based studies are conceptually grounded on the general notion of democracy and have failed to make the crucial distinction between democracy-in-principle and democracy-in-action (Weffort 1989). On the other hand, other studies have approached the multi-phase process of democratization from a holistic or teleological perspective and failed to differentiate democratic consolidation from its prior stage of democratic transition (O'Donnell 1996; Rose & Mishler 1996).

In previous survey-based studies, moreover, affective or evaluative orientations to democracy as an ideal political system are equated, often mistakenly, with behavioral orientations to democratic change. General support for democratic regime change is also mistakenly regarded as indicative of commitment to the expansion of limited democratic practices. For these reasons, prior studies appear to be in agreement over the prevalence of democratic support among the mass publics, especially of new European democracies (Duch 1995; Gibson 1996a; Rose & Mishler 1996; Weil 1993).

Therefore, from most of the survey-based studies to date, little can be learned about the diverse orientations that individual citizens hold toward the consolidation of limited democracy. From the percentages of the citizens who are favorably or unfavorably disposed to democratic political ideals or newly installed democratic political institutions, for example, it is difficult to determine accurately whether they are actually committed to either removing age-old authoritarian practices, or, instead, expanding incipient democratic rule.

Theoretically, survey-based research on the mass publics of new democracies is often predicated on the assumption that orientations to democratic and authoritarian politics are mutually exclusive (Rose & Mishler 1994). Rejection of authoritarianism is assumed to accompany acceptance of democracy. Conversely, preference for a democratic political community is assumed to bring about dissociation from authoritarian rule. Such a theoretical assumption of mutual exclusiveness is, however, highly unrealistic in the real world of new democracies where neither democracy nor dictatorship is widely believed to offer a satisfying solution to the many problems facing them (Adamski 1992; Finifter & Mickiewicz 1992; Simon 1994; Weil 1993; Weil, Huffman & Gautier 1993; Shin & Shyu 1997). Under such uncertainty, many citizens, more often than not, do embrace both democratic and authoritarian political propensities concurrently. This is the reason why many self-avowed democrats in Hungary, Poland, and Russia elected neo-communists to power in their latest parliamentary elections.

Methodologically, prior survey research on democratic support has been concerned mostly with amounts or quantities, such as the degree to which the mass citizenry as a whole is favorably disposed to democracy or democratic reforms.[4] Relatively few surveys have been conducted to ascertain the different kinds or characteristics of such support, nor the exact patterns of relationships among those characteristics and their sources (Gibson 1996b). As a result, little is known about whether various democratic orientations cohere enough to shape democratic political behavior. Much less is known about qualitative differences in the roles that ordinary citizens are actually playing in the course of democratic consolidation.

In summary, survey-based research, to date, has been concerned primarily with levels of affective or evaluative orientations to the ideal of democracy or its institutions (Rose & Mishler 1994: 161). As a result, it has failed to systematically distinguish between people's passion for democracy as a political ideal and their willingness to pursue democratic dreams. Survey-based research has also failed to ascertain accurately the various public dispositions toward the necessary tasks of democratic consolidation. To identify those truly committed citizens from others, surveys should focus on the unique problems and dangers lurking in the particular phase of democratic consolidation rather than the general process of democratization.

Conceptualization

What specific political orientations are required of the mass citizenry for their partially democratic regime to become a fully consolidated

*No clear
orientations
associated
with
consolidation*

democracy? As Eckstein (1998: 19) and O'Donnell (1996: 39) note, the existing study of democratic consolidation is so deficient that there is presently no single theory capable of offering a satisfactory answer to this question. The answer, therefore, has to be explored from the perspective of characteristics that are commonly associated with the notion of democratic consolidation. This examination has yielded three sets of mass political orientations deemed necessary for democratic consolidation.

(1)   The most rudimentary of these sets concerns the popular belief that there are no better alternatives to the existing democratic arrangements in governing the nation (Linz 1990c). "Even in the face of severe

*Properties
of consolidation*

political and economic crises," Linz & Stepan (1996b: 15) argue, "the overwhelming majority of the people [should] believe that any further political change must emerge from within the parameters of democratic procedures." The popular acceptance of democracy as "the only game in town," however, cannot be assumed to be the sole contribution to the expansion and endurance of limited democracy. Such democratic orientation should be interconnected and reinforced by two additional

(2)   properties: (1) endorsement of the essential norms of democratic
(3)   politics, and (2) the willingness to support all needed institutional reforms.

Specifically, individual citizens should become actively involved in the process of reforming any existing deficiencies within democratic institutions while personally cultivating the essential qualities of democratic citizenship. Externally, citizens should be willing to prevent the authoritarian degeneration of existing political institutions and demand the further expansion of current practices of limited democracy (Pridham 1990a, 1995). Internally, they should not only be willing to take part in the democratic decision-making process but also should adhere to democratic rules of the game (O'Donnell 1996). At the individual level, therefore, acquiring such procedural norms constitutes the *internal* dimension of commitment to democratic consolidation. Getting involved in democratic reforms, on the other hand, constitutes its *external* dimension.

Commitment to democratic consolidation, as conceptualized here, involves much more than choosing or projecting democracy alone as a preferable regime. As Przeworski (1991) and Sartori (1987) suggest, a favorable orientation toward democratic change matters only when it is interconnected and reinforced by the disposition to engage in direct action. Embodying both affective and behavioral orientations toward democratic change, commitment to democratic consolidation is viewed in the present study as a dynamic phenomenon with multiple properties, which can shift in both quantity and quality. Its shifting configurations, therefore, cannot be adequately examined by merely estimating the extent to which the mass public favors democracy over authoritarian rule or support for newly installed democratic institutions.

Support for a Democratic Regime

To become fully committed to the consolidation of limited democracy, one must first become an ardent supporter of democracy as a regime in action and not merely an adherent to democratic ideals.[5] The identification of democratic regime supporters is, therefore, the first and most essential step in measuring commitment to democratic consolidation. What specific orientations distinguish supporters from opponents of a democratic regime? Those who not only accept the creation of a democratic state but also project it as the only legitimate way of governing the country are defined in this study as *authentic,* or genuine, supporters. Those who merely accept a democratic regime without fully endorsing its legitimacy are considered as *superficial* supporters.

Approval for democracy-in-action was measured by asking respondents to the 1996 survey how strongly they were supporting or opposing

Figure 3.1 Popular Reactions to the Democratic Transformation of Authoritarian Rule

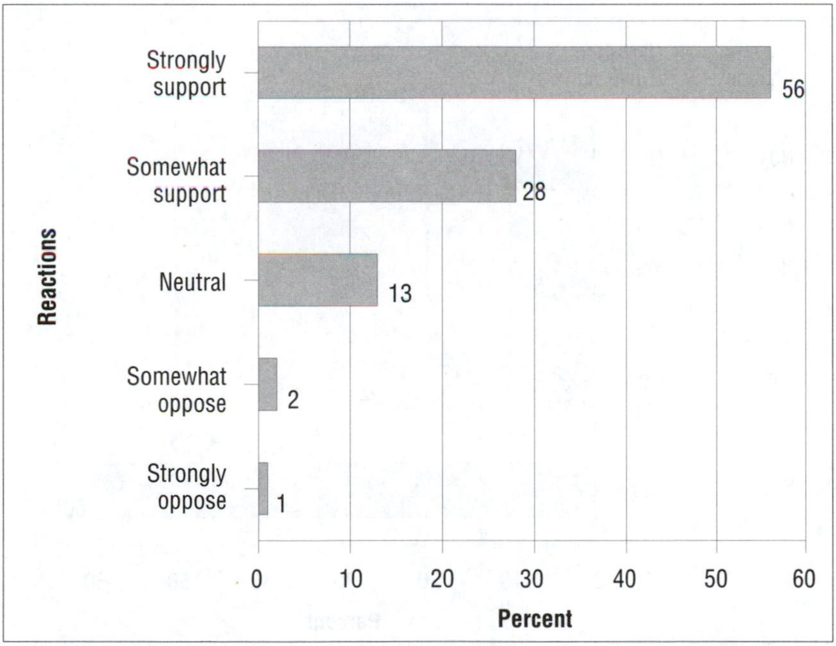

Source: 1996 Korean Democratization Survey

the democratic regime change that ended nearly three decades of
military rule in Korea (see Appendix B E1 for the wording of this
question). The survey found that one in thirty Koreans (3%) opposes
democratic transition while slightly more than four out of five Koreans
(84%) support the change (see Figure 3.1). More notable is that more
than one-half (56%) of the Korean population *strongly* favored installing
the democratic Sixth Republic in which they currently live.

Endorsement for the continuing practice of democratic governance
was measured in terms of the extent to which alternatives to the existing
democratic regime are preferred. Specifically, respondents to the 1996
survey were asked, as shown in Appendix B E2, to choose one of three
alternatives: (1) democratic regime is always preferable to dictatorship,
(2) dictatorship is preferable to democratic regime under some circumstances, and (3) either regime makes no difference. Responses expressing no alternatives to the present democratic arrangements are
considered indicative of unqualified endorsement for the continuing
practice of democratic rule. About two-thirds (65%) expressed unqualified endorsement for their newly installed democratic regime.

How many Koreans can be considered authentic supporters of the
new democratic regime? Figure 3.2 reports their distribution across four

Figure 3.2   Types of Orientations to Democracy as a Viable Political System

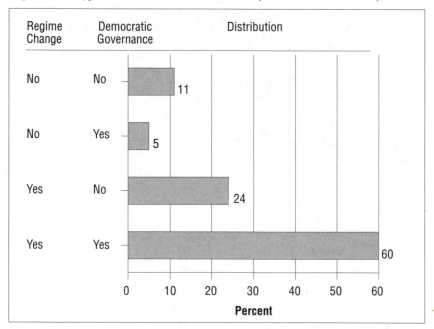

Source: 1996 Korean Democratization Survey

distinctive types of political orientations, including that of authentic supporters endorsing both democratic transition and governance. As expected, not every Korean approving democratic regime change unconditionally endorses democratic governance in the future. Still, 71 percent of those welcoming the new democratic regime subscribe to the unceasing practice of democratic governance. As a result, *authentic* supporters of democratic government comprise only 60 percent of the Korean population. They are over twice as numerous as *superficial* supporters (24%) approving a democratic regime while refusing to endorse it unconditionally. They are, also, over five times more numerous than authentic opponents of democratic rule who neither approve the creation of a democratic regime nor endorse its continuing practice; such staunch opponents comprise only 11 percent of the total Korean population.

Internal Commitment to Democratic Consolidation

For a democracy to function well as a democratic regime in the real world of politics, individual citizens should view themselves as participants, as well as subjects, in the political process. At the same time, they should be willing to accept other participants as political equals and tolerate competition and opposition from their opponents and rivals. The internal dimension of democratic commitment, therefore, focuses on the extent to which individual citizens embrace the two fundamental procedural norms of liberal democracy (Dahl 1971; Gibson & Duch 1993; Held 1987; McClosky & Zaller 1984; Sullivan, Piereson & Marcus 1982). The norms allow: (1) the mass public to take part in politics, and (2) political opponents to freely compete and challenge the actions of government.

How many Koreans have internalized these two procedural norms? To explore this question, respondents to the 1996 survey were asked, as shown in Appendix B E3.1 and 3.2, to report the degree of their agreement or disagreement with the following statements: (1) public participation is not necessary if decision-making is left in the hands of a few trusted, competent leaders, and (2) multi-party competition makes the country's political system stronger. Disagreeing with the first statement and agreeing with the second one are considered indicators of internal commitment to democratic consolidation.

When asked whether mass participation is necessary, even when political leaders are trusted and competent, many Koreans approving democratic change are reluctant to choose the collective wisdom of the masses over the judgment of competent leaders. A substantial minority (42%) reject the democratic norm of mass participation in favor of

Table 3.1 Endorsement for Democratic Norms of Mass Participation and
Free Competition

Levels of Endorsement	Norms (percent)	
	Mass participation	Free competition
Strongly oppose	19	3
Somewhat oppose	23	13
Somewhat support	25	33
Strongly support	28	46
Don't know	5	5
Total	100	100
(N)	(1000)	(1000)

Source: 1996 Korean Democratization Survey

authoritarian leadership. A slim majority (53%) generally subscribe to
the participation norm, which is essential to government by the people.
When asked about free competition among multiple parties, a much
larger majority (79%) endorse it (see Table 3.1).

What can be said about the Korean endorsement of democratic
norms? First, neither of the two norms is strongly endorsed by an overwhelming majority, although each norm is endorsed by more than half
of the Korean population. Levels of their endorsement, moreover, vary
considerably from one norm to another. Of the two norms, the one
guiding mass participation is accepted to a significantly lesser degree
than that of contestation symbolizing the rough-and-tumble aspect of
democratic politics. This is somewhat surprising in view of general agreement among other surveys over relatively lesser acceptance of political
competition (Gibson, Duch & Tedin 1992; Tedin 1994; Weil 1993).

More notable, however, is that only a minority are supportive of both
norms. While more than one-half have embraced none (11%) or only
one norm (46%), slightly over two-fifths (43%) have endorsed both. The
overall level of internal commitment to democratic politics among the
Korean population, therefore, remains relatively low even after eight
years of democratic experience.

Among Koreans, those willing to abide by the two essential norms of
democratic rule are outnumbered greatly by those welcoming the new
democratic regime (43% versus 84%). Moreover, even among authentic
supporters of democratic rule, less than one-half (48%) have internalized the norms of democratic politics. As a result, less than one-third
(32%) of the entire Korean population are the supporters of democratic
rule who have actually internalized the norms of democratic politics.
Therefore, Korea remains a nation of democrats who are yet to
appreciate the art of self-governance.

External Commitment to Democratic Consolidation

For new democracies of a hybrid nature like the one in Korea to be transformed into a consolidated democracy, its people should support institutional as well as other reforms seeking to expand the current practices of limited democracy. At the same time, they should be willing to eradicate the vestiges of authoritarian rule and prevent its return. Support for democratic expansion and opposition to authoritarian tendency constitute, respectively, the positive and negative domains of external commitment to democratic consolidation.

Specifically, the external dimension of commitment to democratic consolidation involves two conceptually distinct categories of behavioral orientations toward political change. These are anti-authoritarian and pro-democratic propensities, which do not operate as mutually exclusive entities. To measure behavioral dispositions against authoritarian regression, respondents to the 1996 survey were asked how much they would agree or disagree with the statement that "for our country these days, a strong leader is needed more than democracy." Responses disagreeing with this statement are considered indicative of anti-authoritarian propensities. To measure behavioral dispositions toward democratic expansion, respondents were asked the degree to which they were in agreement or disagreement with the statement that "our political system should be made a lot more democratic than what it is now." Affirmative responses to this question are considered indicators of pro-democratic propensities.

Koreans enthusiastically support the movement for further democratization. An overwhelming majority (91%) are in agreement with the need to expand their limited democracy. At the same time, however, many of these self-avowed democratic reformers believe that their country is presently more in need of strong leadership than democratic expansion.[6] As Table 3.2 shows, over half of the Korean population chose authoritarian leadership over mass-based participatory democracy. It is indeed a minority (41%), not a majority, who are willing to support anti-authoritarian reforms. While supporting democratic expansion, many Koreans still remain uncommitted to removing authoritarian residues or preventing a reversal to authoritarian rule. So far, this is perhaps the most notable paradox of democratization in Korea. Koreans yearn to be free, yet they crave strong leadership.

Mainly due to the under-development of anti-authoritarian orientations, many Koreans have yet to commit themselves fully to the pro-democratic and anti-authoritarian institutional reforms, which are both necessary for democratic consolidation. More Koreans appear to be either in favor of a hybrid regime combining elements of expanded democracy and limited autocracy or they are in favor of limited

Table 3.2   Percentages Supporting or Opposing Pro-Democratic and Anti-Authoritarian Reforms

| | Reforms (percent) | |
Types of Responses	Pro-Democratic	Anti-Authoritarian
Strongly oppose	1	24
Somewhat oppose	7	29
Somewhat support	36	24
Strongly support	55	17
Don't know	1	6
Total	100	100
(N)	(1000)	(1000)

Source: 1996 Korean Democratization Survey

democracy by supporting anti-authoritarian reforms while opposing any further democratic expansion. Figure 3.3 examines their distribution among the four distinctive types of external commitment to democratic consolidation.

The most notable feature of the data in Figure 3.3 is that Koreans are not placed in just one or two types; instead, they are distributed across all four types. This pattern of distribution suggests that Koreans do not agree on the future direction of the democratic reform movement. They are, instead, in considerable disagreement over what kind of democracy their country should become in the future.

Another notable feature of Figure 3.3 is that a majority (53%) are committed to only one type of necessary reform – either pro-democratic or anti-authoritarian. Of these partially committed Koreans, a simple majority (51%) are supportive of a hybrid regime, i.e. one that expands the current democracy while maintaining some practices of the past authoritarian rule. In striking contrast, a small minority (2%) are in favor of limited democracy by eliminating authoritarian politics without expanding democracy. These are two different types of partial commitment to democratic consolidation.

In addition, there are two other types: totally uncommitted and totally committed. The survey shows that one in every thirteen (7%) is totally uncommitted to further democratization by supporting neither pro-democratic nor anti-authoritarian reforms. Those fully committed to the further democratic movement, by supporting pro-democratic and anti-authoritarian reforms, make up a minority (40%). In Korea today, a minority of fully committed democratic reformers must lead the movement for consolidation of a democratic political system, which operates

Figure 3.3 Types of External Commitment to Democratic Consolidation

Reform Orientations		
Pro-Democratic	Anti-Authoritarian	Distribution
No	No	7
No	Yes	2
Yes	No	51
Yes	Yes	40

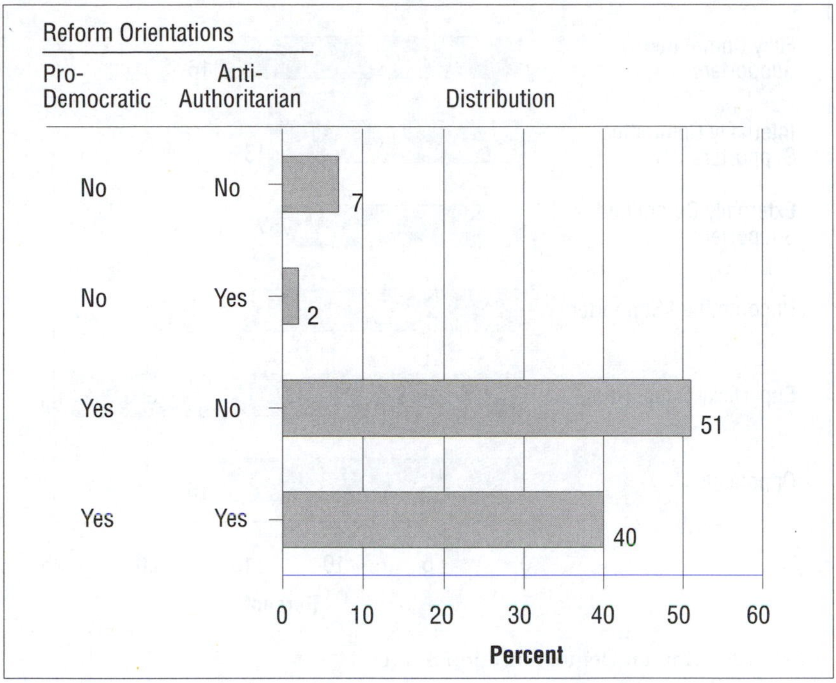

Source: 1996 Korean Democratization Survey

on the principle of majority rule. As O'Donnell (1989) notes, this is indeed "one of the great enigmas of democratic consolidation."

Overall Patterns of Commitment to Democratic Consolidation

A key question emerges at this juncture: What proportion of authentic supporters of democratization among the Korean population is fully (internally as well as externally) committed to democratic consolidation? What proportion of them is merely committed to it either internally or externally? To explore these questions, a typology of commitment to democratic consolidation is constructed by means of the sequential method of combination discussed in Appendix A. Specifically, four separate categories of democratic orientations are considered in the sequence in which democratization tends to proceed naturally at the levels of political system, institutions, and individual citizens. The sequence starts with whether or not ordinary citizens are still endorsing the democratic regime change that took place years ago. Next, it deter-

Figure 3.4   Patterns of Overall Commitment to Democratic Consolidation

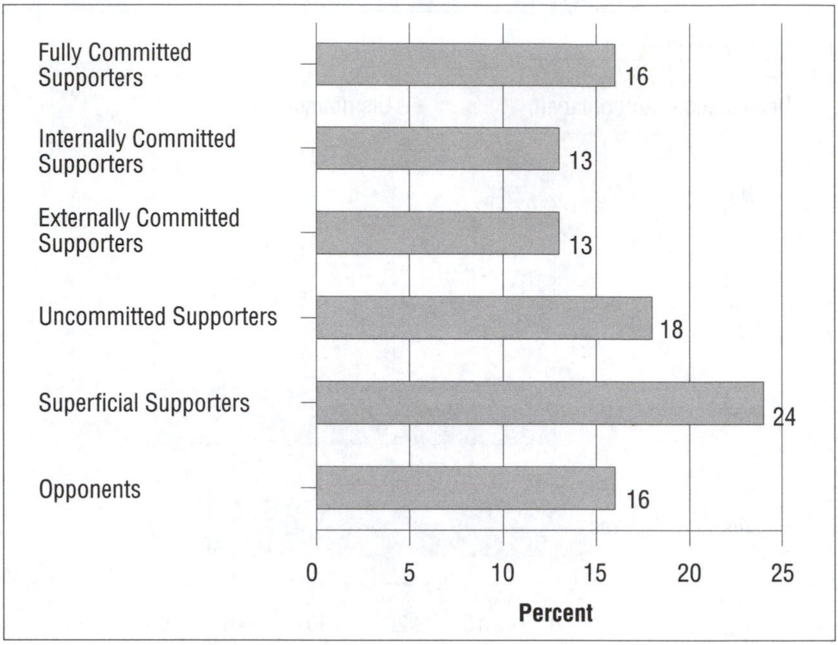

Source: 1996 Korean Democratization Survey

mines whether they are in favor of continuing the practice of democratic governance without any interruption. Then it proceeds to determine whether they are supportive of expanding the current practice of limited democratic rule. Finally, the sequence concludes with whether or not they have already internalized democratic norms. This sequential procedure of typology construction has yielded six distinctive patterns of democratic orientations. Figure 3.4 reports percentages relating to these patterns of roles, which the Korean population is actually playing in the current process of democratic consolidation. These roles are: (1) opponents of democratic consolidation, (2) superficial supporters, (3) uncommitted supporters, (4) externally committed supporters, (5) internally committed supporters, and (6) fully committed supporters.

Opponents of democratic consolidation are those who oppose the recent installation of a democratic state and its necessary institutional reforms. *Superficial supporters* are those who welcome the democratic state but refuse to endorse unconditionally the continuing practice of democratic governance. *Uncommitted supporters* are authentic supporters accepting democratic regime change and fully approving the democratic model of governance; however, they neither embrace democratic procedural norms nor support pro-democratic and anti-authoritarian reforms to the fullest extent. *Externally committed supporters*, on the other hand, differ from uncommitted supporters merely by supporting all the necessary institutional reforms for democratic consolidation. *Internally committed supporters* are the direct opposite of the *externally committed* who refuse to embrace the norms of mass participation and free competition among political opponents. Finally, *fully committed supporters* are authentic supporters who are internally as well as externally committed to democratic consolidation.

The most notable feature of the data reported in Figure 3.4 is that none of the six types constitutes a bare majority or even a substantial minority. With no exception, each and every one of these six types represents a small minority that accounts for less than a quarter of the total population. For instance, superficial supporters are most popular (24%) while externally and internally committed supporters are the least popular (13%).

In contemporary Korea, there are as many as six politically distinct groups of nearly equal strength. None of these groups – including fully committed supporters – is numerically powerful enough to lead the rest. This may be the reason why the Korean nation as a whole remains as highly divided and quarrelsome over the ultimate ends of democratic rule and the appropriate means of democratic governing as it was in 1987 when the first democratic government was elected.

Careful inspection of the data reported in Figure 3.4 reveals significant qualitative differences, especially among the Korean people who support the consolidation of their limited democracy. Fortunately, direct opponents of democratic regime change constitute a relatively small minority (16%). However, partially and fully committed supporters together do not form a majority of the Korean population; they account for only 42 percent. More unfortunate is that fully committed supporters do not form even a plurality; they are not at all numerically superior to opponents of democratic regime change. Worst of all, superficial supporters outnumber either partially or fully committed supporters by substantial margins (ranging from 8% to 11%). The lack of commitment to democratic consolidation is the modal characteristic of the Korean population.

Levels of Commitment to Democratic Consolidation

The typological analysis presented above focuses on qualitative differences in Korean commitment to democratic consolidation. In this mode of analysis, therefore, quantitative variations in such commitment are obscured. To what degree do the Korean people, as a whole, prefer a democratically functioning political system compared to the

Table 3.3 Comparing Popular Commitment to Democratic Consolidation Across Three Dimensions

Index Values	Dimensions (percent)		
	Regime Support	Internal Consolidation	External Consolidation
0	7	11	7
1	10	19	26
2	17	39	38
3	23	15	17
4	43	16	12
[Mean]	[2.8]	[2.2]	[2.1]
Total	100	100	100
(N)	(1000)	(1000)	(1000)

Source: 1996 Korean Democratization Survey

authoritarian system, which they had in the past? How strongly are they committed to the external or internal dimension of consolidation? Is the average Korean a strongly or moderately committed supporter of democratic consolidation? Satisfactory answers to these questions require a different sort of analysis.

In Table 3.3, we report the means of 5-point indexes measuring support for democratic rule as well as internal and external commitment to the consolidation of partial democracy. The scores were calculated according to a 2-step procedure. First, for each index, responses to its two constituent questions were collapsed into a 3-point scale that ranged from being non-positive through partially positive to fully positive. Re-scaled responses to the two questions were then summed up into a 5-point index ranging from a low of 0 to a high of 4.[7] A score of 0 on the index indicates the lack of support or commitment while that of 4 indicates full support or commitment.

The means on these indexes are 2.8 for democratic regime support, 2.2 for internal commitment, and 2.1 for external commitment. All three means are higher than 2.0 – the midpoint of the indexes from which these average scores are derived. The findings show that two of these three means, however, are not significantly higher than the midpoint; instead, they are very close to it. In external commitment, moreover, those scoring higher than the midpoint are fewer than those scoring lower. Undoubtedly, the desire of Koreans to live in a democratically functioning polity is on the relatively high side. Their capacity as democratic citizens and their determination as democratic reformers, however, still remain moderate at best.

Table 3.4 Correlations Among Three-Dimensional Measures of Democratic Commitment

	Regime Support	Internal Commitment	External Commitment
Regime support	——	0.26	0.43
Internal commitment	0.26	——	0.24
External commitment	0.43	0.24	——

Source: 1996 Korean Democratization Survey

Structure of Orientations Toward Democratic Consolidation

One of the widely held assumptions in public opinion research suggests that political orientations and dispositions can affect relevant political behavior more powerfully when they cohere enough to form a syndrome (Converse 1964; Dalton 1996; Gibson, Duch & Tedin 1992; Gibson 1995, 1996a). In light of this assumption, it is important to examine the structural relationships among the three dimensions of orientations toward democratic consolidation. In Table 3.4, we present Pearson's simple correlation coefficients for an assessment of the direction and magnitude of their relationships.

As expected, all three dimensions are positively correlated with each other, indicating that they do belong to the same construct. The magnitude of their relationships, although statistically significant, is too weak to be considered as forming a coherent attitudinal syndrome. All the correlation coefficients registered +0.43 or much lower. This indicates that any combination of three attitudinal dimensions is likely to occur much less than half the time. The very low probability of such occurrence can be interpreted to suggest that democratic orientations have not yet been structured well enough to bring about democratic behavior.

Breadth of Commitment to Democratic Consolidation

New democracies, like the one in Korea, can consolidate only when they evoke generalized acceptance and commitment from all the relevant political forces, including the politically active stratum (Przeworski 1991: 309; see also Dahl 1989; Higley & Gunther 1992; Linz & Stepan 1996a). A fourth question to emerge in this chapter concerns how broadly and equally democratic support and commitment are distributed across various segments of the Korean population. To explore this issue, Table 3.5 contains three columns of percentages for the population groups,

Table 3.5 Levels of Democratic Orientations Among Various Segments of the Korean Population

Personal Characteristics	Support for Democratic Regime	Democratic Commitment	
		Internal	External
Gender			
Male	63	42	39
Female	56	44	36
Age			
20–35	59	52	41
36–50	61	40	36
51+	58	31	35
School			
≤ Middle School	51	28	28
High School	61	46	39
≥ College	67	55	46
Income			
Low	56	33	34
Middle	59	43	39
High	63	50	39
Community			
Large City	61	47	40
Other Cities	60	45	39
Town	55	32	33
Region			
Cholla	68	44	42
Kyongsang	51	34	33
Others	62	47	39

Source: 1996 Korean Democratization Survey

which are defined by gender, age, educational attainment, family income, community, and region of residence.

The second column of the table lists the percentages that not only approve the new democratic regime supplanting three decades of military rule but also endorse its continuity. By comparing these percentages, we can determine whether democracy, as the most preferred type of government, has already evoked broad acceptance among the Korean population.

In the second column, percentages are all in the fifties and sixties. Of those even in the 60s, only one is higher than 67, a figure representing two-thirds of the total population. Two of the figures in the 50s – those with a middle school education or less and residents of Kyongsang province – represent only 1 percent more than one-half the Korean population. Regardless of their personal characteristics, those fully supportive of democracy as a viable political system constitute slim or small majorities of all the population groups considered. Undoubtedly, democracy is yet to be broadly accepted as the best type of political system and the best model of governance for Korea.

Which groups of the Korean population are most and least strongly supportive of democratic consolidation? Based on findings from earlier surveys (Finifter & Mickiewicz 1992; Reisinger et al. 1994; Reisinger, Miller & Hesli, 1995; Gibson & Duch 1993), significantly greater commitment is expected among males, the young, the better educated, and urban residents. All of these groups are supposedly more exposed to the charms of democratic alternatives. In the context of recent memories of authoritarian rule, greater commitment is also expected among residents of the region who suffered most from nearly three decades of political oppression and discrimination. In contrast, lesser support is expected from those benefiting from the status quo or those who benefited most from the authoritarian regime – especially the upper class.

In general, not all of the six variables listed in Table 3.5 follow expected patterns. Between the two genders, for example, little difference is observed on the indexes measuring internal and external commitment to democratic consolidation. More notable is that Korean females are slightly more committed to democratic procedural norms than their male counterparts. Among the three age groups, the young are not always most strongly committed, while the old are always least strongly committed to consolidating Korean democracy, and middle-aged Koreans embrace the new democratic regime more enthusiastically than their younger counterparts. Among the three income groups, it is low-income people, not the wealthiest, who are least committed to regime change and future democratic reforms, not to mention the procedural norms.

The variables of education, community type, and residential region tend to follow expected patterns of variations. Among the three education groups, the most strongly committed group is always that with college education and the least strongly committed are always those with a middle-school education or less. In terms of community types, residents of large metropolitan areas are the most strongly committed, followed by those of middle-size cities and rural areas, in that order. Regionally, residents of the Cholla and Kyongsang provinces are placed

Table 3.6 Types of Democratic Orientations Among Various Segments of the Korean Population

	Opponents	Superficial Supporters	Uncommitted Supporters	Externally Committed	Internally Committed	Fully Committed
Gender						
Male	12	25	19	14	14	16
Female	20	24	17	12	11	17
Age						
20–35	17	24	16	11	14	19
36–50	14	26	19	13	12	16
51+	18	24	20	17	11	11
School						
≤ Middle School	23	26	21	13	9	8
High School	16	24	18	12	13	17
≥ College	9	24	15	15	16	22
Income						
Low	19	25	16	17	12	11
Middle	18	23	19	11	12	17
High	12	26	17	13	15	18
Community						
Large City	17	22	16	13	14	18
Other Cities	13	27	20	12	11	17
Town	19	27	18	15	11	11
Region						
Cholla	11	21	23	15	13	18
Kyongsang	24	25	18	11	11	12
Others	13	25	17	14	14	18

Source: 1996 Korean Democratization Survey

at the opposite ends of the distribution pattern. While the former are consistently the most supportive of democratic consolidation, the latter are consistently the least supportive.

In Table 3.6, demographic differences are highlighted in terms of the six types of overall commitment to democratic consolidation. Of the six types listed in the table, the two genders differ significantly only in one category; far more women are opponents of democratic consolidation. Among the three age groups, the young are most likely to be fully committed while the old are least likely to be so. In terms of education and income, the higher their levels, the more likely it is that they will play the role of fully committed democrats, and it is less likely that they will play the role of opponents. In terms of community size, the larger the community, the higher the proportion of fully committed supporters and the lower the proportion of uncommitted supporters. Residents of Cholla are least likely to oppose democratic consolidation, while those of Kyongsang are the most likely to do so.

Of the six personal characteristics examined above, two are found most salient in differentiating the overall degree of democratic commitment. The first is age; because of the divergent political environments in which they grew up, the young and the old differ significantly in their reactions to democratic reforms. The second characteristic, level of education, is a powerful influence on democratic political outlooks. It directly determines exposure to the ideals and practice of democracy, which is a Western import. These two variables of age and education are trichotomized and combined into a 9-way differentiation of the Korean population. The values of age are divided into the young (20 through 35-years-old), the middle-aged (36 through 50-years-old), and the old (older than 50 years of age). The education variable is divided into the middle-school or less educated, the high-school educated, and the college-educated.

For each of the nine groupings based on these two trichotomies, Table 3.7 reports the percentage of the *fully committed to democratic consolidation* (FCDC). It also reports the extent to which people belonging to each of those groups is over-represented or under-represented in the category of FCDC. The degree of their representativeness is calculated by dividing their percentage share of FCDCs by their percentage of the total population. Scores higher than 1.0 in the last column indicate being over-represented while scores lower than 1.0 indicate being under-represented. The higher the extent to which their values deviate from 1.0, the greater the extent of misrepresentation.

Looking over the figures in the second column, one can see that fully committed democrats are not concentrated into a few groups of the Korean population. Instead, they are distributed across all the nine

Table 3.7   Fully Committed Supporters of Democratic Consolidation by Age and Education

Age Education	Fully Committed Supporters in Each Group (A)	Total Population in Each Group (B)	Representation Ratio (A/B)
Young			
≤ Middle School	2.9	3.5	0.83
High School	24.4	21.3	1.15
≥ College	23.8	18.5	1.29
Middle-Aged			
≤ Middle School	5.2	11.9	0.44
High School	16.9	15.6	1.08
≥ College	12.8	8.2	1.56
Old			
≤ Middle School	7.6	14.7	0.52
High School	4.7	4.8	0.98
≥ College	1.7	1.5	1.13

Source: 1996 Korean Democratization Survey

groups. For example, none of these groups contains more than one-quarter; nor do any two groups together account for a majority. This finding confirms that full commitment to democratic consolidation, although not broadly based, is shown in every segment of the Korean population.

A second notable feature of Table 3.7 concerns the degree of representativeness. A careful inspection of index scores in its fourth column reveals an interesting relationship pattern between education and age on the one hand and representativeness on the other. Regardless of age, those with a middle-school education or less are under-represented among the category of fully committed democrats. Conversely, the college-educated, whether young or old, are always over-represented among those same democrats. In contrast, regardless of education, the young are not always over-represented, nor are the old not always under-represented. This suggests that it is the college-educated, not the young, upon whom the consolidation of Korean democracy depends.

Sources of Commitment to Democratic Consolidation

Why are some Koreans committed to democratic consolidation while others are not? Among those who are committed, why are some Koreans more strongly committed than others? Prior survey research on democratic values and reforms, conducted in both new and advanced democracies, has suggested a number of hypotheses and predictors. Putting these together, we propose a simple model, which features political, economic, and cultural considerations. The model posits that commitment to democratic consolidation develops primarily as a consequence of: (1) reactions to political and economic performance, (2) anticipation of performance changes in the foreseeable future, and (3) exposure to democratic cultural values.

Politically, negative reactions to the past authoritarian rule and fear of its revival are known to dispose individual citizens toward democratic change (Rose & Mishler 1994; Mishler & Rose 1996). Positive evaluations of the workings of newly installed democratic institutions and the ability of electors to be heard are also known to do so (Evans & Whitefield 1995). In order to assess authoritarian experience, respondents to the 1996 survey were asked to express, on a 10-point scale measuring the degree of satisfaction and dissatisfaction, the extent to which they were dissatisfied or satisfied with the Chun Doo Whan government (for the wording of this question, see Appendix B S1.1). For the assessment of democratic experience, they were asked to express their satisfaction or dissatisfaction with the functioning of democracy in their country on the same 10-point scale (Appendix B F2). With respect to being heard in the political process, they were asked to rate the responsiveness of the new government to their preferences on a 4-point verbal scale, which ranged from very much responsive to not at all responsive (Appendix B B4).

In terms of the economy, the general literature on public opinion offers extensive evidence linking political orientations to self-interest (Kinder & Kiewiet 1981; Lewis-Beck 1988; MacKuen, Erikson & Stimson, 1992). In recent surveys, conducted in new European democracies, positive and optimistic evaluations of the personal and national economies are found to lead to greater support for democratic change (McIntosh & Mac Iver 1992; Mishler & Rose 1996). In our survey, as in prior surveys, retrospective and prospective assessments were made on a 5-point verbal scale of the past and future performances of the personal and national economies (Appendix B R1–4). Similarly, retrospective and perspective assessments were made on a 5-point verbal scale of Korea's past and future political situations (Appendix B R5 and R6).

Culturally, in the third wave of democratization, exposure to democratic ideas and practices in the West through the mass media has been considered crucial to the development of support for democratic change in authoritarian societies (Diamond 1996; Fukuyama 1992; Gibson 1996b; Huntington 1991). In the current age of mass communication, the media – especially the electronic media – are believed to powerfully dispose individuals toward democratic change by publicizing events in other countries. To measure exposure to the global wave of democratization, respondents were asked how many days a week they usually watched TV news (Appendix B T1). They were also given a list of six concepts representing alternative models of democracy and asked to identify the ones which they had heard (Appendix B A3). The models were: (1) social democracy, (2) people's democracy, (3) consensus democracy, (4) participatory democracy, (5) guided democracy, and (6) liberal democracy. The number of democratic concepts to which respondents were exposed is considered an indicator of their exposure to democratic values.

In addition to these political, economic, and cultural variables, two personal characteristics are included in the proposed model (Appendix B W2 and W9). Education is widely known to promote democratic support by socializing individuals into accepting democratic values such as freedom, equality, and tolerance (McClosky & Zaller 1984; Nie, Junn & Stehlik-Barry 1996; Putnam 1993; Tedin 1994). In contrast, age is known to detract from democratic support (Sullivan, Piereson & Marcus 1982; Sullivan et al. 1985). For example, the old, as compared to the young, are less receptive to new ideas while upholding the authoritarian values of law and order. The young, on the other hand, are inclined toward post-materialism and libertarianism (Inglehart 1987, 1988, 1990).

A total of twelve predictors are regressed on three composite measures of democratic support and commitment. The *beta* and R^2 statistics from the ordinary least square analyses are presented in Table 3.8. Comparison of the *beta* coefficients in the table makes it possible to determine which predictors are the most and least powerful influences on each dimension of democratic consolidation. Such a comparison also makes it possible to determine how many predictors have a notable independent effect on each dependent variable, after controlling for all other predictors.

Table 3.8 shows that the regression equation involving internal commitment to democratic consolidation stands out from the rest in two respects. First, its R^2 (0.06) is very low and smaller than half the corresponding figures for support for democratic regime (0.16) and external commitment (0.13). This indicates that the twelve predictors, as a whole, do a very poor job of accounting for the internalization of democratic norms. Second, only two predictors are significantly associated with the dependent variable after controlling for all other predictors. These two variables are education and exposure to alternative models of democracy.

Among the Korean population, painful experiences of repressive rule, economic poverty while enduring under it, or the satisfying perform-

Table 3.8 Multiple Regression Analysis of Democratic Commitment:
OLS Regressions (standardized regression coefficients)

	Support for Democratic Regime	Commitment	
		Internal	External
Personal Characteristics			
Age	0.04	−0.07	0.02
Education	0.10*	0.13*	0.07
Political Variables			
Satisfaction with the			
Chun Government	−0.15	0.02	−0.22*
Satisfaction with democracy	0.09*	0.01	0.13*
Regime responsiveness	0.05	0.05	0.02
Political optimism	0.08*	0.03	0.08*
Economic Variables			
Personal economic progress	0.00	0.00	0.01
Personal economic optimism	0.04	0.05	0.06
National economic progress	0.08	0.00	0.00
National economic optimism	0.11	0.02	0.01
Cultural Variables			
Attention to TV news	0.00	0.01	−0.06
Exposure to democratic models	0.17*	0.09*	0.10*
R^2	0.16	0.06	0.13

*Significant at the .05 level
Source: 1996 Korean Democratization Survey

ance of the present and future democratic government have very little independent effect on the willingness to adhere to democratic procedural norms. Such democratic orientations are dependent solely on how much, and what, has been learned about democracy and democratization.

The proposed model does a much better job of accounting for variation in support for democratic rule and commitment to further democratic reforms. The twelve independent variables, as a whole, explain 16 percent of the democratic regime support and 13 percent of external democratic commitment. Understandably, negative reactions to the authoritarian Chun Doo Whan regime and positive reactions to the functioning of a new democracy are significant influences on such democratic orientations. Koreans – like Europeans – are motivated to support past and future democratic change primarily by their fear of authoritarian repression and contentment with the newly installed democratic government (Rose & Mishler 1996).

Of the two sets of economic variables, the one featuring the personal economy is hardly effective in promoting either democratic regime support or commitment to institutional reforms. Unlike Europeans, Koreans are not economically egotistical in orienting and reorienting themselves toward democratization. Even their sense of national economic progress and optimism adds very little to their commitment to pro-democratic and anti-authoritarian reforms; it merely helps them to embrace democratic rule. What Koreans perceive as needed for the future of their limited democracy has nothing to do with their evaluations of the national economy. Based on these findings, it can be concluded that economic factors, in general, are much less potent as an influence on democratization in Korea than in Europe. This is not very difficult to understand because Koreans, unlike Europeans, have been living in growing affluence, not in growing poverty.

Of the two personal characteristics, education has a significant effect on support for the creation and maintenance of the new democratic regime. As expected, the more educated Koreans are, the more strongly they are supportive of the democratic Sixth Republic. Unlike education, however, age has a notable independent effect on neither democratic regime support nor commitment to expanding the limited democracy. Contrary to what is expected from the results of the bivariate analysis presented above, age is found to be positively rather than negatively associated with those orientations when the effects of all other predictors are statistically removed. Why is it that young Koreans are less supportive of the existing democratic regime than old Koreans? Perhaps the former view it, in a substantive sense, as less sufficiently democratic.

Of the two variables measuring exposure to democratic values, attention to TV news has no notable independent effect on any of the three dependent variables reported in Table 3.8. More surprising is that greater exposure to TV news detracts from, rather than contributes to, commitment to further democratic reforms. It appears that direct exposure to rough-and-tumble democratic political practices discourages people from demanding and supporting more of the same.

In sharp contrast to exposure to the electronic media, conceptual exposure to alternative democratic models is significantly associated with all three dependent variables in Table 3.8. More notably, this is the only predictor that has a consistently positive and significant impact on all three dimensions of orientations to democracy and democratization. Of the other eleven predictors, only educational attainment and satisfaction with the old authoritarian government have such impact on two dependent variables. Based on these findings, it can be argued that raising the general level of education among the mass citizenry is essential to the process of democratic consolidation. What is more crucial to the process, however, is the quality of democratic education, which is offered at each level of schooling. Unfortunately, the current literature on democratization has yet to pay attention to this variable.

Cross-National Comparisons

A sixth and final question in this chapter is how the Korean people compare with citizens of other new democracies in terms of commitment to democracy as a viable political system. As reported earlier, Koreans have a greater desire to live in a democracy than those of many other new democracies. More notably, they are attached to the idea of democracy nearly as much as citizens of old consolidated democracies in Western Europe. The question to address now is whether Koreans are committed to democracy, as a viable political system, to the same extent as citizens of other democracies. This question is explored with two other sets of cross-national surveys – the 1992 Eurobarometer surveys and the 1996 Latino Barometer – both of which, like the 1996 Korean survey, asked respondents whether or not they would always prefer democracy to any other kind of political regime.

Of the twelve third-wave democracies listed in Table 3.9, Korea ranks eighth as one of the countries at the bottom in the extent of unconditional popular support for democratic rule. In the extent of preference for authoritarian rule, however, Korea ranks among those at the top and is only behind three other countries (Russia, Brazil, and Chile). A relatively lower level of democratic support and a relatively higher level of authoritarian preference, taken together, make it clear that Korea has been much slower than most other new democracies to legitimatize incipient democratic rule. Why is this so? What has been slowing down the process of democratic legitimation in Korea?

It is understandable that Korea is behind all three consolidated democracies in Southern Europe in the willingness to embrace democracy always "as the only game in town." Koreans trail their peers by more than ten years in Southern Europe in the extent to which they have personally been involved in democratic politics. At the same time, they are trailed by citizens of much younger democracies in Eastern and Central Europe. Obviously the length of democratic experience does not have much to do with the extent to which citizens of new democracies become "subjected to, and habituated to, the resolution of conflict within the specific laws, procedures, and institutions sanctioned by the new democratic process" (Linz & Stepan 1996a: 6). What else affects the process of legitimating democratic rule as "the only game in town"? The type of democracy may do that by affecting levels of citizen satisfaction with it (Anderson & Guillory 1997).

Table 3.9   Comparing Levels of Democratic Legitimacy

Countries (year)	Always Prefer Democracy	Sometimes Prefer Authoritarian	They Are All The Same	Don't Know
Korea (96)	65	17	10	8
Argentina (96)	71	15	11	3
Brazil (96)	50	24	21	5
Chile (96)	54	19	23	4
Czech Rep. (94)	75	11	14	1
Greece (92)	90	4	3	2
Hungary (94)	73	8	16	3
Poland (94)	64	17	16	3
Portugal (92)	83	9	4	4
Russia (94)	50	27	23	1
Slovak Rep. (94)	68	11	19	2
Spain (92)	78	8	7	6

Sources: 1996 Korean Democratization Survey; 1996 Latino Barometer quoted in Marta Lagos (1997); Plasser & Ulram (1994)

Our final comparison involves endorsement for the two fundamental norms of democratic politics. This comparison is based on results from national sample surveys conducted by a University of Iowa team of political scientists in Russia, the Ukraine, and Lithuania in 1995 (Reisinger, Miller & Hesli 1995). The Eastern European and Korean surveys asked identical questions to determine commitment to the norms of mass participation and free competition. Figure 3.5 reports percentages subscribing to each norm.

In the three Eastern European democracies, relatively small minorities (ranging from 30% to 42%) endorsed the norm of mass participation by disagreeing with the statement that "popular participation is not needed if there are strong, trusted leaders." Again, in these countries only small minorities endorsed the norms of free competition among opposing political forces by agreeing with the statement that "multi-party competition makes our political system stronger." In Korea, however, nearly one-half (53%) endorse mass participation while over three-quarters (79%) sanction political competition. Again, Koreans are far ahead of their Eastern European counterparts in commitment to democratic procedural norms.

Summary and Conclusions

The research reported in this chapter is predicated on several assumptions. Substantively, it is taken for granted that democratic and authoritarian values and orientations are not mutually exclusive of each

Figure 3.5 Cross-National Differences in Public Endorsement of Democratic Norms

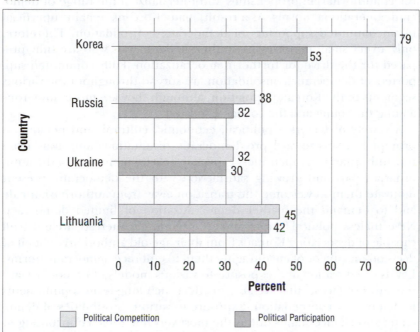

Sources: 1996 Korean Democratization Survey; Reisinger, Miller & Hesli (1995)

other. Theoretically, our research is based on the premise that democratic values and orientations are most likely to affect democratic political behavior when they cohere together to a sufficient extent. Methodologically, it is assumed that quantitative analyses are concerned primarily with amounts, or levels, of those orientations and are incapable of uncovering the true nature and patterns of their relationships – especially with respect to the complex task of consolidating limited democracy.

How well or poorly are ordinary Koreans prepared for consolidating their nascent democracy into a full and stable democracy? What specific roles are they prepared for and willing to play in the consolidation process, and why? To explore these questions, a number of qualitative and quantitative analyses were performed on the 1996 survey data. One notable finding from the data analyses is that an overwhelming majority of Koreans support the installation of a democratic regime, but not every one of these supporters believes that democracy is *always* the best form of government. In Korea, moreover, the relative number of such unwavering supporters is significantly lower than contemporaries in Eastern Europe or its predecessors in Southern Europe.

Many of these Korean democratic supporters, however, have yet to reject authoritarian propensities and internalize a full range of democratic operational norms. As a result, many Koreans remain superficial or uncommitted supporters of democratic consolidation. Therefore, only a very small minority are authentic democrats who are fully prepared for the drive for further democratization. Fully committed supporters of democratic consolidation are spread throughout the various segments of the Korean population, although they are more numerous among the young and the college-educated.

A variety of factors – political, economic, cultural, and personal – prompt Koreans toward pro-democratic orientations and away from pro-authoritarian propensities. Especially fearful memories of the authoritarian past and growing satisfaction with the democratic present motivate them to welcome the transition away from authoritarian rule and to demand the further democratization of limited democracy. Nevertheless, political factors, and even economic interests, are not at all capable of dissociating Koreans from their age-old authoritarian habit of decision-making or of encouraging them to embrace democratic norms. Levels of education and exposure to various models of democracy are the only two factors that are able to effect such long-term commitments to democratic consolidation. Exposure to various possibilities of democratic governance stands out as the most versatile force contributing to every dimension of democratic commitment among the Korean population.

Based on these findings, it is fair to conclude that the consolidation of Korean democracy is not very likely to take place in the near future. It is, indeed, most likely to be a long-term process which will take place over future generations. The satisfactory performance of democratic political institutions alone will not make it possible for a majority of the Korean population to become fully liberated from authoritarian propensities and to embrace all the basic norms of democratic politics in a short span of time. Older and poorly educated generations of the Korean population need to be replaced by younger and more educated citizens. For future generations of Koreans to become better democrats, the quality of education has to be upgraded at every level. This will be an intergenerational process of transformation similar to that in Austria, Germany, Japan, and other old democracies.

CHAPTER 4

Citizen Competence
and Participation

"Participatory democracy must be put into practice; the
people must be respected as masters and must act like
masters."

Kim Dae Jung (1998: 31)

"Citizen participation is at the heart of democracy. Indeed,
democracy is unthinkable without the ability of citizens to
participate freely in the governing process."

Sidney Verba, Kay Schlozman & Henry Brady (1995: 1)

In the aftermath of the installation of the Sixth Republic in 1988, the
Korean people have been offered a variety of new and expanded
opportunities to participate in the political process. For the first time in
more than two decades, for example, they directly elect their president
every five years. Every four years, they also elect legislative and executive
officials of local governments, including those not only of special cities
and provinces but also of urban districts and rural counties in which they
reside. Even in many civic and business associations, Koreans directly
elect their leaders who were once appointed by the government (Seong
1996b; see also Choi & Im 1993; S. Kim 1996, 1998).

Such newly installed and expanded procedures for popular participation, alone, do not necessarily guarantee that government agencies
will act for the people in an accountable and responsive manner. In
order for those procedures to serve as truly viable channels of representative democracy, Korean voters ought to embrace the art of self-
government (Barber 1984; Dahl 1992; Nie, Junn & Stehlik-Barry 1996).
Moreover, they ought to participate actively in the conduct of governmental and public affairs (Dahl 1989; Held 1987; Pateman 1996; Verba,
Schlozman & Brady 1995).

Our main goal in this chapter is to examine and assess how capable
and active Koreans are as citizens within a democratic state. First, the
levels and patterns of citizens' psychological engagement in and cognitive awareness of political life are examined; then their attentiveness to
and involvement in political and associative life are studied. Based on
these examinations, the active and inactive segments of the Korean
population in political and civic life are identified and compared. This is
followed by an exploration of how the change to a democratic regime

95

has affected public activism and how public activism, in turn, has affected the existing commitment to democratic consolidation. Finally, an attempt is made to determine how well mass participation in Korea suits pluralist democratic politics by comparing it to what has been found in certain other consolidated and consolidating democracies.

The Notion of Democratic Citizenship

Democracy, unlike authoritarian rule, is a political system involving the participation of ordinary people in the making of public policy. Moreover, it is a form of government that ought to serve the demands and preferences of its citizens rather than their political leaders. The consolidation of nascent democracy, therefore, requires more than a high level of support for democratic political institutions and strong commitment to democratic procedural norms within the public as a whole. It is also necessary for ordinary citizens to engage themselves in public affairs and take part directly, as well as indirectly, in the governing process itself (Barber 1984; Pateman 1996; Thompson 1970).

In Chile they do not even have this

Democratic theorists are profoundly divided on how and to what extent the average citizen should participate in public affairs as citizens of a democratic political community.[1] Mill, Locke, Barber and many other theorists of participatory democracy have long argued for a high degree of political information, activism, and sophistication. On the other hand, Almond & Verba, Huntington, Lipset, and other theorists of elitist democracy have contended that too much citizen activism is more detrimental than conducive to democratic politics. In this chapter, we see democratic citizenship being, by necessity, participatory in nature. At a minimum, as citizens of a democratic state, Koreans need to be interested in and informed about public affairs on a voluntary basis. In this connection, they need to acquire a set of activist orientations to the political process (Almond & Verba 1963: 138; Gibson, Duch & Tedin 1992; March & Olsen 1995). They also need to acquire a habit of balanced or open-minded thinking (Sniderman 1981). In addition, they should be able to articulate and communicate their interests, needs, and preferences to fellow citizens, government agencies, and elected officials (Dahl 1971; Verba, Schlozman & Brady 1995).

At a maximum, ordinary citizens should be willing to criticize flawed or deficient policies and, when necessary, individually and collectively challenge those in power. They should also become involved in organized social life with other individual citizens and political institutions of representation. Citizen protest is necessary to "focus the attention of the regime on the need for change" and to "focus the minds of elites on the need for an accommodation" (Tarrow 1994; see also Barnes & Kaase

1979). A dense network of civic engagements among the masses, on the other hand, is needed in order to foster civic norms and create effective democratic institutions (Putnam 1993; Diamond 1994b).

Participatory Dispositions

To play an influential role in the process of democratic governance, average Korean citizens should see themselves first as masters of their own political destiny (see Dalton 1996). How many Koreans have acquired such activist orientations? In order to explore this question, respondents to our 1994 survey were asked two separate questions intended to tap general levels of political interest and efficacy (for wording, see Appendix B L1 and L2). Figure 4.1 reports the distributions of their affirmative responses to the questions separately.

A substantial majority (60%) of the Korean population is at least somewhat interested in politics while a small minority (7%) is not interested in it at all. Of those politically interested, however, a large majority (70%) are not "very much" interested. As a result, fewer than one in five (18%) Koreans are "very much" interested in the newly instituted democratic political process for which many took to the streets and even risked their own lives. There is little doubt that an interest in politics inspired a relatively large segment of the Korean masses. The

Int. in politics Higher in S. Korea Began transition in 1988

Figure 4.1   Activist Orientations to Politics

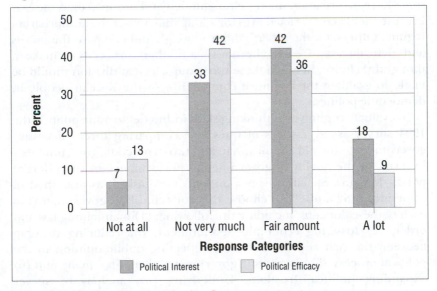

Source: 1994 Korean Democratization Survey

depth of their political interest even under the democratic government, however, remains moderate at best.

political efficacy

In sharp contrast to political interest, a sense of political efficacy is not as broadly based; less than one-half (45%) of the Korean electorate perceive themselves as capable of influencing the process to make governmental decisions and choose public officials. Of this minority, only 9 percent do so strongly. In short, the sense of political efficacy is not only narrowly based but also shallowly rooted.

Even among those who feel politically efficacious, less than two-thirds (63%) are interested in politics. Consequently, only a little over one-quarter (28%) of Korean voters have acquired the fully activist orientations of political interest and efficacy that theorists of participatory democracy demand. Why a majority (54%) of Koreans, who are interested in politics, still perceive themselves as incapable of influencing the political process as they did under the past authoritarian regime remains unknown. Perhaps greater experiences with democratic politics may be needed to transform their authoritarian mindsets, which have been moulded for them over many decades.

Cognitive Competence

As citizens of a democratic state, Koreans should be cognitively capable of making balanced or open-minded judgments in order to arrive at thoughtful political decisions. In considering various policy alternatives, some Koreans are undoubtedly close-minded and prone to extreme bias because they lived restricted lives for a long time under the authoritarian regime. Others, on the other hand, can weigh and compare the merits and deficiencies of each alternative and then proceed to make a thoughtful choice. Between these two groups, a clear division should be made to evaluate the cognitive competence of the Korean people in democratic politics.

To evaluate cognitive, or thinking skills within democratic politics, the 1994 survey asked a series of questions comparing three successive governments – the old authoritarian and two democratic governments – in terms of the quality of governmental performance in six different policy domains. Specifically, respondents were asked, as described in Appendix B S2 and S3, to choose the worst and best governments in each of these domains, including the following: (1) maintaining law and order, (2) fostering economic development, (3) reducing the gap between the rich and the poor, (4) reflecting public opinion in the political process, (5) distributing governmental benefits equally, and (6) expanding political freedom. Underlying this analysis of survey responses is the premise that a democratic regime, for all its virtues, has

Figure 4.2 Cognitive Sophistication

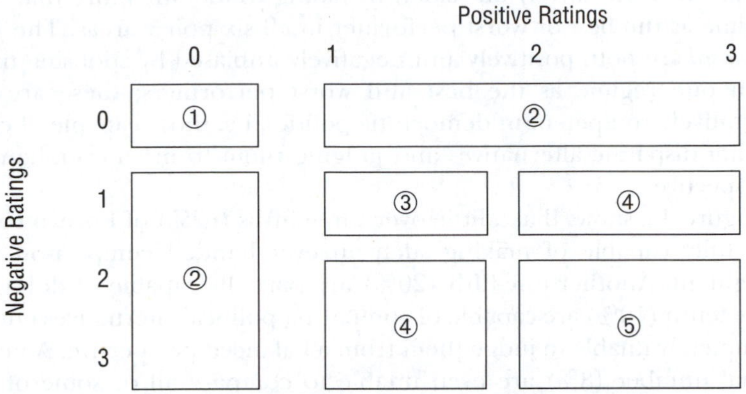

Numerals	Descriptions	Percent
①	Completely uninformed	3
②	Partially uninformed	5
③	Fully biased	10
④	Partially biased	20
⑤	Fully unbiased	62

Source: 1994 Korean Democratization Survey

its own share of faults and shortcomings just as an authoritarian regime (Sniderman 1981).

The overall quality of each respondent's judgment is estimated by counting the number of regimes the person categorized as the best and worst across the six policy domains. The number of the regimes identified as best is considered together with the number of those identified as worst. For each of the best and worst categories, the number can vary from 0 to 3. Figure 4.2 depicts, graphically, the cutting points defining five different levels of cognitive competence, which range from the fully and partially ignorant through the one-sided or closed-minded to the partially and fully unbiased.

As Figure 4.2 shows, the *completely uninformed* are those who are unable to judge the best as well as worst regimes in all of the six policy domains, while the *partially uninformed* were unable to identify either the best or the worst regimes in those domains. The one-sided chose only one of the three regimes as the best performer in all six policy domains and chose another of them as the worst performer in every one of those domains; these are the *fully biased*, praising one regime as the best and blaming another as the worst in all six domains. In contrast to these people who are biased positively as well as negatively, the *partially biased* are either positively or negatively one-sided by failing to identify more than one regime as the best or worst performer in all six policy areas. The *fully unbiased* are both positively and negatively unbiased by choosing more than one regime as the best and worst performers; these are the cognitively competent in democratic politics, i.e. those capable of comparing disparate alternatives and judging them from an even-handed perspective.

Figure 4.2 shows that a little over three-fifths (62%) of Korean voters are fully capable of making such an even-handed comparison and judgment. Another one-fifth (20%) are partially capable of doing so. One-tenth (10%) are capable of comparing political alternatives but are completely unable to judge them from a balanced perspective. A nearly equal number (8%) are even unable to compare all or some of the alternatives they have to consider. In summary, a relatively large majority of the Korean electorate is fully or partially competent in the role of political decision-maker.

Attentiveness to Public Affairs

Cognitive competence alone does not make it possible for the average citizen to choose the best of political candidates and policy alternatives. Unquestionably, such competence is necessary for making the best choice; however, cognitive competence is not a sufficient condition for thoughtful decision-making. To choose the best for themselves and their country, cognitively competent citizens of any democratic state need to remain attentive to public affairs and be sufficiently informed about political issues under debate.

How attentive are Koreans to public affairs? Figure 4.3 shows the percentage of the adult population for each level of attentiveness in the 1994 survey data. This simple summary index of political attentiveness is constructed by totaling responses that affirm frequent viewing of TV news and engagement in political discussion with others (Appendix B L3 and L4.2). Its scores range from a low of 0 (none of the two activities) to a high of 2 (both of those activities).

Over three-quarters (77%) of the Korean adult population often watch TV news covering politics and public affairs. A much smaller majority (52%) have engaged in political discussions with other people. By engaging in at least one of these two activities, a large majority (86%) remain at least minimally attentive to the newly instituted democratic political process. Only a small minority (43%) are adequately attentive to the process by not only following but also discussing public affairs. Yet

[Compare to Chile]

Figure 4.3   Levels of Political Attentiveness

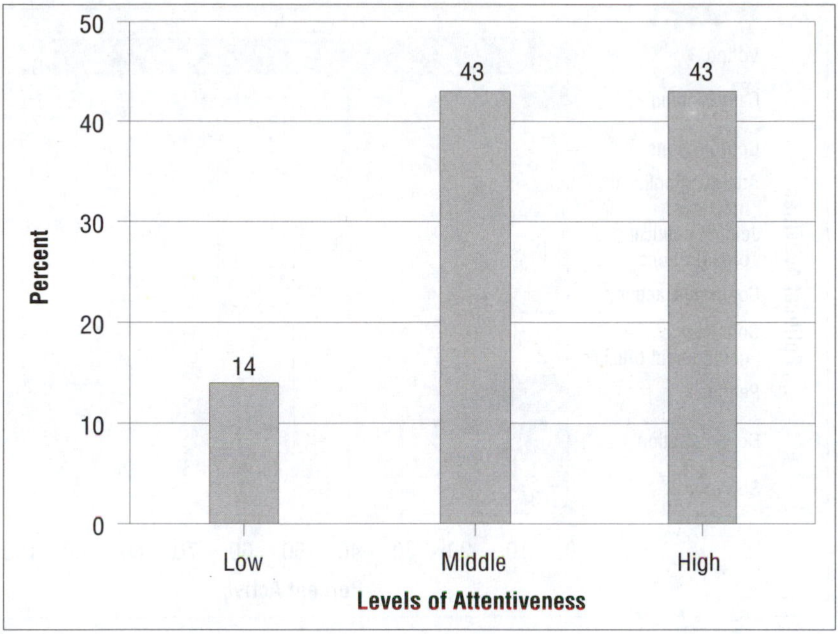

Source: 1994 Korean Democratization Survey

the adequately attentive are over three times more numerous than those who remain completely indifferent to it (43% versus 14%).

The Nature of Political Participation

In democracies, citizens are not forced to get involved in the political process as they are in authoritarian states. Citizens, without their consent, are also not forced to accept or comply with the policies and programs formulated by political leaders. (Ordinarily, their consent is obtained through majority rule.) Therefore, for Korea's nascent democratic regime to consolidate into a full-fledged democracy its mass citizenry needs to go beyond the ballot box.

To what extent have Koreans been involved in the political process since the inauguration of the democratic Sixth Republic in February 1988?[2] Figure 4.4 shows the percentages of the Korean population reported in 1994 as having engaged in each of ten different political acts.[3] As listed in Appendix B L4, the ten activities covered in the November 1994 survey do not, by any means, exhaust the possibilities of involvement in Korea's democratic political process. Yet they include a

Figure 4.4   Percentages Engaging in Ten Political Activities

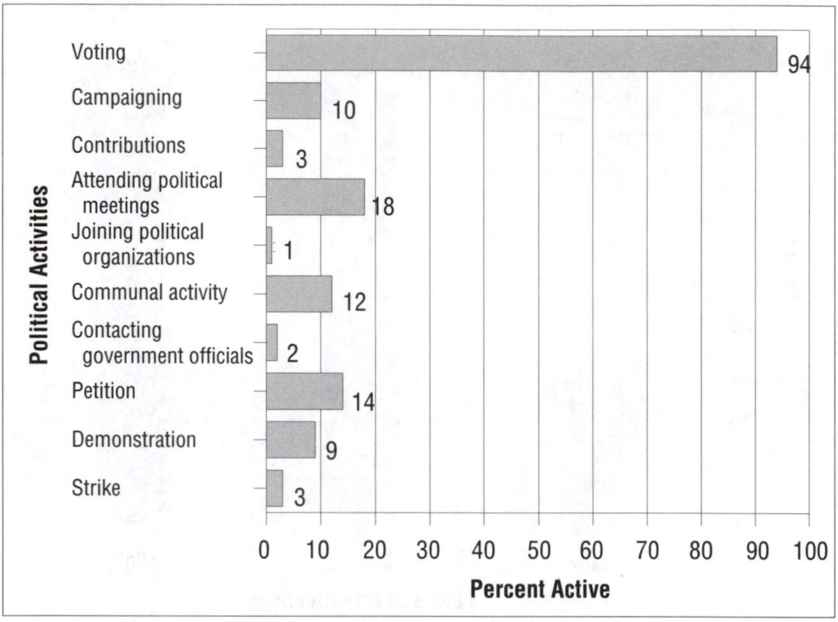

Source: 1994 Korean Democratization Survey

variety of conventional and non-conventional activities directly supporting and challenging the entire process of governance.

As expected, voting in national and local elections is the most commonly reported of all those permitted activities under the current democratic regime. During the six years of democratic rule, an overwhelming
majority (94%) of voting-age Koreans have participated in national or
local elections. Moreover, it is the only political activity in which more
than one-half of the Korean electorate has ever been engaged as citizens
of a democratic state.

All other activities have been performed by relatively small minorities
(ranging from 1% to 18%). Of the nine activities beyond voting, only
three have been embraced by more than one-tenth. These include:
attending political meetings or assemblies (18%), submitting or signing
petitions (14%), and working with others on community problems
(12%). The next group of two, less commonly engaged in, activities are:
campaigning for political parties or candidates (10%) and taking part in
demonstrations (9%). The remaining groups of four activities are each
engaged in by less than 5 percent. They are: making contributions to
political organizations or candidates (3%), joining strikes (3%), seeking

favors from government officials or politicians (2%), and affiliating with political organizations (1%).

Of the nine activities other than voting, none has ever been embraced by a majority of Korean adults for more than half the decade of democratic rule. More notable is that as many as five of the non-voting activities have been appropriated by fewer than one in ten Korean citizens during the same period. These findings clearly indicate that the Korean people have not graduated from the old, authoritarian habit of political detachment. They have yet to take full advantage of democratic reforms. The under-utilization of the many channels and opportunities for political participation is one notable feature of mass politics in democratizing Korea.

How widely have citizens been involved in the entire process of Korean politics? What proportion of the Korean mass citizenry has been very active within the system? What proportion has been completely inactive? To address these questions precisely, each individual citizen's involvement in all ten political activities has to be taken into account. Specifically, we first counted the total number of reported political acts for each respondent in the 1994 survey. Then, the percentage of the entire sample was calculated for each number of the total political acts performed, which range from a low of 0 to a high of 10. The results of this analysis are reported in Figure 4.5a. The results of a similar analysis, exclusive of voting in national and local elections, are also reported in Figure 4.5b.

According to the mean presented in the Figure, the average Korean has engaged in less than two (1.7) of the ten different political acts during the democratization period from 1988 to 1994. In terms of percentages, a little over three-fifths (62%) reported having engaged in only one activity and about one-sixth (17%) did so in two activities. Substantially less than one-tenth (5%) reported having engaged in more than four of the activities surveyed. Those involved in more than half of the ten acts constitute 2 percent while the uninvolved in any of them are 4 percent. The lack of extensive involvement in the political process is a second feature of Korean mass politics during democratization.

Korean involvement in politics becomes more limited when voting in national and local elections is excluded from the overall level of participation; other than voting, nearly two-thirds (65%) have not been involved in any of nine activities. One-quarter (25%) have been involved in one or two non-voting activities, and one-tenth (10%) in three or more. Only 2 percent have engaged in more than half of those activities. From these findings, it is clear that a majority of the Korean people have done very little besides voting. Democratic reforms to date have not

Figure 4.5a   Number of Political Acts (Including Voting)

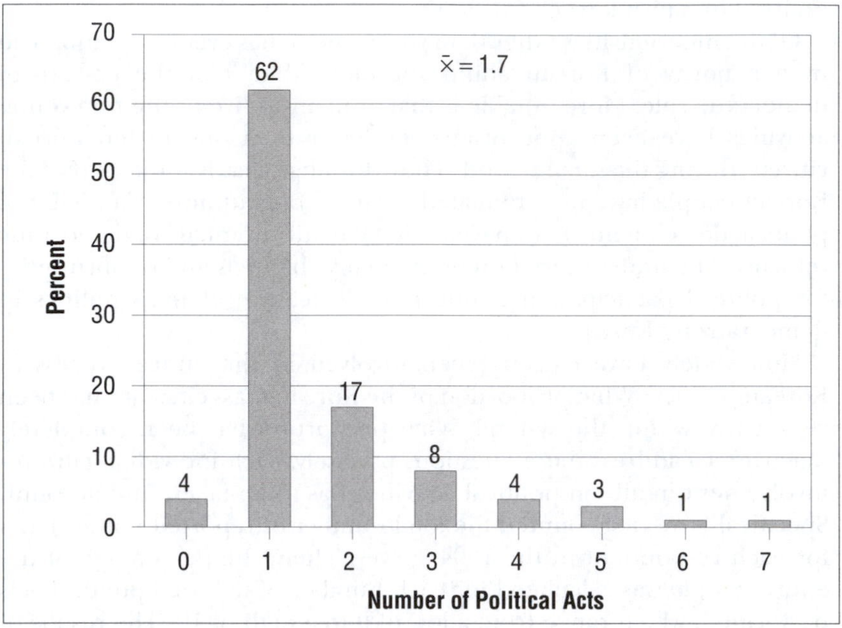

Source: 1994 Korean Democratization Survey

been very instrumental in encouraging the Korean masses to be active beyond voting – the most rudimentary mode of democratic political participation requiring the least amount of time, money, and skills

What types of political activities have been most and least popular among Koreans? We classify ten individual activities into three broad types: two *compliant* (electoral and non-electoral) and one *defiant* (protesting) acts. For each type, the figure provides the percentage of those having taken part in one or more activities. As expected from Figure 4.4, taking part in elections has been the most popular, with 94 percent. This is followed by non-electoral, compliant acts (25%), and protesting (19%) in that order. This order of popularity among the three types is not very surprising. What is surprising is the wide range of percentage differentials between the most and least popular types. Electoral participation is, for example, over three times more popular than either of the other two types.

Even more surprising is the extent to which protesting has been accepted among the Korean masses as a legitimate mode of political participation. Nearly one in every five (19%) Koreans has engaged in one or more activities challenging the government. This figure is nearly four times as large as those very dissatisfied (4%) with the performance

Figure 4.5b Number of Political Acts (Excluding Voting)

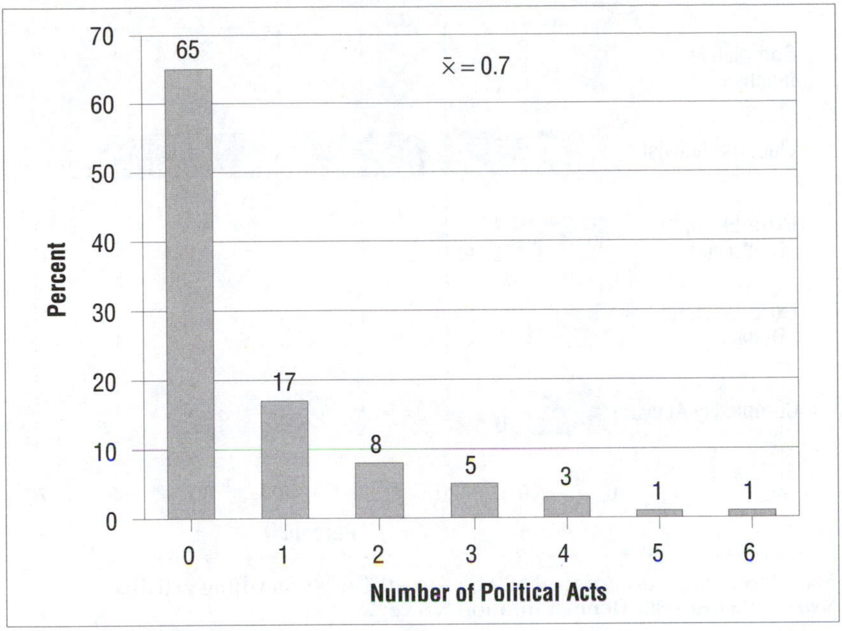

Source: 1994 Korean Democratization Survey

of the Kim Young Sam government. Obviously, protesting is neither confined to a very small segment of the Korean electorate nor is it confined to those disenchanted with the democratically elected government. The advent of democratization has encouraged a substantial proportion of the Korean masses to cultivate a democratic habit of defiant involvement. This is a third notable feature of changing mass politics in Korea.

Do Koreans tend to specialize in only one type of political activity, or do they tend to engage in several types? A large majority (64%) has embraced no more than a single type. A little over one-fifth (22%) have taken part in two types and only one-tenth (10%) in all three types. Among the politically active Korean adults, those involved in a single type constitute nearly twice as many as those embracing multiple types of participatory opportunities, which recent waves of democratic reforms have made available to them.

In what kinds of political activities do a large majority of voting-age Koreans choose to become involved? As described in Figure 4.4, politically active Koreans differ a great deal among themselves in their amount of participation. Do they also differ from each other in how they participate in politics? To answer this question, we need to differentiate

Figure 4.6   Types of Participators

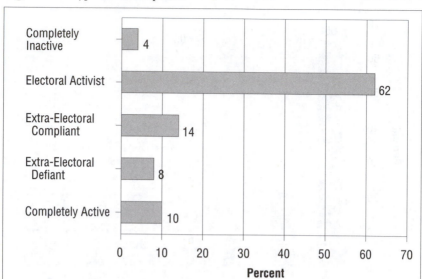

Note: Percentages do not total 100 because 2% are non-voting activists
Source: 1994 Korean Democratization Survey

types of participators. By examining the nature and degree of such political activities as voting and campaigning, non-electioneering, and protesting, five principal types of participators are ascertained: (1) the inactives, (2) electoral activists, (3) extra-electoral compliants, (4) extra-electoral defiants, and (5) complete activists.

The *inactives* are those who have not engaged in any type of political activity. They have neither voted in any of the national and local elections, including two presidential and parliamentary elections, nor have they engaged in any other types of political activity. About one in twenty-five (4%) falls in this segment, which is completely detached from the political process.

Electoral activists are distinguished from the inactives by their involvement in the electoral process. Some of them have merely voted in the elections. Others have worked for a party or candidate. Still others have attempted to persuade their friends or relatives to vote for the candidate they support. Nevertheless, beyond any of these voting and campaigning activities electoral activists have done nothing. A little over three-fifths (62%) have specialized in electoral politics.

Like electoral activists, *extra-electoral compliants* and *defiants* have also taken part in the electoral process. Unlike electoral activists, however, compliants and defiants have engaged in one other political activity. Specifically, compliants have participated in making political contacts, communal work, financial contributions, or other non-challenging activity. Defiants, on the other hand, have taken part in government-challenging activities such as petitioning, demonstrating, or striking. Compliants account for one-seventh (14%) of the Korean adult population and defiants for one-thirteenth (8%).

Unlike any of the three types of activists discussed above, complete activists have taken part in all three types of political activity, including protesting. One in ten Korean adults (10%) has been completely active as a citizen of a nascent democracy.

Of the four types of activists, electoral activists constitute a substantial majority of the entire voting-age population in Korea. About one-third (32%) have been involved in the democratic political process beyond the domains of voting and campaigning. After nearly a decade of experience with democratic politics, Korea still remains a nation of electoral politics. This is a fourth feature of Korean mass politics.

Non-Political Participation

New democracies consolidate as increasing numbers of ordinary citizens organize themselves into groups and associations on a voluntary basis (Diamond 1994b; Foley & Edwards 1996; Putnam 1993; Rose, Mishler & Haerpfer 1997). As an individual, one cannot challenge the authoritarian practices of powerful governmental institutions nor can one deal with a lack of accountability and unresponsive conduct among elected officials. By joining voluntary associations, citizens of new democratic states not only enlarge their hearts and remain civilized, but they also aggregate and represent their interests in the political process and guard against the authoritarian forces re-emerging (de Tocqueville 1956: 198–203; see also Cohen & Rogers 1992).

How active have Koreans been in such voluntary associations? In what type of associations have they been most active?[4] The type and depth of their activism in the non-political process were explored in the 1994 survey data (Appendix B M1). Figure 4.7 reports the percent of Koreans affiliated with the five broad categories of non-political organizations or groups – including fraternal (e.g. alumni and clan associations) and religious associations (churches and temples), economic interest groups (agricultural co-ops and labor unions), and social (charity and environmental protection) and cultural organizations (arts, hobbies, and sports clubs).

Koreans are most commonly affiliated with two categories of associations reminiscent of pre-industrial or traditional village life. Nearly two-thirds (64%) are affiliated with face-to-face friendship or fraternal associations, and almost one-quarter (24%) are members of churches or

Figure 4.7   Civic Engagement by Five Categories of Voluntary Associations

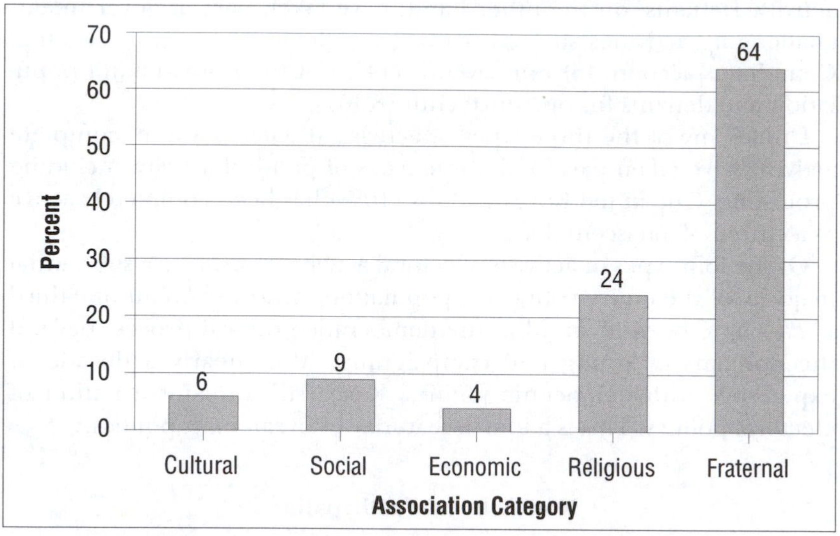

Source: 1994 Korean Democratization Survey

other religious groups. In sharp contrast, no more than one-tenth (9%) are affiliated with any of the three modern types of civic associations, which directly involve those citizens without personal ties. Only 4 percent are affiliated with interest groups or business associations, 9 percent with social associations; and 6 percent with cultural associations. The findings are clear: beyond the organic boundaries of the personal ties deeply rooted in the pre-industrial age, a vast majority of Koreans remain unconnected with each other; they still refuse to join hands with strangers to promote the social capital necessary for national development (Fukuyama 1995a).

In Figure 4.8, we examine the overall depth of non-political participation by tallying memberships in all five types of associations. As the mean (1.1) listed in the Figure indicates, Koreans are, on average, affiliated with a single category of associations. In terms of percentages, one-quarter (25%) are not affiliated with any category. Among the affiliated, those belonging to a single category outnumber those belonging to multiple categories by a substantial margin of two to one (51% versus 24%). Those belonging to more than two categories constitute only 6 percent. In Korea today, involvement in associative life has spread to a large segment of the population. Yet, its activism in the non-political process is very shallow.

The shallowness of non-political activism among Koreans becomes more understandable when levels of their affiliations with voluntary

Figure 4.8   Percentages Engaged in None to All Five Categories of
Associational Affiliations

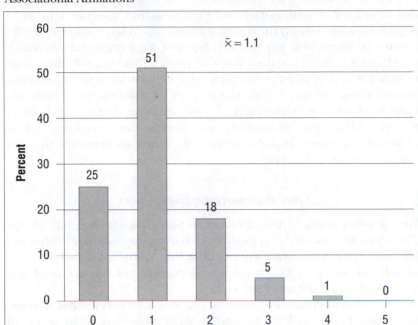

Source: 1994 Korean Democratization Survey

associations are compared across the two distinct types defined by the
historical origins of those associations. Over seven in ten (73%) are affiliated with at least one of the primordial associations built on fraternal,
neighborly, or religious ties. In contrast, only one in six (15%) belongs to
any business or communal institutions that symbolize civic life in modern
society featuring high levels of industrialization and urbanization.

How many Koreans are affiliated merely with associations based on
primordial ties? How many Koreans are affiliated with those built on
similar interests or ideologies rather than their personal identities? To
explore these questions, we need to differentiate types of participators
in associative life. To examine how Koreans divide their total associative
activity into primordial and other associations, they are classified into
two distinct types: *primordialists* and *extra-primordialists.* Three-fifths
(60%) of the Korean population are primordialists whose public life is
still confined within the boundaries of interpersonal or religious ties.
They represent nearly five times as many as extra-primordialists (13%)
who are active beyond those boundaries.

There is little doubt that Koreans tend to be active in associative life. As a nation, however, they are not horizontally integrated to the degree that contemporary industrial and post-industrial societies appear to require for a successfully functioning democracy. A large majority (85%) are not affiliated with any modern types of mass organizations which directly seek to influence the governing process. Additionally, there is no evidence that they attempt to teach their members the art of self-rule. Among those affiliated with these types of associations, which are capable of serving as channels of representative democracy, a small minority (38%) join in multiple and diverse civic associations. This indicates that Korea is still a nation of numerous elements that are closed off from each other.[5]

Overall Democratic Engagement

We will now consider three domains of participation in public affairs. This consideration makes it possible to determine the many distinctive features of Korean involvement in public life. Moreover, it also allows an overall assessment of how much the Korean public has acquired and actually practised the art of self-rule.

In terms of attentiveness to public affairs, six in every seven Koreans (86%) are found at least somewhat attentive to them. In terms of political participation, nineteen out of twenty (96%) are involved in the electoral or governmental process. A comparison of these two percentages indicates that a substantial number of Koreans take part in politics without being adequately informed. Such inattentive political participators comprise as much as one-tenth (10%) of the Korean electorate.

A great deal of difference also exists in the levels of Korean involvement in political and civic life. Those completely inactive in civic life are over six times more numerous than their counterparts in political life (25% versus 4%). Those who are politically active beyond voting and campaigning, on the other hand, represent twice as many as those who are non-politically active beyond fraternal and religious associations (34% versus 15%). These findings contrast sharply with what has been noted recently in the United States where citizens make greater commitments to non-political activities (Verba, Schlozman & Brady 1995: 79). To many Koreans, politics still occupies a central place in their public lives. Within consolidated democracies like the United States, however, it takes a secondary place to churches and to other voluntary activities.

In order to evaluate the overall quality of democratic engagement, it is necessary to consider all three domains of public activities together.

Figure 4.9 Percentages of Koreans Minimally and Adequately Involved in None to All Three Domains of Public Life

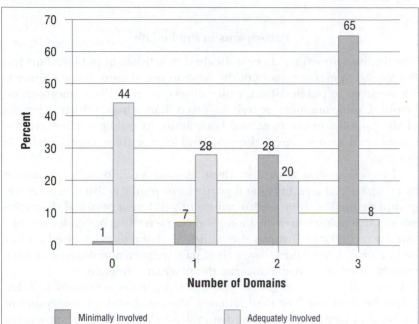

Source: 1994 Korean Democratization Survey

The completely unengaged in most, or all, of the three major domains – political attentiveness, political participation, and associative affiliation – of public life surveyed above account for a very small minority (8%). More impressive is the fact that nearly two-thirds (65%) are engaged in all of the public life domains in one way or another (see Figure 4.9). From this finding, it is clear that a substantial majority are, indeed, not only attentive to public affairs but also involved at least *minimally*.

Among Korean citizens, nonetheless, a very small minority are only adequately active beyond the minimal levels of public life. Precisely, less than one-half (43%) not only follow but also discuss political events with other fellow citizens to the extent that they become *adequately* informed about public affairs. Only one-third (33%) are active beyond voting and campaigning. About one-sixth (15%) are involved in civic associations capable of promoting social cohesion beyond personal ties. Only one in twelve Koreans (8%) is *adequately* engaged in all of these three aspects of public life. In short, Korean activism in public affairs is rather shallow, although it is quite broadly based. The further consolidation of a new democracy in Korea requires qualitative shifts in public activism from electoral to extra-electoral and from primordial to extra-primordial engagements.

Participants in Public Life

The findings presented above indicate that activism in public affairs has not spread to every segment of the Korean population. Some segments are involved in public affairs, while others are not. Even among those involved, some are more actively involved than others. Which segments of the population are most and least active in public affairs? Are the same or different segments the most and least active in every public life domain?

This section seeks to explore these questions of a distributive nature by comparing the amounts and patterns of public activism among the groups defined by three pairs of inherently different personal characteristics. A first pair involves the biological characteristics of gender and age while a second one involves the achieved characteristics of education and income. Unlike these two, a final pair (region, and the type of community based on its size) concerns the place of residence.

In each and every category of public activity, males are shown, in Table 4.1, to be more involved than females. Moreover, with the exception of voting and campaigning, the former lead the latter by a substantial margin. The genders, for example, are nearly equal in the extent to which they take part in the process of electing government leaders (95% versus 93%). Beyond this rudimentary process of democratic politics, however, males register significantly greater levels of political activism than their female counterparts. In attending to public affairs, engaging in non-electoral activity, and joining in voluntary associations, as many as 20 percent more males are involved. When all three domains of public affairs are considered, the gender gap widens to a greater extent. Males are three times (12% to 4%) more numerous among those adequately engaged in public life as a whole, i.e. those who are attentive to public affairs, participate beyond campaigning, and join non-fraternal associations.

Among the three groups defined by age, no single group is consistently more active than others in every category of public life. The most and least active of the age groups vary according to its domains. The young are most active in terms of protesting, but least active in terms of elections. In contrast, the old are most active in elections, but least active in protesting. Those of middle age, on the other hand, are most interested in politics and involved in political activities of a compliant nature. When all domains of public life are considered

Table 4.1 Demographic Characteristics and Public Activism

	Attentiveness		Political Participation			Associational Participation		Overall	
	TV	Discussion	Electoral	Non-electoral	Protest	Primordial	Non-primordial	Minimal	Adequate
Gender									
Male	82	62	95	36	25	79	19	74	12
Female	72	41	93	16	13	67	11	56	4
Age									
Young (20–35)	75	58	90	22	24	78	16	61	8
Middle age (36–50)	81	50	98	31	19	77	17	71	9
Old (50 & older)	75	35	99	26	3	77	9	63	6
School									
Middle School or less	67	32	99	21	8	72	7	56	3
High School	79	53	94	22	17	71	14	65	5
College or more	84	69	90	35	33	77	27	74	17
Income									
Low	69	39	95	23	11	70	9	56	4
Middle	80	53	95	23	22	74	16	68	8
High	79	66	90	35	23	75	22	68	14
Region									
Cholla	70	43	94	34	20	69	16	58	8
Kyongsang	74	47	94	24	21	73	11	62	8
Others	80	55	94	24	18	73	17	68	8
Community									
Large City	80	54	94	25	22	72	14	66	8
Small City	79	54	94	27	20	72	17	66	7
Town	69	43	96	25	12	76	15	61	9

Source: 1994 Korean Democratization Survey

together, middle-aged Koreans are slightly more active than their younger and older counterparts.

Koreans with more formal education tend to be more active politically and non-politically than their less educated counterparts. With only the exception of electoral participation in which the most educated participate in the lowest proportion, the more educated are always more active than the less educated. Therefore, those with less than a high-school education are least active, while the college-educated are the most active in attentiveness to public affairs as well as participation in non-electoral politics and voluntary associations. In some activities, such as protesting and involvement in civic associations, the college-educated are four times more active than those with less than a high-school education. Even among the college-educated, however, about one-fifth (19%) are active beyond the bounds of electoral politics and primordial associations. More striking is that even among the best educated of the Korean population only one in every six (17%) is adequately active in public life as a whole.

As in education, Koreans in the category of high income are least active in electoral politics, while those categorized as low income are most active. In other aspects of public life, the pattern is reversed; high-income Koreans are most active while low-income Koreans are least active. The magnitude of difference between these two income groups, however, is much smaller than that found between the two divergent education groups. Many of the educational differences, moreover, disappear when education is controlled.

Public activism does not vary much across regions nor across urban and rural communities. The only notable difference involves participation in non-electoral politics. Cholla residents, as compared to residents of two other regions, tend to participate more in governmental politics and community affairs. Urban residents tend to engage in protesting to a greater degree than rural residents.

From the above analysis, it is clear that gender and educational attainment affect public activism more powerfully among the Korean population than any other demographic characteristic. These two personal characteristics, therefore, are considered together to identify the most and least active segments of the population in public life. Figure 4.10 lists the six segments defined by these two characteristics and compares their average levels of participation in politics as a whole.

A notable feature of the data in this figure is that every male segment politically outperforms every female segment with a similar education. More notable is that every male segment outperforms any of the three female segments. Whether college-educated or not, males are more involved in politics than their female counterparts. As a result, the

Figure 4.10 Mean Number of Political Activities by Gender and Education

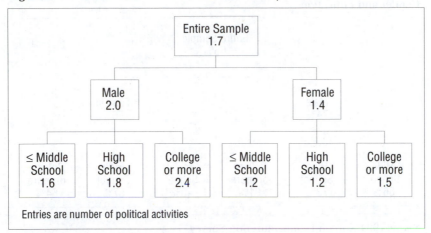

Entries are number of political activities

Source: 1994 Korean Democratization Survey

least involved of the male segments is more active politically than the most involved of the female segments. In other words, Korean males with little or no formal education are more active politically than Korean females with a college education. This definitive evidence indicates that politics in Korea still remains a man's domain – even after several years of democratic rule (see A. Lee & Reinhart 1995).

On the index measuring at least minimal level of involvement in all three domains of public life, the six population segments rank exactly the same as they do on the political participation index (see Figure 4.11). Every population segment representing males ranks higher than any of the three segments involving females. Among both males and females, those who are college-educated rank significantly higher than the less educated. Therefore, of the six segments chosen for this comparison, males with a college education are the most active, and females with a middle-school education or less are least active in political as well as civic life. This constitutes more evidence confirming the secondary role that Korean females play in public life.

The Etiology of Political Participation

Why do some Koreans participate in politics while others do not? Why do more Koreans engage only in voting and campaigning while others are active beyond electoral politics? In this section, we explore the factors contributing to and detracting from the amounts and kinds of political participation. Underlying this exploration is a framework that Verba, Schlozman & Brady (1995) have recently labeled the Civic

Figure 4.11   Percentages Engaged in all Three Domains of Public Activism by Gender and Education

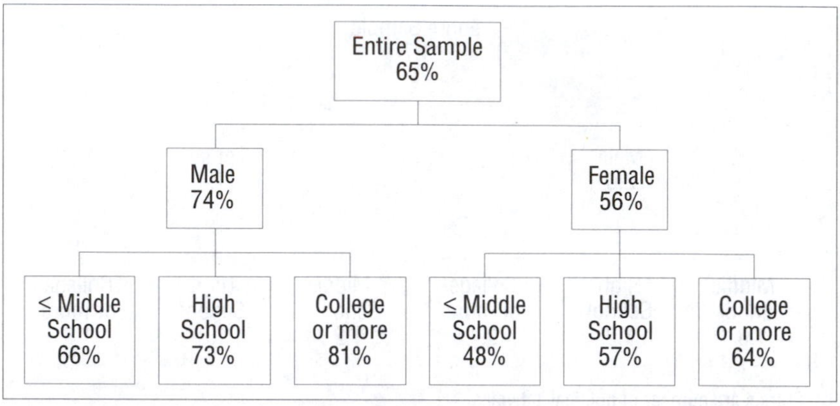

Source: 1994 Korean Democratization Survey

Voluntarism Model (CVM). Unlike the earlier models which stress the importance of individual citizens' political predispositions or socioeconomic status, the CVM emphasizes their involvement in non-political, voluntary associations as the basic foundation of political participation. In a nutshell, the model holds that such civic engagements promote political participation *indirectly* by not only predisposing people to politics, but also providing a variety of valuable opportunities, resources, and skills.

In view of the recent findings that the CVM offers a potent explanation of participation in the United States and other countries (Brady & Kaplan 1996), we used regression analysis (ordinary least square procedure) on three separate measures of political participation with a pair of variables measuring membership in primordial and civic associations together with four other pairs of independent variables. The four other pairs are: (1) personal characteristics (gender and age), (2) political motivations or predispositions (interest and efficacy), (3) political attentiveness (discussing politics and viewing TV news), and (4) socioeconomic resources (education and income). For each of the ten independent variables, Table 4.2 reports five *beta* weights – one for each of three types of political activity and two overall indexes of political participation. Taking these *beta* weights as a rough measure of relative importance, we can identify the individual independent variables and the respective sets that most powerfully influence Korean involvement in electoral and non-electoral politics.

The first interesting feature of the data in Table 4.2 concerns the direction in which each independent variable affects the three types of

Table 4.2 Multiple Regression Analysis of Political Participation: OLS Regressions (standardized regression coefficients)

	Participation Types			Overall Index	
	Electoral	Non-electoral	Protest	With voting	Without voting
Gender	0.03	0.08*	0.12*	0.11*	0.11*
Age	0.13*	0.09*	−0.18*	0.01	−0.01
School	−0.04	0.04	0.05	0.03	0.04
Income	−0.02	0.00	−0.03	−0.01	0.00
Political Interest	0.11	0.12*	0.04	0.12*	0.12*
Political Efficacy	0.00	0.00	−0.04	−0.02	−0.03
TV News	0.08*	0.02	0.00	0.05	0.04
Discuss Politics	0.08*	0.19*	0.16*	0.20*	0.21*
Traditional Organization	0.16*	0.10*	0.07*	0.14*	0.11*
Modern Organization	0.11	0.30*	0.16*	0.27*	0.28*
R^2	0.13	0.26	0.16	0.28	0.28

*Significant at the 0.05 level
Source: 1994 Korean Democratization Survey

political activity – electoral, non-electoral, and protesting. The same variables do not always affect divergent political activities in the same direction; some are consistently positive, while others are not. For example, the variables measuring political attentiveness and institutional affiliations, gender (being male), and political interest promote all three types of political activities. Old age, on the other hand, contributes to electoral and non-electoral participation while detracting from protesting. Educational attainment, in striking contrast, contributes to protesting while detracting from electoral participation. Unlike education, income and political efficacy detract from protesting. Among Koreans, the same demographic, behavioral, and psychological characteristics are not uniformly instrumental in promoting various political activities.

Which specific characteristics or sets of characteristics are most powerful as agents to encourage or discourage Koreans from engaging in each type of political activity? Of ten independent variables, older age and involvement in both types of voluntary associations contribute most when it comes to electoral participation, and involvement in civic (non-primordial) associations and frequent discussions of politics are the prime contributing forces behind non-electoral participation of a compliant nature. With respect to protesting, however, younger age, civic associative involvement, and political discussions contribute most. When the three types of political activity are considered together, associative attachments stand out as one of the two most powerful influences on every type.

In sharp contrast to those organizational attachments, two socio-economic resource variables matter very little to any type of political activity. Neither educational attainment nor family income is statistically significant with *beta* weights much less than 0.07. With respect to any type of political participation, feelings of political efficacy also do not matter significantly. Why is it that the socioeconomic resources, long regarded as "the universal solvent" or "a critical determinant of democratic political behavior," matter little to Korean adults (Nie, Junn & Stehlik-Barry 1996: 3)? Why is it that Koreans remain unmotivated by the key component of participatory predispositions, which is widely believed to "certainly facilitate political activity" (Verba, Schlozman & Brady 1995: 271)? These questions constitute the unknown of political participation in Korean democratic politics.

In fully consolidated democracies like the United States, non-political associations are found to "merely provide a framework for political engagement, resources, and recruitment," and thus have "only a small direct impact on participation" (Brady & Kaplan 1996: 8). In newly democratizing Korea, however, these associations are found to have a very large direct impact on political participation. To estimate their relative importance as compared to other sets of independent variables, Table 4.3 reports squared part correlation coefficients.[6] Of the five sets of independent variables in the table, affiliations with primordial and civic associations constitute the only set adding both *directly and substantially* to the variance explained by all other four sets and confirming their salience as a force directly influencing Korean participation. These findings confirm the contrasting roles that voluntary associations play in consolidating and consolidated democracies.

Table 4.3   Proportions of the Variance in Political Participation Independently Explained by Five Clusters of Variables

	Participation Index	
Clusters	With voting	Without voting
Biological characteristics	0.01	0.01
Socioeconomic resources	0.00	0.02
Political attentiveness	0.04	0.04
Activist orientations	0.01	0.01
Organizational involvement	0.09	0.09

Entries are part correlation coefficients squared
Source: 1994 Korean Democratization Survey

Why is it that organizational affiliations, not personal resources and motivations, powerfully attract the Korean masses to the democratic political process? In the wake of the democratic regime change, all prominent politicians and their followers have been allowed to compete freely with each other. To an extent never accomplished before, these politicians have been able to create an extensive network of new organizations and politicize existing ones for their own political advantage. Through elaborate spectacles of election campaigns and rallies, and by pitting their own home base against other regions, the three most prominent Kims in Korean politics have successfully mobilized the average citizen who had been deprived and kept powerless by authoritarian rule for decades.

Such circumstances, featuring the intense politicization of voluntary associations and the extensive mobilization of the masses by their leaders, have apparently created some anomalies of mass involvement in Korean politics.[7] Under these conditions, citizens are able to compensate for their deficiency in motivations and resources necessary for political participation. In the words of Rosenstone & Hansen (1993: 234), "participation is taken out of the realm of the individual citizen and placed in the sphere of the political system." As they suggest, the political logic of mass mobilization is the key to the puzzle of Korean participation.

The Meaning of Public Activism for Korean Democracy

What does active involvement in public life mean for Korean democracy? Has it oriented or reoriented the Korean people toward democratization? Have Koreans become more committed to democratic change as they have become active in politics and civic affairs? If so, is it political or non-political activism that contributes more to their democratic commitment? This section examines these questions concerning the possible consequences of public activism for democratic political life among the Korean people.

Table 4.4 cross-tabulates measures of public activism with those weighing unwavering commitment to the consolidation of nascent democracy in Korea. The measures of unqualified democratic commitment are percentages expressing: (1) the desire to live in a *perfect* democracy by choosing the highest score of ten on a 10-point democratic preference scale (Appendix B C1.3), (2) unqualified support for the further democratization of Korean politics by *strongly* agreeing with the statement that "our political system should be democratized more than it is now" (Appendix B E3.3), and (3) unqualified opposition to the rebirth of authoritarian political leadership by *strongly* disagreeing with the

Table 4.4 Relationship of Public Activism to Democratic Orientations

	Democratic Preference	Democratic Commitment	
		Positive	Negative
Political Attentiveness			
Low	24	15	6
Middle	26	22	12
High	34	34	19
Levels of Political Involvement			
Low	27	21	11
Middle	28	31	12
High	36	40	29
Types of Political Involvement			
Inactive	27	27	16
Electoral	27	21	10
Extra-electoral	29	36	16
Defiant	27	23	12
Completely active	43	44	39
Levels of Non-Political Involvement			
Low	29	25	9
Middle	28	24	14
High	32	34	21
Types of Non-Political Involvement			
Inactive	29	25	9
Traditional	28	24	14
Modern	33	41	29
Both	31	33	23

Source: 1994 Korean Democratization Survey

statement that "the dictatorial rule led by a strong leader like Park Chung Hee is much better than a democracy to deal with the serious problems facing the country these days" (Appendix B G2.3).

From Table 4.4, it is apparent that more engagement in public life means greater commitment to democratic change and vice versa. All five measures of public activism are found to be positively associated with every measure of democratic commitment. With no exception, the most active in each dimension of public life have cultivated the greatest desire to live in a perfect democracy. To the greatest extent, they have also committed themselves to the positive, as well as negative, political reforms required for further democratic consolidation.

Nonetheless, a careful scrutiny of the data in Table 4.4 reveals that more activism does not always bring about significantly greater preference for a perfect democracy. Nor does it bring about significantly greater commitment to democratic reforms. Among four out of five types of political participators, for example, there is little difference in their desire to live in a perfect democracy. Between the completely inactive in politics and the electoral activists, it is not the latter who are more committed to democratic consolidation. Between low and middle levels of non-political involvement also, it is not those in the latter who are more committed to that change. Koreans appear to be more strongly motivated to embrace democratic political culture by the particular kind of involvement in public affairs than its degree.

Of the three types of political participation considered, electoral participation and protesting appear to be equally ineffective in orienting or reorienting the Korean masses strongly toward complete democratization. On any of three measures of democratic orientations, those who have engaged in elections alone or protesting do not display any more commitment to it than even those who have been completely inactive in the political process during the course of democratization. Instead, the former are shown in Table 4.4 to be less committed, although not significantly, than the latter in all those three measures. Those who have engaged in extra-electoral and compliant mode of political activities, on the other hand, are shown in the same table to be more strongly committed than those who are politically inactive.

Between the two types of organizational involvement considered, it is the involvement in modern (socioeconomic and cultural) associations that contributes to the democratization of mass political orientations. The involvement in traditional (fraternal and religious) associations appears to have discouraged Koreans from reorienting themselves toward democracy. In two of the three dependent variables measuring democratic orientations, members of such traditional associations score lower than those who are not affiliated with any associations at all. Those affiliated only with non-traditional associations, on the other hand, always scored higher than those affiliated with both traditional and non-traditional associations.

Consequences of Democratization for Public Activism

Has the democratic transformation of authoritarian rule in Korea encouraged or discouraged its people from engaging in public life? Are Koreans more active in public life these days than during the earlier period of authoritarian rule? If so, in what domain of public life are they more active? To address these questions adequately, we would need to review the parallel surveys that measured all three domains of public life in both authoritarian and democratic periods. Such surveys, however, are not available for our purpose of longitudinal analysis. During the authoritarian period, all surveys were able to ask only a limited number of questions about a few domains of public life

When the military headed by former General Chun Doo Whan ruled the country with a heavy hand, two nationwide sample surveys were conducted in 1984 to investigate political participation (Han & Auh 1987; Park & Kim 1987). Results of the two 1984 surveys are compiled in Table 4.5 with those of our 1994 and 1996 surveys in order to explore the impact of democratization on political participation. In the table, we see that the percentages taking part in most political activities have neither increased nor declined significantly between the authoritarian and democratic regimes. For example, those taking part in voting, campaigning, and contributing have changed less than 5 percentage points over the period. In attending political meetings and campaign rallies, as well as contacting government agencies and public officials, however, significant changes have taken place. Those attending political meetings have declined by two-thirds (from 40% to 13%). Those attending campaign rallies have also declined by 10 percentage points (from 46% to 36%). In sharp contrast, the proportion contacting government offices

Table 4.5   Political Participation Before and After Democratic Transition (percent)

	Pre-Transition		Post-Transition	
Activity	1984a	1984b	1994	1996
Voting	91	88	94	
National elections				93
Local elections				91
Campaigning	10	9	10	8
Persuading Others to Vote	19			22
Attending Rallies	46			36
Attending Political Meeting		40	18	13
Contributing Money		2	3	2
Contacting Government Officials or Politicians	5		15	
Member of Political Organizations			1	
Community Work			12	14
Petitioning	7	8	14	4
Striking			3	2
Demonstration	10		9	7

Notes: 1984a Survey was done by Han & Auh (1987)
         1984b Survey was done by Park & Kim (1987)
Sources: 1994 & 1996 Korean Democratization Surveys; Han & Auh (1987); Park & Kim (1987)

or public officials has tripled (from 5% to 15%). Those submitting a petition have doubled (from 7% to 14%).

These changes are not difficult to understand in view of the nature of the two different regimes under which the Korean people have lived for the past decade. During the authoritarian era, Koreans were often mobilized by the government and the party in power to take part in political meetings and campaign rallies. At the same time, they were discouraged or prohibited from contacting many government agencies and challenging public officials. With the demise of authoritarian rule, Koreans are no longer required to attend unpopular political meetings. At the same time, they are free from political oppression and at liberty to challenge governmental authorities. For this reason qualitative changes have occurred in the way Koreans have participated in the political process during the past decade.

Have such changes brought about substantial shifts in the *relative* levels of political participation among the various population subgroups? To explore this question, the relative levels of political participation are

Figure 4.12   Levels of Political Participation Before and After Democratic Change by Five Levels of Socioeconomic Resources (in standard score)

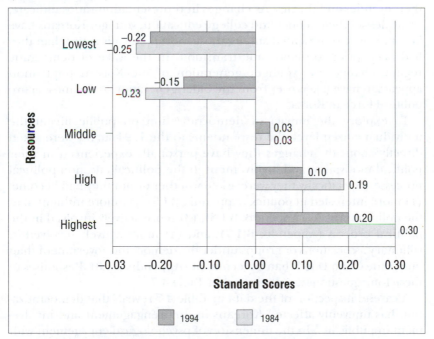

Sources: 1994 Korean Democratization Survey; Park & Kim (1987)

compared across five socioeconomic subgroups over the 1984–94 period.[8] In terms of education and income, the upper classes have become a much less dominant force in the democratic political process than they had been during the authoritarian political process ten years ago. According to the standard scores reported in Figure 4.12,[9] the two lower classes are still significantly less involved in the political process than the two upper classes. Yet, the former are no less involved, relatively, as they were ten years ago. As the difference between the 1984 and 1994 surveys indicates, the participation gap between the lower and upper classes has narrowed over the period. When compared to the authoritarian period, current participation in democratic politics is less heavily concentrated in the hands of the upper classes. The reduction of unequal participation is a notable consequence of Korean democratization.

Democratic change has also brought a significant generational shift in the demographic composition of those most actively involved in the political process.[10] According to the survey conducted by the Korean Legislative Development Institute in 1984,[11] reported in Table 4.6, three-fifths (60%) of those most active in authoritarian politics were concentrated among males and females forty years and older. Among the similarly active in democratic politics ten years later, however, a larger majority (65%) are concentrated among younger males and females in their twenties and thirties. As changes in representation ratios indicate, regardless of their gender and college education, younger Koreans have become more represented among those most politically active than they had been prior to democratic transition. In the wake of democratic regime change, the younger generation of the Korean population appears to have taken over from the older generation as the most active political force in Korea.

To explore the impact of democratization on public life at the individual citizen level, the respondents to the 1994 survey were asked directly about the changes they have personally experienced in their political motivation and involvement in the political and non-political processes. Specifically they were asked whether or not they had become: (1) more interested in politics (Appendix B L6), (2) more influential in the political process (Appendix B B3), (3) more actively involved in the political process (Appendix B L7), and (4) more actively involved in voluntary associations or groups under the democratic government than under the Chun Doo Whan government (Appendix B L8). Responses to these four questions are presented in Table 4.7.

A careful inspection of the data in Table 4.7 reveals that democratization has unevenly affected Koreans in their engagement and involvement in public life. In the dimension of psychological engagement with politics, a large majority perceive themselves to be affected by the demo-

Table 4.6 Distribution of the Most Actively Involved in Authoritarian and Democratic Politics

Demographic Characteristics	Authoritarian Politics (1984) Survey			Democratic Politics (1994 Survey)			
	Percent most active (A)	Percent in population (B)	Representation ratio (C = A/B)	Percent most active (D)	Percent in population (E)	Representation ratio (F = D/E)	Change in representation ratio (F−C)
Male							
No college **Young (20–39)**	13.8	21.5	(0.64)	15.7	14.3	(1.09)	(+0.45)
College	17.6	13.2	(1.33)	28.7	12.5	(2.29)	(+0.96)
No college **Old (40+)**	38.4	24.1	(1.59)	19.9	19.3	(1.03)	(−0.56)
College	15.1	7.5	(2.01)	8.8	4.6	(1.91)	(−0.10)
Female							
No college **Young (20–39)**	5.7	18.9	(0.30)	11.1	24.9	(0.44)	(+0.14)
College	3.1	5.4	(0.57)	9.3	10.0	(0.93)	(+0.36)
No college **Old (40+)**	6.3	9.4	(0.67)	6.5	14.4	(0.45)	(−0.22)
College	—	—	—	—	—	—	
Totals	100.0	100.0		100.0	100.0		

Source: 1994 Korean Democratization Survey

Table 4.7   Perceived Changes in Four Domains of Public Activism Subsequent to Democratic Transition

	Types of Perceived Changes (%)					
Public Life Domains	Much more (A)	Some- what more (B)	Changed little (C)	Some- what less (D)	Much less (E)	Net change ((A+B) − (C+D))
Political interest	9	33	40	14	4	+24
Political efficacy	10	47	33	8	2	+47
Political involvement	2	15	63	11	9	−3
Non-political involvement	4	15	69	7	5	+7

Source: 1994 Korean Democratization Survey

cratic regime change. In the behavioral dimensions of political and organizational involvement, however, a larger majority perceive themselves unaffected, rather than affected, by the same change. From this finding, it is clear that, at the individual level, democratization constitutes a slowly moving, 2-step process in which psychological and behavioral changes take place in sequence. At first, individual citizens become psychologically attracted to public life. Later, they become behaviorally involved in it.

Another notable feature of the data in Table 4.7 concerns the direction in which democratization has affected public life in Korea. Of the four domains surveyed, three have been affected more positively, and one was affected more negatively. In the domains concerning political motivations and organizational involvement, more Koreans claim increases rather than decreases in their public activism as a result of democratic change. In the case of political participation, however, more people claim decreases rather than increases, which is consistent with the declining rates of voting in National Assembly elections, as discussed early in the Introduction to this book. Why is it that newly gained freedom and opportunities for participation have done more to move the Korean people out of, rather than into, the political process? Is it possible that they are finally at ease with their government and no longer see the necessity of getting involved in the process?

These democratic reforms, nonetheless, have contributed to, more than detracted from, the building of a more active community in Korea. When changes in all four dimensions of public life are considered, a

Figure 4.13   Overall Levels of Perceived Changes in Public Activism

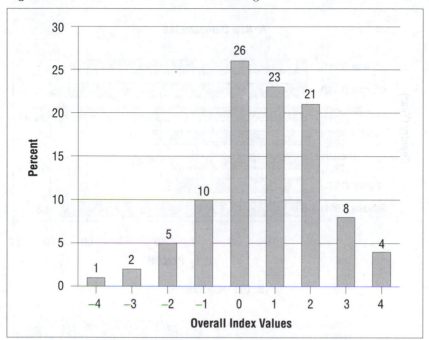

Source: 1994 Korean Democratization Survey

greater number of Koreans have become more active rather than less active in public life. According to Figure 4.13, measuring the overall impact of democratization on public life, nearly three-fifths (56%) have experienced increases in public engagements while a little less than one-fifth (18%) experienced decreases. Clearly, positive changes outweigh the negative ones. Nevertheless, those who have been positively affected in all or most of the public life domains comprise only a small minority (12%), which indicates that Koreans have a long way to go before they become a fully active democratic community.

Cross-National Comparisons

There is no absolute answer to the question of how much activism in public affairs is suitable for the development and maintenance of a fully democratic regime (Verba, Schlozman & Brady 1995: 68). One way of assessing Korean activism in political and civic life is to compare Korea with other democracies. In this section, our survey findings about public activism in Korea are compared with those from old and new democracies, including the United States and Spain.

Figure 4.14 Cross-National Differences in Political Interests

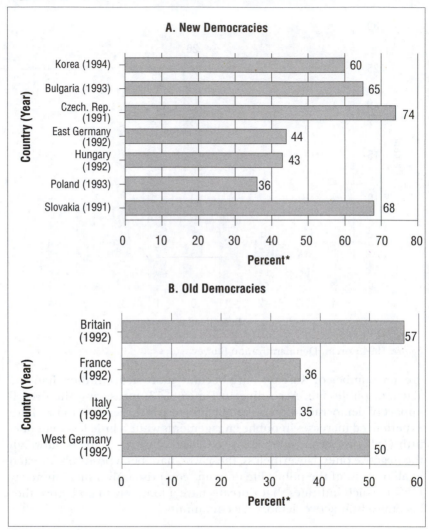

*Percent saying "a great deal" or "a fair amount"
Sources: 1994 Korean Democratization Survey; Mary McIntosh et al. (1993)

Figure 4.14 compares levels of political interest in Korea with ten other democracies, first in terms of new democracies and then old democracies. In terms of the percentage reporting "a great deal" or "a fair amount" of interest in politics, Korea ranks higher than old consolidated democracies such as Britain (57%) and West Germany (50%). When compared to new democracies such as the Czech Republic (74%)

Table 4.8   Cross-National Differences in Political Participation

Activity (Years)	Korea (1996)	Austria (1979)	Netherlands (1979)	United Kingdom (1979)	Germany (1979)
Voting	94	94	84	87	87
Campaigning	10	5	3	4	8
Contact	14	12	11	11	11
Communal Works	14	14	18	17	14
Political Meetings	18	18	6	9	22

Sources: 1996 Korean Democratization Survey; Verba, Schlozman & Brady (1995)

and Slovakia (68%), however, a much smaller proportion (60%) of Koreans is interested in politics. Korean people as a whole are neither too politicized, as citizens of some new democracies are, nor are they too detached from politics, as are citizens of some of the older democracies.

In political and civic involvement, Korea does not lag far behind its predecessors in Europe. As Table 4.8 shows, Koreans are currently (1996) more involved in three of five political activities (voting, campaigning, and contacting) than citizens of four European democracies – Austria, the Netherlands, the United Kingdom, and West Germany – were nearly twenty years ago. In working with others on community problems and attending political meetings, Koreans are slightly ahead of or equal to most of these consolidated democracies two decades ago.

When compared to Americans, however, Koreans are much less active. In six of the nine political activities listed in Table 4.9, Koreans trail Americans. In four of those activities, they lag far behind Americans by over 15 percentage points: 22 points in making campaign contributions, 19 points in contacting government officials, 46 points in affiliating with political organizations, and 16 points in attending political meetings. Only in voting and protesting do Koreans lead Americans by a substantial margin. For Korea to become a fully democratic state, like the United States, it appears that more active participation in the non-electoral process is urgently needed.

Figure 4.15 compares public engagements in non-political associations. In terms of percentages for joining at least one of those voluntary associations, Korea leads other new as well as old democracies – including the United States. Korea is one of the two countries in which more than three-fourths of the population is affiliated with voluntary organizations or groups. Over three-fourths of Koreans (87%) are joiners as

Table 4.9   Political Participation in Korea and the United States

Activity	Korea (1996)	United States (1989)	Difference (Korea − US)
Voting in national elections	93	71	+22
Attending political meetings	13	29	−16
Affiliating with political organizations	2	48	−46
Campaigning	10	8	+2
Contributions	2	24	−22
Communal work	13	17	−4
Contact officials	15	34	−19
Petition	4	6	−2
Protest	8	6	+2

Sources: 1996 Korean Democratization Survey; Verba, Schlozman & Brady (1995)

compared to Spaniards (30%); West Germans (60%); Brazilians (66%), and Americans (79%). These percentage figures make it clear that the shortage of joiners itself is not a serious obstacle to the further development of Korean democracy. What keeps Korean democracy from consolidating further is the shortage of joiners in non-fraternal or non-primordial associations that are capable of articulating and aggregating divergent interests. Therefore, qualitative shifts in associative membership need to take place among the Korean public.

Summary and Conclusions

In order for Korean democracy to consolidate further, its ordinary citizens must be able to embrace and practice the art of self-government. In this chapter, we examined and assessed the capacities and practices of the Korean people regarding participation in public affairs. We first examined how Koreans perceive and evaluate politics and reach their political decisions. Then we analyzed, from the historical and comparative perspective, the levels, patterns, sources, and consequences of their personal involvement in political and civic life.

The data from the 1994 Korean Democratization Survey reveal that a majority of the Korean masses have yet to acquire fully activist orientations toward politics, although they are quite attentive to public affairs and capable of making open-minded decisions in the political process. The same data also reveal that an even larger majority have yet to get involved beyond electoral politics and primordial associations. Based on these findings, it is fair to conclude that a significant shift must take place in the quality of democratic engagements among the Korean mass

Figure 4.15   Cross-National Differences in Organization Membership

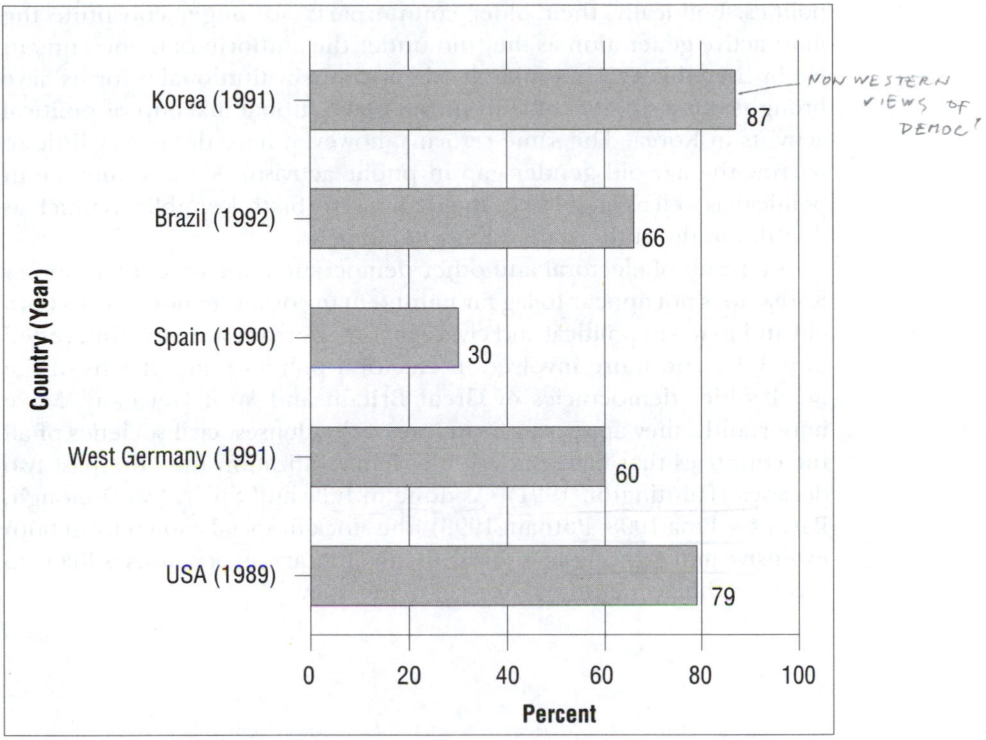

Sources: 1991 Korean Democratization Survey; McDonough, Barnes & Pina (1998); Verba, Schlozman & Brady (1995)

public. Koreans need to reorient themselves from electoral to governmental politics and from fraternal and religious organizations to genuinely communal institutions.

Retrospective self-assessments of public activism and evidence from pre-democratic surveys indicate that the democratic regime change has begun to facilitate such qualitative shifts. Under the current democratic government, Koreans have become more actively predisposed toward politics and more broadly involved in voluntary associations. In addition, the average Korean has also become not only less deferential to governmental authorities but also more active beyond voting and campaigning. It is apparent that a growing number of ordinary Koreans have been slowly learning the art of self-rule from years of personal experience with democratic politics.

Among three different generations of the Korean electorate, those in their twenties and thirties have been the most successful in adjusting to the democratic mode of governance. These younger Koreans now comprise a large majority of those most actively involved in Korean politics. Politically, their older counterparts no longer constitute the most active generation as they did under the authoritarian government led by the military. Undoubtedly, democratic institutional reforms have brought out a significant shift in the generational makeup of political activists in Korea. The same reforms, however, have done very little to narrow the age-old gender gap in public activism. Males dominate in political as well as civic life in the democratic Sixth Republic as much as they did in the authoritarian Fifth Republic.

As a result of electoral and other democratic reforms, contemporary Korea does not appear to lag far behind many other democracies – both old and new – in political and civic activism. Koreans are more interested in politics and more involved in electoral politics than citizens of the much older democracies of Great Britain and West Germany. More importantly, they appear to form one of the densest civil societies of all the countries that have undergone democratization over the past two decades (Huntington 1991). As done in Italy and Spain (McDonough, Barnes & Pina 1998; Putnam 1993), the stock of social capital from both extensive and growing membership in voluntary associations is likely to promote the deepening of Korean democracy.

PART III

Representative Institutions

CHAPTER 5

Legislative Assemblies

"Legislatures are quintessential institutions of democracy."
William Mishler & Richard Rose (1994: 5)
"The legislature, more than any other political institution,
stands at the confluence of democratic theory and
democratic practice."
David Olson & Michael Mezey (1991 xi–xii)

Legislatures are the oldest and most prominent institutions of modern democracy. They are also "the primary representative institution" within democratic government structure (Olson 1994: 3). As nation–states cannot accommodate masses of average citizens to participate directly in policy-making, legislatures have been established and endowed with the authority to represent them. Members of the legislature are elected periodically by the people themselves, and the legislature is, therefore, indispensable to the functioning of all contemporary democracies (Hahn 1996). This is the reason why "legislatures are among the first institutions abolished or subverted when democratic regimes are over-turned, and they are among the first created or revived when democ-racies are instituted or restored" (Mishler & Rose 1994: 6).

In all new democracies, including Korea, legislative assemblies have emerged or re-emerged to assume a central constitutional role in reproducing and keeping their governments genuinely based on the democratic principle of popular consent (Longley 1994). As a result, these legislative institutions have become the most "popular" platforms in the democratic political life of their respective countries – regardless of the disparate functions and authority with which they are formally endowed. As Liebert (1990) notes, national assemblies and parliaments have been the central sites of partisan disputes, negotiations, and important policy debates. They have often become the institution most subject to public criticism and ridicule (Agh 1994; Copeland & Patterson 1994).

As in many other new democracies, the National Assembly in Korea has re-emerged as an autonomous institution of democratic govern-ance since 1988 in the wake of free and competitive elections, which are based on the twin principles of plurality and proportional representation.[1] Since 1991, legislative assemblies have been elected at the two subnational levels of Korean government.[2] As the key representative institution of the democratic Sixth Republic, these legislatures offer new opportunities and additional resources for participation in the political process to a variety of political parties and socioeconomic groups, including many of those banned from participation during the authoritarian period.

At the same time, Korean legislatures provide an arena in which political parties and other organizations can moderate their extreme demands and allow for the mediation of their partisan disputes (C. W. Park 1998b). In addition to the integration of centrifugal forces and peaceful resolution of their conflicts, legislatures also allow the electorate to legitimize representative democracy itself in increasing support for its place in democratic governance. As in Southern Europe, these legislative institutions, like political parties, are crucial for consolidating Korean democracy by "rooting" the new Sixth Republic within the citizenry and organized social forces (see Di Palma 1990b; Hahn 1996; Schmitter 1988).

For the existing legislatures to contribute to the consolidation of Korean democracy, the Korean electorate must embrace them as "a representative and deliberative body symbolizing democratic control of government" (Mishler & Rose 1994: 8; see also Kim & Park 1992). How strongly do Korean voters support the national and local legislatures established to represent themselves in the political process? How broadly based is their legislative support? What motivates them to accept the existence of those institutions as legitimate, i.e. necessary and proper? Is it popular perceptions about how well the National Assembly has been functioning in the new era and environment of representative democracy, or do some other sets of concerns shape legislative support among the Korean electorate?

Addressing these questions, this chapter seeks to examine the commitment of the Korean voters to the ideals and practice of legislative democracy based on the principle of popular representation. Unlike prior research concerned mostly with legislative practices exclusively in new democracies of Southern Europe and Latin America (Liebert & Cotta 1990; Close 1995) or diffuse support for the legislative system in Central and Eastern Europe (Hahn 1996; Hibbing & Patterson 1994; Mishler & Rose 1994; Olson & Norton 1996), our analysis emphasizes the symbiotic relationship between the Korean legislative assemblies and their respective electorates. In doing so, it seeks to trace changes in the evaluation of legislative performance in the National Assembly and assess the impact of such evaluations on the representative process of Korean democracy.

Premises and Hypotheses

The present analysis of legislative support and approval is predicated on two premises, which are well accepted in the literature on legislative politics (Mezey 1979; Olson 1994; Olson & Mezey 1991). The first premise is that legislatures become democratic institutions only when the electorate accepts them as necessary and proper for what they are. Unlike political parties and interest groups, legislatures are popularly elected to represent the interests and preferences of the electorate. Only with the widespread and growing support of the electorate can they assume many important responsibilities of representative governance, including democratic oversight of the executive. Therefore, the greater the popular support for legislatures, the more they are likely to endure and institutionalize as democratic assemblies.

The second premise underlying this study is that legislatures are truly representative institutions only when they are capable of meeting popular demands on a continuing basis. In all new democracies, citizens tend to be highly impatient with government and expect it to tackle the very problems they were subjected to under the authoritarian government. Therefore, when studying the growth of these new legislatures as representative institutions, it is important to know how much they are approved of for what they actually do. The more favorable legislatures and legislators are judged by the electorate, the better they represent its legislative concerns.

In short, democracy is government elected by the people. It should not be run by the few as in oligarchies or autocracies; nor should it be guided by intelligence or professional expertise apart from the people (Lindblom 1977). Ideally, it is majorities of the mass publics – not the politically attentive or elites – that should be assumed to determine the direction and pace of democratizing legislative politics. Therefore, only when supported and approved by the public itself can any legislature qualify as a genuine institution of representative democracy.

Conceptualization

Conceptually, support for legislative democratization is considered a phenomenon with three distinctive characteristics: affect, behavioral disposition, and cognition. The first characteristic concerns preference for parliamentary democracy over authoritarianism as a political ideal. The second deals with the willingness to defend and support the continuing practice of popular representation in the legislative process. The third characteristic concerns the belief that the practice of legislative representation is needed throughout the political system. Following earlier research on democratic norms and practice (Prothro & Grigg 1960), our inquiry distinguishes between legislative democracy as an ideal and legislative democracy as a collective practice. It also makes a distinction between the temporal and spatial aspects of legislative democratic practice.

In principle, citizens who desire to live in a democracy accept representative assemblies as a crucial element in democratic political systems – whether parliamentary or presidential in nature. Such aspiring democrats must also understand that the citizenry can be better served when the process of representation is practised throughout the entire political system rather than when it is confined to the national level. Most of what citizens prefer these days is too complex and diverse to be met solely by the one legislature representing the entire nation. The viability and professionalism of the national legislature are, moreover, enhanced by legislative careerists who can rise in office from local to regional to national legislatures. Therefore, citizens of new democracies must accept legislative assemblies at *all* levels of government as necessary channels of representative democracy.

In practice, citizens should oppose any attempt to suspend the assembly at any level or to subject them to the control of the executive branch. With the suspension of these legislative institutions, the practice of legislative representation ceases to exist. Without any autonomous legislature to oversee and hold the executive branch accountable, representative democracy is reduced to function merely as delegative democracy. The desire of the public to accept legislatures as appropriate and necessary for the established democratic regime and its willingness to defend them on a daily basis constitute two distinct domains of legislative support.

To investigate public approval of legislative performance, this study emphasizes that representative democracy, unlike an authoritarian regime, requires its legislature and elected officials to do much more than formulate new legislation. As Mezey (1979: 6–11) has suggested, the activities of legislatures and their members can be grouped into three broad categories. The first of these is policy-making. A defining characteristic of a legislature is built around whether or not the institution can decide what the law is and is not. Legislatures may differ in the degree to which they control the substance of public policy, but the law-enacting function is central to the meaning of the institution. Making policy includes the aspect of oversight: to be able to examine, question, and redirect the substance of policy according to legislators' findings about how legislative intent is implemented.

The second category of legislative performance refers to representational activities. How do legislators connect the people and their interests to the law-making process? Authorized by popular election, they speak for the interests of constituents. In addition to speaking in the legislature, activities include lobbying bureaucrats and pursuing casework on behalf of constituents. While it is during political campaigns that contacts between legislators and constituents are most commonplace, most legislators interested in re-election keep channels of access between themselves and potential voters open at all times.

Thirdly, the legislature and its members do things to sustain the governing system. Representatives from different parts or sectors of society learn to resolve differences collectively, transforming conflict into consensus, and enhance a national identity for both elites and the masses. Legislators not only articulate demands from constituents, they explain, rationalize, and defend policies to the constituents.[3] Legislation and legislators legitimize the substance and implementation of public policy.

Based on these three categories of activity, legislative performance is not equated in our analysis with an aggregate of institutional activities alone. Instead, it is considered to be a dynamic phenomenon taking place at two different levels: the legislative institution and the individual legislator. Both institutional and individual performances are considered together to offer a comprehensive and dynamic account of legislative democratization in Korea.

Support for Legislative Democratization

For democratically elected legislatures to function as truly representative institutions, public support and approval should be relatively high and widespread. Public support for Korean legislatures and approval of their performance, therefore, are evaluated according to two criteria: central tendency and distribution. The first criterion addresses the degree to which the Korean people, as a whole, support and approve their legislatures. The second criterion deals with the extent to which popular support and approval are distributed across sociological groupings and regional bases.

Types of Legislative Support

The National Assembly is the oldest and most prominent of legislative assemblies in Korea. The nature of its authority and functions has changed a great deal from one regime to another and from one government to another (C. W. Park 1995). Since the installation of the democratic Sixth Republic in 1988, however, it is no longer mocked as a rubber stamp; it has become more independent and diversified than ever before. Clearly the president, the military, and big business must reckon with it on a daily basis.

Respondents to the 1996 survey were asked two questions to determine their degree of support for the democratic reform of the National Assembly. First, they were asked, as shown in Appendix B N2 and N3, how much they agreed or disagreed with the statement: "It is better to abolish the National Assembly and let a strong leader decide everything." Then they were asked: "If the National Assembly was suspended in the future, would you definitely approve, somewhat approve, somewhat disapprove, or definitely disapprove?" By presenting the national legislature as an alternative to an authoritarian regime, the first question tapped their *affect or preference* for popular representation as a principle of democratic governance. The second question, on the other hand, elicited their *behavioral disposition or commitment* to its continuing practice in the legislative process.

In principle, an overwhelming majority (85%) of the Korean electorate rejected an authoritarian system of government based on strong leadership and embraced a democratic system of government with the National Assembly serving as their representative. In practice, an equal proportion of Koreans (85%) expressed disapproval of doing away with their popularly elected National Assembly in favor of its uninterrupted operation. A representative assembly appears to be widely embraced among the Korean people not only as a democratic political ideal but also as a viable institution of democratic governance.

What type of legislative democracy do they most prefer? Is it a democracy requiring a representative assembly to oversee and hold the executive branch accountable? Or, is it a democracy requiring the legislative assembly to delegate to the executive the right to do whatever it deems fit for the country (O'Donnell 1994)? To explore questions concerning the preferred type of legislative politics, individual opinions on the principle and practice of popular representation were combined into a 4-fold typology of legislative political orientations. The four types are: (1) *representative democrats* endorsing the democratic principle of legislative representation and supporting its unqualified practice, (2) *delegative democrats* endorsing such principle and yet refusing to support its unqualified practice, (3) *soft authoritarians* rejecting legislative representation in principle but opposing the suspension of a legislative assembly in existence, and (4) *hard authoritarians* favoring strong executive leaders in place of legislative representatives.

The Korean people are distributed across all four types derived from the above classification. The most numerous are *representative democrats*

(77%) who oppose not only the restoration of undivided government led by powerful executive leadership but also the suspension of the National Assembly. They are followed by *delegative democrats* (8%), *soft authoritarians* (9%), and *hard authoritarians* (6%). In Korea today, the number of representative democrats is over nine times greater than delegative democrats who desire the strengthening of the presidency at the expense of the National Assembly. More notable is that only a very small minority (6%) are *hard authoritarians* committed to a completely non-democratic regime, which denies the National Assembly any independent and major role in Korean politics.

Depth of Legislative Need

New democracies become fully representative when representative assemblies are institutionalized throughout the political system. Therefore, their mass publics should support the functioning of legislatures at all levels of government as necessary and proper rather than questioning their existence. To date, prior research on legislative support in new democracies has focused exclusively on *national* legislative assemblies or parliaments. Disregarding legislatures at the lower levels of government, scholars have merely given a partial picture of legislative support in any of the new democracies surveyed.

How fully do the Korean people support representative democracy? Do they endorse national as well as subnational legislatures as necessary for democratic governance? To explore these questions, the 1996 survey asked respondents to report on a 4-point scale (ranging from "absolutely needed" to "not at all needed") the extent to which they thought of these institutions as a requirement (see Appendix B N1). Table 5.1

Table 5.1 Levels of Perceived Needs for Legislatures at Three Tiers of Korean Government

Types of Legislatures	Need Levels (%)						
	Absolutely	Mostly	Not much	Not at all	Don't know	%	(N)
National Assembly	70	25	3	1	1	100	(1000)
Provincial Assembly	43	36	14	4	3	100	(1000)
Local Assembly	39	34	18	6	3	100	(1000)

Source: 1996 Korean Democratization Survey

compares the levels of perceived need for legislatures at three tiers of Korean government: the National Assembly, metropolitan or provincial assembly, and urban district or rural county assembly.

Remarkably, the legislatures at the regional and local tiers, like the National Assembly, are accepted as necessary by large majorities. While 95 percent rated positively the legislatures at the national tier of the Korean government, 79 percent and 73 percent gave positive ratings to the assemblies at the middle and bottom tiers, respectively. Among the Korean population, the popular sense of need for legislative institutions appears to correspond to the amount of power and resources those institutions command. The greater the power and resources a legislature commands, the greater the number of the Korean people who acknowledge their need for it.

What system of legislative representation do the Korean people support most? Is it the partial system confined to the national level or the full system involving both the middle and bottom levels of their government? Positive responses to all three levels of legislatures were tallied to measure the depth of legislative need. As shown in Figure 5.1,

Figure 5.1   Perceived Need for Legislatures at all Three Levels of Government

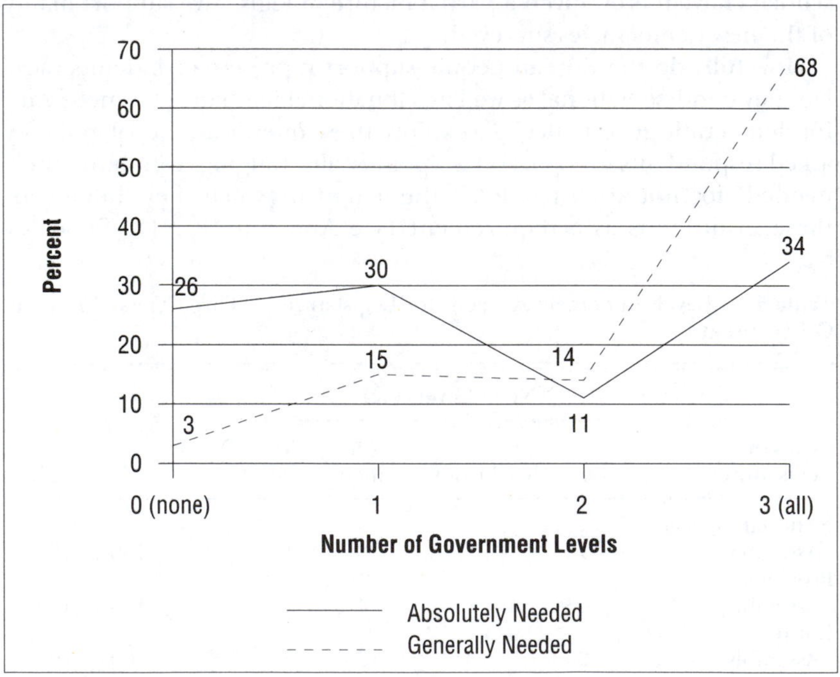

Source: 1996 Korean Democratization Survey

of those who felt that levels of legislature were generally needed, small minorities were supportive of a 1-tier system (15%) or a 2-tier system (14%). Two-thirds (68%), on the other hand, opted for a full 3-tier system of legislative representation and endorsed the recent expansion of legislative representation to the subnational levels of their government. More notable is that only one-third (34%) express unqualified support for the 3-tier system.

Overall Legislative Support

In Figure 5.2, types and depth of legislative support are considered together in order to distinguish two types – full and partial – of supporters of representative democracy. Those who endorse legislative representation at all three levels of government are listed in the figure as full supporters, while those endorsing it only at the national level are listed as partial supporters. Among the Korean people, full supporters of representative democracy are most numerous, constituting a majority (55%). They are over twice as many as partial supporters (22%) of repre-

Figure 5.2 Types of Legislative Supporters

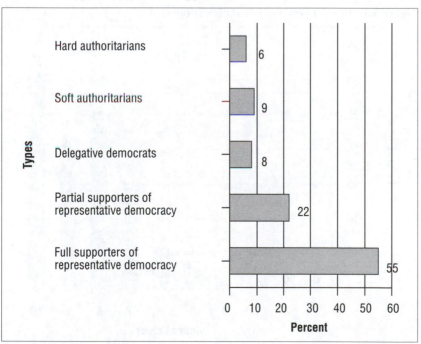

Source: 1996 Korean Democratization Survey

sentative democracy and six times as many as those supporting delegative democracy (8%)

On the whole, how strongly are the Korean people supportive of the
current full system of legislative representation? The three dimensions
of legislative support – preference, commitment, and need – are considered together to estimate overall magnitude. Figure 5.3 reports the
distribution of the Korean people on an index, which adds up responses
on each of the three dimensional scales (ranging from a low of 1 to a
high of 4). Scores of this index are re-scaled to run from a low of 1 to
a high of 10. A score of 1 indicates no support, while a score of 10 indicates unqualified support for legislative democratization.

Careful inspection of the means and percentages in the figure reveals
that Koreans as a whole are supportive of abandoning the old authoritarian system in which the strong executive branch dominated a tame
legislature. Only a few want to restore the old authoritarian system by
opposing any measure of its democratization. Among those Koreans
supporting legislative democratization, however, there is some notable
variation about the appropriate scope of democratic change.

In short, the Korean legislative system has undergone two significant
changes in the wake of the institutional reforms that have taken place

Figure 5.3   Overall Levels of Legislative Support

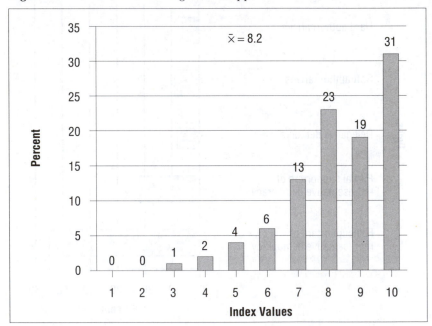

Source: 1996 Korean Democratization Survey

since 1988. Horizontally, the National Assembly has become a legislative institution, increasingly independent of the executive, that represents the electorate.[4] Vertically, it has become a 3-tier legislative system of popular representation. Between these two dimensions of legislative democratization, the horizontal one appears to be more popular than the vertical one. A majority (52%) support both dimensions of democratic change, which have made Korea a fully representative system of legislative democracy. More remarkable is that nearly one-third (31%) are unqualified supporters of the system.

The National Legislature in Action

The transition to democracy in 1988 has brought about significant changes in the formal standing of the National Assembly. The new constitution of the Sixth Republic upgraded the Korean national legislature to make it more equal to the executive branch. Formally, it is no longer "the handmaiden" of the executive branch headed by the powerful presidency. Under the authoritarian Fifth Republic, the president was empowered to dissolve the legislature under the pretext of national security or a crisis. In contrast, under the constitution of the current Sixth Republic, the National Assembly cannot be dissolved by the president under any circumstances, including those of national emergencies. It is no longer required to be in session for a maximum of only 150 days a year in order to work on the agenda set by the executive branch. Constitutionally, the current legislature is provided with the independent authority to represent its electorate in policy-making and to check the executive branch on a year-round basis.

Although provided with the appropriate constitutional authority to establish its autonomy as a supreme legislative organ and equipped with the increased staffing and other resources, the Assembly remains subservient to the executive branch. According to the political scientist Park Chan Wook (1998a: 2), the National Assembly is "hardly autonomous in its interactions with external actors and forces." Even under the leadership of civilian President Kim Young Sam, the president, as the head of the party in power, chose the Assembly Speaker, as was done under the military dictatorships. More often than not, the president and his close associates at the Blue House without much co-operation among the Assembly's opposition parties set the major legislative agenda and the appropriate floor strategies, especially for controversial bills.

Imposing strict internal discipline on their members, moreover, the ruling and opposition parties, alike, require individual legislators to follow the directives from their respective party leaders. Any party member who defies those directives on major policy issues does so at the risk of being expelled from his or her own party (C. W. Park 1997: 101). Even the Speaker of the National Assembly is not immune from his party directives and guidelines. In this regard, the Assembly, despite a decade of democratic rule, is yet to be transformed into a truly democratic institution representing the preferences of the electorate rather than those of political leaders. Although independently and democratically elected, the Assembly remains far from being an institution of representative democracy that is not only externally autonomous but also internally cohesive.

The National Assembly has made serious efforts recently to improve its legislative performance. A plethora of formal rules and regulations concerning legislative proceedings, internal order, and discipline have been introduced and revised for a more democratic and effective management of its affairs. None of these changes, however, has contributed much to the effective accommodation of policy differences among opposing parties nor to the orderly management of their partisan conflicts (C. W. Park 1993: 11). This is because both the ruling and opposition parties are not strongly committed to the formal rules of the democratic game requiring civility, decorum, and tolerance.[5] Instead of searching for a compromise, the ruling party still employs the extra-legal *blitzkrieg* tactics of ramming through legislation, while the opposition party engages in illegal disruptive tactics of sit-ins, hunger strikes, or boycotting plenary or committee meetings. As long as political parties resort to these extra-legal and illegal obstructionist tactics, many Koreans may find it difficult to distinguish the current National Assembly from the one they had under the military government a decade ago

Approval of Legislative Performance
Current Performance

How effective has the freely elected National Assembly been perceived in its dealings with the various problems inherited from the old days of the military dictatorship? How responsive has the legislature been in meeting the newly emerging preferences of the Korean electorate? To make an overall assessment of the performance of the most powerful legislature as a representative assembly, we asked respondents in the 1996 survey to indicate how well or poorly they thought the National Assembly had been performing its duties for their nation (see Appendix B O1).

The continuum of responses was divided into four categories ranging from "very well" to "very poorly." "Somewhat poorly" was the modal response. In fact, a substantial majority (57%) replied that the National Assembly was doing "somewhat poorly" in the current democratic setting

Figure 5:4   Levels of Approval of Legislative Performance

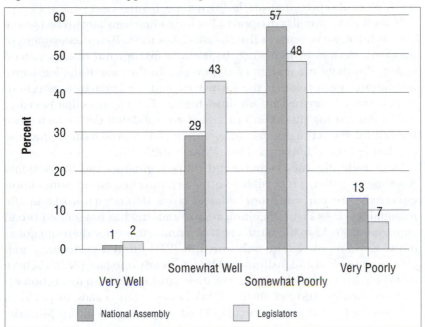

Source: 1996 Korean Democratization Survey

of the Sixth Republic. Another one-eighth (13%) said "very poorly." These two categories of negative responses, when considered together, indicate that seven out of ten (70%) Koreans are less than satisfied with the way their National Assembly has been functioning as a representative institution.[6] Even among a small minority (30%) of the satisfied, moreover, very few (1%) believe that it has been doing "very well." In the eyes of Korean voters, there is broad agreement that the National Assembly has been functioning inadequately, despite being reorganized and democratically elected.

How well or poorly are individual legislators of the current National Assembly fulfilling their roles as representatives of their electoral districts? Respondents to the 1996 survey were asked to rate their performance on a 4-point verbal scale (see Appendix B O2). As in the case of the National Assembly, the performance of representatives is judged more negatively than positively in their performance. Over one-half of our respondents (55%) believe that their legislators are doing "somewhat poorly" or "very poorly." A smaller proportion (45%), on the other hand, think that those legislators are doing "somewhat well" or "very well." A comparison of these two percentage ratings makes it clear that the Korean people tend to disapprove rather than approve of their freely elected representatives' individual performance.

Nonetheless, popular disapproval of individual legislators is less severe than similar assessments of the National Assembly. In the assessment of personal services by individual legislators, disapproval ratings exceed approval ratings by a margin of 10 percent. In the case of the legislative institution's performance, the former exceed the latter by a margin of 40 percent, a figure nearly four times higher. This suggests that Koreans, unlike Americans and other citizens of consolidated democracies, are less critical about the performance of their own representatives than the legislature itself (Hibbing & Theiss-Morse 1995: 45).

By considering assessments of individual legislators and the National Assembly together, it is possible to offer a comprehensive account of how effectively the current model of legislative democracy works at the national level. As Figure 5.5 indicates, the model has not gained broad approval. It works to the satisfaction of a minority rather than a majority of the Korean population; only one-fifth (21%) find it performing well at both individual and institutional levels. Nearly one-half (45%) believe that the current model falls short of their satisfaction both institutionally and personally. Another third (33%) believe that it fails to perform well enough either institutionally (24%) or personally (9%). Minority

Figure 5.5   Overall Approval of Legislative Performance at the National Level

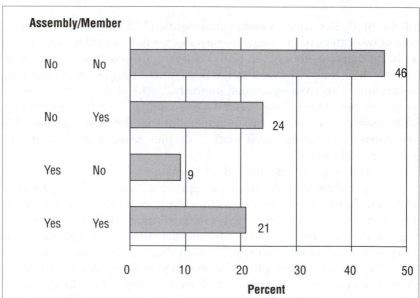

Source: 1996 Korean Democratization Survey

representation by the legislature, to a greater degree than its individual members, is a notable feature of the current model of representative democracy.

Performance Change

Dissatisfaction with the national legislature is not unique to Korea. However, it is important to assess how the current National Assembly compares with the one under the authoritarian regime. Has the democratic legislature been doing a better job than its authoritarian predecessor during the past decade? According to the 1996 survey which asked respondents to rate its performance change on a 5-point verbal scale (Appendix B O3), democratic regime change has not convinced Koreans that there are many substantial improvements in the way the Korean National Assembly does its business. As shown in Figure 5.6, nearly half (46%) believe that the legislature still performs "about the

Figure 5.6 Approval of Performance Change: Comparing the Authoritarian Assembly with Its Democratic Successor

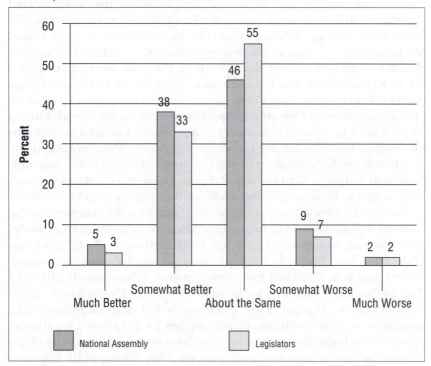

Source: 1996 Korean Democratization Survey

same way" as it did prior to democratic transition. Among Koreans who perceive changes in legislative performance, a few (11%) report that it has changed for the worse. However, four times as many (43%) report that it has changed for the better.

There is little doubt that democratic regime change in Korea has received more approval than disapproval for the performance of the National Assembly. Nevertheless, the benefits of regime change so far have been perceived by only a minority; a greater number of Koreans have yet to sense a clear benefit from it. In Korea, it appears that free elections and other institutional reforms alone have not yet convinced the people of significant improvements in the Assembly's performance. In order for the Assembly to function more satisfactorily, perhaps a new generation of politicians needs to be elected to the legislative body. Also, they may have to be further socialized into the norms of democratic parliamentary politics, including those of compromise and negotiation.

Do members of the current National Assembly perform better at serving their district needs than those who were elected under the authoritarian regime? The 1996 survey asked respondents to rate any changes in their performance on a 5-point verbal scale (see Appendix B O4). A majority (55%) of the Korean people believe that freely elected legislators provide about the same services as the ones they had prior to democratic change. While a relatively small proportion (9%) report declines in the services, a little over one-third (36%) believe that current legislators perform better than those of the authoritarian Assembly. More Koreans sense that representation from their freely elected legislators is better rather than worse. Yet, it is only a minority who perceive improvement from free and competitive elections. Obviously, limited experience with elected legislators has not broadly changed perceptions of political behavior among individual legislators. More notable is the fact that since the authoritarian era, the image of the National Assembly has improved more than the popular perception that current legislators are doing a little better job than those of the earlier era (43% to 36%).

Koreans are divided in their sense of approval for the changes that the current National Assembly brings compared to the authoritarian model it supplanted. As shown in Figure 5.7, fewer than one-half (45%) see it as little improved, both institutionally and personally, over that experienced under the authoritarian government. Nearly one-third (31%) believe that it has improved in one of the two levels. Only a fourth (24%) believe that the current model performs better than its authoritarian predecessor at the institutional and member level. In short, the democratization of legislative politics, to date, has convinced a majority of the Korean people of improvement; however, most see room for improvement in performance.

Figure 5.7 Overall Approval of Legislative Performance Change Viewed both Institutionally and Personally

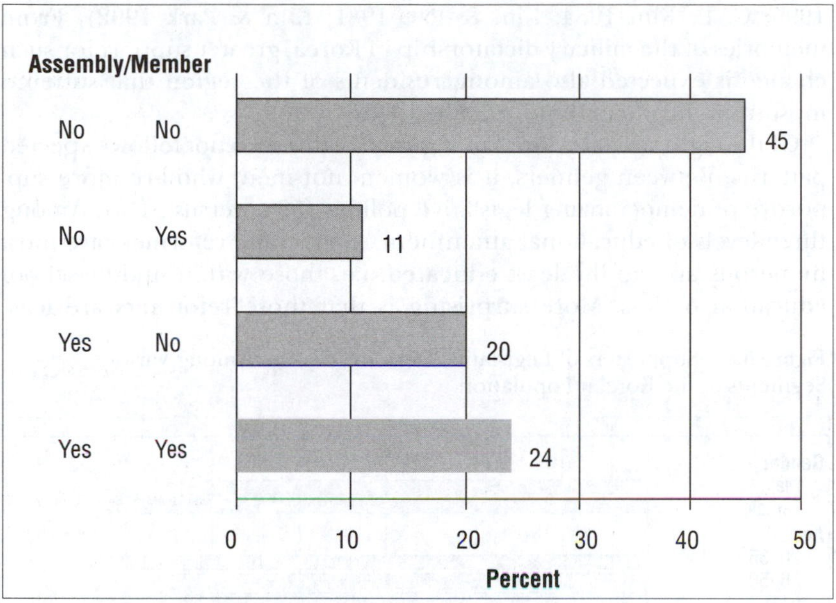

Source: 1996 Korean Democratization Survey

The Distribution of Legislative Support and Approval

By now, two things are clear about the relationship between the Korean public and legislative politics. First, its support for legislative democracy is substantial but not uniform. Second, popular approval of legislative practices is neither very deep nor very strong. In light of these findings, we chose to determine the precise identities of those supporting a full model of representative democracy and those approving the performance of the National Assembly and its legislators. This section explores their identities through behavioral, demographic, psychological, and community characteristics.

Who Fully Supports Representative Democracy?

Supporters of the complete and full practice of legislative representation, as described in Figure 5.2, are identified in terms of the specific categories, which include their gender, age, education and income levels, place of residence, ideology, and political efficacy and involvement. From results of prior survey research on democratic reforms, greater support for legislative democratization is expected among males, the young, the socioeconomically better-off, the ideologically left, and the politically efficacious and actively involved (Hibbing & Theiss-Morse 1995; C. L. Kim 1984; Kim & Pae 1981; Kim & Park 1992). From memories of the military dictatorship in Korea, greater support for such change is expected also among residents of the region that suffered most from the old authoritarian legislative system.

Of the eight variables listed in Figure 5.8, three do not follow expected patterns. Between genders, it is women, not men, who are more supportive of democratizing legislative politics (59% versus 51%). Among three levels of educational attainment, democratic reformers are most numerous among the least educated, i.e. those with a middle-school education or less. More surprising is that those reformers are least

Figure 5.8 Supporters of Legislative Democratization Among Various Segments of the Korean Population

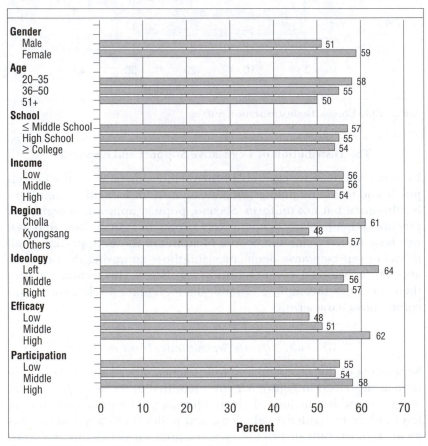

Source: 1996 Korean Democratization Survey

numerous among the college-educated. The more educated Koreans are, the less they support the radical transformation of the old authoritarian legislative system. The same pattern of inverse relationship is observed between levels of income and support for legislative change; the most affluent support the change least. It appears that the socioeconomically advantaged of Koreans are interested in protecting what they have already acquired.

Why is it that among the Korean people, men, the college-educated and the relatively rich support the expansion of democratic reform in the legislative process least? Why is it that women, the middle-school or less educated, and the relatively poor support the same change most? Those Koreans most supportive of the legislative change have one thing in common: they were the most deprived during the old system. Those Koreans least supportive of the change, on the other hand, appear to have benefited a great deal from the same system. The relative sense of deprivation from the old system motivates many Koreans to support more strongly the new system of legislative politics. This is the reason why residents of the Cholla province are the most supportive while those of Kyongsang are the least supportive of the fully democratic legislative system.

Age, ideology, and political involvement follow the patterns we have expected. The young are more supportive of democratic reforms than the middle-aged or the elderly. Ideologically, those on the left are more supportive of the reforms than those who are either moderate or on the right.[7] Psychologically, the most efficacious are most supportive of those changes (Appendix B L2). Behaviorally, the most actively involved are also the most supportive.[8] This is not surprising in light of what has already been observed in other new democracies. What is surprising is that none of the most supportive groups identified above is overwhelmingly supportive of democratic change. In none of these groups, for example, do more than two-thirds support the change.

Who Approves Legislative Performance?

As we reported earlier, perceptions of legislative performance and its changes among the Korean population vary considerably from one domain to another. Many Koreans do not see the institutional and personal domains in the same light, nor do they interpret changes of those in the same light. This finding says nothing about the group of Koreans who approve of each or both domains of legislative performance. Nothing is also known about the type of Koreans who endorse *change* in such performance. In this section, Table 5.2 provides data on those Koreans in terms of their demographic, socioeconomic, behavioral, and psychological characteristics.

Table 5.2 Demographic and Other Differences in Approval of Legislative Performance

Personal Characteristics	Current Performance		Performance Change	
	Institutional	Personal	Institutional	Personal
Gender				
Male	29	39	44	33
Female	30	51	43	40
Age				
20–35	31	47	44	38
35–50	27	42	40	33
50+	32	48	49	41
School				
≤ Middle School	33	44	41	37
High School	33	46	45	39
≥ College	22	46	44	33
Income				
Low	36	47	50	45
Middle	30	46	41	34
High	25	42	44	34
Region				
Cholla	37	52	63	57
Kyongsang	28	46	34	30
Other Areas	29	43	44	35
Ideology				
Left	30	40	49	23
Middle	30	48	42	22
Right	29	43	46	25
Efficacy				
Low	33	42	43	23
Middle	26	43	41	24
High	33	48	47	24
Participation				
Low	33	47	39	24
Middle	32	46	45	22
High	22	40	49	25

Source: 1996 Korean Democratization Survey

In terms of the gender characteristic, little difference exists in the overwhelming reluctance to approve of institutional performance and its subsequent change to democratic transition. Equally small proportions of men and women approve of the current National Assembly's performance (29% versus 30%). Nearly identical proportions of the two genders think that democratic change has brought about improvements in institutional performance (44% versus 43%). In judging the personal performance of individual legislators, however, the genders differ significantly. For example, while men tend to judge their district legislators negatively, women tend to judge them positively (39% versus 51%, respectively). Also, when comparing the legislators under the democratic and authoritarian governments, a significantly greater proportion of women believe that members of the current democratic Assembly perform better than those of its authoritarian predecessor (40% versus 33%). It may be that free and competitive elections have prompted legislators to be more attentive to, or at least less oppressive to, women voters than the authoritarian system was.

All three age groups are in agreement that their National Assembly, as an institution, performs more poorly than individual legislators do. They are also in agreement that democratic regime change has brought about greater improvements in the performance of the former than in that of the latter. Of the three age groups, however, the middle-age group consistently provides the least positive ratings, while the old-age group provides the most positive ratings in every assessment of legislative performance and its changes. The oldest Koreans are the most positive about the current legislative system because they remember the corrupt and unresponsive nature of the authoritarian legislative system. It appears that the middle-aged respondents take a more sceptical wait-and-see attitude about the current system.

Of the two socioeconomic resource variables – education and income – reported in Table 5.2, only income follows the pattern we expected from the analysis of legislative support presented above. More than those in middle and high-income groups, low-income people approve of the way in which the current legislative system performs. They also compare it with what they had before in the most favorable terms. Differences in education seem unrelated to variations in approval of the current system, although the college-educated are much less approving of institutional performance than the less educated.

Among residents of three regions, Cholla residents stand out again. In other regions, majorities are not satisfied with every aspect of legislative politics. In Cholla, however, respondents reveal the strongest levels of approval. A little more than one-half (52%) think that their district legislators are doing not only well but also better than those of the previous authoritarian Assembly. Nearly two-thirds (63%), moreover, judge the current National Assembly to be an improvement over what they had before. It is expected that residents of Cholla believe to a greater extent that they have benefited most from the democratization of legislative politics, given their treatment under the previous military and quasi-military governments.

Political psychology and behavior did not follow exactly the pattern observed in legislative support. Regardless of ideological propensities, political efficacy, and political involvement, a majority of the Korean people are not satisfied with the current legislative system. Among the various categories of these variables, moreover, none is consistently associated with the highest level of performance approval.

In summary, the current model of representative democracy does not function effectively enough to satisfy a majority of the Korean population. However, all respondents did find something to praise in the new system. Unlike the former regime, democratic representation has been quite effective in rescuing victims of the past military dictatorship. While women and Cholla residents are cheering on legislative reforms, the socioeconomically advantaged are expressing concern.

Sources of Support for Legislative Democracy

Why do some Koreans fully and strongly support the democratization of legislative politics while others do not? Prior research on new democracies in Europe suggests three alternative explanations for support for popular representation in the legislative process among the Korean public (Hibbing & Patterson 1994; Mishler & Rose 1994; Rose & Mishler 1996). The first of these models emphasizes general commitment to democracy and democratization as principal influences on legislative support. The second model, on the other hand, focuses on the effective performance of the National Assembly and its representatives. The third model holds that the economy is of foremost public concern in new democracies and that its good performance disposes people toward legislative and other democratic reforms.

For each of these models, we chose a set of four predictors. Specifically, general levels of democratic commitment were measured in terms of preference for democracy over authoritarianism as a political ideal, desire for further democratization, commitment to the norm of mass participation, and commitment to the norm of political competition.[9] The effectiveness of legislative performance, as discussed above, was also measured according to four variables including the perceptions of institutional and personal legislative performances and changes in those performances, which are attributable to democratic transition. Similarly, the effectiveness of economic performance was measured according to the four variables of retrospective and prospective assessments of personal and national economic conditions (see Appendix B R1–R4).

Which one of these three models is more capable of explaining Korean support for legislative representation, which was measured on the 10-point index introduced in Figure 5.3? Table 5.3 addresses this

Table 5.3 Multiple Regression Analysis of Support for Legislative Democratization: OLS Regressions (standardized regression coefficients)

	Equations						
	1	2	3	4	5	6	7
Democratic Commitment							
Preference for democracy	0.09*			0.08*	0.07*		0.07*
Support for democratic expansion	0.24*			0.21*	0.23*		0.21*
Support for mass participation	0.07*			0.08*	0.07*		0.08*
Tolerance for competition	0.14*			0.16*	0.14*		0.16*
Legislative Approval							
Current institutional performance		0.01		0.00		0.02	0.00
Current personal performance		0.02		0.02		0.02	0.00
Change in institutional performance		0.11		0.11*		0.14	0.10*
Change in personal performance		0.04		0.02		0.03	0.01
Economic Consequences							
National economic progress			0.05		0.02	0.04	0.03
Personal economic progress			0.08*		0.06	0.07*	0.08*
National economic optimism			0.10*		0.07*	0.07*	0.04
Personal economic optimism			0.02		0.01	0.02	0.02
Variance explained (R^2)	0.10	0.03	0.03	0.13	0.12	0.05	0.14
Squared part correlation coefficient	0.09	0.02	0.01	0.11	0.11	0.03	—

*Statistically significant at the 0.05 level

Source: 1996 Korean Democratization Survey

question by estimating and comparing their relative explanatory powers. The relative potency of each model is estimated by the means of the squared part correlation coefficient, which measures the difference between the values of two coefficients of multiple determination (R^2) (for further details, see Bohrnstedt & Knoke 1982: chap. 11).

Table 5.3 shows that all four variables of democratic commitment alone account for 10 percent of the total variance in legislative support. The four variables of legislative performance and the four measures of economic performance explain 3 percent and 3 percent, respectively. All three sets of democratic, legislative, and economic variables together explain only 14 percent of the total variance. Two inferences can be made from these findings. First, Korean legislative support cannot adequately be explained solely in terms of these sets of independent variables. Second, the set of four democratic variables is far more potent than the other two sets.

A comparison of the sixth and seventh R^2s in the last row of Table 5.3 reveals that the squared part correlation between democratic commitment and legislative support is 0.09. This means that the four variables of democratic commitment add an increment of about 9 percent to the variance explained by the other two sets of legislative and economic variables. In sharp contrast, the legislative performance cluster raises the potency of explanation by 2 percent and the economic performance cluster also does by 1 percent. A comparison of the 3-part correlation coefficients indicates clearly that Koreans are motivated to support legislative democratization over six times more by their general orientations toward democratic politics than by their positive evaluations of either legislative or economic performances.

A comparison of the *betas* listed in the last column of Table 5.3 allows us to estimate the relative importance of each of the twelve predictors in the final equation. What are the individual factors that dispose Koreans most powerfully toward representative democracy? According to the *betas* in Table 5.3, there are two political variables: desire for the further expansion of incomplete democracy (0.21) and tolerance for political competition among political rivals without which any political system degenerates into an autocracy (0.16). The more the Korean people are willing to support democratic expansion and the more they are willing to tolerate a variety of political ideas, the more they are likely to support the advancement of legislative democracy.

Other significant influences on support for legislative democratization include approval of institutional legislative performance change (0.10), support for mass participation in politics (0.08), approval of personal economic change (0.08), and preference for democracy (0.07). This list of predictors makes it clear that while all four democratic variables are significant influences on legislative democratic reform, most of the legislative and economic variables fail to contribute to or detract from it to a degree that is statistically significant. Among the people in Korea, where growing economic prosperity fueled their initial demand for democratic regime change, the sagging economy is not a deterrent to support for legislative democratization. Nor does the dismal performance of their national legislature and representatives discourage citizens from supporting it.

Cross-National Comparisons
Legislative Support

How do Koreans compare with citizens of other new democracies in supporting the democratization of legislative politics? Levels of legislative support are compared in terms of the extent to which they disapprove of the abolition and suspension of their national legislatures. Types of such support, on the other hand, are compared in terms of percentages of citizens who prefer divided government over a strong leader and disapprove of suspension of national legislature. For these comparisons, we used New Democracies Barometer IV directed by Richard Rose and Christian Haerpfer in 1996.

In Table 5.4, we see that Korea compares quite favorably with the new Eastern and Central European democracies in supporting legislative democratization. Of the eleven countries listed in the table, Korea (with an 85% rating) ranks third behind the citizens of Croatia (94%) and the Czech Republic (86%) in rejecting strong leadership in favor of a democratic government divided between the executive and legislative branches. Korean respondents are broadly united in opposing suspension of the national legislature; with an 85 percent rating, again, the country ranks second – slightly behind Romania (87%). When these two dimensions of legislative democratic orientations are considered together, Korea stands out as one of only two new democracies in which more than three-quarters of the mass public choose representative democracy over delegative democracy or authoritarian rule.

Legislative Approval

To date, cross-national surveys of new democracies have been overly concerned with the survival of their legislatures. As a result, surveys have not asked their respondents to directly evaluate the performance of the legislative institutions or individual legislators as our survey did. Instead, the other surveys often asked the respondents how much they can trust what their legislatures do. Such a measure of public trust in the

Table 5.4 Cross-National Differences in Legislative Support

	Korea	Belarus	Bulgaria	Croatia	Czech R.	Hungary	Poland	Romania	Slovakia	Slovenia	Ukraine
1. Best to get rid of Parliament											
Strongly agree	3	27	8	2	4	8	10	14	5	11	37
Somewhat agree	12	29	15	3	10	13	23	15	14	18	30
Somewhat disagree	34	16	31	11	26	23	34	17	27	18	14
Strongly disagree	51	27	46	83	60	56	33	56	54	52	19
2. If Parliament was Suspended											
Definitely approve	4	9	6	3	6	4	5	4	2	4	21
Somewhat approve	10	31	21	15	16	22	27	8	14	16	40
Somewhat oppose	23	37	38	29	39	37	50	23	47	50	23
Strongly oppose	62	23	35	53	39	38	17	64	36	30	16
3. Typology of Support											
Representative democrats	76	36	65	79	75	65	51	66	69	69	22
Delegative democrats	9	24	12	3	8	10	17	21	9	12	17
Soft Authoritarians	9	8	12	15	11	14	16	5	12	7	12
Hard Authoritarians	6	32	10	3	6	11	16	8	9	12	49

Sources: 1996 Korean Democratization Survey; Rose & Haerpfer (1996)

Figure 5.9 Cross-National Differences in Trust in Legislatures

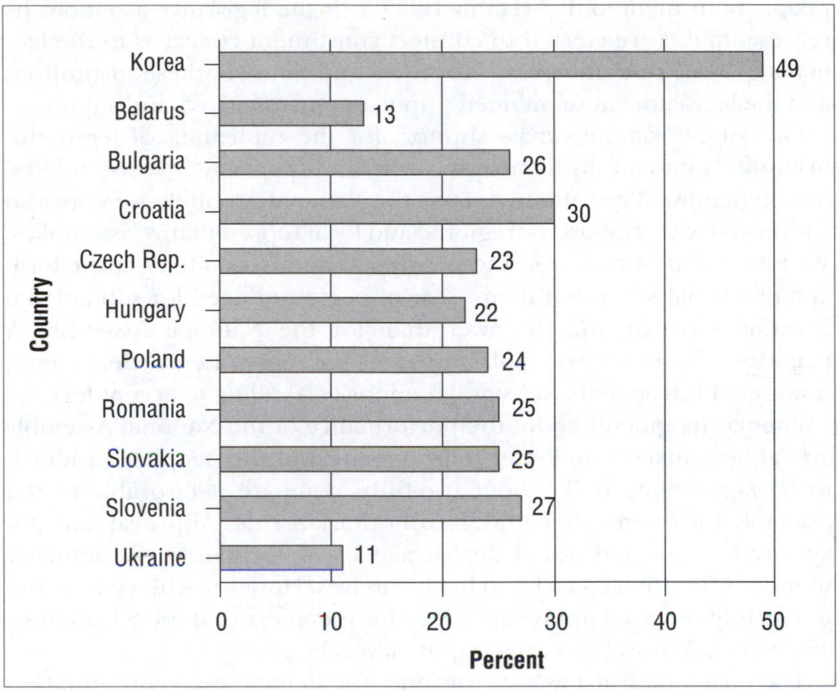

Sources: 1996 Korean Democratization Survey; Rose & Haerpfer (1996)

legislature is chosen for our cross-national comparison as an indicator of legislative performance approval. Figure 5.9 lists legislative trust ratings for Korea and the ten European new democracies covered in *New Democracies Barometer IV.*

Do Koreans approve of their legislature more than their European counterparts do? According to Figure 5.9, the answer is an unqualified "Yes." More Koreans than any European citizenry approve of the national legislature. They do so as much as four times and over. From 11 percent to 30 percent of European mass publics judged their legislatures to be trustworthy. Among the Korean people, however, nearly one-half (49%) trust the National Assembly. Relatively high levels of support and approval of representative democracy are a notable feature of Korean democratization.

Summary and Conclusions

Around the world, representative democracy is energizing societies previously governed by authoritarian regimes. The institution that "serves as the principal link between what government does and what people want them to do" (Hahn 1996: 5) is the legislative assembly. Its representatives are elected to connect constituent concerns to the law-making arena. If democracy is to thrive and flourish, these institutions and the legislators in them need popular approval, trust, and support.

Our study examines mass support for the reforming of legislative institutions into a fully democratic system of representative assemblies. Although most of our attention is on the National Assembly, we were also concerned with support for regional and local representative assemblies. We found that Koreans tend to be supportive of assemblies at the local and provincial levels, but their sense of perceived need for subnational assemblies is substantially lower than for the National Assembly. A majority of Koreans favor a full-scale model of representative democracy; however, it is true that a substantial minority is willing to accept less.

Popular judgments about the performance of the National Assembly are, at best, lukewarm. Fewer than one-third of the people consider it to be performing well. About two-fifths compare it favorably to the assembly they remember under authoritarian rule. Approval and dis-approval of the individual performances of legislators are similarly unimpressive when considered by themselves. However, when compared to recently reported approval ratings for members of the US Congress, 45 percent approval in Korea is quite favorable.

The sociopolitical bases of support for democratic representation were not quite what we expected. We anticipated and found that support was stronger among the young rather than the old, among those with left-wing rather than right-wing ideology, among those with a high sense of personal efficacy, and those whose civic participation was high. We also expected and found the highest support from those in the Cholla region, which suffered most during authoritarian rule. We were sur-prised to find women more supportive than men, the least educated more supportive than those with college educations, and more support from those with low incomes rather than high incomes. Apparently, the people most disadvantaged under the old regime – women, the under-educated and those with low incomes – find more to support under representative democracy than their counterparts.

To account for variations in positive support for legislative democ-ratization, we considered three alternative explanations: (1) a general-ized commitment to democratic principles, (2) the degree of approval people express regarding contemporary legislative performance, and (3) perceptions of economic well-being. The findings of our regression analysis were disappointing in that they only explain 14 percent of the total variance we measured in support of legislative democracy. Clearly, most of the variance we seek to explain goes unaccounted for by the independent variables we brought to bear by our inquiry. Despite that disappointment, however, it is important to note what predictors have, or fail to have, explanatory power. Support for representative democratization is unexplained by perceptions of economic well-being. Korean society has been powerfully transformed by an economic bonanza, which has increased productivity by the people and has raised their standard of living. Despite that broad ranging change, the assessments that the people have regarding economic well-being are mostly unrelated to support for legislative democratization.

By contrast, almost all the explanatory power that we have uncovered is, in general, oriented toward democratic politics. The key ideas are desire for further democratization and tolerance for political competition. The only attitude specific to legislatures that is of consequence is approval of legislative performance change in the wake of democratic regime change.

Our results, modest as they are, confirm Mishler & Rose (1994: 25) in that democratic commitment precedes and shapes support for the legislature. Institutions of democracy require the sustenance of democratic commitment by the people. But we note that improvements in legislative performance do evoke support for the democratic reform of the legislature. Thus, the prospect exists that continuing performance of legislative tasks in the National Assembly, as well as in regional and local assemblies, can produce growing support for democratization.

When assessed with the New Democracies Barometer, which has been used successfully to measure legislative support in Eastern European countries (Rose & Haerpfer 1996), the Korean results reveal an impressive level of commitment to legislative democratization. More Koreans chose representative democracy over delegative democracy or authoritarian rule than did citizens in nine out of ten emerging European democracies. Koreans show stronger trust in their legislators than do any of the European publics. Approval of the national legislature is substantially higher in Korea than in comparison states. When examined comparatively, support for representative democracy is more robust.

CHAPTER 6

Political Parties

"Democratic government is unlikely and may not be possible
in the absence of political parties."

William C. Crotty (1993: 664)

"Unless stable parties can be formed, competitive
democratic politics is not likely to last in many of the new
Eastern European and Central Asian polities."

Seymour Martin Lipset (1994: 15)

Of the various institutions in new democracies, political parties occupy a central place in consolidating democratic gains (Rueschemeyer, Stephens & Stephens 1992: 168). Unlike other democratic institutions, parties can be effective in preventing a reversal to authoritarian rule. "In the absence of free competing parties," Rustow (1994: 55) observes, "the organizational vacuum of newly proclaimed democracies might be filled by military coups, as it was in much of the Third World in the 1960s and 1970s, or by populist or quasi-fascist movements, as it might be in some of the post-communist states of Central and Eastern Europe."

Besides removing authoritarian challenges to nascent democracies, strong and competitive political parties can make a significant contribution to the expansion of limited democracy. Unlike interest groups and other voluntary political associations, parties are usually both territorially based and electorally oriented organizations, which always seek to manage and win competitive elections (Schmitter 1992: 444). Parties can expand channels of political participation to the widest spectrum of the mass public by offering alternative policies and appealing to heterogeneous segments of the electorate.

Moreover, by aggregating the conflicting interests of the masses and assuring the accountability of political leaders, parties with a broad popular base throughout the nation can directly promote the legitimacy of nascent democracy. Such parties, as compared with interest groups and other narrowly based professional associations, are more capable of mobilizing and representing the public in the policy-making process. This is the reason why Pasquino (1990: 52) argues that "democratic consolidation is a party-dominated process while this is not so always with democratic transition." This is also why Pridham (1990a: 7) and Lipset

(1994: 15) regard the political party as a crucial agent of democratic consolidation.

Although they are indispensable as agents of democratic consolidation, political parties have received relatively less attention from the scholarly community and government circles than other democratic institutions and procedures such as governmental structure and electoral formulae. There is little doubt that the choices between presidential and parliamentary governments, as well as between the plurality and proportional representation systems of election, affect the survival of new democracies, especially in culturally or ethnically divided societies.[1] These democracies, however, will not be able to consolidate without the development of truly competitive and mass-based political parties. Such parties alone are capable of facilitating peaceful and stable alternation in political power between competing forces. As Huntington (1991: 266–7) and Lawson (1993: 194) maintain, there is no possibility of genuine democracy and democratic consolidation as long as there is no alternation in power between competing parties.

To date, relatively little research has been conducted in approaching democratic consolidation from the perspective of building competitive and strong parties with a nationwide popular base. As Levine (1990: 379) discusses in his review of the general literature on democratization, political parties are notable mostly by their absence. In the many works dealing with political parties in new democracies, on the other hand, the observation is often made that parties are notable mostly either in their operation and structure or in their ties to the mass electorate (Huang 1997; Kitschelt 1995; Mainwaring & Scully 1995a; Miller & Erb 1996; Morlino 1995b; Pridham 1990b; Rueschemeyer, Stephens & Stephens 1992; Toka 1997; Weil, Huffman & Gautier 1993).

In short, empirical research on political parties in newly democratizing countries has been too limited to offer a comprehensive and balanced account of party politics unfolding during the course of democratic consolidation (Olson 1993). Substantively, the research has focused mainly on the structural and performance characteristics of individual parties. The remaining research has concentrated merely on the amounts and sources of support that parties receive from the mass public. Consequently, this kind of research has not been able to systematically determine how the structure and performance of political parties and their public support are related to each other.

As Bermeo (1990) and Crotty (1993) urge, we should bring political parties back into the study of democratic consolidation in order to give a fuller account of the complexities and uncertainties involved in its process. We should also employ different approaches to measuring and monitoring party integration in the standard practices of representative democracy. This chapter, then, seeks to propose and test an approach that deals with both the performance and support dimensions in which political parties figure as the most important mediating organizations between the citizenry and the democratic state.

The chapter begins with a brief review of the theoretical literature concerning the development of partisan support. The notion of democratic consolidation and its key variables are then outlined from the perspective of building competitive and strong parties with a nationwide popular base. The 1993 and 1996 surveys are analyzed to examine the level of popular support for Korean parties and its relationship with assessments of their performance. Next, the results of this analysis are discussed from comparative and historical perspectives. Finally, the chapter concludes with the implications of the findings that point to the difficulty and uncertainty of consolidating Korean democracy.

Theoretical Considerations

In recent years there have been increases in major survey research efforts to monitor the growth of partisanship among mass publics in new democracies (Barnes, McDonough & Pina 1985; McDonough, Shin & Moises 1998; Miller & Erb 1996; Moises 1993; Reisinger & Nitkin 1993; Tedin 1994). The most puzzling elements of their respective findings are: (1) that a majority of the mass publics of new democracies remain unattached to any of a number of political parties, and (2) the acquisition of stable partisan loyalties has been very slow and erratic in spite of what has been expected from recent theories of associative or participatory democracy.

Why do so many ordinary citizens of new democracies refuse to identify themselves with this standard institutional vehicle of representative democracy? And why is it that these citizens remain unidentified with parties while they are strongly attached to political ideologies and personalities? Also, what factors inhibit the growth of their identification with parties, which play a crucial role in undergirding stable democracy? Four different theoretical models have recently been introduced to explore these questions.

The first model focuses on the length of personal experience with democratic politics. According to Converse (1969), stable partisanship is a function of the passage of democratic time, which features personal involvement in elections and party politics – two procedural minima of representative democracy. Based on the political experiences of old democracies in which competitive elections and parties emerged slowly over a long period of time, this socialization model holds that stable partisanship is not an intra-generational phenomenon. It is, instead, an inter-generational affair, which can only be completed over a long period of more than two generations.

A second model emphasizes the role of the mass media, especially the electronic media, in exposing average citizens to the political process (Butler & Ranney 1992; Kellner 1991; Lawson & Merkl 1988; Ward 1993). In this age of mass communications, parties must compete with television and other media of mass persuasion as informational sources for voters and also as agents of change, which shape their political preferences and promote their participation in politics. According to this model, the more attentive people are to the mass media, the less they are likely to be identified with and involved in political parties.

In contrast to the media model, a third model emphasizes the increasingly important role that interest groups and professional associations play as intermediaries between citizens and the state (Cohen & Rogers 1992; Hirst 1994; Putnam 1993). According to Schmitter (1992: 426), today's citizens have "a much more variegated set of interests" and "quite different organizational skills." On an increasing basis, therefore, they do not rely on political parties to defend and represent those interests to the state. Instead, citizens are turning to alternative channels of representation where interest groups and professional associations are key players. According to this neo-corporatist model, the more involved people are in associational life, the less likely they are to be attached to political parties and involved in partisan politics.

Finally, a fourth model concentrates on the democratic performance of political parties. For individual citizens to be attracted to parties, each of those parties should distinguish itself from others by offering clear policy alternatives on a continuing basis (Barnes, McDonough & Pina 1985: 715). The inaction or inability of parties to effectively perform this and other important tasks of representative democracy would discourage citizens from identifying with them. According to this model of democratic performance, the more positively people evaluate the performance of political parties, the more closely they are attached to those parties.

As such, these are the four competing models of popular attachment and involvement in political parties. Of these four, three – media, neo-corporatist, and performance – are tested in this analysis with a cross-sectional survey conducted in 1993. However, the political socialization model cannot be tested in this study because it requires longitudinal surveys.

Conceptualization

The democratic consolidation of political parties is conceptualized in this study as a dynamic process of interactions between parties and the people who need to be represented in the policy-making process. Specifically, it consists of two conceptually distinct dimensions: (1) improvements in the parties' capacity to represent the people, and (2) increases in the people's support for parties as representative institutions. Underlying this conceptualization are two simple premises. First, individual parties in a democracy can continue to exist and function only if they have a stable popular base upon which to rely. Second, democratic parties can establish such a base only if they are perceived to serve the people on a continuing basis.

Political parties in democratic regimes need a permanent base of popular support throughout the nation in order to survive their electoral defeats or policy failures (Lipset 1994: 14). Without a loyal support base, parties can be wiped out easily, thus eliminating effective opposition, or "the *sine qua non* of contemporary democracy" (Lawson 1993: 192). The absence of such a support base has recently led to the decline, and even demise, of several ruling as well as opposition parties in many newly democratizing countries, including the Civic Union in East Germany, the People's Party in Korea, and the Union of Democratic Center in Spain. As shown during recent parliamentary elections in Eastern European democracies, the absence of a stable support base has also reduced the ability of other remaining democratic parties to represent the interests of a democratic minority among the population.

In sharp contrast to those ill-fated new democratic parties, several ex-communist parties, with a solid support base in Eastern and Central Europe, have either survived the collapse of communism or regained their strength in post-authoritarian parliaments. For example, the Democratic Left Alliance in Poland, the Democratic Labor Party in Lithuania, and the Socialist Party in Hungary are now back in power by regrouping ex-communists (Knight & Pope 1994; Perlez 1994). As such, the survival of political parties depends largely upon the extent to which they are supported by broad segments of the mass public. Therefore, "having at least two parties with an uncritically loyal mass base comes close to being a necessary condition for a stable democracy" (Lipset 1994: 14).

In the United States and other old democracies, psychological identification with an individual party has long been equated with support for political parties. Unfortunately, this research practice, though overly simplistic, has been uncritically accepted in the study of political parties in new democracies (Barnes, McDonough & Pina 1985; McDonough, Shin & Moises 1988). Such a unidimensional model of party support is not, however, suitable for an accurate and meaningful understanding of what has been taking place between the masses and political parties in many countries during the current wave of democratization.

The existing model of mass support for parties is asserted on two critical assumptions about the democratic political sophistication of the mass citizenry – neither of which can be met in new democracies. The first one is that the masses, as a whole, are in favor of a democratic party system that consists of two or more competitive political parties. The second is the assumption that citizens are adequately informed about the changing configurations of their democratic party system. Only when they are able to choose between parties that are committed to the rules of democratic politics can their new democracies consolidate (Reisinger et al. 1994: 217).

Contrary to these assumptions, democratic political parties are not supported by a majority or a plurality of the masses in some new democracies; this was revealed in recent parliamentary elections held in Bulgaria, Hungary, Lithuania, Poland, Romania, and Russia. Instead, citizens remain supportive of anti-democratic system parties which are based on the principles of authoritarian or totalitarian politics. Unquestionably, a recent surge in popular attachment to these anti-system parties cannot be accepted as a valid indicator of democratic consolidation. A crucial distinction should, therefore, be made between democratic and anti-democratic types of partisanship because "anti-system parties have consequences for the outcome of democratic consolidation and the rate at which it is achieved" (Pridham 1990a: 33).

In new democracies, moreover, political parties are not consolidating as they did in old democracies. Instead of being clustered and stable, they are highly fragmented and extremely volatile. Consequently, many political parties tend to come and go between elections. In a short span of time, many existing parties disappear while an equal number of new ones emerge. In some countries, for example, Poland, Hungary, and Russia, several dozen political parties took part in the latest parliamentary elections. On the other hand, in the new democracy of Korea, the leaders of three conservative parties suddenly and secretively agreed to merge while keeping their party loyalists in complete darkness. In such situations of extreme fragmentation, instability, and secrecy, the masses cannot be assumed to be adequately informed about the rapidly changing configurations of their party system. For these reasons, meaningful research on party support in new democracies should deal with more than levels of psychological attachment to parties among the mass electorate. It should examine also the more fundamental questions of how greatly the masses are in favor of a democratic party system and how well informed they are about it.

Support for the democratic party system is conceptualized in this study as a multifaceted phenomenon consisting of four distinct dimensions. First, it is a political evaluation that a party system with two or more competitive parties is better than one with a single party or non-competitive parties. Second, as an evaluative orientation, support is based on varying levels of factual information about the party system in operation. Third, it involves varying levels of affect for constituent members of the system. Finally, it includes physical involvement in the various activities of those parties.

As conceptualized here, party system support refers to a dynamic phenomenon with four qualitatively distinct properties: (1) evaluation, (2) cognition, (3) affect, and (4) behavior. As each constituent property shifts in both quantity and quality in the process of democratization, its entire dynamics cannot be adequately understood solely in terms of the changes taking place in one or two properties (such as partisan attachment and involvement). An accurate picture of popular support for the democratic party system can be depicted only when changes in all four dimensions are taken into account.

What should democratic political parties do in order to secure a loyal mass base? The key to this policy-oriented question lies in the quality of their performance. Parties in representative democracies are fundamentally different from those of non-democratic regimes in their *raison d'être*. They do not operate according to the totalitarian principles that the people have a unitary interest and that there is only one correct solution to organizing their interests. Instead, democratic parties operate according to the principles of pluralism and social interaction (Lindblom 1977: chap. 19). Therefore, to secure a support base throughout the nation, democratic parties have to do much more than mobilizing personal support for their leadership and policies.

Specifically, political parties in new democracies should be capable of encouraging citizens to formulate and express their preferences by individual and collective political action. In addition, democratic parties should be capable of representing citizens' preferences in the policy-making process rather than the personal interests of the leadership. Most importantly, the parties should be able to offer alternative governments to the electorate by developing policy alternatives and criticizing each other. Only when two or more parties in each new democracy perform all these tasks effectively can its party system become consolidated democratically. Otherwise, it will drift either as a hybrid regime that combines elements of autocracy and democracy or as an unconsolidated democracy such as *dictablandas* or *democraduras*.[2]

In appraising the democratic development of partisan politics in Korea, this chapter focuses on the link between popular support for political parties and perceptions of their performance as a representative institution. By considering both dimensions of democratic party politics, it seeks to generate more reliable information concerning the difficulty and uncertainty of democratic consolidation than has been done in prior research on political parties.

Support for a Democratic Party System
Preference

What type of political party system do average citizens in Korea favor for the further development of their new political system? Are they in favor of a multi-party system premised on the principle of free and open competition? The 1993 survey asked these questions (see Appendix B P1.1 and P1.2). As expected, an overwhelming majority (95%) of respondents to the 1993 survey were in agreement that parties are necessary for democratic development. A large majority (89%) also chose a multi-party system by disagreeing with the statement that Korea would be much better-off with only one party.

Nonetheless, many of these supporters of a multi-party system were unwilling to endorse the principle of free competition among parties for

Figure 6.1 Preferred System of Political Parties

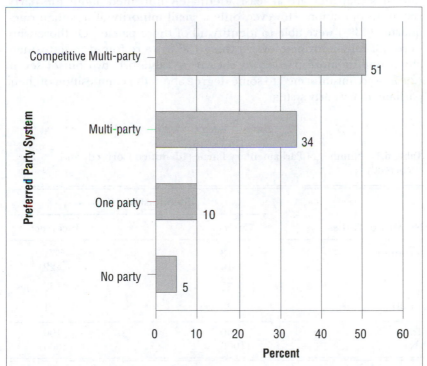

Source: 1993 Korean Democratization Survey

democratic development. When asked whether or not any political organization or group in opposition of democratization should be out-lawed (Appendix B P2), less than three-fifths (60%) endorsed this principle by expressing their disagreement with the statement. Although nearly nine out of ten Koreans (89%) are in favor of a multi-party system, only one out of two (51%) are in favor of a truly competitive, multi-party system. This finding makes it clear that the notion of a competitive, adversarial party system has yet to be accepted among broad segments of the Korean population.

Knowledge

How well are average citizens informed about their party affairs? Table 6.1 and Figure 6.2 report data relevant to this question (for the wording of this question, see Appendix B P3). Of the four parties represented in the National Assembly, nearly nine out of ten respondents (87%) were able to correctly name at least one or more parties, and over one-half (54%) were able to identify most or all of the parties surveyed. This indicates that they are at least adequately informed about the party system in operation. However, only a small minority of less than one-quarter (23%) were able to identify all of those parties. Of those who were not fully informed, over a third (36%) were found misinformed about one or more parties. As shown in Table 6.1, two out of seven (29%) were misinformed to some degree about the composition of their parliamentary party system.

Table 6.1   Number of Parliamentary Parties Identified Correctly and Incorrectly

	Identification (%)	
Number of Parties	Correct	Incorrect
0 (none)	13	71
1	10	22
2	23	5
3	31	1
4 (all)	23	1
Total	100	100
(N)	(1000)	(1000)

Source: 1993 Korean Democratization Survey

Figure 6.2 Patterns of Being Informed about the Parliamentary Party System

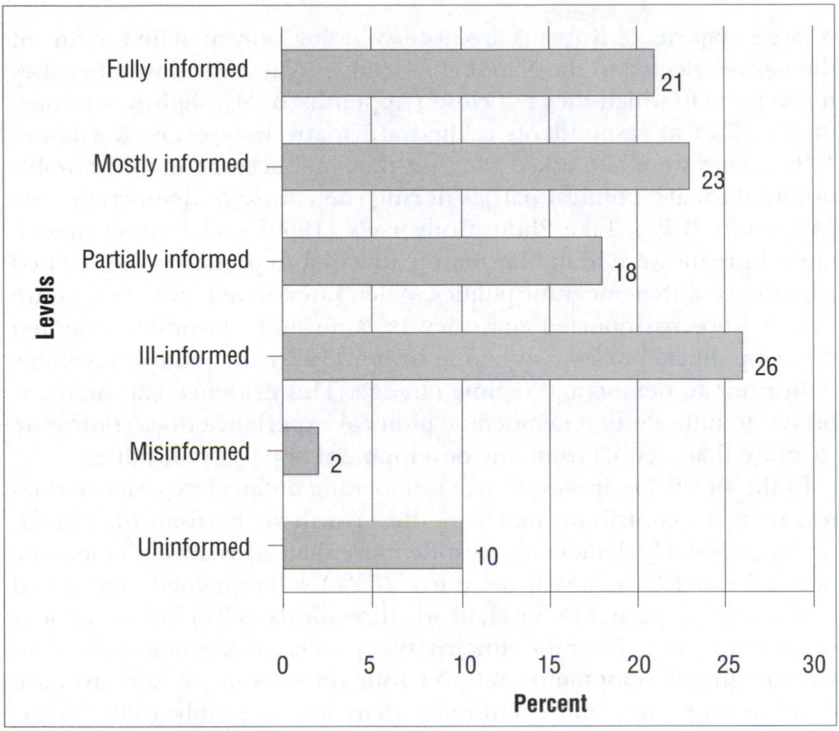

Source: 1993 Korean Democratization Survey

When correct and incorrect answers to the question were considered together, one-tenth (10%) of the Koreans were uninformed as they were unable to identify any party either correctly or incorrectly. About one in fifty (2%) Koreans who are designated as "misinformed" were able to identify some or all of those parties incorrectly only. About a quarter (26%) were "ill-informed" by virtue of identifying political parties both correctly and incorrectly. Of the over three-fifths (62%) who were correctly informed, 21 percent were "fully informed" as they were able to identify all four parties correctly; 23 percent were "mostly informed" by being able to identify three of the four parties; and 18 percent designated as "partially informed" were able to identify one or two of them only. On the whole, the Korean people tend to believe in the principle of a competitive multi-party system for democratic development. In practice, however, they are not well informed about political parties in action.

Affect

A large majority of Koreans are not psychologically attached to any of the parties elected to the National Assembly. When asked whether they had a party to which they felt close (Appendix B P4), slightly over one-third (37%) of respondents replied affirmatively (see Lee & Glasure 1995). They were also asked whether they had become more favorably oriented toward political parties during the course of democratic rule (Appendix B P5). Like Philip Converse's (1969) socialization model, more Koreans were found becoming attached to parties as they gained experience with democratic politics. When interviewed, two of every five (43%) Koreans reported that they became more favorably oriented toward political parties, while one in ten (10%) turned less favorably than prior to democratic regime change. This evidence can be interpreted to indicate that democratic political experience does contribute to, more than detract from, the development of partisan loyalties.

In the short run, however, such democratic political experience does not seem to contribute much to the growth of partisanship, which undergirds stable democracy. Despite more than six years of democratic political experience, nearly two-thirds (63%) still remained unattached to any political party. Moreover, nearly three-fifths (57%) failed to orient themselves more favorably toward the parties. Nonetheless, it is an encouraging development that over four times as many Koreans have become reoriented more favorably than less favorably (43% versus 10%). Even among those who were not emotionally attached to any party, those who had experienced favorable reorientations are shown in Table 6.2 to lead those who had experienced less favorable changes by a margin of 33 to 12 percent.

Table 6.2   Types of Orientations Toward Political Parties (percent)

Shifts in Orientation	Attachment to Party		Totals
	No	Yes	
More favorable	33	59	43
No change	55	33	47
Less favorable	12	8	10
Row total	63	37	100
Column total	100	100	
(N)	(697)	(413)	(1100)

Source: 1993 Korean Democratization Survey

Involvement

How actively are the Korean people involved in party politics? The 1993 survey asked two separate questions each of which deals with a different aspect of partisan behavior (see Appendix B P6 and P7). As expected from the low level of their partisanship, they were found mostly unwilling to get involved. A small minority (18%) reported that they had worked for a party in some capacity. Only one in twenty (5%) said that they were formal members of a political party at the time of the survey. When these two activities were considered together, less than a fifth (19%) were involved in party politics as a member or non-member of a political party.

Figure 6.3 compares the levels of popular support for a democratic party system across the dimensions of preference, knowledge, affect, and involvement. The support levels for these four dimensions are estimated in terms of the percentages of Koreans in the 1993 survey sample who:

Figure 6.3 Comparing Popular Support for the Democratic Party System Across Four Dimensions

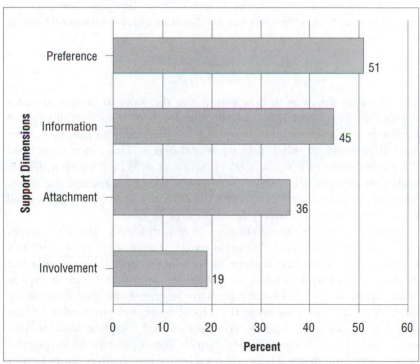

Source: 1993 Korean Democratization Survey

(1) were in favor of a competitive multi-party system, (2) were accurately informed about most or all of four parliamentary parties, (3) identified themselves with one of those parties, and (4) worked for a party as a member or in some other capacity.

Of the four dimensions, the preference dimension registered the highest level of support with 51 percent. This is followed by those of knowledge (45%), psychological attachment (36%), and behavioral involvement (19%) in that order. It is not surprising that only a small minority of the Korean public identify with and are involved with political parties. In old democracies as well, the affective and behavioral dimensions of democratic party politics are known to grow slowly over generations. What is surprising is that a political party's cognitive and evaluative dimensions have grown at a relatively slow pace. Even with two rounds of quadrennial parliamentary and quinquennial presidential elections for five years (1988–93), nearly half the Korean electorate remained unwilling to endorse the principle of a truly competitive multi-party system, even though nearly all of them desired to live in a democratic political system. In addition, a majority were yet to be adequately informed about the parties that are competing for their votes before they chose one party over the others. These findings attest to the difficulties and uncertainties involved in the consolidation of Korean democracy.

Overall Support

The question arises as to how supportive the Korean people are of a democratic party system as a whole. The levels of their overall support for the system are estimated by an index tallying up the number of the four dimensions in which they were supporters. This index runs from the lowest score of 0 to the highest score of 4. When a respondent is found non-supportive in every one of the four dimensions, the index takes on the lowest score of 0. When the person is found supportive in all those dimensions, it takes on the highest value of 4.

Figure 6.4 reports the distribution of respondents in the 1993 survey across five levels of overall democratic party system support as measured by the index. A notable feature of the data in this figure is that the distribution of respondents is skewed to the low end of the index. Specifically, a plurality (36%) were supportive in one of the four dimensions only, while a substantial minority (16%) were not supportive in any dimension. These two figures, when considered together, make it clear that a majority (52%) were either entirely non-supportive or supportive in only one dimension. This combined figure is over three times higher than the 15 percent for those who were supportive in most or all of the

Figure 6.4 Levels of Overall Support for the Democratic Party System

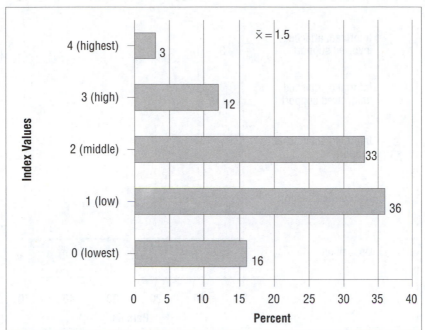

Source: 1993 Korean Democratization Survey

four dimensions. On average, the Korean electorate was found to be supportive of a democratic party system in fewer than half of its four dimensions. To be precise, the average Korean voter scored 1.5 on the index, indicating that in Korea popular support for democratic party politics remains largely under-developed.

In Figure 6.5, we further analyze democratic party support among the Korean people in terms of its qualitative differences. Such differences are ascertained in terms of five distinctive types. These types are determined by considering each respondent's scores on four support dimensions in sequence, beginning with the preference dimension through those of information and affect to involvement in party affairs. Underlying this sequential analysis are two premises. The first is that the preference dimension constitutes the most essential component of democratic party support. The second is that average citizens tend to develop their democratic party support cognitively and affectively before they do it behaviorally.

Of the five types listed in Figure 6.5, the first one is that of *opposition* toward the democratic party system featuring free competition among multiple parties; nearly half (49%) are opponents of the system. The

Figure 6.5   Five Types of Affinity Toward the Democratic Party System

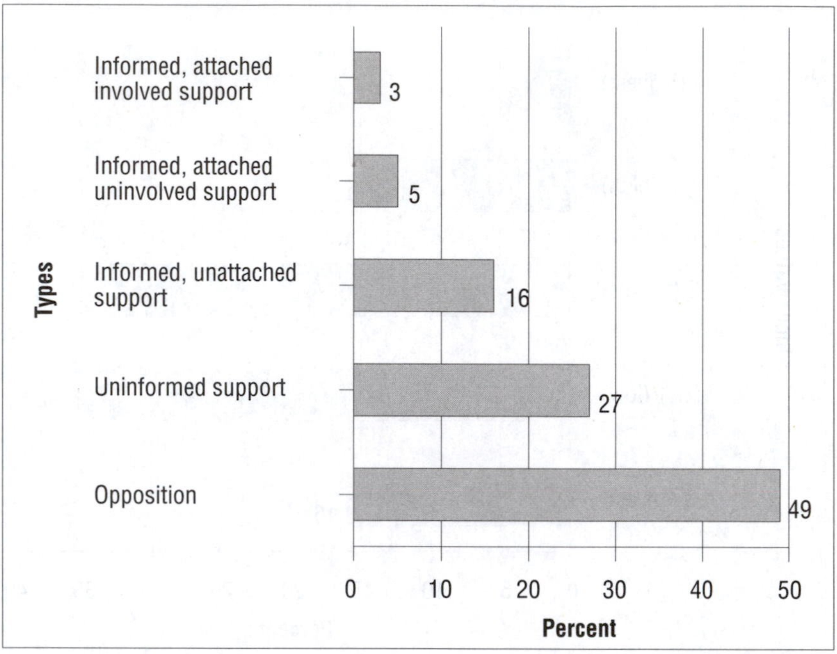

Source: 1993 Korean Democratization Survey

second type involves *uninformed support* in which slightly over one-quarter (27%) are supportive of such a system – although not adequately informed about the political parties competing. The third type is *informed unattached*; one-sixth (16%) consist of supporters of the democratic party system who are not closely attached to any political party despite being well informed about them. The fourth type is *informed, attached, uninvolved support*; one-twentieth (5%) consist of the adequately informed partisan supporters who are not directly involved in party affairs. The fifth, and final, type is *unqualified support* in which a very small minority (3%) fall into this type of supporter; those who are not only well informed and attached to a party but also are involved in its activities.

A comparison of percentage figures across the five types reconfirms that Korean support for democratic party politics remains, by and large, not only under-developed but also undifferentiated. A substantial majority of three-quarters (76%) of the Korean electorate are either outright opponents or merely uninformed supporters of a democratic party system. In striking contrast, a small minority of less than a tenth (8%) are psychologically attached or behaviorally involved supporters.

Most notable is that a very small proportion (3%) are mature supporters who are not only well informed about democratic parties in action but also attached and involved in those parties. In short, Korea is a nation of democrats without many active supporters of a democratic party system.[3]

Party Politics in Action

Political parties in Korea have recently undergone considerable changes in their organizational structure and membership, but the parties have failed to achieve even a minimum level of institutionalization, not to mention democratization (Jaung 1998).[4] As intermediaries between the government and the electorate, Korean political parties remain as highly unstable and deeply fragmented as they did under the military dictatorships. Of the four major parties that competed in the first founding election of the Sixth Republic in 1987, not one has kept its initial name nor maintained its original organizational structure.

Roh Tae Woo's Democratic Justice Party, Kim Young Sam's Reunification Democratic Party, and Kim Jong Pil's New Democratic Republican Party, for example, jointly formed the Democratic Liberal Party through a merger in January 1990.[5] Likewise, Kim Dae Jung's Party for Peace and Democracy joined with Lee Ki Taek's party in September 1991 and formed the new Democratic Party. In March 1995, Kim Jong Pil broke with the ruling Democratic Justice Party led by President Kim Young Sam and established his own party called the United Liberal Democrats. Kim Dae Jung came out of his short retirement in September 1995 and took his faction away from the Democratic Party to form the National Congress for New Politics. Two weeks after Kim Dae Jung and Kim Jong Pil joined their parties into a presidential electoral coalition in early November 1997, the ruling New Korea Party, which was once called the Democratic Justice Party, merged with the Democratic Party and formed the Grand National Party.

Every major political party in Korea has experienced at least one merger or breakup since the democratic transition ten years ago. In Korea today, there is not a single political party or party name that has survived more than two of the country's six republics (S. Yang 1995: 23). There is no doubt that Korean political parties, whether in power or opposition, remain highly unstable and lack the requisite capacity to adapt to the changing political environment (Jaung, 1998, 11). Such a high level of institutional instability, in turn, has made it difficult for those parties to build broad bases of popular loyalty and support (Huang 1997: 152).

Even after a decade of democratic rule, Korean political parties remain firmly entrenched in amorphous and primordial regionalism;

they are all minority parties that are regionally based and focused (Ahn 1995; Kim & Suh 1997). Not one party has been willing to tear down the iron wall erected around its own regional basis of support. In all three rounds of presidential and parliamentary elections, no political party has achieved the status of a majority party by tearing down the walls erected by other parties in the Honam, Yongnam, and Choongchung provinces.

All Korean political parties are ideologically conservative "cadre" parties; they have failed to recruit active members from among the masses and offer no ideologically alternative policies or programs of policy action (B. K. Kim 1996: 7). Organizationally, they have also failed to build any network capable of aggregating and representing interest groups and other civic associations in the policy-making process. As Byung-Kook Kim (1994: 33) sums up, "the political parties usually limit themselves to the discussion on the allocation of ministerial posts and the regional distribution of investment resources."

Lacking a concrete organization and a specific program of action, the political parties continue to serve as "the mere vehicle of their leaders to obtain or retain power," as Steinberg (1996: 13) notes. For decades political leaders, such as Kim Young Sam, Kim Dae Jung, and Kim Jong Pil, have repeated the same cycle of founding, dissolving, re-establishing, and renaming their own parties at will. During this period, members of these parties had to faithfully follow the guidance and leadership of their party bosses (S. Yang 1995: 20). Like a father in a traditional Korean family who, alone, makes all the important decisions, every party boss exclusively controls the nomination of his party candidates for each and every electoral district of the National Assembly. Once the candidates are elected, the boss tells elected representatives how to vote on every major issue and censures them when they defy the guidelines. A revolt of assembly workers against their party boss has rarely occurred because their political future lies exclusively in their employers' hands. Such systems of autocratic decision-making and party management have served to inhibit the furtherance of democratic politics rather than to promote it (Huang 1997: 152; Steinberg 1996: 14; see also B. K. Kim & J. Y. Suh 1997: 20)

Assessments of Party Performance

Political parties in a democracy, unlike those in a non-democracy, must perform a variety of functions related to the formulation, expression, and representation of citizen preferences in the policy-making process. To assess the quality of their performance as democratic parties, the 1993 survey asked three questions (see Appendix B P1.3–P1.5). To the question of whether their parties had been facilitating participation of the mass public in politics, a slight majority (57%) replied affirmatively. When asked about the interests that the parties represented, a larger majority (73%) replied that they tended to serve the interests of party leaders rather than those of the mass citizenry. The largest majority (75%) reported that all political parties differed very little in terms of political ideology or in the public policies they were advocating.

These findings make it clear that Korean political parties have been a positive influence only in bringing a greater number of ordinary citizens into the political process. But beyond this rudimentary stage of mass mobilization, political parties in Korea appear to have contributed little to the further development of representative democracy. For a majority of the Korean electorate, parties still serve primarily as a political instrument of elites and do not offer any meaningful alternative to the extant government.

Figure 6.6 summarizes public evaluations of the performance of political parties from three functional areas into an overall index. This index, which offers a summary account of party performance, is constructed by tallying up the number of the three functional areas that each respondent rated as democratically performing. The summative

Figure 6.6   Overall Assessments of Political Party Performance

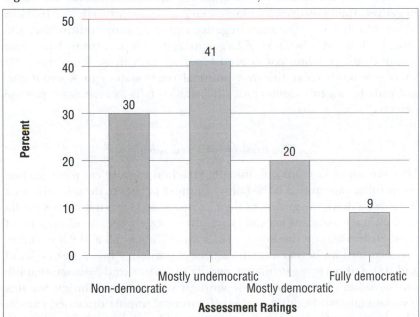

Source: 1993 Korean Democratization Survey

index takes on the lowest value of 0 when all three functional areas are rated as performing non-democratically. When all those areas are rated as performing democratically, on the other hand, it takes on the highest value of 3.

As expected from the earlier discussion of parties in action, Korean parties as a whole scored 1.1 – a score indicating that they perform democratically only in one of three functional areas. The undemocratic character of their performance can be detected more easily from the percentage figures in Figure 6.6; twice as many respondents are placed at the low end of the index than at its high end. About seven-tenths (71%) judged Korean political parties to have been performing non-democratically rather than democratically. More than two-fifths (41%) of these respondents rated the performance of those parties as mostly non-democratic. More notable is that the percentage ratings (30%) denoting completely non-democratic performance are over three times larger than those (9%) that indicate party performance as completely democratic.

How well or poorly do political parties in Korea perform as institutions of representative democracy? This question was asked of respondents in the 1996 survey conducted by the Korea-Gallup (Appendix B P8). Once again, Koreans rated the overall performance of their political parties as a channel of representation far more negatively than positively by a large margin of nearly two to one (65% to 35%). Much worse, the most negative of their ratings outnumber the most positive ones by an even larger margin of 9 percent to 1 percent. These findings, when considered together with those from the 1993 survey, make it clear that the political party system in Korea today not only is run non-democratically but also fails to represent average citizens.

The Etiology of Partisanship

Why are some Koreans emotionally attached to political parties while many others are not? Is it the failure of those parties to democratize that has slowed down the growth of their partisan ties? Or is it the mass media or voluntary associations that have discouraged the development of partisanship among the Korean electorate? Tables 6.3 and 6.4 examine the relationships between two measures of partisanship on the one hand and those of party performance, media exposure, and associational life on the other. These three independent variables are chosen for this bivariate analysis because of their theoretical import discussed earlier. The 4-point indexes of media exposure and membership in voluntary associations are constructed on the basis of responses to the questions listed in Appendix B T2 and M2.[6]

Table 6.3 Attachment to Political Parties by Indexes of Party Performance, Civic Involvement, and Media Exposure

Variable Names	Index Values				Statistic (eta)
	0	1	2	3	
Party assessments	23	35	48	60	0.23
Civic involvement	35	35	36	40	0.04
Media exposure	40	32	40	34	0.08

Entries are the percentages of respondents at each index value who are attached to political parties
Source: 1993 Korean Democratization Survey

From the percentage and *eta* statistics reported in Table 6.3, it is clear that there are positive and statistically significant relationships between the perceived quality of party performance and both measures of partisanship. In the table, for example, we see that the percentage of those closely attached to a party rises steadily and sharply from the completely non-democratic to the completely democratic categories of performance assessment. The percentage of those partisans is shown in the table to be nearly three times more numerous among those who rate party performance as completely democratic than those who rate it as completely non-democratic (60% to 23%). Therefore, the more democratically the Korean people evaluate the performance of their political parties, the more closely they become attached to them. This is an important piece of evidence to support the instrumental or functional model of partisanship.

In Table 6.4, we see also that less non-democratic and more democratic assessments of party performance are positively associated with favorable shifts in partisan orientations and negatively associated with unfavorable shifts in those orientations. When asked whether their orientations toward parties have become more or less favorable since the democratic transition in 1988, more favorable responses lead less favorable ones by a margin of 30 to 14 percent among the respondents who rated parties as completely non-democratic. Among those who rated the same parties as completely democratic, however, more favorable responses lead less favorable ones by a significantly greater margin of 59 to 6 percent. As shown in the fourth column of Table 6.4, the percentage differential between the favorable and unfavorable changes in partisanship becomes steadily and significantly larger as the performance of parties is judged to be more democratic. Between the two extreme perceptions of party performance, there is a large difference – 37 percentage points. This evidence reconfirms the functional hypothesis that the more Koreans perceive their parties to function democratically, the more favorably they orient themselves toward those parties.

Table 6.4   Shifts in Partisan Orientations by Indexes of Party Performance
Quality, Civic Involvement, and Media Exposure (percent)

Index Values	Party Assessments			Civic Involvement			Media Exposure		
	Fav.	Unf.	Dif.	Fav.	Unf.	Dif.	Fav.	Unf.	Dif.
0 (lowest)	30	14	16	44	8	36	44	11	33
1	43	11	32	40	11	29	41	10	31
2	53	6	47	43	10	33	46	13	33
3 (highest)	59	6	53	46	13	33	39	7	32

Keys: Fav.   Favorable shift
        Unf.   Unfavorable shift
        Dif.   Difference
Source: 1993 Korean Democratization Survey

Contrary to what is expected from the neo-corporatist theory of representative democracy, levels of partisanship and its temporal shifts vary not only little but also inconsistently across the four groups involved in voluntary associations. Between the most inactive and active groups in civic life, for example, there is a relatively small difference of 5 percentage points in the emotionally attached to any political parties (35% to 40%) in favor of the latter rather than the former (see the third row of Table 6.3). In reorienting more favorably toward political parties over time, there is an even smaller difference of 3 percentage points between those two extreme groups (36% to 33%). What contradicts the theory more directly is the finding that those more active in civic affairs are not always less attached or less favorably reoriented toward parties than their less active peers. Instead, the former are slightly more attached and even more favorably oriented to parties than the latter. These findings run directly counter to the neo-corporatist theory that political parties are being displaced by proliferating interest groups and professional associations.

In Tables 6.3 and 6.4 also, we do not see much evidence that the mass media are displacing political parties as an instrument of representative democracy – at the least during the initial stage of democratic consolidation. As the theory predicts, those least exposed to the news media are more attached to political parties than those who are most exposed (40% to 34%). Nonetheless, those less exposed are not always more attached to those parties than their more exposed peers. In Table 6.3, two groups at considerably varying levels of media exposure (the most inactive and second most active) are shown to be exactly identical (40%) in the percentage of those emotionally attached to parties. In experiencing favorable shifts in partisan orientations over time, moreover, the least exposed to the news media did not experience such positive changes most frequently. Those changes occurred most frequently among those in the second most exposed group. All in all, there is no consistently negative relationship between media exposure and partisan orientations among the Korean people, as the theory of media exposure holds.

The bivariate analyses presented above have ruled out that media exposure and civic involvement are the two major forces inhibiting the growth of partisan orientations among Koreans. The same analysis, however, has firmly established that the performance quality of political parties can be one of the forces powerfully promoting those orientations. How does the party performance variable compare with regional ties, education, and other factors that are widely known in the literature on Korean politics to shape partisanship powerfully? To explore this question, the 4-point index measuring the overall quality of party performance was analyzed together with the four other independent variables of gender, age, educational attainment, and regional ties. Since two of these five independent variables (regional ties and gender) are nominal-scale measures, multiple classification analysis (MCA) was employed to estimate and compare their relative power of accounting for partisanship and its shifts (Andrews 1973).[7] Results of this analysis are reported in Table 6.5.

The second and third columns of the table, respectively, list *beta* coefficients for two different indicators of affect for political parties. The first indicator is a dichotomous measure of psychological attachment to those parties, and the second is a trichotomous measure of changes in general orientation toward political parties. A comparison of *beta* coefficients across the rows in the columns of the table makes it possible to estimate the relative importance of each independent

Table 6.5 Multiple Classification Analysis of Partisanship and its Shifts

Predictors	Partisan Attachment *beta*	Shift in Partisanship *beta*
Gender	0.09*	0.04
Age	0.07	0.06
Education	0.07	0.09*
Region	0.18*	0.06
Performance assessments	0.21*	0.20*
R^2	0.11	0.06

*Statistically significant at the .05 level
Source: 1993 Korean Democratization Survey

variable against the other four as an influence on partisan loyalty or its change over time.

Which variable most strongly influences partisan attachment among the Korean people? According to the magnitude of *beta* coefficients reported in the second column of Table 6.5, party performance is the strongest influence on their partisan loyalty. Of the five *beta* coefficients listed in that column, three coefficients are larger than 0.07, where *betas* become significant statistically as well as in substantive meaning. Of these three, the one for the variable measuring the quality of party performance is largest with 0.21. It is followed by regional ties (0.18) and gender (0.09). Based on this finding, it is fair to conclude that Koreans' attachments to political parties are shaped by a combination of divergent forces, yet such attachments are shaped most powerfully by how well or poorly parties are judged to perform.

Beta coefficients in the third column of Table 6.5 were then compared to determine the relative importance of five independent variables in shifting partisan loyalty over time. Of these five variables, the perceived quality of party performance is one of the only two predictors (the other being education) whose coefficients are significant both statistically and substantively. According to the *betas*, the performance variable is over two to five times more powerful in reorienting Koreans toward or away from political parties than the other four variables included in the MCA equation. Moreover, better assessments of party performance among the Korean people are always accompanied by more favorable shifts or less unfavorable shifts in their attitudes toward parties. In striking contrast, greater educational attainment among Koreans, especially those with a college education, is found weakening, rather than strengthening, their partisan loyalty. The improvement of party performance is, therefore, the only way to broaden the support bases of Korean political parties to a significant degree.

In view of the findings presented above, it is reasonable to argue that the democratization of all the political parties currently operative in Korea is crucial to building a democratic party system with broad bases of popular support in that country. Party leaders must transform the current undemocratic system of cadre parties, based on the principle of bossism, into a truly open and competitive system of democratic governance before they can expect the mass citizenry to support their parties on a broader continuing basis.

Discussions

The multivariate analyses presented considered five variables to explain the support of the Korean mass public for political parties in the current era of democratic politics. As coefficients of multiple determination (R^2) in the last row of Table 6.5 indicate, those five variables, as a set, fail to offer a satisfactory account of popular support for Korean parties. The amount of its explained variation is small, ranging from 6 percent for shifts in partisan orientations to 11 percent for psychological attachment to parties. In this connection, the question arises as to what other variables orient the Korean mass citizenry more powerfully than the ones considered in the present analysis toward or against political parties in action.

Traditional Confucian culture appears to hold the key to the slow growth of partisanship in Korea by "engendering a peculiar system of political parties incapable of interest aggregation and political integration" (Kim & Suh 1997: 9). As Im Hyug Baeg (1997b: 1) notes, Confucianism has long been defunct as the ruling ideology of the Korean state, and only a very small minority (2%) nowadays identify themselves as Confucianists. As a system of cultural norms and values, nevertheless, it remains an all-powerful influence on interpersonal relationships among all segments of the Korean population (Steinberg 1997: 153). Confucianism, particularly in the political sphere, continues to exert a profound influence by inculcating the personal value that emphasizes "the rule of man" over "the rule of law" (Hahm & Rhyu 1997: 43; see also Kihl 1994; K. D. Kim 1997).

The Kim Young Sam government, for example, swiftly lost its moral authority to rule and became completely immobilized as soon as it became known that Kim's second son was a major player in the Hanbo scandal. The popularity of Lee Hoi Chang, the candidate of the ruling party in the last presidential election, also plummeted from first to third place among the four leading candidates as soon as it became public knowledge that his two sons had been excused from military service for being underweight. "Beholden to the Confucian political discourse with its strong moralistic bent" (Hahm 1997: 73) – Koreans still expect their political leaders, like President Kim and Mr Lee, to merit moral authority and only thereafter to exercise such authority. In Korea, which must be seen as a deeply Confucian society, therefore, it is the moral character of individual political leaders, not their affiliation with a political party, that matters most to many Korean voters.

Table 6.6 reports data from a series of parallel surveys concerning the factors that have been selected as most decisive among the Korean electorate in selecting candidates for the National Assembly elections over a period of forty years. In every election survey since 1954, candidates have been found to influence the electorate far more decisively than their political parties or policy orientations. Even in the parliamentary elections held in 1992, 42 percent of Korean voters reported

Table 6.6 Personal Character and Political Party as Influences on Parliamentary Elections (percent)

Year	Personal Character (A)	Political Party (B)	Difference (A–B)
1954	72	7	+65
1958	39	11	+28
1960	28	17	+11
1963	63	10	+53
1967*	44	19	+25
1969	41	13	+28
1973	80	5	+75
1985	46	22	+24
1992*	42	16	+26

*Figures for 1967 and 1992 are averages of percentages from multiple surveys reported
Source: M. Shin (1993)

that they chose their candidate solely on the basis of his or her personal character rather than political party or policy commitment.

More remarkable is that the Confucian tradition of personality-based politics has never lost its vigor during a period in which Korea, as one of the most successful economic powerhouses, has witnessed the proliferation of corporate agencies and the diffusion of powerful technologies of mass communication networks. As few as one in six Korean voters (16%) seriously take into account political parties in the election of political leadership – about the nearly identical percentage as in 1960 (17%). In Confucian nations like Korea, culture must be reintroduced in order to unravel the mystery surrounding the slow growth of a democratic political party system. The mystery will not be resolved by theories of neo-corporatism or electronic media.

Cross-National Comparisons

Are the Korean people more supportive of a democratic party system than those in other new democracies? This question cannot be addressed fully with the data currently available from other national and cross-national surveys. Yet, the data reported in Figure 6.7 indicate that Koreans lead other citizens in embracing political parties for democratic governance. In most new democracies of Central/Eastern Europe, more than 10 percent still refuse to accept the democratic norm of multi-partyism. The corresponding percentage for Korea is only 5 percent, a negligible proportion. In principle, Koreans appear to be more supportive of a democratic party system than their counterparts in other new democracies.

Figure 6.7 Cross-National Differences in the Percentages Agreeing with the Statement that "We Need Political Parties If We Want Democratic Development"

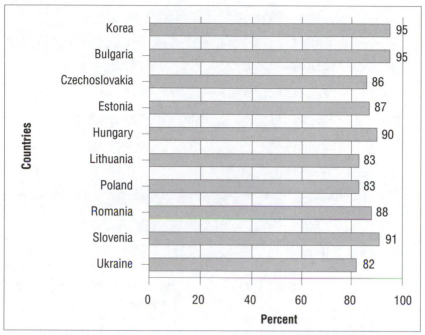

Sources: 1993 Korean Democratization Survey; Bruszt & Simon (1990–91)

In taking part in party politics, however, Koreans are far behind the citizens of most new European and Latin American democracies. The percentage of Koreans who are attached to any political party compares very poorly with eight of nine European democracies (see Figure 6.8). Poland is the only country that registered a lower percentage of partisans than Korea. The discrepancy between the democratic principle and practice of party politics appears to be more pronounced in Korea than in its counterparts elsewhere. This can be attributable to the fact that Koreans are significantly less satisfied with their parties than Europeans are.

How well do Korean political parties, as compared with those in nine East European democracies, fulfil their functions as a pivotal institution of representative democracy? In all of the three functions surveyed, Korean parties are shown in Table 6.7 to rank lowest. For example, 46% to 64% of Eastern Europeans reported that they did not agree that their political parties were only serving their party leaders' interests. Among the Korean mass public, however, only 27 percent gave the same response. It appears that while political parties in European democracies

Figure 6.8   Cross-National Differences in the Percentages of the Mass
Citizenry Attached to Political Parties

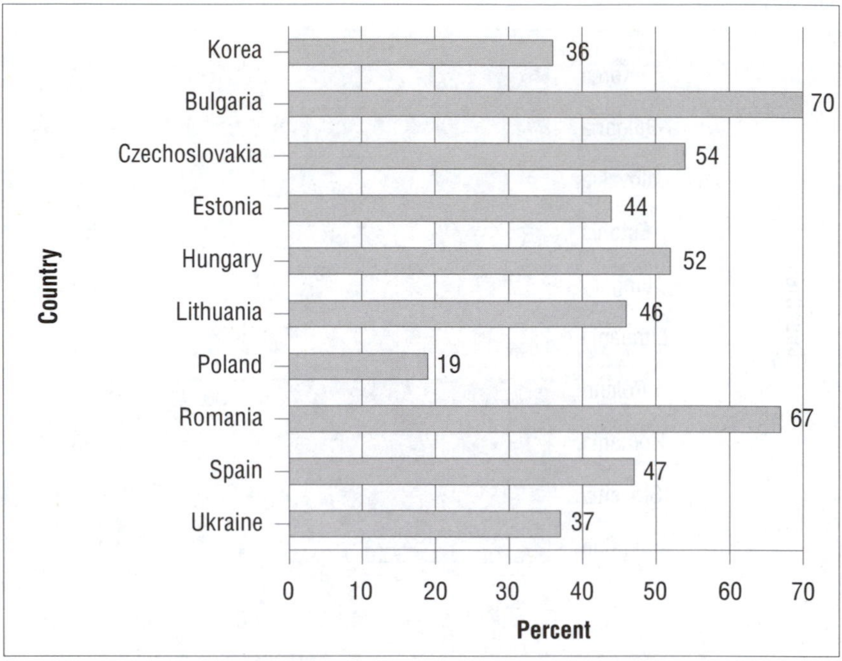

Source: 1993 Korean Democratization Survey; Bruszt & Simon (1990–91);
McDonough, Barnes & Pina (1998).

are serving a majority of their citizenry, Korean parties are working only
for a small minority, which consists of their political leaders. All these
findings, when considered together, suggest that very little has been
accomplished in the democratization of Korea's political parties. The
findings also suggest that political parties may be more difficult to
democratize than other political institutions such as the military or the
civil service.

Summary and Conclusions

This chapter has sought to contribute to the systematic exploration of
the difficulties and uncertainties associated with the development of a
democratic party system. Democratic consolidation, unlike democratic
transition, requires the development of a competitive multi-party system.
For a competitive multi-party system to become democratically consolidated, constituent parties must establish a broad and stable base of
popular support capable of fulfilling the representational functions of
modern democracy.

Table 6.7 Cross-National Differences in Public Assessments of Party
Performance (percent)

Country	Performance Area (%)		
	Provide opportunity to participate in politics	Serve the interests of the public	Offer different policies
Korea	57	27	25
Bulgaria	92	64	28
Czechoslovakia	84	62	28
Estonia	84	49	32
Hungary	87	52	32
Lithuania	78	55	34
Poland	89	47	46
Romania	84	69	35
Slovenia	84	56	26
Ukraine	82	46	42

Sources: 1993 Korean Democratization Survey; Bruszt & Simon (1990–91)

From the survey findings presented in this chapter, however, it is clear that an abundance of presidential, parliamentary, and local elections over the past six years has failed to transform the multi-party system in Korea into a truly democratic party system. As in the period of authoritarian rule, Korean parties do not have broad and reliable ties to a vast majority of the mass citizenry. Unlike political parties in consolidated democracies, both the ruling and opposition parties in Korea lack an army of loyal supporters or dues-paying members; they manage every election with staffs of salaried workers and paid campaigners (Y. H. Kim 1994; M. Shin 1993). Korean parties, moreover, are not capable of formulating and offering viable alternatives in democratic governance, and they appear to be similar to the organizations that served the previous authoritarian regimes of Park Chung Hee and Chun Doo Whan as mobilizing tools of political leaders.

The Korean task of developing a semi-democratic party system into a fully democratic one appears to be extremely difficult. As a multifaceted phenomenon, the development of democratic party politics is affected differently by a variety of forces; most cannot be subjected directly to any policy manipulation. The most intractable of these forces is the political culture that is rooted deeply in the age-old principles of Confucianism. It emphasizes the personal quality of individual leaders over their organizational affiliations. Over the past forty years, the Confucian culture has refused to wane; it still "saturates the Korean people's lives and is the core of Korean culture" (quoted in Steinberg 1997: 153). In the foreseeable future, therefore, it is not likely to be transformed into a culture that is conducive to the development of a fully democratic party system.

The Korean prospect for a fully democratic party system is, therefore, highly uncertain. Political leaders are committed to the task of democratizing the military and other anti-democratic government agencies. Yet, in their refusal to open the policy-making process to the electorate, they are not strongly committed to the task of democratizing their own party organizations. Members of the electorate, on the other hand, are not willing to embrace political parties until the parties are democratized enough to serve *their* interests rather than those of party leaders. Obviously, there is a dynamic tension between the two processes of democratizing the performance of political parties and mustering popular support for them. The complex interactions of these processes mean that the failure of one process would have grave consequences for the other. Under this catch-22 situation, it is highly uncertain whether or not a competitive multi-party system, with a broad and stable popular support base, will emerge in Korea in the near future.

PART IV

Non-Western Roads to Democratization

CHAPTER 7

Consolidating a Nascent Democracy

"Now, we have just begun setting the distortions of history
straight in order to build a true community which is ruled by
law, justice, conscience and ethics. This undertaking designed
to right past wrongs is indeed a signal for the birth of a new
society and a proud beginning for building a new nation."
Kim Young Sam (1996: 568)
"Why must you speak of profit? . . . Superios and inferios will
try to seize profit from another. And state will be endangered."
Mencius (1970: 92)

The current wave of democratization has been rapidly moving from the phase of expansion to that of consolidation (Diamond et al. 1997; Huntington 1996b; Linz & Stepan 1996b; O'Donnell 1996). With frequent setbacks in the global movement toward democracy occurring over the past few years, the problems of consolidating new democracies have recently become a subject of increasing and widespread concern not only in the scholarly community but also in government circles (Diamond 1999; Hadenius 1992, 1997; Huntington 1997; Przeworski et al. 1996; Schmitter & Santiso 1998; D. Shin 1994). What can, and should, be done to consolidate incomplete democratic rule? The former President Kim Young Sam advocated an exceptional, non-Western model of democratic consolidation.

In both substance and style, this model contrasts strikingly with what has been observed in all other countries during the current wave of democratization (Bratton & van de Walle 1997; Chu 1992; Desmond 1995; Gunther, Puhle & Diamandouros 1995; Linz & Stepan 1996a; McDonough, Barnes & Pina 1998; Rose, Mishler & Haerpfer 1998; Rosenberg 1995). "In almost all these countries [new democracies]," Huntington (1991: 215) emphasizes, "no effective prosecution and punishment [of authoritarian crimes] occurred (see also Rosenberg 1995: 149). In Korea, however, Kim, as the second president of the democratic Sixth Republic (1993–98), has relentlessly dismantled the old power base as well as the *modus operandi* of the *ancien* military regime. As *Time* reported in its December 18, 1995, issue, "Few countries that have gone from dictatorship to democracy have the past on trial in such a sweeping, abrupt way" (Desmond 1995: 18).

As will be discussed below, President Kim's successive waves of democratic reforms and anti-authoritarian campaigns have run directly counter to what many political scientists and policy advocates of liberal democracy often prescribe for consolidating democracies (Ackerman 1992; Di Palma 1990a, 1993; Huntington 1991, 1996b; Linz & Stepan 1996a; Przeworski 1991). Indeed, Kim has offered a truly alternative model of consolidating nascent democracies in post-authoritarian societies to the scholarly community as well as government circles. Even Russian President Boris Yeltsin was known to have followed closely Kim's model of legitimating democracy through the search for truth about the authoritarian past (Knight 1996: 49).

What constitutes the Kim Young Sam model of democratic consolidation? What institutional reforms and political campaigns have been carried out under his leadership? How much do those reforms and campaigns depart from the existing theories and practices of democratic consolidation? How effective have they been in consolidating democratic political institutions and reorienting the masses toward democratic rule? Which specific reform measures have been most and which least effective in promoting the consolidation of democratic institutions and culture?

An examination of Kim's presidency in the past has been far more descriptive and speculative than analytical and evaluative. Much of the existing literature on the subject has been devoted to extensive descriptions of various individual reform measures or to speculation of Kim's political motives behind those measures (B. Y. Ahn 1995; Cotton 1995a; Hahm 1996; B. Han 1997; Kil 1993; Kihl 1995; D. Kim 1993; K. Kim 1995; M. Kim 1994; Manning 1995; Paik 1995; Yang 1995). As a result, little effort has been made to systematically assess the relative effectiveness and uniqueness of his democratic reforms.

The primary objective of this chapter is to distinguish President Kim's model of democratic consolidation from other Western models and to evaluate its *raison d'être* and capability from a strategic perspective. Specifically, the chapter begins with a critical review of existing models of democratic consolidation. Based on this review, the chapter identifies and highlights the most distinguishing characteristics of the Kim Young Sam model, which seeks to build a democratic community. The audacious campaigns to rectify the authoritarian past and eradicate political corruption are discussed and assessed by means of the survey conducted in January 1996, when the campaigns were in full swing. The consequences of these campaigns for democratizing political culture are explored at both the aggregate and individual levels. The chapter concludes with the implications of the Kim Young Sam model for democratizing limited democracies in Asia and elsewhere.

Existing Models of Democratic Consolidation

What do the empirical and theoretical studies of democratization offer for political leaders of new democracies who are seriously interested and directly involved in consolidating the "frozen" or "incomplete" democratic polity? These studies, as a whole, make it clear that democratic consolidation is neither unidimensional nor inevitable nor unidirectional (Gunther, Puhle & Diamandouros 1995: 19–20; see also Mainwaring, O'Donnell & Valenzuela 1992; Morlino 1995a; Schmitter 1995b). They also emphasize that its dynamics are shaped by a multitude of factors and forces, which vary a great deal from one country to another – not only in duration but also in pattern (Munck 1994; Remmer 1995).

What has been offered by the theoretical and empirical literature so far is known to be of little use to those seeking to effect the dynamic and uncertain process of democratic consolidation. Schneider (1995: 219), for example, points out that prior research on democratic consolidation has failed to offer "a fully satisfying and empirically serviceable definition." Moreover, O'Donnell (1996: 18) notes that "there is no theory that would tell us why and how the new polyarchies that have institutionalized elections will 'complete' their institutional set, or otherwise become 'consolidated'."

With few exceptions, democratic consolidation has been equated exclusively with the establishment and acceptance of political institutions and electoral procedures representing individual citizens and their organized interests. The widely accepted minimalist definition offered by Linz (1990c) and many others, for example, emphasizes the institutionalization of free and fair elections, majority rule, multi-party competition, a popularly elected president, and other representative procedures as essential characteristics of democratic consolidation. According to Schmitter (1995b: 544), "consolidation of democracy is over when the rules and resources of basic democratic institutions are sufficiently entrenched." For Przeworski (1991: x, 26), moreover, consolidation requires spontaneous, *self-interested* compliance: political actors come to view democratic procedures as serving their long-term self-interest.

Existing definitions of democratic consolidation are concerned primarily with aggregate procedural characteristics of new democracies; therefore, they have "nothing to do with the issues of quality and performance" (O'Donnell 1996: 17). In addition, those definitions are all based on the liberal democratic notion of self-interest (Barber 1984: 4). Assuming that the public good derives from personal desires and interests of individual citizens, the liberal model disregards the role of community, or social setting, within which those desires and interests are actually nurtured and given content. In this model, therefore, "the claims of particularistic identities" are not seen to be in serious conflict with "the claims of democratic citizenship and officialdom" (March & Olsen 1995: 39).

As was documented in the recent works of communitarian and institutional critics (Caney 1992; Fukuyama 1995a; Gould 1988; March & Olsen 1995; Marcus & Hanson 1993; Warren 1992), *self-interested* individuals alone, however, cannot form a democratic political community that would be viable over any length of time. For nascent democracies to survive and consolidate, therefore, their people should understand and embrace democratic procedures as serving more than their own self-interest. In addition, they need to participate in the political process as *public-spirited* citizens.

Unfortunately, many individual voters and their elected representatives in these new democracies do not act according to norms and formal rules associated with their respective roles within a democratic state. Instead, they are more often than not in pursuit of personal advantage and gains as *self-interested* citizens or public officials (O'Donnell 1996). The newly gained freedom and rights from democratic regime change have served as expanded opportunities to pursue personal advantages and interests at the expense of the community (Manent 1996). Such conflicts and dilemmas facing all new democracies cannot adequately be taken into account in the liberal model of democratic consolidation. For this reason, Fukuyama (1995a: 351) argues that liberal democracy cannot work well as a political system unless "its individualism is moderated by public spirit."

Based on the notions of voluntary exchange and free competition, the liberal model over-estimates the importance of co-operation and consensus among elites as a strategy for promoting democratic consolidation (Gunther, Diamandouros & Puhle 1995; Huntington 1991). "For consolidation to take place," Morlino (1995a: 579) claims, "compromise must be maintained and strengthened." According to Burton, Gunther & Higley (1992), new democracies consolidate when their political elites reach a consensus either by convergence or settlement. Settlement occurs through explicit pacts between previously disunified elites. Convergence is achieved when the opposition drops its anti-system discourse, wins elections, and exercises power according to established democratic procedures. Both arrangements are intended to incorporate all politically relevant elites within the democratic consensus.

Rueschemeyer, Stephens & Stephens (1992: 156), on the other hand, argue for "close articulation of political and economic elites" in the process of democratic consolidation. Przeworski (1991: 31) also argues for the protection of powerful institutions, including the military and bourgeoisie. Any attempt by new democracies to directly challenge established interests is viewed as dangerous and detrimental to the survival of these democracies – not to mention their consolidation.

As such, the existing models of democratic consolidation assume that co-operation and consensus among powerful political and economic elites are essential to the institutionalization of democratic institutions and procedures. They also assume that the formal rules of democratic political games are potent enough to effect their co-operation and consensus.[1] In the real world of new democracies, the elites more often than not *collude* rather than *co-operate* in order to seek the best personal outcome at the expense of the powerless masses. In this world, therefore, the formal rules of democratic politics are very poor guides to the processes of aggregating competing interests and formulating public policy. As March & Olsen (1995: 21) correctly observe, rules that actually guide those processes are manifested not only in formal institutions but also within the political culture of a given community. In regulating political participation and competition among citizens and government officials, informal rules, rooted deeply in their political culture, often overpower the formal rules prescribed in a given country's democratic constitution (Robinson 1994; Song 1997).

Kim Young Sam's Vision of a Democratic Community

Kim Young Sam assumed the second presidency of the democratic Sixth Republic of Korea on February 25, 1993. Before he became the first civilian president following thirty-two years of military domination, President Kim had long been a champion of democracy. In 1979, when former General Park Chung Hee was in power, Kim was expelled from the National Assembly for labeling the Park regime "dictatorial" in his interview with the *New York Times* and calling on the United States to support Korea's democratization. In 1983, when former General Chun Doo Whan was in power, Kim staged a 23-day hunger strike in his demand for democratic reform. Before the hunger strike, which almost led to his death, Kim was under house arrest for more than three years.

Unlike his immediate predecessor Roh Tae Woo, who was a leader of the 1979 military coup d'etat, President Kim was a seasoned parliamentarian and a veteran party politician (Yang 1995). He had won nine elections to the National Assembly and served five times as an opposition floor leader. He had also served as the leader of four different opposition parties after he broke with the first president of Korea, Rhee Syngman, who amended the constitution to permit a third term.

Kim's role as the leader of an opposition party ended in January 1990 when his party and another opposition party merged with the then-ruling Democratic Justice Party to form a majority party for the Roh government (1988–93).[2] As the nominee of the new ruling Democratic Liberal Party, Kim was elected to the presidency on December 25, 1992.[3] Being the leader of a minority faction within the ruling party, he had to share power with the majority faction of that party, which had served as the authoritarian political machinery for the military dictatorship headed by former General Chun Doo Whan (1980–88), and Kim negotiated a peaceful transition to democracy.

As the first civilian president of a country dominated by former military elites, President Kim had to assert the principle of civilian supremacy over the military, which for three decades had been the most powerful institution in Korea. As the head of a state long dominated by the tradition of collusive ties between government and business, Kim inveighed against the common practice of demanding and accepting donations in exchange for favorable business deals. As the first president of democratic Korea with no direct ties to the previous military governments, he had to confront mistakes of the authoritarian past in order to build a fully democratic state.

Undoubtedly the Western model of liberal democratization was of little use to President Kim in dealing with any of the problems that stood in his way to democratize age-old practices of authoritarian politics and Confucian-based cultural values (B. K. Kim 1994; Steinberg 1996). To Kim, a democratic state must embody more than the institutions and procedures of popular representation allowing voluntary exchange and free competition for the pursuit of self-interests. Its citizens must recognize also that the common good should take priority over all other political values, including individual preferences and minority rights, and its government should serve those citizens rather than their leaders. His notion of democracy, therefore, must have a more communitarian than libertarian nature and involve both substantive outcomes and representative procedures.[4]

In his inaugural address on February 25, 1993, President Kim outlined a communitarian model of democratic consolidation under the name of a New Korea. His vision of the New Korea was to create a freer and more mature democratic society in which "freedom must serve society" (Y. S. Kim 1993: 76). His New Korea was also "a sharing community, working and living together in harmony" in which "justice will flow like a river" and "a higher quality of life will flourish." It was also an honorable society that would no longer "give currency to the immoral notion that the end justifies the means."

To build such a democratic community, President Kim stressed the importance of changing unethical habits and corrupt practices among citizens and officials in addition to that of building democratic institutions and procedures, which are often outlined in a minimal definition of consolidated democracy. Specifically, he stressed the following changes: "stop considering narrow self-interests and demanding one's own share too greedily," "give greater consideration to the larger common good," "root out misconduct and corruption and restore national discipline," and "cultivate wholesome character and unwavering democratic belief."

President Kim's notion of democracy contrasts sharply with Dahl's (1971; see also Schmitter & Karl 1991) liberal notion that has served for decades as a foundation for a minimal definition of democratic consolidation. By putting the community ahead of its individual members, Kim chose to become a communitarian democrat subscribing to the notion that "democracy is partly a structure of laws and incentives by which less-than-perfect individuals are induced to act for the common good while pursuing their own goals" (March & Olsen 1995: 41; see also Manent 1996: 10). By infusing democracy with a moral framework, President Kim found it immoral and undemocratic to continue cooperation with former dictators and their supporters who seized power by military coups and who massacred people demanding political freedom and equality.

For Kim Young Sam, democratic consolidation required the building of a truly moral community by removing every authoritarian enclave rather than sustaining an alliance with it – even if this operation "may cost the ruling party a considerable number of National Assembly seats in the April general elections" (D. Han 1996: 13). Consequently, institutionalization and elite convergence do not figure prominently in his model of democratic consolidation. Instead, purification and purgation are its most critical elements. In the Geoffrey Pridham (1995: 173) formulation (see also Morlino & Montero 1995), the Kim Young Sam model is intended more for negative, rather than positive, democratic consolidation. "Negative consolidation includes the solution of any problems remaining from the transition, and, in general, the containment or reduction, if not removal, of any serious challenges to democratization."

Negative Democratic Consolidation under Kim Young Sam

After his inauguration as the second president of democratic Korea in February 1993, President Kim carried out his democratic reform program in four successive waves.[5] Among these waves, the fourth accorded most closely with the ultimate goal of a new democratic community as outlined in his vision of a New Korea. It was also the wave that made Japan and other Asian neighbors wonder "if – and when – their own people would discover the same impulse that has driven Korea to confront a system built on graft" (Brull 1995: 52).

The fourth wave of Kim's democratic reforms is often called "the campaign to rectify the past" or "a revolution to restore our honor." It began on October 19, 1995, with an investigation of the political slush fund amassed by former President Roh Tae Woo, Kim's immediate predecessor. Since then, the slush fund scandal has opened the way for reviving the democratic reforms that were badly compromised by President Kim's association with close colleagues of the former military rulers. The reform has been transformed successfully into a battle to shape Korea's democratic destiny by waging a fundamental assault on the old ruling triad of generals, politicians, and businessmen and by uncovering the truth about the abuses and brutality of the old authoritarian regime.

Former presidents Chun Doo Whan and Roh Tae Woo, who ruled the country from 1980 to 1993, were sentenced to life in prison and seventeen years, respectively, on numerous charges, including those of an illegal army mutiny in 1979 and the sanctioning of the 1980 massacre of pro-democracy demonstrators in the city of Kwangju (Clarke 1988; see also Kristof 1995, 1996a). Thirteen more generals were sentenced to four to ten years in prison on charges related to this massacre, which killed at least 240 people and wounded 1800. Former President Roh Tae Woo was convicted of administering a political slush fund of US$350 million while in office. His predecessor Chun Doo Whan was also convicted of controlling a US$276 million slush fund, and four of Chun's associates have been convicted of taking bribes.[6] Related to this slush fund scandal, leaders of nine major *chaebols* were also convicted of offering bribes and kickbacks; however, most of them have not been imprisoned.

In his 1996 New Year's speech to the nation, President Kim (1996: 570) emphasized that "the campaign to rectify the distortions of Korean history is a signal for the birth of a new community which is ruled by law, justice, conscience and ethics." He added: "We can no longer overlook in the name of national reconciliation, the acts and attitudes that disgraced the people and our history." Rather than leaving past misdeeds to the judgment of history, Kim decided to expose these activities and punish those responsible for their misdeeds. What mattered more to him in building a democratic community was no longer national reconciliation or consensus; instead, it was the purging of past ills and the purifying of past wrongs.

The slush fund scandal served as a timely opportunity for President Kim to remove the authoritarian enclave of the *minjong* (liberal justice) faction from the ruling Democratic Liberal Party. Linking the Chun Doo

Whan government and its Liberal Justice Party to the corruption and brutality of the authoritarian past, Kim was able to purge congressmen and party district heads who belonged to the *minjong* faction and to replace them with younger political newcomers for the forthcoming 15th National Assembly election on April 11, 1996. On December 6, 1995, Kim even changed the name of the ruling Democratic Liberal Party to the New Korea Party in order to demonstrate a clean break with the authoritarian past. The new name symbolized his vision of the new, democratic Korean community that was outlined in his 1993 inaugural address.

Besides the special legislation that allowed his government to pursue an aggressive investigation of the 1979 military rebellion and the 1980 Kwangju massacre, President Kim actively supported the enactment of local autonomy legislation and reform campaign legislation. In his model of democratic consolidation, however, the institutionalization of these democratic procedures matters little unless primordial or particularistic political habits and corrupt practices of the authoritarian past are transformed into communitarian and universalistic ones. To ensure such a democratic transformation, individual citizens would be made aware of all the illegal acts and injustices of the old military governments, and they would be encouraged also to reorient themselves toward the community in which they live with others. Furthermore, their elected officials should depart from an alliance with those responsible for the authoritarian ills. These officials and civil servants should also sever their collusive ties with the business community.

Anti-Authoritarian Campaign

To what degree did the Korean people support their president's campaign to rectify the authoritarian past? To explore this question, the 1996 survey first asked its respondents to express, on a 5-point verbal scale, the extent to which they were supporting or opposing each of the seven specific measures implemented as part of his anti-authoritarian campaign (see Appendix B Q1). The seven measures include: (1) arrest of former President Roh Tae Woo, (2) arrest of former President Chun Doo Whan, (3) prosecution of the principal leaders of the 1979 military coup, (4) prosecution of the principal leaders of the 1980 Kwangju Incident, (5) prosecution of businessmen who donated the secret funds, (6) prosecution of politicians who managed the secret funds, and (7) purging of Fifth and Sixth Republic leaders from public offices.

For each of these seven measures, Table 7.1 shows summary statistics and the distribution of respondents across five categories ranging from "strongly oppose" to "strongly support." The measures intended for the

Table 7.1 Public Support and Opposition to the Campaign to Rectify the Authoritarian Past

Rectification Measure	Five-Point Verbal Scale					Summary Statistics		Percentages		
	Strongly oppose	Somewhat oppose	Neutral	Somewhat support	Strongly support	Mean	Rank	Support (A)	Oppose (B)	Balance (A–B)
Arrest of former President Roh Tae Woo	1.6%	6.0%	10.1%	16.7%	65.6%	(1.4)	2	82.3%	7.6%	+74.7%
Arrest of former President Chun Doo Whan	2.3	7.2	8.3	15.7	66.5	(1.3)	4	82.2	9.5	+72.7
Prosecution of 1979 coup plotters	1.5	3.8	9.6	19.1	65.9	(1.4)	2	85.1	5.3	+79.8
Prosecution of those responsible for the 1980 Kwangju massacre	1.5	3.6	8.7	18.4	67.7	(1.5)	1	86.1	5.1	+81.0
Prosecution of businessmen who contributed to slush fund	4.6	15.6	19.9	22.0	37.8	(0.7)	7	59.8	20.2	+39.6
Prosecution of slush fund managers	0.9	4.3	12.8	27.1	54.9	(1.3)	4	82.0	5.2	+76.8
Exclusion of 5th and 6th Republic leaders from public offices	2.1	8.6	16.1	23.3	49.9	(1.3)	4	73.2	10.7	+62.5

Source: 1996 Korean Democratiation Survey

effective prosecution and punishment of authoritarian crimes as a whole were supported by 60 percent or more. With the exception of two measures: (1) prosecuting corrupt businessmen, and (2) purging tainted politicians for the political process, President Kim's anti-authoritarian reform measures were opposed by less than 10 percent and supported strongly by majorities. By and large, Koreans enthusiastically joined their president in the campaign to examine the brutal actions of previous military dictators and to unravel the large institutional fabric of corruption.

Levels of support and opposition, however, vary considerably across the categories of authoritarian crimes and targeted wrong-doers for punishment. Of the four categories of wrong-doers, namely, presidents, generals, businessmen, and politicians, Koreans were most supportive of punishing the military leaders who plotted a coup in 1979 and ordered the massacre of Kwangju residents in 1980. They were least supportive of punishing the businessmen who contributed to the slush funds controlled by Korea's last two presidents. As Table 7.1 shows, three out of five Koreans (60%) supported the prosecution of those businessmen

Figure 7.1   Overall Levels of Public Support for the Campaign to Rectify the Authoritarian Past

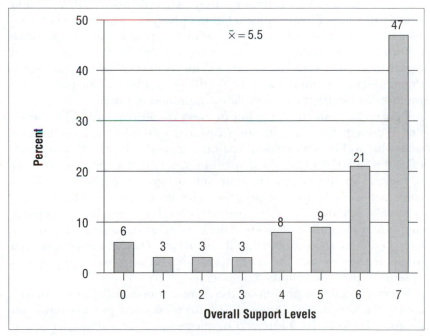

Source: 1996 Korean Democratization Survey

while more than five out of six (82%) supported the arrest of the two former presidents who illegally amassed the slush funds. When choosing between former presidents and their political cronies who managed the slush funds, Koreans were more willing to punish the former. In the eyes of the Korean people, their last two presidents were wrong-doers who should be subjected to harsher punishment because they were the leaders of brutal oppression and massive corruption.

Figure 7.1 shows the amount of overall support among the Korean people for President Kim's rectification campaign as a whole. Support was measured by tallying the number of times respondents supported the seven reform measures reported in Table 7.1. The Figure also shows how they are distributed across eight different levels of such support ranging from none to all of the seven measures. According to the means reported in the table, the average Korean supported more than five (5.5) of the seven rectification measures. Percentage figures, on the other hand, show that more than two-thirds (68%) were supportive of most or all measures while less than one-tenth support none. More striking is that nearly one-half (47%) of the Korean population was supportive of all seven measures. In short, the Korean people were strongly supportive of President Kim's efforts to rectify the authoritarian past.

Why did most Koreans support their president's anti-authoritarian reform measures? Was it because they believed those reforms would contribute to the further consolidation of Korean democracy? Or, were they supportive mainly because they wanted to punish those responsible for brutal acts and corrupt practices? To explore the real motive behind their support, respondents to the 1996 survey were asked to what degree they thought measures taken to rectify the authoritarian past would promote or hinder the further democratization of Korea.

Figure 7.2 shows that nine out of every ten Koreans (90%) believed that President Kim's rectification campaign would contribute at least somewhat to Korean democratization (Appendix B Q2). It also shows that one-half (50%) would contribute a lot to that process. Among supporters of the campaign, nine out of ten (90%) believed in its contribution to democratic progress. The punishment of authoritarian criminals was not the only reason behind overwhelming popular support for the most audacious of the anti-authoritarian campaigns ever launched in newly consolidating democracies. The Korean people, as a whole, tended to back President Kim's anti-authoritarian campaign in order to expand their limited democracy.

Which specific components of the rectification campaign were viewed among the Korean people as contributing most to the process of Korean democratization? To address this question, all seven items tapping support or opposition to the individual reform measures implemented

Figure 7.2   Perceived Impact of the Rectification Campaign on Democratization

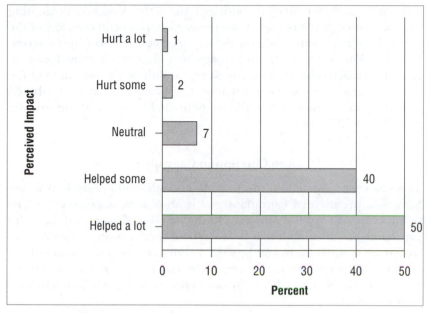

Source: 1996 Korean Democratization Survey

as part of the campaign were regressed on the item measuring its overall impact on the democratic process in a stepwise mode. Table 7.2 shows the coefficient of multiple determination and standardized multiple coefficients (*betas*) that resulted from this regression analysis.

The arrest of former president Chun Doo Whan, the prosecution of the 1979 coup plotters, the prosecution of principal leaders in the 1980 Kwangju massacre, and the exclusion of the Fifth and Sixth Republic

Table 7.2   Predicting the Perceived Impact of the Rectification Campaign on Democratization: OLS Regressions (standardized regression coefficients)

Predictors	Beta
Arrest of former President Chun Doo Whan	0.26*
Prosecution of 1979 coup plotters	0.12*
Prosecution of principal leaders of the Kwangju massacre	0.13*
Exclusion of Fifth and Sixth Republic leaders from public offices	0.11*
R^2	0.29

*Significant at the 0.01 level
Source: 1996 Democratization Survey

leaders from public offices are significantly associated with positive assessments of the reform campaign. Of these four measures, Chun's arrest is the most potent contributing factor to the process of promoting Korean democracy; it is at least two times more powerful than any of the other three rectification measures. In sharp contrast to Chun's arrest, Roh Tae Woo's arrest was not a significantly contributing factor to Korean democratization. To many Koreans, Roh, as the president of the first democratically elected government, appeared to have contributed to Korean democracy as much as he detracted from it with his involvement in the 1979 coup.

Anti-Corruption Campaign

To set Korea on a path toward a fully democratic community, Kim Young Sam as a presidential candidate saw it absolutely necessary "to free politics from the yoke of money." On the first day of his presidency, Kim proclaimed to the nation that he would not receive a single penny from the business community, and he would eliminate the old style of politics characterized by collusion between politics and business. Until his 5-year term ended in February 1998, President Kim was widely believed to have kept this promise.

Obviously, Kim made a clean break with the age-old Korean presidential politics of illicitly amassing political funds. His immediate predecessor Roh Tae Woo was widely known (or generally believed) to have controlled a US$650 million political slush fund from 1988 to 1993. For the 1980–88 period, Chun Doo Whan was also widely known to have amassed an even larger fund, totaling more than US$900 million, by accepting bribes and kickbacks from large conglomerates (Jordan 1995; Pollack 1996).

In addition to his refusal to accept political donations from various businesses, President Kim worked to bring the country's institutionalized corruption under control. He initiated a series of ethical standards and anti-corruption laws, including the Public Servants' Ethics Law (Kil 1993; M. Kim 1994). Those engaged in the illegal practices of bribery and kickbacks or the unethical practices of real estate speculation have been purged and barred from assuming public office under his government. All elected officials and high-ranking public servants are now legally required to reveal their assets on an annual basis. More notably, a new "real name" system of financial transactions has replaced the former system based on aliases, which served as the main device for illicit transactions of politicians and government officials with businessmen and other patrons.

Undoubtedly, such a broad range of anti-corruption reforms for the promotion of democratic consolidation is hardly prescribed in the

Table 7.3 Perceptions of Elected Politicians and Civil Servants as "Corrupt" (from none to all, of every ten)

Number Mentioned	Elected Politicians	Civil Servants
0 (none)	0.0	0.0
1	0.3	1.5
2	2.0	4.6
3	3.4	7.7
4	3.0	5.2
5	17.9	25.4
6	9.1	9.1
7	12.7	10.7
8	17.6	11.7
9	13.0	7.7
10 (all)	9.8	4.5
No answer	11.2	11.9
Total	100.0	100.0
(N)	(1000)	(1000)
[Mean]	[6.9]	[5.9]

Source: 1996 Korean Democratization Survey

current literature on the subject. And, many advocates of liberal or consociational democracy would naturally question whether those anti-corruption measures are really needed for a country that has, peacefully and successfully, established all the institutions and procedures required of a democratic political order. In an attempt to test the rationale of President Kim's unconventional campaign, the 1996 survey asked two sets of questions: one tapped the extent of corrupt practices among public officials, the other measured inclinations toward corruption among the mass citizenry.

Table 7.3 reports responses to the questions of how many of every ten elected officials and civil servants Koreans would think were engaged in corrupt practices (see Appendix B H2 and H3). These survey responses, although highly speculative, offer a new light on the darkest arena of Korean politics. Of the 88 percent of the sample who agreed to answer the questions, none said that every politician or civil servant is unmarred by political corruption. More surprisingly, two in every three Koreans (69%) rated half or more of their civil servants as corrupt, and eight out of ten (80%) rated more than half of elected officials that way. Only a small minority (19%) believed that less than one-half of their politicians and government officials were corrupt. Clearly, these findings illustrate the fact that neither the promulgation of a new democratic constitution nor the competitive election of public officials has brought about any significant shift in the rules by which the political game is actually played

Table 7.4 Public Approval and Disapproval of Specific Corrupt Practices (percent)

Corrupt Practices	Very bad (A)	Bad (B)	Not bad (C)	Not bad at all (D)	No answer (DK)	Subtotal (A+B)
To receive a gift at election time	64.4	19.9	12.8	1.2	1.7	84.3
To be treated to a meal at election time	59.1	21.9	15.0	2.4	1.6	81.0
To receive compensation for work performed at election time	53.0	22.9	17.9	4.8	1.4	75.9
To give a gift to government workers	70.0	20.8	7.0	0.8	1.4	90.8
To give pocket money to government workers for holidays	65.7	21.1	9.5	2.2	1.5	86.8
To treat government workers to meals in the course of conducting one's business	46.5	22.9	24.2	5.0	1.4	69.4
To donate money to politicians for the benefit of one's business	64.3	21.7	10.4	2.1	1.5	86.0

Source: 1996 Korean Democratization Survey

in Korea. The game is still, more often than not, played by its age-old informal rules of *particularism.*

To what degree are average Koreans inclined to play the political game by the universalistic rules of democratic politics? In the 1996 survey, we asked respondents to judge seven common practices in Korean politics from the ethical point of view that involves selling and buying gifts or favors for personal political gain (Appendix B H1). The practices surveyed were: (1) receiving a gift at election time, (2) being treated to a meal at election time, (3) receiving compensation for work performed at election time, (4) giving a gift to government workers, (5) giving pocket money to government workers for holidays, (6) treating government workers to meals in the course of conducting one's business, and (7) donating money to politicians for the benefit of one's business.

As Table 7.4 shows, large majorities (ranging from 69% to 91%), judged those practices as ethically wrong by saying that they are "somewhat bad" or "very bad." The percentages condemning them as "very bad" range, however, from a low of 47 percent to a high of 70 percent. In the case of treating government officials to meals, a majority (53%) did not judge it as "very bad." These findings, taken together, indicate that nearly one-third or more are not completely dissociated or liberated from most of the corrupt practices of the authoritarian past.

When all seven practices are considered together, a majority (56%) did not judge all or most of them as "very bad." As Figure 7.3 shows, nearly one-fifth (19%) refused to reject any of them as "very bad" while less than one-third (32%) found all of the old habits of corrupt politics unacceptable. This indicates that particularistic orientations of toleration for corruption are still highly resilient and widely pervasive among the Korean population. Many Koreans are not yet ready to commit themselves to the constitutional rules of their democratic game, which assert that trading favorable political and governmental decisions for money is neither appropriate nor legitimate.

There is little doubt that in Korea, as in other new democracies, two democratically elected governments have failed to create a *Rechtsstaat*, a law-bound state. Its state apparatus is not always subjected to the rule of law that Linz & Stepan (1996b) characterize as an indispensable condition for democratic consolidation. As an illustration, major business executives are still known to pay top government officials "rice-cake expenses" of between US$6500 and US$19,500 on major holidays (Glain 1995). The Korean people, as voters as well as elected officials, are far from a fully democratic community, which is habituated to constitutionalism and the rule of law. For this reason, President Kim Young Sam

Figure 7.3   Percentages Assessing Corrupt Practices as "Very Bad"
(from none to all of seven practices)

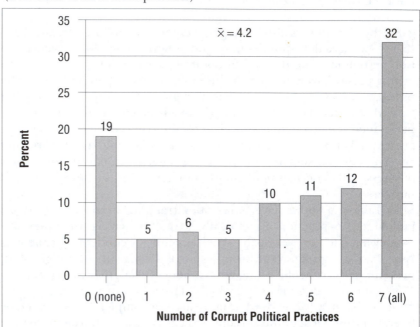

Source: 1996 Korean Democratization Survey

launched successive waves of anti-corruption campaigns for the consolidation of nascent democracy.

How effective have President Kim's anti-corruption campaigns been
in controlling and eradicating political corruption, which is endemic in
Korea and fueled by thirty years of authoritarian rule? How effective has
his moral crusade against illicit and unethical behavior been in transforming the primordial and particularistic standards of behavior among
the Korean people? To explore these questions, we asked respondents
to the 1996 survey whether they had experienced any change in the level
of political corruption under the Kim Young Sam government
(Appendix B H4).

As Table 7.5 shows, a large majority (71%) reported having experienced at least some degree of decrease in political corruption. A small
minority (4%), on the other hand, reported having experienced
increases. By a large margin of eighteen to one, the experience of
decreased corruption overwhelms that of increased corruption. Thus,
the evidence was supportive of the view that "the corrupt old system is
gradually giving way to one that is more transparent and market-
oriented" (Brull 1995: 26). Nevertheless, Kim's anti-corruption

Table 7.5 Corruption Change During the Kim Young Sam Government

Changes	Percent	(N)
Decreased a lot	16	(163)
Decreased somewhat	55	(553)
Changed little	23	(225)
Increased somewhat	3	(33)
Increased a lot	1	(5)
No answer	2	(21)
(Total)	(100.0)	(1000)

Source: 1996 Korean Democratization Survey

measures have been cut short by the age-old, Confucian cultural norm of reciprocity, and those measures have become impotent in the rising tide of materialism and personal greed.

In the latest 1997 survey we further attempted to assess the lasting impact of President Kim's earlier anti-corruption campaigns by asking respondents to describe the extent to which the Kim Young Sam govern-

Figure 7.4 Perceptions of the Level of Political Corruption of the Kim Young Sam Government

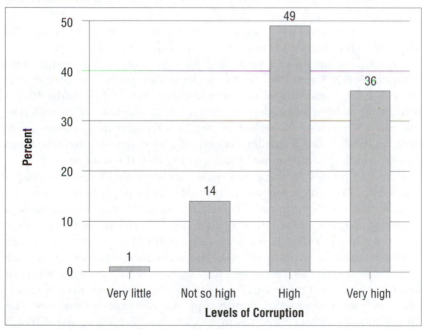

Source: 1997 Korean Democratization Survey

ment was corrupt (Appendix B H5). As expected from the massive incidence of corruption involving one of the largest conglomerates, cabinet
ministers, National Assemblymen, and his own son, nearly one-half
(49%) replied that the current level of corruption of Kim's government
is "high," and over one-third (36%) even said that it was "very high."
Only a small minority perceived it as either "not so high" (14%) or "very
little" (1%). This finding illustrates the fact that for all the important
steps Kim took for the 1993–97 period, the age-old custom of corruption
was not dying at all in the Korean political marketplace; instead, the
informal norms were still overpowering the formal rules of the newly
implanted democratic political game (H. B. Im 1997c: 15).

Civic Orientations

How effective have President Kim's campaigns been in transforming
particularistic Koreans into communitarian people? In order to build a
democratic community, Koreans should acquire a strong sense of a
common identity and attend to the obligation of democratic citizenship
(March & Olsen 1995). As citizens of a democratic community, they
"should have empathic sympathy for the feelings and desires of others,
and, in some circumstances, should subordinate their own individual or
group interests to the collective good of the community" (March &
Olsen 1995: 38).

How civic-minded are Koreans in their political and social lives? To
determine the degree of their civic-mindedness, the 1996 survey asked
two questions: one on social trust and the other on political compromise
(Appendix B M3 and M4). To the question, "In general, to what extent
do you trust a majority of the people these days?" three-fifths (60%)
expressed at least some degree of trust in a majority of their fellow
Koreans. When asked whether or not "it is dangerous to compromise
with political rivals," a smaller majority (52%) expressed their desire to
opt for political compromise by disagreeing with the statement.

When responses to these two questions are considered together, a
majority of Korean citizens are found to be lacking a coherent view of a
democratic civic community. Nearly one-fifth (19%) neither trust a
majority of other citizens nor accept them as equals in the political
process. On the other hand, about one-half (51%) trust many other
fellow citizens but refuse to make political compromises with those
citizens, or they are at least willing to compromise with others but do not
trust them much. Only a small minority (30%) have acquired a strong
sense of both a communal identity and civic obligations to others. The
implication is that President Kim was far from achieving the difficult
goal he personally set for the creation of a democratic community.

Consequences for Cultural Democratization

How has President Kim's anti-authoritarian and anti-corruption campaign, undertaken in the latter part of 1995, affected the cultural process of democratic consolidation? To assess its impact on cultural democratization, we first selected two orientations: one toward democracy and the other against authoritarianism (Appendix B C1.3 and S1.1). Then, the aggregate ratings of pro-democratic and anti-authoritarian orientations among the entire Korean population are compared before and after two former presidents and their cronies were arrested and imprisoned on charges of authoritarian crimes and amassing illicit fortunes.

A comparison of percentage ratings for 1994 and 1996 in Table 7.6 indicates that this campaign was instrumental mostly in delegitimating authoritarian rule. By uncovering authoritarian brutalities and corruptions, the campaign helped over one-tenth (11%) to discontinue their affinity for authoritarian rule. On the other hand, it contributed little to reorienting non-democrats toward democracy. As measured on a 10-point scale, the average level of Korean desire to live in a democracy remained at 8.6 – the same as it was before the campaign began.

In Figure 7.5, we now explore, at the individual level, the impact of President Kim's rectification campaign on anti-authoritarian and pro-democratic orientations. Underlying this exploration is the hypothesis that stronger supporters of the campaign, if it is conducive, are more pro-democratic and anti-authoritarian than others. Figure 7.5 cross-tabulates the combined level of support for President Kim's anti-authoritarian and anti-corruption campaign with the means of preference for democracy-in-principle and dissatisfaction with the Chun Doo Whan regime, both of which are measured on a 10-point scale.

As expected, the higher the level of support for President Kim's campaign, the higher the level of democratic preference and the greater

Table 7.6 Democratic and Authoritarian Orientations Before and After the Anti-Authoritarian Campaign (percent)

Year	Dissatisfaction with Authoritarian Rule	Preference for Democracy	Both*	(N)
1994	70	92	66	(1500)
1996	81	94	77	(1000)

*Expressing dissatisfaction with authoritarian rule and preference for democracy
Sources: Korean Democratization Surveys (1994 & 1996)

Figure 7.5 Orientations to the Chun Doo Whan Government and Democracy by Levels of Support for the Rectification Campaign

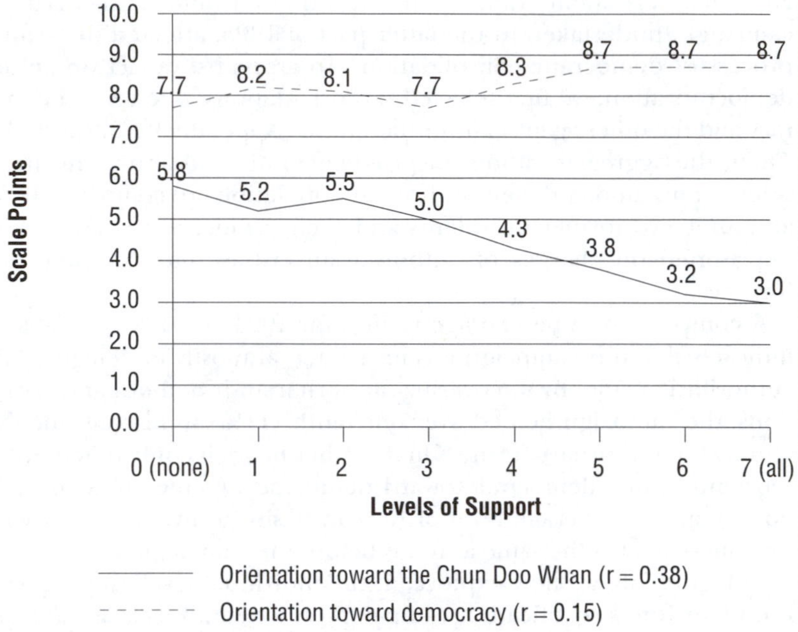

Source: 1996 Korean Democratization Survey

the level of dissatisfaction with the old authoritarian government. As simple correlation coefficients of 0.38 and 0.15 indicate, however, anti-authoritarian orientations, as compared to pro-democratic ones, are over two times more strongly associated with the same experience in the campaign to expose the painful truth about the authoritarian past. This is another piece of evidence suggesting that President Kim's democratic reform program was far more conducive to delegitimating authoritarianism than legitimating democracy.

Rewriting History

Correcting or righting the distortions of history concerning the brutality and corruption of the past governments was one of the main objectives President Kim Young Sam personally set for the rectification campaign. To what degree has progress been made in achieving this goal of rewriting history? This question requires an examination of what was and was not written about the past governments and their presidents before the campaign began.

It is fair to say that history was overly kind to Chun Doo Whan and Roh Tae Woo, who led the 1979 military mutiny and the Kwangju massacre, until President Kim Young Sam ordered a full investigation of Roh's slush fund scandal on October 19, 1995. As former presidents, they lived extremely well in expensive homes with government pensions and perquisites worth about US$250,000 a year. They were described admirably in Korean school textbooks as national leaders who contributed to economic development and democratic transition. Nowhere in the textbooks was a single line written about the Kwangju massacre, in which at least 240 people were reported dead, nor Chun's and Roh's leading roles both in this national tragedy and the 1979 illegal mutiny (Desmond 1995: 21).

These two past presidents were arrested, detained, and tried for a variety of charges – including their involvement in the mutiny and massacre. Did witnessing these extraordinary events serve as an opportunity for average Koreans to recover their history as President Kim

Figure 7.6   Changing Perceptions of the Chun Doo Whan and Roh Tae Woo Governments (on a 1–100 point index)

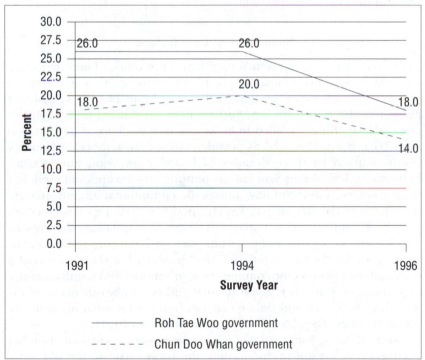

Source: Korean Democratization Surveys (1991, 1994 & 1996)

initially hoped? To explore this question, individual perceptions and judgments of the governments led by Kim's two immediate predecessors are considered together and compared to discern any notable trend over the 1994 to 1996 period. Figure 7.6 presents their combined ratings on a scale in which a score of 1 indicates being fully dissatisfied with a complete dictatorship, and a score of 100 indicates being fully satisfied with a complete democracy.[7]

In November 1994, when Chun and Roh were not only immensely rich with slush funds but also were untouchable by existing laws, the Korean public placed their government on the 1–100 numeric scale at 20 and 26, respectively. In January 1996, when they were standing humbled in white prison uniforms, the same public rated the two governments far more negatively than ever before; they were rated at lows of 14 and 18, respectively. Comparison of the pre-campaign and post-campaign ratings indicates that the Korean public devalued both governments equally – by as much as 30 percent during the first three months of the rectification campaign alone. Based on this finding, it is fair to say that in the wake of the campaign, in their own minds, the Korean people were rewriting the two most painful chapters of recent political history (*Economist* 1996).

Summary and Conclusions

There is little doubt that Kim Young Sam is not much of an intellectual – especially when compared to presidents of some other new democracies, such as Czech President Václav Havel and Brazilian President Fernando Henrique Cardoso. Furthermore, in shifting tides of democratic change Kim has failed to be as steadfast as many of his counterparts have been. However, as president of a new democratic country deeply scarred by three decades of brutal oppression and massive corruption, Kim Young Sam has propounded an exceptional model of democratic consolidation that utilizes the communitarian and substantive notion of democratic politics. His model, unlike the ones based on the liberal and related notions of democracy, emphasizes the importance of purifying the authoritarian past and purging authoritarian elements from the democratic political process. For the creation of a truly and fully democratic community, Kim's model also emphasizes the importance of transforming primordial and particularistic orientations of ordinary citizens and public officials into communitarian and universalistic ones (Fox 1994; Roniger & Gunes-Ayata 1994).

The Kim Young Sam model of negative democratic consolidation has been quite successful in dismantling the power base of the old authoritarian governments and delegitimating authoritarian rule itself.

However, Kim's model has not been very effective in consolidating democratic institutions and legitimating democratic values. At the same time, while it has prevented the kind of overwhelming wrong-doing that was common among his predecessors, the model has failed to uproot the endemic political corruption and irregularities in Korean business and politics and to transform primordial and particularistic political habits. Political corruption, therefore, remains as Korean as *Kimchi* (Kristof 1997a).

Nonetheless, President Kim's conscious efforts to rectify the various sins of the authoritarian past and to confront directly the chronic ills as well as paradoxes of the democratic present constitute significant evidence that Korean democracy is very much in the process of consolidation, which features not only representational procedures but also the following substantive outcomes: human dignity, justice, and truth. To advance these outcomes further, every citizen and public official may need to be reminded that democratic governance is impossible if they are concerned only with their own self-interest and ignore the common good. From the spectacle of President Kim's second son being led to court in a prison uniform and sentenced to three years in prison for bribery and tax evasion, all present and future leaders in government, big business, and the military have now received ample notice that the rule of law, which once was applied only to the powerless and deprived, will now apply to them as well. In the words of Kristof (1997a), an astute observer of Korean democratization, this development constitutes "a stunning demonstration of how Korean democracy has come to apply the rule of law even to the nation's most powerful family."

With the imprisonment of his two immediate predecessors and his own son, President Kim has already established a formidable legacy of negative consolidation for Korea and the rest of the democratizing world. To China, Singapore, and other authoritarian regimes, Kim's rectification campaign has unequivocally illustrated that the mass public will neither forgive nor forget the political oppression even if it is mixed with rapidly rising income (Kristof 1995). To Brazil, Italy, Japan, and other stalled democracies, his anti-corruption campaign has illustrated that their incomplete democracies will never be able to consolidate fully unless collusive institutional ties between political power and business are severed by astutely applied shock therapies or radical surgeries (Brull 1995).

As the *New York Times* (1995) reported, President Kim Young Sam has erected, for his own nation, the institutional foundation that will keep the Korean political process transparent and accountable to ordinary citizens.[8] For younger generations of politically active Koreans, Kim has created an invaluable opportunity to enter politics and manage it professionally. There is little doubt that, in the long run, President Kim's rectification model is more suitable for steering Korea in the direction of becoming a fully democratic community. It can do this by redefining the meaning of democratization and raising the standards of democratic politics itself rather than either the liberal model, which is advocated in the Western scholarly literature on new democracies, or the cohabitation model, which he inherited from his predecessor. In the short run, however, President Kim's democratic reform program has driven Korean democracy more deeply into a multi-party presidential system, a most thorny combination of democratic institutions (Mainwaring 1993). Furthermore, while its successes have infuriated many authoritarians, its failures have disenchanted equally many democrats. For this reason, the Kim Young Sam government ended immensely unpopular, even with those Koreans who elected him to the presidency in 1992.[9]

CHAPTER 8

Acquiring Democratic Orientations

"Human beings do not have some natural affinity for
democratic political orders; inclusive democracy, even if
properly instituted, cannot be expected to develop of itself."
Harry Eckstein (1998: 4)
"Attitudinally, democracy becomes the only game in town
when, even in the face of severe political and economic
crises, the overwhelming majority of the people believe that
any further political change must emerge from within the
parameters of democratic procedures."
Juan Linz & Alfred Stepan (1996a: 5)

The supposition that a civic culture emerges as a necessary or sufficient condition prior to democratization (Inglehart 1988) has been
challenged by the hypothesis that changes in political culture may
be more likely to follow than precede the onset of democratization
(Muller & Seligson 1994; see also Jackman & Miller 1996). Whatever
the status of the controversy over sequencing and causation, however,
how political culture changes during the course of democratization
remains a matter of some uncertainty. In thinking about the dynamics
of popular support for new democracies, therefore, a number of
questions arise. In what ways do citizens orient themselves toward
democratization once the process gets underway? What motivates
citizens to modify their support for the transition to democracy? Does
a changing economy or some other set of concerns alter commitment
to democratization?

This chapter compares the dynamics of popular reactions to democratization in Korea and other new democracies. Beginning with a review
of survey research on mass culture in new democracies, we next develop
a theoretical framework for understanding how and why citizens react to
democratization. The key determinants of such shifts are conceptualized, and their empirical indicators are outlined. Then, we analyze how
and why Korean citizens have adjusted their views on democratization.
Finally, the patterns and sources of shifting orientations in Korea are
compared with the results of research on other new democracies.

Research on Political Culture and Democratization

Numerous surveys have been conducted documenting the levels and origins of support for democratization in Asia (Fu & Chu 1996; Mangahas 1994; Nathan & Shi 1993; Shin & Shyu 1997), Eastern and Central Europe (Evans & Whitefield 1995; Klingemann 1997; McIntosh & Abele 1993; Rose & Haerpfer 1994; Rose, Mishler & Haerpfer 1998; Weil 1993), Southern Europe (McDonough, Barnes & Lopez Pina 1986; Montero, Gunther & Torcal 1997), and Latin America (Moises 1993; Lagos 1997; Seligson & Booth 1993). Instructive as it is, for our purposes this body of work suffers from two deficiencies.

First, as Rose & Mishler (1994: 161) note, most studies have failed to deal adequately with the dynamics of individual responses to democratization. To some extent, this omission reflects a temporal constraint. In some countries democratization is so recent that first-in-the-field studies can only register provisional cross-sections of opinion. Moreover, the logistics of systematically monitoring public opinion under precarious political conditions can be daunting. Yet even when sufficient time has passed and periodic data gathering proves to be feasible, surveys have rarely provided a methodological basis for unraveling the dynamics of political orientations. With few exceptions (Gibson 1996a), prior surveys do not employ a panel design that involves interviewing and reinterviewing the same respondents, and even the panel studies confine themselves to the attitudinal dynamics within democratic regimes, since they lack data for inter-regime comparisons. Nor, again with few exceptions (Rose & Haerpfer 1996), do surveys taken at a single point in time make an effort to estimate change by asking respondents to recollect how their attitudes may have shifted as democratization unfolds.

Second, most of these surveys are based on a liberal notion of democratic politics, which Barber (1984: 4) characterizes as "a 'thin' theory of democracy." Predicated on the assumption that what is personally desirable and preferable to individual citizens is the paramount determinant of their commitment, or lack of it, to democracy, the approach is open to a pair of criticisms.

The strong criticism, advanced by communitarian and institutional theorists (Barber 1984; Caney 1992; Fukuyama 1995b; Marcus & Hanson 1993; March & Olsen 1995; Warren 1992), is that the liberal model, as discussed in Chapter 7, disregards the role of community, or social setting, within which personal desires and preferences for democratic politics develop. Largely ungrounded in the historical and cultural configurations that shape personal values, surveys adhering to the liberal democratic model (Dahl 1971) convey a picture of democratization that may not travel well.[1]

A second limitation entails a variant on the difficulties of inferring aggregate *culture* from individual *opinion*. While personal preferences for or against democracy may be of interest, individual opinions are not equivalent to judgments of how suitable democracy may be for the country as a whole (Evans & Whitefield 1995; Thomassen 1995). In this instance, the distinction is more between individual desires, on the one hand, and perceptions of collective feasibility on the other than between contending definitions of democratic norms as liberal or communitarian. Though they may be connected, opinions about democracy-in-principle ("desirability") and perceptions of democracy-in-practice ("suitability") are not equivalent to one another.

While we do not engage in the debate over liberal versus communitarian models of democracy, the ensuing analysis does stress the distinction between: (1) democratic principles as statements of individual preferences, and (2) perceptions of the viability of the democratic venture as a collective undertaking. In effect, we treat the latter set of orientations as sociotropic – as attitudes that, by taking into account collective conditions, may be related loosely to personal conviction.

Theoretical Considerations

Why do people maintain or shift their support for democratization? Functional theories of attitude change suggest the opposite of what has been offered to explain the apparent resilience of support for democratization in Central and Eastern Europe. The functional approach argues that citizens either remain committed to or withdraw their support for regime change based on how such change serves various functions or goals to which they give priority (Gastil 1992; see also Schwartz 1987). If they feel that democratization promotes those goals, citizens become more supportive of the process; if they feel that it hinders them, they become less supportive.

A functional perspective on the attitudinal dynamics associated with democratization clashes with explanations of popular support for regime change in Central and Eastern Europe. In his research on the former Soviet Union, for example, Duch (1995: 135) argues:

> They [Soviet citizens] did not reject democratization because support for democratic institutions is not instrumental, i.e. it is not seen simply as a means to achieve a specific political or economic goal such as economic prosperity or better sanitation services. Rather, individual preferences for democratic institutions are the result of more diffuse effects such as education, exposure to Western media, and what might be called the "fad" of democracy that was pervasive in Soviet society at the time.

The difficulty here derives from a confusion between broad, shallow ("fashionable") dispositions and deep-rooted values. This problem is compounded by the fact that the middle ground occupied by assessments of rather concrete political operations is not considered at all. Preference for democracy as a remote and probably vague political ideal or principle and commitment to democracy as a project that involves the installation of new institutions and procedures are conceptually distinct (Weffort 1993: 253). It is far-fetched to suppose that endorsement of democratic institutions and procedures can be sustained diffusely, even if it can "take off" or get on the political agenda this way, without regard to performance. Like citizens of the United States and other consolidated democracies who have withdrawn trust in various democratic institutions (Dogan 1997; Lipset 1994; Miller & Borrelli 1991; Nye, Zelikow & King 1997), citizens of new democracies may decline to support democratic institutions unless the institutions serve certain functions.

What are these functions? Rousseau, Mill, Dewey, Pateman, Barber, and other theorists have argued that democracy fulfils a variety of specific ends (Caney 1992; Dahl 1989; Powell 1982; Warren 1992). While all of these functions can be said to involve payoffs, for example, physical well-being, autonomy, social identity and a sense of belonging, not all of them are reducible to narrowly material or directly instrumental returns (March & Olsen 1995: 55). In particular, citizens can be expected to judge democratization in light of both its economic and non-economic repercussions. Almost certainly, assessments of economic welfare alone provide an inadequate rationale for changes in popular orientations toward democratization.

Recent evidence lends support to the claim that citizens expect more than improved economic well-being from democratization (Drakulic 1993; Finifter & Mickiewicz 1992; McIntosh & Abele 1993; Song 1997). Material considerations may not be the primary, much less the only, reasons why ordinary citizens support and participate in democratic transitions (Sartori 1991; Weffort 1989). A growing collection of empirical clues suggests an approach to the democratization of political culture that goes beyond the usual economic line-up (Abramson & Inglehart 1995; Huntington 1996a; Klingemann & Fuchs 1995).

By itself, the argument that economic factors alone fail to explain what impels citizens to support democratization does not reveal much. We need to specify what these other factors are and how they operate. With appropriate refinements (to be detailed in the next section) we divide the causal factors behind support for democratization into three major categories: (1) perceptions of economic conditions, (2) assessments of the repercussions of democratization on the quality of life, and (3) evaluations of the political performance of democratic governments.

Modeling the Dynamics of Support for Democratization

As already discussed in Chapter 2, classical and contemporary theory contends that citizens embrace democratization to improve their economic lot and to enhance other dimensions of their lives and, perhaps, the collective good. From the perspective of functional theories of attitude change, citizens modify their political sentiments in response to perceptions of how democratic reforms have affected their personal and collective lives in the past and in accord with expectations of how the process will do so in the future.

The repercussions of democratic reform on: (a) economic well-being and (b) quality of life can themselves be visualized along a pair of dimensions, each following (c) an egocentric/sociotropic distinction and (d) a retrospective/prospective split. The combinations produce a total of eight evaluations: (1) egocentric–retrospective economic, (2) egocentric–prospective economic, (3) sociotropic–retrospective economic, (4) sociotropic–prospective economic, (5) egocentric–retrospective life quality, (6) egocentric–prospective life quality, (7) sociotropic–retrospective life quality, and (8) sociotropic–prospective life quality.

We hypothesize that evaluations of life quality alter democratic support more than economic assessments do, for two reasons. In general, the notion of "life quality" allows for a more comprehensive account of human life than does an exclusive focus on economic well-being (Campbell 1981; Campbell, Converse & Rodgers 1976). Perhaps more decisively, in a newly industrialized country like Korea, where economic prosperity contributed to undermining an authoritarian state, democratization tends to be viewed as more than an escape from economic poverty and hardship (H. B. Im 1994; S. Han 1990; S. Kim 1997).

In addition, sociotropic evaluations can be expected to drive democratic support more powerfully than egocentric evaluations do, while retrospective evaluations are expected to do so more than prospective evaluations. This set of propositions flows directly from the literature on electoral behavior, which has shown that citizens are more likely to view political change as a means of improving (or jeopardizing) collective, rather than individual, well-being. Citizens are also more likely to modify their views in response to past experiences than as a function of future expectations (Lewis-Beck 1988; MacKuen, Erikson & Stimson, 1992; Mishler & Rose 1994).

An expressly political set of perceptions, focused on governmental performance, rounds out the factors expected to influence support for democratization. As with economic and quality-of-life perceptions, the retrospective–prospective distinction makes sense for evaluations and expectations of governmental performance. However, since political repercussions are collective virtually by definition, we do not press the egocentric–sociotropic division for this dimension. As for the effects of judgments and expectations of political performance, we hypothesize that their impact will tend to be at least as powerful, and perhaps greater, than the force of judgments about the economy and quality of life. In nascent democracies, perceptions of governmental performance may be barely distinguishable from evaluations of democratic governance itself. In this sense assessments of the performance of a particular government may be easily confused with judgments of the legitimacy of democracy.

Measurement
Dependent Variables

Respondents to the 1994 survey were first asked to indicate their personal *desire* for democratic change under the current government and to recall how desirable they felt democracy was during the previous governments: one democratic and the other authoritarian. They were then asked to reflect upon the condition of their country during each regime, and were also asked to indicate the extent to which they felt democratization was *suitable* for the country during those times. This series of questions makes a simple, but crucial, distinction between the *desirability* of democracy as a matter of personal preference or principle and perceptions of the *suitability* of democracy as collective practice. This corresponds to the distinction between egocentric and sociotropic opinion.

To estimate how these views might have changed as democratization unfolded, respondents were asked to recall their past opinions and to state their present ones (see Appendix B C1 for the wording of these questions). How much did they want to democratize the political system while they lived under authoritarian rule (1980–88)? How much did they want to democratize it under the first democratically elected government of Roh Tae Woo (1988–93)? And how much did they want to push democratization under the second democratic government of Kim Young Sam (1993–98)?

To gauge support for democratization as a collective enterprise in the Korean context, respondents were given a set of three questions inquiring, in effect, how ready they felt the country was for democracy. For each of the last three governments, respondents were asked, as shown in Appendix B D1, to judge the *suitability* of a democratic political system for the nation as a whole on a 10-point scale, with a score of 1 representing complete unsuitability and a score of 10 indicating complete suitability.[2]

The dependent variables, democratic desirability and suitability, are handled as inter-regime differences once we get the introductory, univariate presentation. The key contrast is the algebraic differences between support for democracy at the present time, during the second democratic government (t_3), and support for democracy during military rule (t_1). Thus, for example, the dependent variable becomes support for democracy-in-principle during the Kim Young Sam government, minus support for democracy as recollected under the Chun Doo Whan dictatorship.

Independent Variables

Unlike its counterparts in Central and Eastern Europe, Korea became an economic powerhouse while under authoritarian rule (Sakong 1993). In a manner similar to Spain's experience, economic prosperity, rather than hardship, preceded the demise of the authoritarian regime. To be sure, concern with the economy did not vanish as Korea modernized, and democratization probably introduced a degree of uncertainty about the economic direction of the country. Nevertheless, the standard of living continued to rise (Moon & Kim 1996b). It is this situation, which contrasts with the relatively desperate economic straits of some post-communist democracies, that led us to stress a range of economic and non-economic correlates of popular support for democratization.

To assess the impact of the changing economy on democratic support, we asked a set of four questions concerning retrospective and prospective evaluations of personal and collective economic conditions (Appendix B R1–R4). For retrospective assessments, respondents were asked whether they felt: (1) their family, and (2) the country as a whole were better-off than they had been under the authoritarian government. For prospective evaluations, they were asked how they believed their: (3) family, and (4) the nation as a whole would fare economically over the coming five years.

The impact of democratization on perceptions of the quality of life was measured according to Cantril's (1965) "self-anchoring striving scale," which is widely used in studying life quality around the world (Andrews & Withey 1976; Campbell, Converse & Rodgers 1976). This device asks individuals to imagine "the best life" and "the worst life" and to indicate their past, present, and future locations on a 10-point scale spanning the two extremes. Comparison of ratings across points in time allows us to estimate experienced and expected changes in the quality of life.

The quality-of-life series contains six items rather than the four tallied for perceptions of economic conditions; the extra pair comes from assessments of life quality at the present time in addition to evaluations of the past and projecting of the future. Thus, respondents were asked two sets of three questions: one set was to determine individual concerns and the other was to assess their perceptions of the collective, or national, quality of life (see Appendixes B I1 and J1). The questions were: (1) where they (and the nation) stood on the scale while living under the authoritarian regime, (2) where they (and the nation) stand at the present time while living under the democratic government, and (3) where they would expect themselves (and the nation) to be five years hence if Korea continued to democratize. Present and past ratings furnish the ingredients for comparisons that estimate the experienced impact of democratization on personal lives and perceptions of the nation as a whole. Similarly, present and future ratings establish the basis for comparisons to estimate the expected impact of democratization on individuals and on the nation.[3]

The experienced and expected impacts of democratization on political life and governmental performance in general were measured in terms of a cluster of three variables, two single-item measures and one composite measure. The single-item measures: (1) retrospective assessments of the political changes that have taken place since the birth of the Sixth Republic (Appendix B R5), and (2) prospective assessments of political changes over the next five years (Appendix B R6). The composite measure was designed to tap changes in satisfaction with governmental performance in the wake of democratic regime change (Appendix B S1).[4]

Univariate Analysis
Levels and Types of Support for Democratization

Table 8.1 reports three pieces of information concerning the personal and collective domains of support across three successive governments. For each of the two domains, the table presents the percentage who expressed an opinion by choosing one of the ten steps shown on a ladder scale and the percentage of those who refused to do so. The table also reports the mean scores of respondent ratings on the 10-point scale.

Inspection of the percentages and means across the three governments (Chun 1980–88; Roh 1988–93; and Kim 1993–98) shows that as the regime or government changed, support for democratization changed also. For example, the incidence of respondents choosing one of the top three steps (8 through 10) on the scale, expressing a strong desire for democratic change, rose sharply from 43 percent under the authoritarian Chun Doo Whan regime to 54 percent under the first democratic government of Roh Tae Woo, to 81 percent under the

Table 8.1 Variations in Support for Democratization Across Three Government Periods (percent)

Scale points	Democratic Desire			Democratic Suitability		
	Chun period	Roh period	Kim period	Chun period	Roh period	Kim period
1	0.3	0.1	0.1	2.5	1.3	0.7
2	0.3	0.1	0.2	5.5	3.0	0.7
3	1.3	0.5	0.4	14.7	8.1	2.8
4	2.2	1.0	0.7	16.4	11.7	5.3
5	11.4	7.2	2.3	17.3	21.6	10.8
6	13.1	12.5	2.4	13.5	19.7	17.6
7	17.7	17.0	9.2	9.5	14.7	22.3
8	21.6	26.3	25.9	7.9	8.9	20.2
9	8.5	12.5	25.6	1.9	2.5	10.2
10	13.1	15.0	29.0	1.3	1.1	3.6
No opinion	10.5	7.9	4.2	9.5	7.5	5.8
(Mean score)	(7.3)	(7.7)	(8.6)	(5.0)	(5.5)	(6.8)

Source: 1994 Korean Democratization Survey

second democratic government period of Kim Young Sam. The percentage claiming that democratization was highly suitable for Korea (again using the top of the scale – 8 through 10 – criterion) more than tripled from 11 percent under authoritarianism to 34 percent under the second democratic period. Over the same period, non-respondents decreased (from 11% to 6%). As Koreans became more familiar with democratic politics, those once among the undecided leaned toward democratization.

Table 8.1 also reveals significant differences between the two domains of support for democratization. While both increase over time, Koreans' avowed desire for democracy is consistently higher than their assessment of democracy's suitability for the country. For example, a large majority (74%) claim to have acquired democratic preferences or sympathies while living under authoritarian rule. However, a majority (56%) felt that democratization would *not* have been suitable for their country during the same period. Even under the civilian democratic government of Kim Young Sam, substantially fewer Koreans consider democratization suitable for the country than those who declare their support of democracy-in-principle. What political system Koreans say they admire as an ideal and what they feel is suitable for Korea differ. Desirability is one thing, and suitability is another.

Table 8.2 summarizes changes in democratic support by tracking the combinations of personal preference and judgments of suitability across three government periods. A plurality (46%) assert that while they personally favored democratization in the authoritarian period, at the time, they refused to endorse it for the nation. However, by the time of the first democratic government period, a plurality (42%) favored democracy as a personal preference *and* viewed it as suitable for the nation. And during the second democratic government, a large majority (71%) had become both personally and "collectively" supportive of democracy. Thus, during the seven years of democratization in Korea,

Table 8.2 Variations in Types of Support for Democratization Across Three Government Periods (percent)

Types		Government Periods		
Desire	Suitability	Chun	Roh	Kim
No	No	20.0	12.0	5.1
No	Yes	5.9	4.7	2.8
Yes	No	45.9	41.3	21.0
Yes	Yes	28.2	42.0	71.1

Source: 1994 Korean Democratization Survey

the number of those who saw democracy as both desirable and feasible increased by two-and-a-half times (28% to 71%). Conversely, the fraction of those neither personally nor nationally supportive of change decreased sharply (from 20% to 5%). As democracy took hold, negative dispositions toward democratization became positive more readily than positive attitudes became negative.

Dynamics of Support for Democratization

Table 8.3 documents the dynamics of support for democratization from a larger perspective. The array was generated by combining the preference and suitability indicators for each of the three governments. This enables us to estimate the proportions of "pure" democrats – those who claim to have consistently favored democratization from the authoritarian period onward – as well as the pure anti-democrats – those who admitted to rejecting the democratic option throughout the entire period. The incidence of these unequivocal types is just about the same, between a fifth and a quarter of the respondents in either case.

Beyond this symmetry, of perhaps greater diagnostic interest is the fact that the largest category, nearly one-third (31%) is formed by Koreans who recall starting out as unconvinced about democracy during the authoritarian years. They persisted in their doubts during the first democratic government and finally acceded to the appeal of democracy by the time of the second democratic government. Significantly, the second largest category of changers (16%) consists of those who started out as sceptics and claim to have opted for democracy "the first time around," during the Roh Tae Woo government. By contrast, switchers

Table 8.3 Comparing and Summarizing the Dynamics of Support for Democratization (percent)

Patterns	Government Periods			Dimensions		
	Chun	Roh	Kim	Personal desire	Collective suitability	Both
A	No	No	No	4.7	20.0	23.5
B	No	No	Yes	9.5	29.1	30.8
C	No	Yes	Yes	11.0	15.3	15.6
D	Yes	No	No	0.7	1.7	1.3
E	Yes	Yes	No	1.9	2.9	2.3
F	Yes	Yes	Yes	69.7	27.1	22.2
G	Other patterns			2.5	3.9	4.3

Source: 1994 Korean Democratization Survey

from an initial pro-democratic to an eventually anti-democratic stance constitute a very small fraction (less than 4%) of the total.

These empirical patterns suggest two related points. One is that, while over two-thirds (69%) of the respondents are self-described democrats by the time the transition had shown its promise by managing to constitute two governments in a row, nearly half (46%) of the respondents are those who came to side with democratization only after exhibiting considerable caution about the process during its early and middle years. The most characteristic pattern is one that shows democratization picking up support as the process unfolds rather than reflecting popular consensus or euphoria from the beginning.

Second, this ambivalence and provisional commitment rings true in the Korean case where democratization entailed a measure of risk in the wake of the prosperity associated with authoritarian rule. There was clearly some scepticism about fixing a political system, which in the eyes of many did not appear to be grievously broken. This baseline helps account for the gradualistic, prudent air of democratic "values" surrounding the Korean transition as opposed to the early reports of diffuse and pervasive enthusiasm in Eastern and Central Europe (Dalton 1994; Duch 1995; Gibson, Duch & Tedin 1992; Huntington 1991; Weil 1993).

Bivariate Analysis

As a first step in exploring the forces that shape mass opinion during democratization, we examine the relationships between perceptions of economic conditions and life quality, on the one hand, and changes in personal desire for and commitment to democratic change as suitable to the nation, on the other. The rationale is straightforward: to check for signs that the economic and quality-of-life perceptions might be worth analyzing further as determinants of support for democracy-in-principle or as judgments of its suitability, or both. Table 8.4 reports the correlation coefficients summarizing the relationships between the four pairs of predictors and the two dependent variables.

The personal desire of Koreans for democratization varies very little across perceptions of economic conditions or quality of life. Shifts in personal democratic preferences bear almost no connection to retrospective or prospective evaluations of economic conditions or life quality, whether viewed individually or as descriptions of collective circumstances. By contrast, these perceptions are significantly related to judgments concerning the country's readiness for democracies; as the economy or quality of life was perceived to improve, Korea was considered better prepared for democratic change.

Table 8.4 Correlations Between Changes in Democratic Support and Perceptions of Economic Conditions and Life Quality (Pearson correlation coefficients)

Perspectives Variables	Democratic Support	
	Personal desire	Collective suitability
Egocentric Retrospective		
Economic conditions	0.03	0.25*
Life quality	0.05	0.31*
Egocentric Prospective		
Economic conditions	0.03	0.16*
Life quality	0.00	0.07*
Sociotropic Retrospective		
Economic conditions	0.05	0.26*
Life quality	0.05	0.36*
Sociotropic Prospective		
Economic conditions	0.03	0.21*
Life quality	0.05	0.07*

*Significant at the 0.05 level
Source: 1994 Korean Democratization Survey

Table 8.5 documents how the dynamics of support for democratization are affected by negative perceptions of its consequences for economic well-being and life quality. A summary index of such negative perceptions was constructed by tallying the number of times in which democratization was retrospectively and prospectively thought to detract from the personal and national spheres of economic well-being or life quality. The index ranges from a low of 0 to a high of 4; it reaches the highest value of 4 only when both spheres are perceived to be continuously affected adversely by democratic change. The low of 0 occurs when none of the spheres is perceived to be adversely affected from the past to the future.

Not surprisingly, Koreans are reluctant to strengthen their support for democratic change if they perceive its consequences for economic well-being and the quality of life as harmful. There is also a strong indication, as we might expect from studies of sociotropic voting, that perceived deterioration in collective conditions matters more than evaluations of personal economic fortunes for judgments about the viability of democracy. Perhaps most intriguing is the suggestion that perceptions of the collective quality of life more powerfully affect assessments of democratic suitability than do perceptions of the economy in the aggregate. This finding is the most significant evidence that supports Jean-Jacques Rousseau, James Madison, Alexis de Tocqueville, and other theorists who argue that democracy maximizes the public good by aggregating and reconciling conflicting interests among divergent citizen groups.

Table 8.5   Magnitude of Changes in Support for Democratization by Negative
Perceptions of Economic Conditions and Life Quality*

| | Economic Conditions | | Life Quality | |
	Personal desire	Collective suitability	Personal desire	Collective suitability
(None) 0	1.3	2.1	1.4	2.1
1	1.2	1.6	1.1	1.3
2	1.1	0.9	1.0	0.6
3	1.1	0.4	1.3	−0.7
(All) 4	0.9	0.5	−0.2	−1.8
Pearson correlation	−0.05	−0.23	−0.09	−0.28

*Changes in personal desire and collective suitability are calculated by
subtracting the scores for the authoritarian government from those for
the current democratic government
Source: 1994 Korean Democratization Survey

The differential impact of economics and life quality becomes clearer
in Figure 8.1, which compares the percentages expressing declines in
either of the two domains of democratic support as a function of negative
perceptions of: (a) economic conditions, and (b) quality of life. Clearly,
the fall-off in support is steeper when quality of life, rather than economic
circumstances, is taken into account. At the extreme, when democratization is viewed as lowering the quality of life, 60 percent moved away
from supporting change. When the same change is viewed as lowering
economic well-being, however, a minority (33%) retreat from supporting
the idea of democratization. It is the declining quality of life, not just
economic ill-being, that turns average Koreans away from democracy.

Our first-cut analysis suggests, then, that declarations of personal
desirability and collective suitability regarding democracy do not shift at
the same pace and do not react similarly to the same forces. Of the two
domains, the personal tends to be far steadier than the collective. The
former reacts weakly, if at all, to signals from the economic and social
environment. Also, evaluations of economic conditions appear to be less
powerful than perceptions of life quality when forces shaping changes
in estimates of suitability of democracy are considered.

Multivariate Analysis

How do perceptions of the economy and life quality prompt Koreans to
modify their attitudes toward democratization? To explore this question,
the measures of support along the personal and collective dimensions of

Figure 8.1   Percentages Expressing Declines in Support of Democratization by Negative Perceptions of Economic Conditions and Life Quality

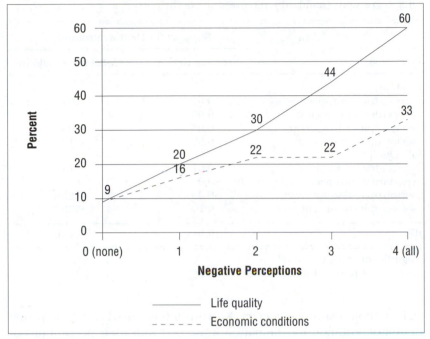

Source: 1994 Korean Democratization Survey

democracy were separately regressed on assessments of economic conditions and life quality from retrospective and prospective perspectives. Standardized multiple regression coefficients and the coefficients of determination for each analysis are reported in Table 8.6.

Only one of the eight predictors is significantly associated with variation in personal desire for democratization. Moreover, the predictors as a whole account for only 1 percent of the variance. In effect, the personal desire for democratic change has nothing to do with how well or poorly the economy and the quality of life are perceived. In this sense, the desire for democracy can be understood to be acquired *diffusely* rather than instrumentally. It appears more to be held or rejected in principle than to be conditioned by material circumstances. Therefore, the desirability-in-principle of democracy seems to be resilient to fluctuations in the larger economic and social world of Koreans.

When it comes to change in commitment to democratization as suitable for the country as a whole, however, the eight predictors measuring economic well-being and life quality account for as much as 18 percent of the variance and four of these variables are significantly associated

Table 8.6   Multiple Regression Analysis of Changes in Personal Desire and
Collective Suitability for Democratization
OLS Regressions (standardized regression coefficients)

	Support for Democratization	
Predictors	Personal desire	Collective suitability
Economy		
egocentric–retrospective	−0.01	0.07*
egocentric–prospective	0.00	0.00
sociotropic–retrospective	0.03	0.06*
sociotropic–prospective	0.00	0.10*
Life Quality		
egocentric–retrospective	0.01	0.15*
egocentric–prospective	−0.04	0.05
sociotropic–retrospective	0.06	0.20*
sociotropic–prospective	0.10*	0.05
R^2	(0.01)	(0.18)

*Significant at the 0.05 level
Source: 1994 Korean Democratization Survey

with commitment to democracy. Koreans tend to modify their approval
of democratization for the nation in accord with their perceptions of
whether the process contributes to or detracts from economic well-being
and the quality of life in the aggregate. Unlike personal desire for the
realization of an ideal, approval of democracy as a collective venture is
more circumstantially than diffusely determined. The dynamics of mass
support for democratization cannot be understood without taking into
consideration citizens' judgment that they are "ready for democracy"
collectively. Support for democracy-in-practice stands, to some extent,
apart from approval of democracy-in-principle.

We are now in a position to test these preliminary inferences from
the theoretical perspectives introduced earlier. To begin, we group the
eight independent variables according to three pairs of competing
approaches (outlined below). We then regress the measure of democratic suitability on two sets of four independent variables in each pair.
For each set of predictors, we estimated the multiple coefficients of
determination and the multiple part correlation coefficient. For each
predictor, we estimated standardized multiple regression coefficients
(*betas*). Table 8.7 reports these statistics.

Our primary objective is to estimate the relative importance of contrasting models, which explains the dynamics of popular support for
democratization as measured in terms of its collective suitability. To this

Table 8.7 Testing Three Sets of Theoretical Perspectives on the Dynamics of Collective Suitability for Democratization

| | Theoretical Perspectives | | | | | | |
| Sets of Predictors | Pair 1 | | Pair 2 | | Pair 3 | | All together |
	Retrospection	Prospection	Economy	Life quality	Private life	Public life	
Experienced Impact							
Economy							
Family	0.07*		0.13*		0.15*		0.07*
Nation	0.09*		0.13*			0.09*	0.06
Life Quality							
Person	0.13*			0.14	0.26*		0.15*
Nation	0.23*			0.26*		0.30*	0.20*
Expected Impact							
Economy							
Family		0.09*	0.03		0.06		0.00
Nation		0.17*	0.14*			0.10*	0.10*
Life Quality							
Person		0.04		0.06	0.10*		0.05
Nation		0.00		0.06		0.08*	0.05
Variance Explained							
R^2	(0.17)	(0.06)	(0.10)	(0.16)	(0.13)	(0.16)	(0.18)
Part Correlation							
Coefficient Squared	(0.12)	(0.01)	(0.02)	(0.08)	(0.02)	(0.05)	—

*Significant at the 0.05 level

Source: 1994 Korean Democratization Survey

end, we chose the multiple part correlation approach, which was employed in earlier analysis. Unlike the multiple partial correlation approach, this strategy estimates the unique contributions of each theoretical cluster of independent variables. The squared part correlation coefficients indicate how much of the variance a cluster of variables accounts for in the dependent variable, which is left unexplained by other clusters of variables. The multiple part correlation approach is an appropriate device for testing contrasting models of the psychological dynamics of democratization (Bohrnstedt & Knoke 1982: 370).

A first pair of regression equations in Table 8.7 concerns retrospective versus prospective perspectives on the dynamics of democratic attitudes. From the squared multiple part correlation coefficients for the first two sets of variables, we see that retrospective measures of economic conditions and life quality add an increment of 12 percentage points to the variance already explained by prospective measures of the same variables. The prospective measures raise explanatory power by 1 percentage point. By and large, Koreans are retrospectively motivated when they adjust their attitudes toward regime change. Their orientations toward democracy are significantly performance-based.

A second pair of regressions concerns whether Koreans support democratic change primarily as a means of improving their economic well-being or their overall life quality. Again comparing the squared multiple part correlation coefficients for the third and fourth regression equations, we find that the economic well-being and life-quality models uniquely explain 2 percent and 8 percent of the variance, respectively. The percentage of the variance explained by the life-quality model is three times higher than that of the economic model. It is also significantly higher than that explained jointly by the two models (8% versus 6%).[5] Quality of life, somewhat more than economic welfare, drives support for democratization in Korea, as expected from communitarian and participatory theories of democracy.

A final, third pair concerns egocentric versus sociotropic perspectives. Do Koreans become more, or less, attached to democratic change mainly out of consideration for their own personal well-being or by way of perceptions of the collective repercussions of democratization? Or have they been egocentric as well as sociotropic in readjusting themselves toward democratization? Comparison of the squared multiple part correlation coefficients for the fifth and sixth equations reveals that each of the egocentric and sociotropic models uniquely accounts for less than one-third of the total explained variance in the dependent variable (2% and 5%, respectively, out of 18 percent); the outcome gives sociotropic perceptions an edge in explanatory power. In summary, 11 percent – more than half of the total explained variance – is accounted for jointly by the egocentric and sociotropic models. To Koreans, democratic regime change has figured as a means of personal gain as well as national development, with a modest but significant tilt toward an appreciation of democratization as favoring collective improvement.

Of all sets of independent variables considered together in the final regression equation, the two measuring retrospective perceptions of life quality stand out as the most powerful influences on the dynamics of support for democratization. As the standardized multiple regression coefficients for these two measures of life quality show, their explanatory role is two or more times greater than that found for most of other predictors considered in the regression analysis reported in the last column of Table 8.7. These two variables are also over two times more powerful than the two variables measuring similar consequences for economic well-being. In addition, of the two variables measuring retrospective perceptions of life quality, the perceived quality of collective life exerts the more powerful influence. Perceptions of how democratization has changed the nation as a place to live constitute a vital key to understanding the mass psychology of Korean democratization. This is an additional piece of evidence to support the communitarian model of democracy that was discussed in Chapter 2.

In addition to all four retrospective perceptions, one other standardized multiple regression coefficient is statistically significant: the indicator measuring prospective perceptions of the national economy. Similar perceptions of personal economic well-being and life quality have neither a statistically nor a substantively significant effect on changes in democratic support when controlling for all other variables. In deciding the extent of their support for, or opposition to, democratization, Koreans are typically, though not massively, more concerned with how the process will affect the nation than with their personal lot.

Perceptions of Political Change

The analysis presented up to this point, while encouraging insofar as it provides some confirmation for the theoretical priority given to sociotropic over egocentric and quality of life over economic perceptions, is still inadequate as an account of the process of attitudinal dynamics in the course of democratization. The two clusters of economic and life-quality predictors explain less than one-fifth of the variation in democratic support. A fuller account can be attained by incorporating a cluster of three political predictors (see Lipset 1994: 8).

To the three clusters of variables – economic, life quality, and political – a stepwise regression procedure was applied to identify the most parsimonious subset of independent variables that could explain the

Table 8.8   Stepwise Regression Analysis of the Dynamics of Collective
Suitability for Democratization

Predictors	Beta
Past change in governmental performance	0.32
Past change in the quality of national life	0.09
Past change in the quality of personal life	0.08
Future change in the national economy	0.08
Future change in political situations	0.07
R^2	(0.24)

All *beta* coefficients are significant at the 0.05 level
Source: 1994 Korean Democratization Survey

most substantial part of the variance in support for democracy. Table 8.8
reports the results of this procedure by listing only the predictors that,
taken one-by-one, turn out to be significant in order of impact.

The exercise suggests that the dynamics of popular democratic
support are determined jointly by: (1) retrospective assessments of
governmental performance, (2) retrospective assessments of the quality
of national life, (3) retrospective assessments of the quality of private life,
(4) prospective assessments of the national economy, and (5) prospective assessments of political situations.

The five variables represented in this final model do not come from
one cluster, such as economic conditions or life quality. Instead, they
derive from all three clusters of variables, including the political cluster.
They represent retrospective and prospective perspectives as well as
egocentric and sociotropic concerns. Attempts to explain the dynamics
of democratic support in terms of a single cluster of economic variables,
therefore, are unlikely to produce a satisfactory explanation.

The most notable feature of the model in Table 8.8 is that, *ceteris
paribus*, Koreans discontinue or withdraw their support for democratization when they feel that the democratic governments perform more
poorly than the old authoritarian regime. Indeed, decline in the perceived quality of governmental performance undermines public support
for democratic change to a significantly greater degree than democratization's perceived impact on economic well-being or life quality.
Comparisons of the *betas* reported in Table 8.8 indicate that the former
does so as much as from three to four-and-a-half times more than
the latter.

The implication is that ordinary people in fledgling democracies tend
to blame democratic institutions when their government proves incapable of effectively tackling problems facing the nation. Citizens of new

democracies may not distinguish clearly between the quality of governmental performance and the legitimacy of democratic institutions. As
Evans & Whitefield (1995: 503) argue, "people support democracies
because they are seen to work, reflecting respondents' experience of the
pay-offs from democracy itself, rather than on the basis of a simple 'cash
nexus'." Unless they reach the decision that the new democratic government performs better than the old authoritarian government under
which they lived, average Koreans may be characterized as prudent,
rather than enthusiastic, about supporting democratic reform. Democratic legitimacy, in short, has to be earned.

Summary and Conclusions

Several studies contend that citizens of former communist countries in
Eastern and Central Europe acquired a strong preference for democracy
primarily through global diffusion of its message prior to the demise of
communism (Dalton 1994; Duch 1995; McIntosh & Abele 1993; Mishler
& Rose 1994; Tedin 1994). Furthermore, some of these studies have
claimed that mass publics have provided continuing, pervasive support
for democratic change by directing their dissatisfaction against incumbent government *officials* rather than at newly installed democratic
institutions. New European democracies, the argument goes, have
commanded the resilient and pervasive support of the public.

However, the evolution of commitment to democracy in Korea and,
we suspect, in many other countries has followed a more complex
trajectory. Even though they lived under an authoritarian regime that
permitted greater exposure to democratic cues than its communist
counterparts, Koreans were initially reticent about democratization.
Only after they had positive experience with democratic reforms, did
they begin to increase their support for those reforms *instrumentally* and
incrementally. Their attachment to the reforms shifted significantly
during the transition and responded to the performance of democratic
governments. A wait-and-see attitude, prevailed over unequivocal
support.

A major clue to this discrepancy lies in the distinction between a
personal preference for democracy – its close-to-consensual desirability
– and the assessment of its suitability for the country as the transition
unfolds. The viability of democracy-in-practice is seen as more
problematic than the desirability of democracy-in-principle.

Much of the gap between the results reported in earlier studies and
our own may be attributed to the way in which support for democratic
change is conceptualized and measured. Surveys of post-communist
publics have routinely neglected to distinguish between democratic

"norms and values," which are invariably measured as personal preferences, and perceptions about the sheer suitability of democracy.[6] Our
study taps both dimensions of attitudes toward democratization and
strongly suggests that the "diffuse" and surprisingly "steady" attributes,
thought to characterize popular orientations in post-communist
societies, reflect a failure to specify properly how mass publics may
become democratic, or less so, during the course of democratization.

The design of previous studies tended to foist a unidimensional
rendition of political transformation on citizens whose perceptions of
the workability of democracy are probably as important as their avowals
of the desirability of democracy-in-principle. Relying on an economic
perspective adapted from studies of electoral choice in advanced democracies, the same line of research has generally failed to consider the life-
quality concerns that impel citizens toward or away from democratization. These omissions undoubtedly contributed to the characterization
of European mass support for democratic reforms as highly pervasive
and resilient to socioeconomic crises.

On the one hand, changes in perceptions of democratic suitability are
determined to a modest though significant degree by perceived changes
in the quality of life and economic conditions during democratization,
as compared to achievements under authoritarianism. Quality-of-life
concerns appear to count for a bit more than assessments of the economy probably because, in the wake of a developmental dictatorship
that was largely successful in improving the standard of living, economic
performance itself is not a sharply distinguishing feature of democracy
in Korea. Some functional conditions of the growth of democratic
support, notably changes in perceptions of the overall quality of life, are
less material but no less powerful than the narrowly economic, at least in
countries that democratize under propitious economic conditions.

On the other hand, outweighing both these ingredients of our functional explanation of commitment to democracy-in-practice is the process of political learning. Koreans update their appreciation of democracy by keeping a tally not just of the changing socioeconomic situation
but of what they perceive to be the performance of the new regime.
While the desirability of democracy appears to spread by diffusion,
convictions about its "fit" follow a learning curve. Commitment to
democracy-in-practice is contingent not only on functional payoffs,
having to do with economic and quality-of-life issues, but also on estimates of how democratic government works – i.e. how efficiently it
implements policies. This type of democratic learning may be particularly important in the Korean case because it is in the political domain,
more than in regard to economic performance or even in the area of life
quality, that the separation between an authoritarian system identified
with prosperity and an uncertain democracy emerges most clearly.

Our analysis calls into question the conventional notion that support for democracy is equivalent to diffuse commitment reflecting deep-seated values. Contrary to what Easton (1975) and others (Di Palma 1993; Kornberg & Clarke 1983) have argued, popular support for a democratic political system is not impervious to change; instead, it grows and declines in response to a variety of forces. Our study lends further support to recent evidence that civic attitudes are a result, rather than a cause, of democratic politics (Seligson & Booth 1993; Muller & Seligson 1994). Finally, the tendency for democratic support to be conditioned by the perceived quality of governmental performance testifies to the instrumental theory of system support according to which established regimes are supported at least as much for what they do as for what they are or claim to be (Lipset 1994; Przeworski 1991, 1993).

The gist of our analysis is that popular commitment to democracy encompasses two dimensions. A preference for democracy in the abstract, untested by experience, may be a promising start – an improvement over the outright hostility that in some cultures views democratic ideals as corrupt, decadent, and otherwise insidious. But it is not a commitment to the collective suitability of democracy. It seems unlikely that mass publics of nascent democracies acquire a robust stake in democracy, that is, something approaching an enduring commitment to it, diffusively through exposure to Western media and education, even if these agencies are crucial to putting democracy on the screen of popular culture in the first place. Equally if not more important is the tendency for a democratic political culture to develop through a learning process that includes first-hand experience with democratic politics (Fukuyama 1995a; Putnam 1993; Weil 1994). During this process, mass publics may, as some theorists argue, learn the art of self-government while conforming to "universalistic and public-oriented rules rather than their particularistic interests" (O'Donnell 1996: 32; see also Dahl 1992; Fukuyama 1995b; Putnam 1993). Perhaps more realistically, ordinary citizens may come to the realization that "democracy is a structure of laws and incentives by which less than perfect individuals are induced to act in the common good while pursuing their own" (March & Olsen 1995: 41).

In short, it is fair to conclude that new democracies consolidate fully only when each of their respective citizen bodies is capable of balancing their own self-interests. This task of balancing self-interests with the common good at the micro level is far more difficult to achieve than the initial installation of democratic institutions or directing popular dissatisfaction at public officials rather than the democratic institutions themselves.

PART V

Conclusion

CHAPTER 9

Korean Democracy:
Problems and Prospects

"Democracy has often been compared to a slow-growing
plant which must be carefully nurtured and sometimes even
replanted before it is well enough rooted to survive."
Sanford Lakoff (1996: 25)
"The development of democracy, like the erosion of support
for authoritarianism, takes time."
Richard Rose (1994: 80, 86)

The global wave of democratization has established a large family of new
democracies in regions that were once widely viewed as inhospitable to
democratic political development (Pinkney 1994). In the past decade
alone, the number of new democracies has expanded from 69 in 1987
to 118 in 1997 (Karatnycky 1997: 6). There are now over five dozen in
this family of new democracies, and Korea, which joined in the wave
more than a decade after it began in the Southern Europe of the mid-
1970s, is a major Asian member of the family. Korea is also one of twelve
in the family that are generally regarded as influential new democracies
in terms of the relative size of the population and gross domestic product. Of these twelve, only Korea and Poland are known to have consistently maintained and even improved political rights and civil liberties
since the transition to democracy (Diamond 1996: 30).

With a population of 44 million and a Gross Domestic Product larger
than ten of the fifteen states in the European Union, Korea is, indeed,
an influential new democracy by any standard. Of over seventy countries
in the current wave of democratization, Korea is the only non-Western
new democracy that has recently been admitted to the OECD. Among new
democracies in Asia, moreover, it is the first country that has peacefully
transferred power to an opposition party. As one of the most successful
democratic transitions in the past decade, Korea occupies a prominent
place in the current wave of democratization. Furthermore, its democratic experience for the past decade, as documented in Chapters 7 and 8,
offers non-Western alternatives to institutional and cultural democratization and, thus, merits a careful study across time and space.

By analyzing Korean democratization from both temporal and spatial
perspectives, this volume was designed to promote a more accurate and
meaningful understanding of its contours, dynamics, consequences, and

problems. It also sought to test the prevailing wisdom of the theoretical and empirical literature on democratic transition and consolidation. The study was conceptually grounded in the notion that democracy is more than a set of political institutions and procedures and that democratization involves a fundamental transformation of the way in which cultural values, political structure, and individual citizens interact. It was also based on the supposition that repeated surveys of a cross-section of the adult population over time make it possible to unravel and compare the trajectories of democratic change across different countries. In light of the major findings presented above, this final chapter seeks to identify the key elements of the Korean experience of democratization, determine its relevance as a Confucian model, and assess Korea's prospects for becoming a fully consolidated democracy in the near future.

Distinctive Characteristics
Legacies of the Authoritarian Regime

What constitutes the distinctive features of democratization that have been unfolding in Korea during the past decade? One notable feature concerns the legacies of authoritarian rule that contrast markedly with what has been noted in many other democratizing countries. As compared especially to those in Central and Eastern Europe and Latin America, Korea began its transition to democracy with much less painful and fearful memories of its non-democratic past. Memories of political repression, economic poverty, and social inequality were neither pervasive nor deeply ingrained in Korean minds to the extent to which they were in the citizenry of former communist and military regimes elsewhere (see Dominguez 1994; Rose, Mishler & Haerpfer 1998).

In its regime character, the military rule in Korea resembled many other right-wing military dictatorships, particularly those in Latin America. The Korean and Latin American militaries were infused with a highly developed anti-communist ideology that served as an effective means of suppressing dissent (J. Choi 1996, 1997; Karl 1990, 1995). Unlike left-wing communist parties in Eastern and Central Europe, which sought public participation in the political process, these ruling juntas sought to enforce public silence by severely restricting civil liberties and abusing civil rights (Bunce 1995).

The legacies of the military rule in Korea contrast sharply in detail with those of their counterparts in Latin America and communist Europe. In suppressing political dissidents, for example, Korean generals were much less forceful and were highly selective. They neither executed nor sent political dissidents and their relatives to concentration camps en masse. While countless numbers of Latin American and

European citizens were murdered, only a few Koreans were killed by the Korean military. According to the survey conducted in 1994, only 3 percent of the Korean population remembered that they themselves, someone else in their family, or their close friends suffered political oppression by the military government.

More notably, Korean generals did a far better job than the military dictators of Latin America and communist rulers of Europe in managing economic affairs. Under military leadership, the Korean economy, with the average annual rate of growth at 10 percent, became one of the fastest growing economies in the world. In sharp contrast, Latin American economies became either stagnant or considerably depressed, and communist economies went bankrupt. While economic failures in those countries forced their dictators to relinquish power, economic success in Korea led the military to include the rapidly expanding middle class in the political process. As Im Hyug Baeg (1996) aptly points out, it was a crisis of economic success that conditioned the demise of military rule in Korea, not a crisis of economic failure as in Latin America as well as in communist Europe.

The absence of economic difficulties made it possible for Korean generals to negotiate a series of pacts with democratic forces and set the course of democratic transition on a narrow path and at a slow pace (S. J. Kim 1994; H. B. Im 1995). In communist Europe, the agenda for democratic transition even involved the transforming of a socialist economy into capitalism (Rose, Mishler & Haerpfer 1998). In Latin America, it involved the restructuring of malfunctioning and disparity-ridden capitalism by "making the government more of a regulator than an owner" (Lagos 1997: 126). In Korea, on the other hand, a democratic agenda was set to replace an authoritarian constitutional structure with democratic ones, not to restructure its development-oriented capitalist system, which had worked reasonably well for decades (Moon & Mo 1998). Not surprisingly, the task of democratic regime change was completed quickly with a great deal of success, and Korea has shortly become a more vigorous democracy than Japan.

Korea's quick success in democratic regime change, however, was not accompanied by a similar success in replacing its authoritarian leadership.[1] As evidenced by the election of former general Roh Tae Woo as the president of the first democratic government, democratic transition did not entail a fundamental shift in the authoritarian nature of political leadership. Authoritarians and democrats were allowed to cohabit and dwell on procedural reforms under the new regime called "the democratic Sixth Republic of Korea." This was the most notable feature of democratic transition in Korea, and this was attributable to the huge success of *dirigiste* capitalism with which the Korean military was credited. This suggests, therefore, that an authoritarian regime's economic success can become a double-edged sword for its subsequent democratization.

Overall Trajectory of Korean Democratization

The second feature of the Korean model concerns the overall trajectory of democratic change in the way in which political culture and structure operate and interact with each other. As described in Chapter 1, the trajectory was mapped by monitoring public opinion on democratic politics and reforms through a series of six nationwide sample surveys taken over the past decade. Contrary to what was expected during the promising transition from military rule, the consolidation of democratic political structure has advanced neither quickly nor steadily. Nor has political culture consolidated in a quick and steady fashion over the past decade of democratic reform.

For the first two-thirds of the decade the structural or regime character of the Korean political system, as perceived by the mass public, consistently and substantially shifted toward the more democratic especially in the wake of governmental change in 1993. Soon after, the upward trajectory leveled off and then was followed by a slightly downward movement. This pattern of curvilinear trajectory was also observed in the cultural domain of the Korean political system, and the interactions between the structural and cultural domains also displayed the same pattern.

Thus, in the eyes of the Korean people, their regime was less democratic in 1997 when a third round of presidential elections was underway to choose a successor to President Kim Young Sam than it was when President Kim Young Sam was inaugurated as the second president of the Sixth Republic four years previously. For all the democratic reforms and anti-authoritarian campaigns President Kim carried out for over four years, the regime remained only partially democratic. Much worse, it began to reverse its path toward further consolidation. The character of Korean political culture, as measured by the popular desire to live in a perfect democracy, also stopped growing in 1997. Both structurally as well as culturally, therefore, Korean democratization represented a stalled progression at the time of our sixth Korean Democratization Barometer survey in June 1997. More precisely, it appeared to be in a state of deconsolidation and re-equilibrium.[2] A successful transition followed by stalled consolidation is a second feature of Korean democratization. This confirms that a successful transition from authoritarian rule is one thing, but a successful consolidation of an incipient democracy is another.

Quality of Governance

If democracy means government *for* the people, democratization should bring about significant improvements in the quality of governmental performance. Can Korean democratization be equated with a greater quality of governance? To explore this question, we compared over time the percentages of those satisfied and those unsatisfied with the authoritarian and democratic governments under which they have lived during the past decade.

In all three surveys spanning the 5-year period of 1991–96, vast majorities (87% in 1991, 84% in 1994, and 88% in 1996) replied that the Chun regime had not performed to their satisfaction (Appendix B S1.1). In the same surveys, smaller majorities (85% in 1991, 65% in 1994, and 61% in 1996) reported that neither of the two democratically elected governments had performed to their satisfaction either. Although the number of unsatisfied Koreans is less under democratic rule, a substantial majority (61%) still remain unsatisfied. This suggests that all the institutional reforms so far have failed to bring about substantive democratization, i.e. a qualitative shift in governmental performance from unsatisfactory to satisfactory.

In an attempt to further examine such failures in substantive democratization, we divided 1996 survey respondents into four groups by collapsing and combining their assessments of the old authoritarian and new democratic governments. The four groups include: (1) sceptics who are unsatisfied with both the old and new regimes, (2) allegiants who are unsatisfied with the old regime but satisfied with the new one, (3) the disaffected who are satisfied with the authoritarian regime but unsatisfied with the democratic one, and (4) the indifferent who are satisfied with both regimes. When a majority fall into the category of allegiants, it is evident that democratic regime change has brought about a qualitative shift in governmental performance. Conversely, when a majority fall into the category of sceptics, no such shift has occurred.

Of the four groups examined, the largest one consists of those who disliked the performance of the old regime and still dislike the new regime. This group of sceptics is followed by allegiants, the disaffected, and the indifferent, in that order. More notable is that sceptics constitute about one-half (54%) of the Korean population and that they comprise one-and-one-half times as many as the allegiants who saw a positive transformation of governmental performance. This pattern of distribution supports the view that change in the quality of governmental performance has been mostly a matter of degree, from being *highly unsatisfying* to somewhat *less unsatisfying*. In short, Korean democratization does not mean greater citizen *satisfaction* with governmental performance; instead, it merely means *less dissatisfaction* with it.

Commitment to Democracy-in-Practice

If democracy is government *by* the people, democratization cannot be completed without improvements in citizens' orientations toward, and capacity in, democratic politics (Alfonsin 1992; Linz & Stepan 1996a; Rose, Mishler & Haerpfer 1998). As discussed in Chapters 1 and 8, the past decade has witnessed remarkable increases in the orientation toward democracy as preferable to all other types of non-democratic regimes and that democratization is also desirable for improvements in the quality of personal and public life. Such increases in democratic preferences, however, have not been accompanied by corresponding shifts within the internalization and habituation of the basic norms of democratic politics and the commitment to necessary measures for democratic consolidation.

Consequently, while a large majority of those Koreans are favorably oriented to the ideals of democracy and democratization, they remain detached from the real world of democratic politics and reforms. For example, in the 1993 survey, respondents were asked to rate the priority of democratization as a national development goal in relation to economic development (Appendix B D2). While about one-half (49%) were in favor of economic development over democratic reform, about one-quarter (26%) chose democratization over economic development. In 1997, however, less than one-tenth (9%) replied that democratization is more important than economic development for their nation (see Table 9.1). Even among those who believe that democracy is always the best form of government, moreover, economic development outweighs democratic development by an overwhelming margin of 52 to 11 percent. The implication is that a majority of the Korean people would withdraw their support for democratic reforms whenever they saw those reforms interfering with economic development (see Hahm & Rhyu 1997: 41).

To further examine the depth of commitment to democratic expansion, our 1994 survey asked respondents whether they personally would approve or disapprove of three specific reform measures aimed at expanding the current practices of limited procedural democracy (Appendix B D3.1–D3.3). They are to: (1) revise the existing national security laws, the most oppressive of legacies from the past military dictatorship, (2) allow the labor unions to engage in political activities as their business counterparts do, and (3) lower the voting-age limit to eighteen from twenty as in other consolidated democracies.

None of these three necessary measures for democratic expansion was strongly endorsed by a majority of the Korean electorate. All three measures received unqualified approval by small minorities (ranging from 13% to 30%). More notable is that three-fifths (61%) are not

Table 9.1 Assessing the Relative Priority of Democratization Against Economic Development (percent)

	Year		Change
Relative Priority	1993	1997	(97–93)
Democratization is more important	26	9	−17
Economic development is more important	49	53	+4
Democratization and economic development are equally important	25	38	+13
Total	100	100	
(N)	(1198)	(1117)	

Sources: 1993 & 1997 Korean Democratization Surveys

strongly committed to any of the three measures surveyed. Most notable is that a little over one-tenth (13%) are *generally* (strongly or somewhat) committed to all three measures, while a minuscule proportion (3%) are strongly committed (see Table 9.2). Even among those who strongly believe that more democratization is needed, less than one-quarter (22%) only are committed to the fullest spectrum of democratic reforms. This evidence confirms the shallowness and slow growth of Korean commitment to democracy-in-practice.

Even after a decade of democratization, little progress has been achieved in the willingness of the Korean people to commit themselves to the expansion of limited democracy-in-action. As a result, their desire to live in a greater democracy remains, by and large, an abstract political

Table 9.2 Commitment to Democracy-in-Practice

	Types of Commitment (percent)	
Commitment Levels	General	Strong
0 (none)	19	61
1	37	26
2	31	10
3 (all)	13	3
Total	100	100
(N)	(1500)	(1500)

Note: General commitment includes both strong and somewhat approval of democratic practices while strong commitment includes strong approval of those practices only
Source: 1994 Korean Democratization Survey

ideal signifying few of the concrete practices of democratic change. A great deal of *unevenness* in the growth of affective and behavioral domains of democratic culture is a fourth notable feature of Korean democratization.

Dissociation from Authoritarianism-in-Practice

Democratization at the individual citizen level involves more than embracing democratic norms and reform measures. Besides committing themselves to those norms and measures, citizens must dissociate themselves from the ideals and practices of age-old authoritarianism and particularism, which are widely known to pose enormous impediments to democratization. Koreans have lived all, or most, of their lives in the Confucian culture, which emphasizes the values of both authoritarianism and particularism.

As an ethical system, Confucianism does not endorse the notion of either individual freedom or human rights from which the democratic practices of mass participation and competition in the West emanated (Hahm 1997; Kihl 1994; H. B. Im 1997b). Nor does it embrace the rule of law, which is widely accepted as an indispensable condition of democratic consolidation. Instead, Confucianism emphasizes the rule of man, the supremacy of the group over the individual, the family over the community, discipline over freedom, duties over rights, and personal wisdom over impersonal law.[3]

In principle, an overwhelming majority (85%) of Koreans oppose the idea of restoring military rule (Appendix B G2.1). Nearly as many Koreans (81%) reject the idea of abolishing the National Assembly so that a powerful dictator can control decision-making (Appendix B G2.2). In practice, however, there has been very little decline in the extent to which Koreans, whether democrats or non-democrats, are committed to the authoritarian means of dealing with national problems. As they did during the first democratic government, a large majority (66%) remain subscribed to the belief that a powerful dictator, like former General Park Chung Hee, is more effective in handling those problems than a democratically elected government (Appendix B G2.3). Even among those who believe that democracy is always the best form of government, a majority (58%) reject the democratic method of conflict resolution in favor of the authoritarian method.

Adherence to such authoritarian practice remains linked with the economic gains that many Koreans personally experienced during three decades of military rule. Such economic experiences prior to democratic regime change still discourage many Koreans from relinquishing the old habit of equating dictatorship with effective leadership or good

Figure 9.1 Relating Assessments of Economic Life under the Authoritarian Government to Strong Attachment to Authoritarianism-in-Practice

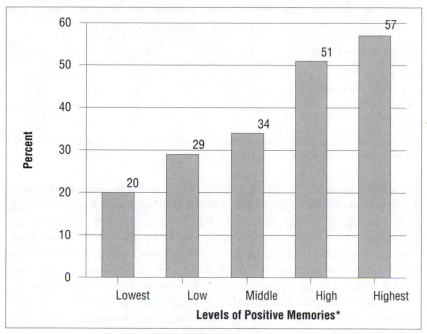

Entries are the percentages who *strongly* agreed with the statement that "the dictatorial rule like that of a strong leader like Park Chung Hee would be much better than a democracy to handle the serious problems facing these days"
*Levels of positive memories are measured by adding up positive ratings of national and personal economic life under the authoritarian government against the current democratic government
Source: 1997 Korean Democratization Survey

governance. In Figure 9.1, we see that those with a lot of positive memories of economic life under the authoritarian government are more than twice as likely to cling to that authoritarian habit than those with none of those memories (57% versus 20%). A taste of good life in the authoritarian past inhibits many Koreans from dissociating themselves from authoritarianism-in-action.

Likewise, many Koreans refuse to give up their support for the unitary structure of authoritarian governance that limits mass participation in the political process. In October 1984, when former General Chun Doo Whan (as the president of the old authoritarian government) was waging all-out campaigns against the incipient democracy movement, a substantial minority (45%) expressed the view that "local autonomy should be implemented on a broad basis in Korea because it is a basic

Table 9.3   Support for the Full Spectrum of Legislative Democracy by
Educational Attainment

	Types of Support (percent)		
Education Level	General	Strong	(N)
No school	68	34	(44)
Elementary School	68	42	(111)
Middle School	70	36	(146)
High School	70	34	(417)
College or more	63	28	(282)

Source: 1996 Korean Democratization Survey

element of democracy" (Park & Kim 1987). In November 1991, when
the first democratic regime of the Sixth Republic was three years old,
about one-third (34%) believed that local autonomy had little or
nothing to do with democracy. Again, in November 1996, when both
provincial and county assemblies were in full operation, nearly as many
(31%) refused to endorse the full practice of local autonomy (Appendix
B N1.2 and N1.3). More surprisingly, those with college educations are
less willing to support this practice of democratic politics than the less
educated (see Table 9.3). In Korea, a college education does not always
mean greater support for democracy-in-practice.

Among the Korean population, sharp increases in the preference for
democracy as an ideal have not brought about parallel declines in the
preference for the authoritarian mode of governance. Nor have remarkable increases in college education over the past decade reduced popular attachment to the age-old practice of authoritarianism. In Korea,
there is considerable independence between democratic preference and
authoritarianism. There is also considerable independence between a
college education and authoritarian propensities. This constitutes a fifth
characteristic of the Korean experience of democratization.

Dissociation from Particularism-in-Practice

For a new democracy like the one in Korea to endure and mature,
citizens and officials should be freed from the particularistic identities
that are inconsistent with the obligations of democratic citizenship
(March & Olsen 1995: 39). Instead of relying on self-interests or group-
based identities which are contradictory to a democratic community,
citizens should acquire civic identities and act accordingly. Otherwise,
their democracy will never consolidate fully; instead, it will degenerate
into an amoral laissez-faire state (Huntington 1996b: 7).

After a decade of democratic rule, Koreans remain bound largely by their ties to the groups or organizations that are inconsistent with the public good. These ties are built primarily on primordial identities that are neither changeable nor inclusive. Between the national and local communities, for example, a large majority (70%) still identify more closely with the latter, according to the 1997 survey (Appendix B V8). As demonstrated in Chapter 4 through a careful analysis of their engagement in civic life, Koreans are also confined mostly to fraternal and religious associations (see Steinberg 1995, 1997). Their legislative assemblies and political parties continue to serve the interests of the rich and powerful few as they did in the authoritarian past. To build a truly democratic civil society, Koreans must be freed from such particularistic ties and be able to develop multiple and complementary identities (J. Choi 1997: 121; see also Linz & Stepan 1996b: 27).

In pursuing particularistic claims, moreover, Koreans are not strongly motivated to abide by the rule of law. In the 1997 survey we sought to determine the extent to which Koreans were inclined toward the "illegal services" of offering bribes or using connections to get rules waived and cheating as when an individual makes a false claim that officials accept without a bribe. Specifically, the survey, as described in Appendix B H6, asked respondents whether they would advise friends to use any of these services for the problems involving: (1) the assignment of a military draftee to a job in a remote area, (2) a child whose poor grades do not guarantee admission to a college, (3) obtaining a permit from a government agency promptly, and (4) securing a government-subsidized apartment.

Over two-fifths (42%) openly replied that they would advise friends to disobey the law in order to avoid an unfavorable decision by the government on at least one of those four problems. Fortunately, such inclinations toward illegal services are significantly lower for democrats than for authoritarians (39% versus 52%). Between those with college educations and those with less education, however, the former are significantly more inclined toward those services than the latter (55% versus 38%). As Figure 9.2 shows, the more Koreans are educated, the more they are inclined to disobey the law for their own good. Unfortunately, in Korea today, rule-breaking has become a normal way of getting things done, especially among the privileged.

In defining and pursuing political interests, Koreans also rely heavily on identities of a primordial nature. In every local and national election, an overwhelming majority of Koreans supported candidates of the party led by one of three Kims (Kim Young Sam, Kim Dae Jung, and Kim Jong Pil) from their own region (Bae 1995; N. Lee 1993). Voters' gender, age, education, income, and political efficacy do not matter much in

Figure 9.2   Public Dispositions Against the Rule of Law by Educational
Attainment

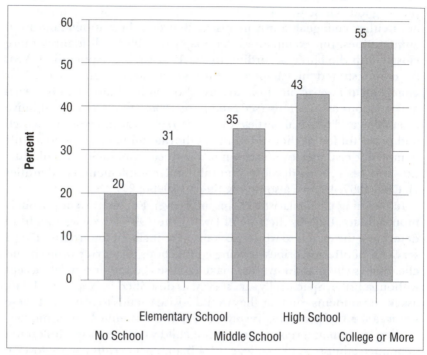

Source: 1997 Korean Democratization Survey

candidate selection. Candidates' personal character, ideology, and policy
orientations are also not of great concern when compared to the
regional identities of voters and their candidates (H. B. Im 1997a: 26).
Even in reaching decisions on democratic expansion and authoritarian
removal, this primordial identity often overwhelms those, such as education and income, that are based on personal achievements. On the
whole, Korea is still a nation disjointed by high levels of particularism
and clientelism.

A Confucian Model of Democratization

Korea's experience of democratic change, as highlighted above, needs
to be compared to what has been observed in its neighbors in order to
determine whether Korea can be characterized as a Confucian model of
democratization.[4] For this comparison, Taiwan was chosen for a number
of reasons. First, Taiwan is one of the only two other democratizing
countries (the other being Mongolia) in the region. China, North

Korea, and Singapore as yet have not completed the demise of authoritarian rule, the first stage of democratization. In 1987, when Korea began to terminate three decades of military rule, Taiwan also began dismantling four decades of one-party dictatorship. Since then, these two countries, known internationally as East Asian dragons or little tigers, have jointly become "two of the most promising democratic transitions of the past decade" (International Forum for Democratic Studies 1996: 5).[5]

The contours of democratization in the two dragon states are similar. They were shaped by the same forces that are known to set them apart in the current wave of democratization as "two quintessential outlier states" (Eberstadt 1992). The two countries, for example, remain both highly imbued with the values of Confucianism and are ambivalent toward the Western values of individualism and pluralism. They also remain territorially and ideologically divided nations. For decades, military threats and ideological challenges from the communist regime in mainland China justified the existence of the anti-communist dictatorship in Taiwan. Those threats and challenges also denied the opportunity for the Taiwanese to learn the values and norms of democratic politics. Under a right-wing dictatorship, Taiwan became an economic powerhouse envied throughout the world. That prosperity in Taiwan, as in Korea, created the means for democratic regime change (Chu 1996).

In the wake of change, the menace of communism and the economic legacy of *dirigiste* capitalism have collaborated to keep Taiwanese democratization within the bounds of political conservatism and economic pragmatism. Therefore, the progress of democratic reform in Taiwan has been gradual with no fundamental restructuring of the development-oriented capitalist system. Culturally, new subcultures of Western liberalism and pluralism have been merely grafted onto the dominant cultures of authoritarianism and collectivism (Soong 1992). As in Korea, the combination of these forces has uniquely shaped Taiwan into an outlier state among the newly democratizing countries of the world. As outlier states, Taiwan and Korea together form the East Asian contours of democratization (Shin & Shyu 1997).

As expected from such contours, over the past decade Korea and Taiwan have been on very similar paths to democracy. In terms of the direction and trajectory of popular support for democratic change, for example, the two countries differ very little from each other. In Taiwan, a series of national sample surveys was conducted to monitor the trajectory of its cultural democratization over time. Specifically, respondents to these surveys were asked whether or not they agreed with the view that did not favor further democratization, i.e. "Our political system has democratized enough; we should not expect too much." The percentage of the respondents who disagreed with this view was chosen as a measure of the desire of Taiwanese to expand their limited democracy.

As in Korea, the percentage in favor of more democratic change in Taiwan continued to rise for the first half of the democratic decade and then stopped rising (see Figure 9.3). Specifically, the relative number of democratic reformers rose steadily from 50 percent in 1991, to 60 percent in 1992, and to 66 percent in 1993 when constitutional reforms formally ended the one-party dictatorship and instituted a multi-party representative democracy. Since 1993, however, the percentage of democrats among the Taiwanese has declined. According to the latest 1995 survey the figure stands at 61 percent. This trajectory, which features a steady upward movement followed by a slight downward movement, is virtually identical to the one observed in Korea (see Figure 1.2).

Besides similar trajectories, the two countries are very much alike in current levels of popular desire for the expansion of limited democracy. In the 1997 survey, in which some of the 1995 Taiwanese survey questions were replicated, Korean respondents responded to the statement: "Since our political system has democratized enough, we should not expect too much." By voicing disagreement with the statement,

Figure 9.3   Percentage of Taiwanese Supporting Democratic Expansion

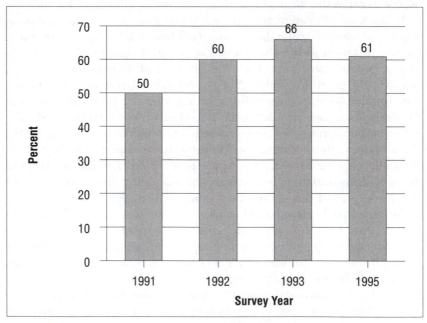

Source: Taiwanese General Surveys on Social Change and Legislative Yuan Electoral Surveys quoted in Shin & Shyu (1997)

59 percent expressed support for democratic expansion. This figure is 2 percentage points apart from the latest figure (61%) available for the Taiwanese population.

To further compare the depth of cultural democratization, the 1997 Korean survey replicated four more questions concerning the Confucian ideal and practice of authoritarian rule (Appendix B G1). They are: (1) "We can leave all things to morally upright leaders," (2) "If a government is often restrained by an assembly, it will be unable to achieve great accomplishments," (3) "Too many social groups would undermine social harmony"; and (4) "Heterogeneous opinions would undermine social order." The percentage of Korean and Taiwanese respondents who expressed disagreement with these statements and the mean of the statements they disagreed to were calculated to estimate and compare the overall levels of dissociation from authoritarianism in the two East Asian new democracies.

As Table 9.4 shows, more than half of the Korean (57%) and Taiwanese (52%) populations objected to none or only one aspect of the authoritarian practices surveyed. In both countries, it is a small minority of less than one-tenth (7% in Korea and 6% in Taiwan) who are fully detached from all of those four authoritarian practices. Furthermore, the average levels of dissociation from Confucian authoritarianism in the two countries are virtually identical, as shown by the means (1.5) reported in Table 9.4. On average, both Koreans and the Taiwanese are dissociated from one-and-one-half of four legacies of authoritarian rule, indicating that they are only 38 percent dissociated from those legacies.

Table 9.4 Levels of Dissociation from Authoritarian Practices in Korea and Taiwan

	Country			
	Korea		Taiwan	
Dissociation Level	%	(N)	%	(N)
0 (lowest)	28	(309)	27	(569)
1	29	(321)	25	(515)
2	21	(234)	25	(523)
3	15	(173)	17	(352)
4 (highest)	7	(80)	6	(134)
Total	100	(1117)	100	(2093)
Mean ($\bar{x}$)	(1.5)		(1.5)	

Sources: 1997 Korean Democratization Survey; 1995 Legislative Yuan Electoral Survey in Taiwan quoted in Shin & Shyu (1997)

Results of these comparisons strongly indicate that Korea and Taiwan have been on similar contours and trajectories of democratization. Their mass publics are presently at nearly identical levels of positive and negative commitment to democratic consolidation, i.e. support for democratic expansion and dissociation from authoritarianism. As was the case in West Germany decades ago, their political ambivalence reflects "the juxtaposition of two valued goals: order and democracy" (Dalton 1994: 477). In view of all these findings, it is reasonable to argue that Korea represents a Confucian model of democratization.[6]

The Future of Korean Democratization

As Schmitter (1994: 59) points out, new democracies like the one in Korea face "no simple choice between regression to autocracy and progression to democracy." They can remain hybrid regimes, combining elements of autocracy and democracy, or they may persist as unconsolidated "delegative" democracies (O'Donnell 1994).

What does the future hold for Korean democracy?[7] The analyses of public opinion data reported in this book suggest that Korea is likely to tread on a very unsteady and long march toward consolidation for many years, and even decades, to come. Unlike many new democracies in Africa, Europe, Latin America, and Southeast Asia, Korea is an ethnically homogeneous and highly industrialized country. These may be the only factors that separate Korea from the rest of the new democracies and make it look better positioned for democratic consolidation. What is *present* from the authoritarian past, however, may not be as powerful as what is *missing* from it in determining the ultimate destiny of democratic consolidation (Eckstein 1998; Rose, Mishler & and Haerpfer 1998).

The old military regimes have left a powerful legacy of autocracy featuring the arbitrary exercise of power and a strong president unaccountable to an elected assembly. They have also left an equally powerful legacy of personalizing and privatizing political authorities and powers. What is absent from Korea's authoritarian past, therefore, includes both the rule of law and accountability, which are often called *positive* legacies for democratization. The absence of these legacies alone forms the *hard* prospect of consolidating Korean democracy, as Rose, Mishler & Haerpfer (1998) note.

Korea today remains a nation deeply plagued by the legacy of authoritarianism (Kristof 1996b; Steinberg 1996). To date, democratic change in Korea has not been accompanied by the necessary transformation of authoritarian political orientations into democratic ones. There have been no significant declines in the authoritarian political habits into which Koreans and their institutions have long been socialized. A majority of Koreans still believe that authoritarian solutions are more effective than democratic ones for tackling the nation's most serious problems. Furthermore, sharp increases have recently been reported in the belief that another Park Chung Hee is needed for the country. This confirms that Koreans are "inadequately vaccinated against regression to totalitarian government" (Shim 1997b). In short, Korean political culture lacks what Lipset (1994) calls the *effectiveness domain of democratic culture.*

Moreover, recent waves of anti-corruption reforms and campaigns have failed to serve as a major deterrent against the age-old, corrupt way of doing politics in Korea. Two former presidents and their associates have been imprisoned after being convicted of bribery and other corruption charges. While they were in jail, a son of the incumbent president was engaged in similar illegal practices. Many Koreans, especially the college-educated, whether democrats or authoritarians, show little respect for the rule of law. As they were in the authoritarian past, laws are perceived to be made only for those who are powerless and unfortunate. Politics is viewed as a personal game in which winners become rich and famous. Thus, the promotion of the quality of life among ordinary citizens is not a primary concern among many public officials, whether elected or not.

The signs are ubiquitous that democratization in Korea is rapidly turning into a highly uncertain, long march (Diamond & Kim 1998; Diamond, Henriksen & Shin 1999; Korean Political Science and Sociological Associations 1997). Both procedurally and substantively, it has also been of a limited nature. That is to say, while Korea, like many other new democracies, has passed a first test toward democratic consolidation by exchanging powers between opposing parties, its political parties have not been transformed into institutions of representative democracy. They remain not only hierarchically organized but also regionally based. Substantively, very little progress has been made in dismantling the structure of economic and political domination by the *chaebol* conglomerates and redistributing political power and economic resources on a broad basis. Political powers and economic wealth continue to remain in the same hands (Y. T. Jung 1997: 16).

In Korea today, moreover, the authoritarian past is far from being completely gone. It persists in the beliefs, values, and attitudes of its voters and elected officials who were all socialized to accept the cultural norms of the previous undemocratic regimes (Flanagan & Lee 1998; A. Lee 1994, 1998; Steinberg 1997). Consequently, most Koreans remain no more than diffusely attached to the ideals of democracy as the preferred political system and civic community. Being merely "fair weather" or "convenient" democrats, they are far from being committed to removing the residue of authoritarian rule and expanding the currently limited democracy-in-action. At the deepest and most important level, remoulding authoritarian cultural codes, fostering democratic behaviors, and liberalizing Confucian values may take several generations (see Dahrendorf 1990; Sztompka 1991).

Legislative assemblies, political parties, and other newly established democratic institutions, therefore, "must consolidate themselves without yet benefiting from democratic culture and democratic socialization" (Friedman 1994: 45). Otherwise, the continuing existence of ideological as well as military threats from the communist rival regime in the north together with the formidable legacy of authoritarian-sponsored prosperity might keep Korea merely drifting along as a "delegative" democracy.[8]

The furtherance of democratization is absolutely essential for the greater quality of private and public life in Korea, as documented in Chapter 2. Given the slow and uncertain process of its cultural democratization for the past decade (Auh 1992; A. Lee 1994; C. M. Park 1997), however, it seems a highly optimistic suggestion that Koreans will form a truly democratic nation in a single generation. It would be more accurate to think that they are in a "long march" that requires several generations rather than a single generation (see Jowitt 1992; see also Abramson & Inglehart 1995; Inglehart 1997; Rose, Mishler & Haerpfer 1998). This may be the reason why Alexis de Tocqueville (1956: 133) admonished us more than 160 years ago to approach the establishment of democracy as "the greatest political problem of our times."

More than anything else that has occurred since the democratic transition in 1988, the sudden outbreak of an economic crisis is complicating the current process of Korean democratization by entailing an unprecedented challenge to, as well as an opportunity for, the consolidation of its democracy. In the wake of the economic crisis that erupted in November 1997, questions are being raised about the continuing validity of democracy as a system conducive to economic prosperity. As the effects of financial dislocation are beginning to ripple through the economy, the question is also being raised about democratization itself being a probable cause of the economic crisis (Mo & Moon 1998). As unemployment and bankruptcies are reaching new heights and the economic dislocation is becoming more apparent with few signs of a turnaround in sight, doubts are being voiced about the continuing commitment of the Korean mass public to democracy.

Culturally, Korean democracy is now facing the challenge of whether ordinary citizens will continue their support for democratic reform under the worsening economic situation by directing their economic dissatisfaction at their key political leaders rather than at democracy itself. New democracies, such as Korea, are known to strive and mature when their citizens are sophisticated enough to distinguish between the poor quality of government performance and the legitimacy of democracy itself (Duch 1995; Huntington 1991).

Institutionally, the worsening economic crisis has occasioned calls for a comprehensive and critical assessment of the Korean democratic experience over the past ten years. It has simultaneously provided an opportunity to search for an alternative model of democratization. In revealing the dark side of the earlier model of democratization, the economic turmoil has served as an impetus for facilitating the transformation of crony capitalism which transformed Korea from its status as an economic powerhouse into that of an international pauper. Under pressure from foreign creditors, which some analysts call a blessing in disguise, Korea has begun to dismantle the age-old structure of crony capitalism that has been the most recalcitrant institutional legacy of the past military regimes. With the implementation of genuinely pro-market economic reforms, Korea has been afforded a new opportunity to promote democracy and the free market in parallel (The Republic of Korea Ministry of Finance and Economy & the Korea Development Institute 1998).

These new developments of cultural challenge and institutional opportunity will determine in large measure the direction and pace of the current democratization process in Korea during its second decade. Korea will emerge as a new East Asian model of democratic consolidation and economic prosperity only with the growth of sophistication about democratic politics among the mass public along with the successful management of a large-scale economic restructuring by the democratically elected Kim Dae Jung government.

Notes

Preface

1   The nature of the authoritarian rule led by the military is examined in J. Choi (1996); Cotton (1992); Cumings (1997); H. B. Im (1987); Jacobs (1985); Kihl (1984); Moon & Kang (1995); H. C. Sohn (1995); H. K. Sohn (1989); and Yoon (1990).

2   According to Freedom House's 1996–97 surveys of civil liberties and political rights, Korea is a "free" country with a combined average rating of 2 on a 7-point scale (for further details, see Karatnycky 1997).

3   There is a growing body of Korean-language literature devoted to the study of democratization in Korea. Representative of this literature are Ahn (1994); J. Choi (1993a, 1996, 1997); the Korean Consortium of Academic Associations (1997); the Korean Political Science and Sociological Associations (1997); Im & Song (1995); Park & Kim (1987); Seong (1996a); Shin, Kim, Chey & Park (1990); and H. C. Sohn (1995).

4   The Korean Consortium of Academic Associations (1997) and K. Wells (1995) are two notable exceptions to this generalization.

5   In the December 18 1997 presidential election, for example, the Agency for National Security Planning conducted a clandestine operation to smear Kim Dae Jung, an opposition party candidate.

6   Chey, Kwon & Hong (1989) and Shin & Rose (1997) describe sampling and other fieldwork procedures in detail.

Introduction

1   Cumings (1997), S. Han (1974), and Wade & Kang (1993) have examined the pro-democracy movements that existed in the earlier Republics of Korea. Their assessments of these movements provide a basis for concluding that there is an increasing desire on the part of the Korean people to live in a democracy. At the same time, however, these movements should not be seen as nations with a growing commitment to the various practices of democratic politics. Chapters 3 and 8 will provide empirical evidence that there is a large gulf between popular yearning for democracy on the one hand and actual commitment to it on the other.

266

2   See D. Clarke (1988) for the details of the Kwanju uprising.
3   For further details of this mass movement, see the Korean Consortium of Academic Associations (1997).
4   It is generally believed that Roh Tae Woo was not the author of the Declaration. For its full text, see Bedeski (1994: 169–70).
5   Y. J. Lee (1998) examines the direction and trajectories of President Kim's popularity with the time–series data gathered by the Korea-Gallup.
6   From the recent debate over why this happened, three things are clear. First, Kim Young Sam was not intellectually capable of understanding any major issue facing the nation. Second, his moral authority as the President collapsed completely when his second son and close associates were implicated in corruption scandals. Third, Korea is still a nation based on the rule of man, not the rule of law.
7   Results of the 15th presidential election are analyzed in the Korean Political Science Association (1998). See also C. W. Park (1998b) and Steinberg (1998).
8   These two Kims joined forces solely for the reason of political opportunity rather than policy.

1 Uncertain Dynamics of Democratization

1   For the evolution of the current wave of global democratization, see Huntington (1991); Diamond (1992, 1999); Karatnycky (1997), Schmitter & Santiso (1998); and D. Shin (1994).
2   Cumings (1997: chap. 7); the Korean Consortium of Academic Associations (1997, vol. 1); Im & Song (1995: part 2), and Seoul National University Institute of Social Development (1996: chaps. 13–16) offer historical accounts of the democratic movement in Korea for the period of 1960–96.
3   Barber (1984); Boyte (1990); Held (1987); Isaac (1994); Huber, Rueschemeyer & Stephens (1997); Macpherson (1977); Pateman (1970, 1994); and Weyland (1995) examine the various limitations associated with the minimal, procedural definitions of democracy.
4   The relationships between electoral democracy and the Confucian norms of *minbon* and *wimin* are discussed in B. K. Kim (1997: 21).
5   It should be noted that the present study differs significantly from the extant literature based on the dubious assumption that substantive change or democratization takes place at the systemic level only.
6   The conservative nature of Korean democratization was examined from a variety of perspectives in several papers presented at a recent conference organized by the Korean Political Science and Sociological Associations (1997). See also J. Choi (1996); H. C. Sohn (1995); and McDonough & Shin (1995).
7   During the last two months of 1997 when business conglomerates and merchant banks were unable to pay their huge short-term debts to foreign creditors, the Korean model of economic development was branded as crony capitalism. At the same time, the restructuring of this corruption-ridden model became the most controversial issue in Korean politics. The Kim Dae Jung government's first decision was to close five small and weak banks.
8   Regional disparities in the recruitment of government leaders and allocation of government benefits are carefully analyzed in Hwang (1997) and Park & Jang (1998).

9 The democratic Sixth Republic of Korea is not much different from its·
authoritarian Fifth Republic in terms of their commitment to social welfare.
As in pre-democratic Korea, social welfare programs in the Sixth Republic
account for less than 1 percent of its Gross National Product. In sharp
contrast, advanced countries are known to have committed from 10% to
20% of their GNPs to social welfare. Even middle-income countries are
known to spend five to seven times more for social welfare than democratic
Korea does. For further details, see K. Park (1997: 14).

2 The Human Meaning of Democratization

1 According to a survey conducted in 1996, a majority of Russians feel
negative about the present regime and positive about the old communist
regime. Specifically, a majority (55%) refuse to reject communism and
two other undemocratic alternatives. For further details, see Rose (1997:
101, 104).
2 Negative consequences of democratization for human life are highlighted in
Pateman (1996: 5–12) and Knight (1996).
3 One notable exception is Rose's (1995) comparative study of freedom in
Eastern and Central Europe.
4 This literature is reviewed in Caney (1992).
5 Temporal and spatial differences in the meaning of democracy are discussed
in Lakoff (1996) and Collier & Levitsky (1997).
6 The 1997 survey asked respondents whether they would welcome back
undemocratic alternatives, rule by the army and rule by a dictator. Only a
small minority were supportive of a return to military rule (16%) or dictatorship by a strong man (19%).

3 Commitment to Democratic Consolidation

1 Steinberg (1997) discusses some of these norms and mores in detail.
2 The authoritarian nature of Korean political culture and its impact on
democratization are explored in Auh (1992); Han & Auh (1987); A. Lee
(1993, 1994, 1998); C. M. Park (1991); and Park & Kim (1987).
3 Some of these failures are debated in the recent exchanges between
O'Donnell (1996) and Gunther, Diamandouros & Puhle (1996).
4 A few exceptions to this generalization include Rose (1992); Rose & Mishler
(1994); and D. Shin (1995).
5 C. M. Park (1997) examines democratic support among the Korean people
in terms of system affect, institution affect, and incumbent affect.
6 In principle, democracy and strong leadership can be mutually reinforcing.
In practice, however, people who have lived all their lives under authoritarian regimes often accept strong leaders who ignore democratic institutions, as Rose & Mishler (1996) note.
7 Responses to each of these two questions are weighted equally in constructing a 5-point summary index.

4 Citizen Competence and Participation

1 Major theoretical works on political participation are reviewed in Dahl
(1992); Dalton (1996); and Parry, Moyser & Day (1992).

2 Recent analyses of electoral and non-electoral political participation can be found in Bae (1995); Bae & Cotton (1993); H. Choi (1996); Korea-Gallup (1996); N. Lee (1993); and C. M. Park (1994).

3 The number of political acts examined in this study is relatively smaller than that reported in other national and cross-national studies, such as Barnes & Kaase (1979); Parry, Moyser & Day (1992); and Verba, Nie & Kim (1978). Nonetheless, it is sufficient enough to examine the significant modes of participation among the Korean people.

4 For a recent development in Korean civil society, see Choi & Im (1993); S. Kim (1997, 1998); and Seong (1996b).

5 H. B. Im (1996: 25) points out another problem with Korean civil society: "The proliferation of interest associations have not developed institutional-ized channels for mediating differences among them. Korean interest politics is still amorphous, centrifugal, hyperbolic, and unruly."

6 The squared part correlation coefficients indicate how much a cluster of predictors accounts for the variance in the dependent variable which is left unexplained by other clusters of variables. For details, see Bohrnstedt & Knoke (1982: 370).

7 For earlier research on the mobilized participation of the Korean electorate in politics, see C. L. Kim (1980).

8 These five subgroups are identified according to a 3-step procedure First, respondents were divided into roughly three equivalent groups in terms of their educational attainment and family income. Then their relative stand-ing on each variable was coded as: 1 = low; 2 = middle; and 3 = high. Finally their scores on both variables were summed to create five different groups: (1) lowest, (2) low, (3) middle, (4) high, and (5) highest. For each of these groups, we calculated the average of political acts in which its members engaged in 1984 and 1994.

9 Standard scores are more commonly called Z scores. They are calculated by subtracting the mean from each score and dividing by the standard deviation. These scores, unlike original ones, allow for making comparisons across distributions with different means and standard deviations.

10 The most active in politics represent the highest fifth of each sample on an overall participation index.

11 This pre-democratic survey asked 952 respondents whether they had engaged in any of the following during the past few years: (1) saying that a particular candidate is better than others, (2) voting in an election, (3) persuading someone outside own family to vote, (4) taking part in a political meeting, (5) becoming a party member or campaigning for a candidate, (6) visiting a politician or a government office for an official business, (7) visiting a government office as a representative of residential committee, (8) writing a letter to a newspaper or a radio station, (9) taking part in a petition drive, and (10) contributing money to a politician. For further details, see Park & Kim (1987).

5 Legislative Assemblies

1 Choe (1997) examines the electoral system from comparative and historical perspectives.

2 For the consequences of these local elections for the consolidation of Korean democracy, see Seong (1998).

3   C. W. Park (1990) identifies the various ways in which members of the National Assembly contact their district voters.

4   C. W. Park (1998a) offers a balanced account of the changing relationship between the presidency and the national legislature in the wake of the democratic transition in 1988.

5   The informal norms of hierarchy and obedience in the National Assembly are examined from a game-theoretic perspective in Kim & Kim (1995).

6   Earlier surveys conducted by *The Chosun Ilbo* in 1989 and 1990 reported similar patterns of prevailingly negative assessments. For further details, see Kim & Park (1992: 84–5).

7   These three categories of political ideology were constructed by collapsing original responses on a 10-point scale (Appendix B U1) as follows: left = 1, 2, 3, and 4; moderate = 5 and 6; and right = 7, 8, 9, and 10.

8   Three levels of political participation were determined by dividing the 1996 survey sample into three roughly equivalent groups according to their scores on an overall index of political participation. The participation index was constructed by summing the number of political acts in which each respondent reported being engaged. Appendix B L5 lists the specific political acts asked in the 1996 survey.

9   The four items on democratic preference, desire for further democratization, support for mass participation, and commitment to political competition are listed in Appendix B C1.3, E3.3, E3.1, and E3.2 in that order.

6 Political Parties

1   For recent debates on perils and virtues of parliamentary systems and proportional representation, see Horowitz (1990); Linz (1990a, 1990b); Lijphart (1991); Mainwaring & Shugart (1997); and Quade (1991).

2   The significant differences between these hybrid regimes are discussed in Schmitter (1994: 60).

3   In view of this finding, one naturally comes to wonder why Koreans are more reluctant to support political parties than legislative assemblies. One answer to this question is that many Koreans view political parties as constituting "the weakest link in the democratic process" (Steinberg 1998: 80). They trust political parties much less than the two other representative institutions of the National Assembly and the presidency (for details, see Shin & Rose 1997).

4   The various problems of building a democratic party system in post-authoritarian Korea are examined in Jaung (1997, 1998); Y. H. Kim (1994); and H. Yang (1996). According to Y. H. Kim (1994: 179), "its [Korean] political parties have become major actors in the political process, yet they have played a limited role in consolidating the nascent democracy."

5   For an analysis of this merger from the perspective of rational choice, see H. Kim (1995, 1997).

6   To construct these indexes, we first counted the number of news media respondents identified as sources of their political news and the number of associations with which they reported being affiliated. On the basis of each count, we divided them into four roughly equivalent groups.

7   For the MCA, regional ties were considered as a categorical variable and measured in terms of the regions of Korea in which respondents were residing at the time of survey. The five categories are: (1) Seoul, (2) Kyonggi and Kangwon, (3) Choongchung, (4) Cholla, and (5) Kyongsang.

7 Consolidating a Nascent Democracy

1 These and other issues concerning the liberal model of democratization are discussed in Beetham (1992) and Schmitter (1995a).

2 This merger has led many Koreans to question Kim Young Sam's sincerity as a democratic reformer and to wonder whether he is more of a political opportunist than a genuine democrat.

3 It should be noted that President Kim's successful presidential campaign was financed by the slush fund illegally amassed and controlled by his immediate predecessor, Roh Tae Woo. In his recent court appearance, Roh testified that as much as 70 billion won ($90 million) was funneled into Kim's presidential campaign chest. For this reason, Roh's defense lawyers argued that "if past military governments were illegitimate, as the prosecution argues, then the legality of the current administration must also be open to question" (*Economist* 1996: 33).

4 President Kim's ideology of democratic reform is discussed in Y. D. Jung (1993).

5 For the first three waves, see Kihl (1995); Kil (1993); D. Kim (1993); M. Kim (1994); and Paik (1995).

6 According to the Ministry of Justice, 66 percent of Roh Tae Woo's slush fund penalties and 14 percent of Chun Doo Whan's penalties have been collected and returned to the national treasury as of October 1998.

7 This index was constructed by multiplying two 10-point scales, one on regime character and the other on regime performance. Appendix B B1.1 and S1.1 list the two scales for the Chun Doo Whan government, while Appendix B B1.2 and S1.2 list those for the Roh Tae Woo government.

8 It should be noted that many critics of President Kim have accused him of being a "civilian dictator." They have also charged that his anti-authoritarian campaign has had far more to do with the desire to bolster his sagging popularity than with "righting the wrongs of the authoritarian past."

9 President Kim's democratic reforms are critically assessed in Kim & Hahm (1997); G. Lee (1993); Y. Lee (1997, 1998); and H. C. Sohn (1995).

8 Acquiring Democratic Orientations

1 The most notable premise distinguishing the communitarian from liberal conceptions of democratic politics concerns the priority of the common good and self-interest. According to the former, many human goods are irreducibly social. The common good, therefore, should take priority over all other political values, including individual preferences and rights. For further discussion of this debate, see Bell et al. (1995); Dietz (1993); and Schmitter (1995a).

2 A natural objection to this procedure is that, given the progress of the transition, respondents may be inclined to adjust upwards, in hindsight, their estimates of the desirability and suitability of democracy under the authoritarian and first democratic governments. While this possibility cannot be ruled out completely, data drawn from a survey we conducted in 1991 generate mean estimates of satisfaction with these earlier governments that are not significantly different from the satisfaction estimates for the same governments reported in 1994. Thus, there is no empirical evidence that the constancy in "satisfaction" should not hold for "desirability" and "suitability." In addition, what matters more than the absolute values is the relative

ordering of recollected as compared to current evaluations. If, for example, feelings conjured up in memory about the suitability of democracy turned out to be higher under the authoritarian regime than during the current democracy, there would be serious reason to doubt the validity of the data. But, empirically, as will be shown, this is not the case. It should also be noted that our results are consistent with the longitudinal stability of comparable retrospective indicators registered by Rose and his associates in their New Democracies Barometer annual surveys of Eastern and Central Europe since 1991.

3   Past and present ratings were compared to estimate the experienced impact of democratization on life quality. Present and future ratings were compared to estimate the expected impact of further democratization on life quality. These comparisons yielded indexes ranging from −9 to +9. Negative and positive scores of this composite measure were collapsed into two broad categories so that its scores could range from −2 to +2.

4   An index ranging from −9 to +9 was first constructed by subtracting ratings for the Chun Doo Whan government from those for the Kim Young Sam government. Negative and positive scores of this index were then collapsed into 2 broad categories so that its scores can range from −2 to +2.

5   The 6 percent of variance explained jointly by the two models is calculated by subtracting the sum (10%) of the variance explained uniquely by each model from the total (18%) variance explained jointly by the two models, which is listed in the last column of Table 8.7.

6   Many, though not all, studies of democratization fail to distinguish between the ideals and practice of democracy. For some exceptions, see Fuchs et al. (1995); Toka (1995); and Kaase (1994).

9 Korean Democracy: Problems and Prospects

1   The impact of democratic regime change on political leadership is examined in Hwang (1997).

2   For an example of a recent reversion to authoritarian practice in Korea, see Pollack (1997).

3   Nonetheless, it should be noted that Confucianism is opposed to totalitarian rule "for it has placed culture above politics, and not the reverse" (U. Kim 1993: 163). For further discussions of Confucianism and democracy, see Fukuyama (1995a); Hahm (1997); Hahm & Rhyu (1997); B. K. Kim (1997); K. D. Kim (1997); Kim & Suh (1997); B. I. Koh (1996); and Tu (1996).

4   The general problems of and prospects of democratization in East Asia are examined in Alagappa (1995); Cotton (1995b); Curtis (1997); Fukuyama (1997); and Scalapino (1993, 1997).

5   For comparative analyses of institutional democratization in these two countries, see Chan & Clark (1992–93); Eberstadt (1992); and Scalapino (1993).

6   The obvious caveat is that there are significant differences in the practice of Confucianism between Korea and its Asian neighbors. For discussions of these differences, see Fukuyama (1995a) and Tu (1996).

7   H. B. Im (1996) addresses this question, analyzing a variety of forces facilitating and impeding the consolidation of Korean democracy.

8   Similar conclusions are offered in J. Choi (1996, 1997), Cumings (1989, 1997); H. B. Im (1997a); M. Lee (1990); C. W. Park (1998a); H. C. Sohn (1995); Steinberg (1996); and Ziegler (1997).

Appendix A

Index Construction and Missing Data

Advances in the study of democratization have been slowed by the lack of systematic efforts to develop new, innovative measures of the multifarious and dynamic phenomenon (for a comprehensive review of its existing measures, see Diamond 1999: chap. 5). The measurements of democratization taking place at the macro and micro levels to date have mostly been one-dimensional indexes of a quantitative nature. While these indexes differ a great deal, they have two things in common. Conceptually, these composite measures are based on the assumption that all significant attributes of democracy, or popular orientations to those attributes, can be reduced to one dimension (Rose & Shin 1997: 5). At the macro level, therefore, this unidimensional approach makes it difficult to meaningfully differentiate the differences that may be emerging among Western and non-Western versions of democracy, as Huntington (1996a: 10) points out. At the micro level also, the same approach makes it difficult to unravel the dynamics of mass political orientations, each of which often shifts at a different pace.

Technically, indexes, either unidimensional or multi-dimensional, in the literature on democracy and democratization are constructed mostly by means of factor analysis. With few exceptions, original values of each individual indicator are first standardized using the Z-score transformation. These standardized measures are subject to a principle–component analysis. A summary score for each unit of measurement is obtained by multiplying the factor loading for each standardized item by its respective standardized score. This procedure is repeated for all component indicators. The sum of their resultant products is the values for each unit on a given index. The index's values, however, are laden with two limitations. The first is that substantive meaning cannot be attached to the values of the index. The second is that those values are extremely difficult to interpret for political leaders, government officials, and the concerned citizenry with little or no background in statistical analysis.

The measurements of democratization need to be enhanced in such a way that they are capable of differentiating the qualitative differences among an increasing number of individual citizens and their countries subject to such change. The measurements also need to be enhanced in such a way that index values can be easily understood especially by those who are key players and active supporters of the democratic reform movement. In view of these needs, a large number of nominal (qualitative) as well as metric (quantitative) indexes, which can be replicated easily in future research, were constructed for this study of Korean democratization. In addition, simple algebraic procedures of addition, subtraction, and counting or enumerating are chosen over the statistical technique of factor analysis in constructing metric indexes.

Nominal Indexes

Nominal indexes are typologies seeking to identify distinctive types or patterns among units of measurement. Most frequently, they are constructed by considering the dichotomous or trichotomous characteristics of two variables *simultaneously*. Less frequently, they are constructed by considering those characteristics of more than two variables *sequentially*. These two methods of combination are used throughout the book. Listed below are the names of the specific indexes based on each method and the chapters in which they are reported.

1. Indexes Based on the Simultaneous Method of Combination

(1)   Overall patterns of impact from democratization on Korean life (Chap. 2)
(2)   Types of orientations to democracy as a viable political system (Chap. 3)
(3)   Types of external commitment to democratic consolidation (Chap. 3)
(4)   Types of cognitive sophistication (Chap. 4)
(5)   Types of legislative orientations (Chap. 5)
(6)   Types of legislative supporters (Chap. 5)
(7)   Types of overall approval of legislative performance (Chap. 5)
(8)   Types of overall approval of legislative performance change (Chap. 5)
(9)   Patterns of being informed about legislative parties (Chap. 6)
(10)   Types of orientations toward political parties (Chap. 6)
(11)   Types of party support (Chap. 6)
(12)   Types of support for democratization (Chap. 8).

2. Indexes Based on the Sequential Method of Combination

(1)   Patterns of overall commitment to democratic consolidation (Chap. 3)
(2)   Types of political participators (Chap. 4)
(3)   Types of the preferred party system (Chap. 6)
(4)   Patterns of orientations toward the democratic party system (Chap. 6)
(5)   Types summarizing the dynamics of democratization (Chap. 8).

Metric Indexes

Metric indexes, like nominal ones, are intended to offer a comprehensive, balanced, and summary account of complex phenomena in terms of multiple indicators. Unlike the latter, the former merely estimate the extent to which the combined values of those indicators are present or absent. Throughout the book, five simple methods are used to combine multiple indicators into summary indexes. They are: (1) counting the number of indicators that register positive or negative values, (2) adding all the legitimate values of component indicators, (3) subtracting the legitimate values of one indicator from those of another, (4) counting the number of indicators scoring positive values for each dimension first and then adding the resultant numbers for all dimensions, (5) counting the number of indicators with positive and negative values separately first and subtracting the number of negative indicators from that of positive indicators. Listed below are the names of specific indexes based on each of these five procedures and the chapters in which they are reported.

3. Indexes Based on Counting

(1) Exposure to democratic values (Chap. 3)
(2) Number of political acts with or without voting (Chap. 4)
(3) Number of associational affiliations (Chap. 4)
(4) Depth of non-political participation (Chap. 4)
(5) Minimal involvement in public life (Chap. 4)
(6) Adequate involvement in public life (Chap. 4)
(7) Depth of legislative needs (Chap. 5)
(8) Number of parliamentary parties identified correctly and incorrectly (Chap. 6)
(9) Overall support for the democratic party system (Chap. 6)
(10) Overall assessments of political party performance (Chap. 6)
(11) Media exposure (Chap. 6)
(12) Civic involvement (Chap. 6)
(13) Overall support for President Kim Young Sam's rectification campaign (Chap. 7)
(14) Corruption propensity (Chap. 6)
(15) Negative perceptions of economic conditions and life quality (Chap. 8)
(16) Commitment to democracy-in-practice (Chap. 9)
(17) Inclinations toward illegal services (Chap. 9)
(18) Levels of dissociation from authoritarian rule (Chap. 9).

4. Indexes Based on Adding

(1) Substantive democratization (Chap. 1)
(2) Democratic regime support (Chap. 3)
(3) Internal and external commitment to democratic consolidation (Chap. 3)
(4) Political attentiveness (Chap. 4)
(5) Index of overall legislative support (Chap. 5)
(6) Positive memories of authoritarian rule (Chap. 9).

5. Indexes Based on Subtracting

(1) The experienced impact of democratization on private and public life (Chap. 2)
(2) The expected impact of democratization on private and public life (Chap. 2)
(3) Shifts in democratic desirability and suitability (Chap. 8).

6. Indexes Based on Multiplication

(1) The perceived quality of the Chun Doo Whan and Roh Tae Woo governments (Chap. 7).

7. Indexes Based on Counting and Subtracting

(1) The overall experienced impact of democratization on the quality of life (Chap. 2)
(2) The overall expected impact of democratic consolidation on the quality of life (Chap. 2)

(3)   The overall expected impact of authoritarian reversal on the quality of Korean life (Chap. 2)

(4)   The overall impact of democratization on involvement in public life (Chap. 4).

In constructing these nominal and metric indexes, two different procedures are employed to treat missing data. Missing data were all included in the processes of constructing nominal indexes by means of the sequential method of combination and metric indexes by the counting procedure only. In constructing indexes by all other procedures, missing data were excluded. In univariate analyses, missing data were excluded only when those data were small (less than 2 percent of each sample). Missing data were excluded in all bivariate and multivariate statistical analyses. As always, the exclusion of missing data reduced the number of cases and sampling problems in the analyses reported throughout the book. Fortunately, missing data for most variables turned out to be relatively small.

Appendix B

Survey Questions

A. Understanding of Democracy

A1   [SHOW CARD]. People expect several different things from democratic change. Please look over the statements listed on this card and identify all those you personally consider important to democratic political development in our country.

(1)   Expansion of political freedom
(2)   Participation of the mass public in politics
(3)   Economic development in the country
(4)   Guarantees for people's economic livelihood
(5)   Free competition among political parties
(6)   System of justice that treats everyone fairly
(7)   Reducing the gap between the rich and the poor
(8)   Achieving equality between the genders.

A2   [SHOW CARD]. Please look over the six statements on this card and tell me the one that you consider most important to our country's democratic development.

(1)   Political freedom
(2)   Economic development
(3)   Fair justice system
(4)   Free competition among political parties
(5)   Economic equality
(6)   Economic security.

A3   [SHOW CARD]. There are several different types of democracies, as shown on this card. Please tell me the types you have heard of.

(1)   Social democracy
(2)   People's democracy
(3)   Consensus democracy
(4)   Participatory democracy
(5)   Guided democracy
(6)   Liberal democracy.

A4   [SHOW CARD]. People associate democracy with diverse meanings such as those on this card. For each of them, please tell me whether, for you, democracy has a lot, something, not much, or nothing to do with . . .
(1)   Political freedom
(2)   Social equality
(3)   Local autonomy
(4)   Less corruption and less selling of influence
(5)   Mass participation in politics
(6)   Equal justice before law
(7)   Governmental control of big businesses
(8)   Equal rights for women
(9)   Reflecting public opinion in policy-making
(10)   Improvement of economic life
(11)   Free competition among political parties
(12)   Politics of compromises and negotiations.

B. The Experience of Democratization

B1   [SHOW CARD]. On this scale ranging from a low of 1 to a high of 10, 1 means complete dictatorship and 10 means complete democracy. The closer to 1 the score is, the more dictatorial our country is; the closer to 10 the score is, the more democratic our country is.
(1)   On this scale, where would you place our country under the Chun Doo Whan government?
(2)   Where would you place our country under the Roh Tae Woo government?
(3)   Where would you place our country at the present time?
B2   How much or little influence do you think people like you have on the government's policy-making – a lot, some, a little, or none?
B3   How would you say the influence that people like you have on the government has changed since the end of the Chun Doo Whan period – increased a lot, increased a little, stayed about the same, decreased a little, or decreased a lot?
B4   How much effect do you think the government has on people like you – a lot, some, a little, or none?
B5   How would you say the effect on people like yourself of what the government decides has changed – increased a lot, increased a little, stayed the same, decreased a little, or decreased a lot?

C. Preference for Democracy-in-Principle

C1   [SHOW CARD]. Here is a scale measuring the extent to which people desire democracy. On this scale, 1 means complete dictatorship and 10 means complete democracy.
(1)   Where would you place the extent to which you desired democracy for our country during President Chun Doo Whan's Fifth Republic period?
(2)   Where would you place the extent to which you desired democracy for our country during the period of President Roh Tae Woo's Sixth Republic?
(3)   Where would you place the extent to which you desire democracy nowadays?
C2   Let us consider the idea of democracy, not its practice. In principle, how much are you for or against the idea of democracy – for very much, for somewhat, against somewhat, or against very much?

D. Support for Democracy-in-Action

D1 [SHOW CARD]. Here is a scale measuring the extent to which people think democracy is suitable. One means complete unsuitability while 10 means complete suitability.

(1) During the period of the Chun Doo Whan government, to what extent was democracy suitable for our country?

(2) During the period of the Roh Tae Woo government, to what extent was democracy suitable for our country?

(3) Under the present Kim Young Sam government, to what extent is democracy suitable for our country?

D2 Between the two national goals of democratization and economic development, which goal do you think is more important?

(1) Economic development is more important

(2) Democratization is more important

(3) Equally important.

D3 How much do you agree or disagree with the following statement – strongly agree, somewhat agree, somewhat disagree, or strongly disagree?

(1) Our national security laws should be revised

(2) Labor unions should be allowed to engage in political activities

(3) Current voting ages of 20 or older should be lowered to 18

(4) Our political system is democratized enough; we should not expect too much.

E. Commitment to Democratic Consolidation

E1 Some people support that our country has changed to a democracy while others oppose it. Do you strongly support, somewhat support, somewhat oppose, or strongly oppose the change to democratic regime?

E2 Which of the following statements do you agree with most?

(1) Democracy is always preferable to any other kind of government

(2) Under certain situations, a dictatorship is preferable

(3) For people like me, it does not matter whether we have a democratic government or non-democratic government.

E3 How strongly do you agree or disagree with the following statement – very strongly agree, somewhat agree, somewhat disagree, or strongly disagree?

(1) Political participation is not necessary if decision-making is left in the hands of a few trusted, competent leaders

(2) Multi-party competition makes the country's political system stronger

(3) Our political system should be made a lot more democratic than it is now.

F. Satisfaction with Democracy-in-Practice

F1 How satisfied or dissatisfied are you with the way democracy works in Korea these days – very satisfied, fairly satisfied, not very satisfied, or not at all satisfied?

F2 [SHOW CARD]. How satisfied or dissatisfied are you with the way democracy works in our country these days? Please choose a number on this scale in which 1 means complete dissatisfaction and 10 means complete satisfaction.

F3 With which of the following statements do you agree most?

(1) Our democracy works well

(2) Our democracy has many defects, but it works

(3) Our democracy is getting worse, and soon it will not work at all.

G. Dissociation from Authoritarianism

G1   Please tell me whether you strongly agree, somewhat agree, somewhat disagree, or strongly disagree with each of the following statements.

(1)   If a government is often restrained by an assembly, it will be unable to achieve great accomplishments

(2)   We can leave all things to morally upright leaders

(3)   Too many social groups would undermine social harmony

(4)   Heterogeneous opinions would undermine social order.

G2   Our present system of government is not the only one that this country has had, and some people say we would be better off if the country was governed differently.

How much do you agree or disagree with their views in favor of the following? Please tell me whether you strongly agree, somewhat agree, somewhat disagree, or strongly disagree.

(1)   The army should govern the country

(2)   Better to get rid of Parliament and elections, and have a strong leader decide everything

(3)   The dictatorial rule led by a strong leader like Park Chung Hee is much better than a democracy to deal with the serious problems facing the country these days

(4)   For our country these days, a strong leader is needed more than democracy

(5)   The most important decisions about the economy should be made by experts and not the government and Parliament.

H. Dissociation from Particularism

H1   How do you feel about the following activities? Please tell me whether you feel very bad, somewhat bad, not much bad, or not at all bad.

(1)   To receive a gift at election time

(2)   To be treated to a meal at election time

(3)   To receive compensation for the work performed at election time

(4)   To give a gift to a government official

(5)   To give pocket money to a government official for holidays

(6)   To treat a government official to a meal for one's own business

(7)   To contribute money to politicians for one's own business.

H2   Out of 10 established politicians, how many do you feel are corrupt?

H3   Out of 10 civil servants, how many do you feel are corrupt?

H4   Since the inauguration of President Kim Young Sam, do you think political corruption has decreased a lot, decreased a little, changed little, increased a little, or increased a lot?

H5   How would you describe the level of political corruption of the Kim Young Sam government? Is it very high, high, not so high, or very little?

H6   People often have problems getting organizations to do what they would like. What do you think a person should do if they had the following problems?

(1)   A military draftee is told that he will be sent to a remote part of the country. How could he try to avoid this undesirable assignment? Do you think he should offer a bribe, use connections, make up an excuse to rescind the undesirable assignment, submit a petition to delay the undesirable assignment, or nothing can be done, accept it?

(2)   What should a parent do for a high-school student whose grades aren't good enough to be admitted to a university? Offer a bribe, use connections, make up an excuse that would help discount poor grades, pay a tutor and take exams again to do better, or nothing can be done, accept?

(3)   What should a person who needs a governmental permit do if an official says: "just be patient, wait"? Offer a bribe, use connections, write a letter to the head office, don't worry; the permit will turn up, or nothing can be done, just accept?

(4)   What should a family do to get a government-subsidized apartment, even if not entitled to it according to the regulations? Offer a bribe, use connections, tell a story to make the household appear eligible, save money to buy a private apartment, house, or nothing can be done?

I. Change in the Quality of National Life

I1   [SHOW CARD]. Here is a picture of a ladder with ten rungs. Imagine that the top (tenth rung) of the ladder represents the best possible place to live and the bottom (first rung) of the ladder represents the worst possible place to live.

(1)   Where do you think our country stood on the ladder during the Chun Doo Whan period?

(2)   Where do you think that our country stands at the present time?

(3)   Where do you think that our country stands presently if the Chun Doo Whan government continued to rule?

(4)   Where do you think our country will stand in five years if President Kim Young Sam's democratic reforms succeed completely?

(5)   Where do you think our country will stand in five years if his reforms fail and the military seizes power again?

J. Change in the Quality of Personal Life

J1   [SHOW CARD]. Here is a picture of another ladder with ten rungs. Imagine that the top (tenth rung) of the ladder represents the best possible life for you and the bottom (first rung) the worst possible life for you.

(1)   On which step of the ladder would you say you personally stood during the Chun Doo Whan government period?

(2)   On which step do you stand at the present time?

(3)   On which step do you think you would stand now if the Chun Doo Whan government continued to rule?

(4)   On which step do you think you will stand in five years if President Kim Young Sam's democratic reforms succeed completely?

(5)   Where do you feel you will stand in five years if his reforms fail and the military seizes power again.

K. Citizen Competence

K1   For the past decade we have lived under the three different governments led by Presidents Chun Doo Whan, Roh Tae Woo, and Kim Young Sam, respectively. Of these three, which one do you think is the best government in dealing with each of the following problems? Which one is the worst government?

(1)   Preventing crimes and maintaining order

(2)   Economic development
(3)   Reducing the gap between the rich and the poor
(4)   Reflecting public opinion in policy-making
(5)   Fair distribution of governmental benefits
(6)   Expanding political freedom.

L. Political Attentiveness and Involvement

L1   How much are you interested in politics these days? Are you very much, somewhat, not very much, or not at all?

L2   How much influence do you think you have on what the government does? Very much, somewhat, not very much, or not at all?

L3   How often do you watch TV news? Always, often, not often, or rarely?

L4   [SHOW CARD]. Have you participated in any of the political activities listed on this card since the Sixth Republic was inaugurated with the Roh Tae Woo government in 1988?

(1)   Voting
(2)   Discussing politics with others
(3)   Participating in a political meeting or assembly
(4)   Campaigning for a particular candidate
(5)   Contributing money to a politician or political party
(6)   Working with others for a community problem
(7)   Contacting a civil servant or politician
(8)   Signing or submitting a petition
(9)   Taking part in a demonstration
(10)   Taking part in a strike.

L5   I am going to tell you a variety of political activities. Please tell me whether you have done any of those activities for the past seven years since the beginning of the Sixth Republic in 1988.

(1)   Voting in presidential or parliamentary elections
(2)   Voting in local elections
(3)   Persuading others to vote
(4)   Campaigning for a particular candidate
(5)   Discussing politics with others
(6)   Participating in a political meeting or assembly
(7)   Campaigning for a particular political party or candidate
(8)   Contacting a civil servant or politician
(9)   Contributing money to a politician or political party
(10)   Working with others for a community problem
(11)   Signing or submitting a petition
(12)   Taking part in a demonstration
(13)   Taking part in a strike.

L6   As compared to the Chun Doo Whan government period, would you say your interest in politics these days has increased a lot, increased somewhat, changed little, decreased somewhat, or decreased a lot?

L7   As compared to the Chun Doo Whan government period, has your involvement in political activities increased a lot, increased somewhat, changed little, decreased somewhat, or decreased a lot?

L8   As compared to the Chun Doo Whan government period, has your involvement in groups or voluntary associations increased a lot, increased somewhat, changed little, decreased somewhat, or decreased a lot?

M. Involvement in Civic Life

M1 [SHOW CARD]. This card lists six categories of organizations and associations. In which categories do you currently participate?

(1) Fraternal organization or association
(2) Religious organization or association
(3) Interest organization or association
(4) Social organization or association
(5) Cultural organization or association
(6) Political organization or association.

M2 With which of the following associations or groups are you currently affiliated or a member of?

(1) Fraternal association or group
(2) Neighborhood association
(3) Religious organization or group
(4) Hobby or sports club
(5) Arts, music, or educational association or group
(6) Labor union
(7) Agricultural or business organization or group
(8) Professional association
(9) Political party or organization
(10) Charity or social service organization or group
(11) Environmental protection organization or group
(12) Consumer protection organization or group
(13) Civil defense organization or group.

M3 Generally speaking, to what extent do you think the majority of people can be trusted? Would you say a lot, somewhat, a little, or not at all?

M4 How much do you agree or disagree with the view that "it is dangerous to compromise with political rivals"? Strongly agree, somewhat agree, somewhat disagree, or strongly disagree?

N. Support for Legislative Democracy

N1 How much do you think each of the following legislative assemblies is needed? Absolutely, generally, not very much, or not at all?

(1) National Assembly
(2) Metropolitan or provincial assembly
(3) City district or rural county assembly.

N2 How much do you agree or disagree with the view that it is better to abolish the National Assembly and let a strong leader decide? Strongly agree, somewhat agree, somewhat disagree, or strongly disagree?

N3 If the National Assembly was suspended, would you definitely approve, somewhat approve, somewhat disapprove, or definitely disapprove?

O. Approval of Legislative Performance

O1 How do you think the National Assembly has been performing what it is supposed to do? Very well, well, poorly, or very poorly?

O2 How do you think your district representative has been performing what he/she is supposed to do? Very well, well, poorly, or very poorly?

O3 Compared to the National Assembly during the Fifth Republic, how do you think the current National Assembly is performing? Much better, somewhat better, about the same, somewhat worse, or much worse?

O4 Compared to the representative from your own district during the Fifth

Republic, how do you think the incumbent representative is performing? Much better, somewhat better, about the same, somewhat worse, or much worse?

P. Support for a Democratic Party System

P1   How strongly do you agree or disagree with the following views? Strongly agree, somewhat agree, somewhat disagree, or strongly disagree?

(1)   Political parties are absolutely needed for our democratic political development

(2)   Our country would be better-off if there is only one political party

(3)   Political parties provide the opportunities for citizens to participate in politics

(4)   Political parties tend to serve in the interests of their leaders

(5)   There is little difference among political parties.

P2   People have different views about groups or organizations opposing democratization. Are you in favor of or against the view that such groups or organizations should be outlawed?

P3   Do you remember the names of the political parties currently represented in the National Assembly?

P4   Do you feel close to any of these parties?

P5   In general, how do you feel about political parties these days as compared to the Chun Doo Whan government period? More favorable, about the same, or less favorable?

P6   Have you ever worked for a political party?

P7   Are you currently a member of any political party?

P8   How well do you think our political parties fulfil what they are supposed to do as a representative institution? Very well, well, poorly or very poorly?

Q. Support for Anti-Authoritarian Campaign

Q1   For the past three months, the President Kim Young Sam government has been conducting the campaign to rectify the various ills of the authoritarian past. How much do you support or oppose each of the following measures? Strongly support, somewhat support, somewhat oppose, or strongly oppose?

(1)   Arrest of former President Chun Doo Whan

(2)   Arrest of former President Roh Tae Woo

(3)   Arrest of 1979 coup d'etat plotters

(4)   Arrest of participants in the 1990 Kwangju massacre

(5)   Prosecution of businessmen who provided slush funds

(6)   Prosecution of politicians who managed slush funds

(7)   Exclusion politicians of the Fifth and Sixth Republic leaders from public offices.

Q2   How much do you think the rectification campaign would help or harm the maturing of our democracy? Help a great deal, help somewhat, affect little, harm somewhat, or harm a great deal?

R. Economic and Political Changes

R1   How would you compare the economic condition of our country today with what it was during the Chun Doo Whan period? Would you say it is much better, a little better, about the same, a little worse, or much worse today?

R2   How do you think our national economy will be in five years? Much better, a little better, about the same, a little worse, or much worse?

R3   How would you compare the economic situation of your household today with what it was during the Chun Doo Whan period? Is it much better, a little better, about the same, a little worse, or much worse?

R4   What do you think your household economic situation will be like in five years? Much better, somewhat better, about the same, somewhat worse, or much worse?

R5   How do you think the political situation of our country has changed since the inauguration of the Sixth Republic? Has it changed much better, a little better, a little worse, or much worse, or stayed about the same?

R6   How do you think the political situation of our country will be in five years? Much better, a little better, about the same, a little worse, or much worse?

S. Satisfaction with Governmental Performance

S1   [SHOW CARD]. On the whole, how satisfied or dissatisfied are you with the way the following governments handled the problems facing our society? Please choose a number on this scale where 1 means complete dissatisfaction and 10 means complete satisfaction.

(1)   How much would you say you were satisfied with the Chun Doo Whan government?

(2)   How about the Roh Tae Woo government?

(3)   How about the Kim Young Sam government?

S2   Of the Chun Doo Whan, Roh Tae Woo, and Kim Young Sam governments, which one do you think was most successful in dealing with each of the following problems?

(1)   Preventing crimes and maintaining order

(2)   Economic development

(3)   Reflecting public opinion in governance

(4)   Fair distribution of government benefits

(5)   Expanding political freedom

(6)   Economic equality.

S3   Which government do you think was least successful in dealing with each of the following problems?

(1)   Preventing crimes and maintaining order

(2)   Economic development

(3)   Reflecting public opinion in governance

(4)   Fair distribution of government benefits

(5)   Expanding political freedom

(6)   Economic equality.

T. Exposure to the New Media

T1   How many days a week do you usually watch TV news?

T2   Do you rely on any of the following news media to learn about political events?

(1)   Television

(2)   Radio

(3)   Newspapers

(4)   Magazines.

U. Political Ideology

U1   [SHOW CARD]. Here is a scale measuring political attitudes from 1
      (extreme left) to 10 (extreme right). Where would you put yourself?

V.   Demographics

V1   Gender
(1)   Male
(2)   Female.
V2   What is your age?
V3   Are you married?
(1)   Not married
(2)   Married
(3)   Divorced
(4)   Widowed.
V4   Region of residence

(1)	Seoul	(8)	Kangwon
(2)	Pusan	(9)	Choongbook
(3)	Taegu	(10)	Choongnam
(4)	Inchon	(11)	Jeonbook
(5)	Kwangju	(12)	Jeonnam
(6)	Daejon	(13)	Kyongbook
(7)	Kyonggi	(14)	Kyongnam.

V5   Size of community
(1)   Metropolitan area
(2)   Medium-size and small city
(3)   Town
(4)   Village.
V6   Where were you born?
(1)   South Korea
(2)   North Korea
(3)   China
(4)   Japan
(5)   Another.
V7   How long have you lived in this area (city/county)?
       _____ years.
V8   With which of the following do you most closely identify yourself?
(1)   Local community or city in which I live: e.g. Seoul
(2)   Region
(3)   South Korea
(4)   North Korea
(5)   The whole of Korea – North and South
(6)   Asia
(7)   Other
(8)   Don't know.
V9   How much education have you had?
(1)   No schooling
(2)   Primary school
(3)   Middle school
(4)   High school
(5)   College
(6)   Graduate school.

V10 Do you think you belong to upper, upper-middle, middle, lower-middle, or lower class?
(1)   upper class
(2)   upper-middle class
(3)   middle class
(4)   lower-middle class
(5)   lower class.
V11 Do you have a job in order to earn some money? If you do, what kind of job do you have?
(1)   Agriculture/fishery
(2)   Self-employed (owners of small-scale businesses with less than nine employees and family members, such as shop owners)
(3)   Sales/services
(4)   Technical/skilled
(5)   Blue-collar
(6)   White-collar and technician
(7)   Administrative and managerial
(8)   Professional and artists
(9)   Housewife
(10) Student
(11) Unemployed.
V12 What is your average monthly total household income? Please include the incomes of all your family members?
(1)   Less than 1 million won
(2)   1.00 – 1.50 million won
(3)   1.51 – 2.00 million won
(4)   2.01 – 2.50 million won
(5)   2.51 – 3.00 million
(6)   more than 3 million.
V13 Do you have a religion? If so, which?
(1)   Buddhism
(2)   Protestantism
(3)   Catholicism
(4)   Others
(5)   None.
V14 Do you own the place in which you live now?
(1)   Own
(2)   Rent/lease
(3)   Other arrangements.

References

Abramson Paul R. & Ronald Inglehart (1995). *Value Change in Global Perspective.* Ann Arbor, MI.: University of Michigan Press.

Ackerman, Bruce (1992). *The Future of Liberal Revolution.* New Haven: Yale University Press.

Adamski, Wkadtskaw (1992). "Privatization Versus Group Interests of the Working Class and Bureaucracy: The Case of Poland," in Peter M. E. Volten, ed., *Bound to Change: Consolidating in East Central Europe.* Boulder, CO.: Westview Press, 212–17.

Agh, Attila (1994). *The Emergence of East Central European Parliaments.* Budapest: Hungarian Center for Democracy.

Ahn, Byung-Young (1995). "Korean Politics After Slush Fund Scandal," *Korea Focus* 3 (6): 5–16.

Ahn, Chung Si, ed. (1994). *Junhwangiei Hankuk Minjujuui* (Korean Democracy in the Transition Period). Seoul: Bupmoonsa.

Alagappa, Muthiah (1995). "The Asian Spectrum," *Journal of Democracy* 6 (1): 29–36.

Alfonsin, Raul (1992). "What Democracy Needs is Democrats," *International Herald Tribune* (April 20): 4.

Almond, Gabriel & Sidney Verba (1963). *The Civic Culture: Political Attitudes and Democracy in Five Nations.* Princeton, NJ.: Princeton University Press.

Anderson, Christopher & Christian A. Guillory (1997). "Political Institutions and Satisfaction with Democracy," *American Political Science Review* 91: 66–81.

Andrews, Frank (1973). *Multiple Classification Analysis.* Ann Arbor, MI.: Survey Research Center, University of Michigan.

Andrews, Frank, ed. (1986). *Research on the Quality of Life.* Ann Arbor, MI.: Survey Research Center, University of Michigan.

Andrews, Frank & Stephen Withey (1976). *Indicators of Well-Being.* New York: Plenum Press.

Auchincloss, Kenneth (1992). "The Limits of Democracy," *Newsweek* (January 27): 28–30.

Auh, Soo Young (1992). "*Hankukinui Gachigbyonhwawa Minjuhwa* (Korean Value Shifts and Democratization)," *Korean Political Science Review* 25: 137–70.

Bae, Sun-Kwang (1995). "Korean Elections and Voters in the Transition to Democracy, 1985–1992," a Ph.D thesis submitted to the Australian National University.

Bae, Sun-Kwang & James Cotton (1993). "Regionalism in Electoral Politics," in James Cotton, ed., *Korea under Roh Tae Woo*. Sydney, Australia: Allen & Unwin, 170–84.

Barber, Benjamin (1984). *Strong Democracy: Participatory Politics in New Age*. Berkeley, CA.: University of California Press.

Barnes, Samuel (1982). "Changing Popular Attitudes Toward Progress," in Gabriel Almond, M. Chodorow & R. Pearce, eds., *Progress and Discontents*. Berkeley: University of California Press, 403–25.

Barnes, Samuel H., Barbara G. Farah & Felix Heunks (1979). "Personal Dissatisfaction," in Samuel H. Barnes & Max Kaase, eds., *Political Action*. Beverly Hills, CA.: Sage Publications, 381–408.

Barnes, Samuel H. & Max Kaase (1979). *Political Action*. Beverly Hills, CA.: Sage.

Barnes, Samuel, Peter McDonough & Antonio Lopez Pina (1985). "The Development of Partisanship in New Democracies: The Case of Spain," *American Journal of Political Science* 29: 695–721.

Barrow, Robert J. (1994). "Democracy: A Recipe for Growth," *Wall Street Journal* (December 1): 18.

Bedeski, Robert E. (1994). *The Transformation of South Korea*. London: Routledge.

Beetham, David (1992). "Liberal Democracy and the Limits of Democratization," *Political Studies* 40: 40–53.

Bell, Daniel A., David Brown, Kashka Jayasuriya & David Martin Jones (1995). *Towards Illiberal Democracy in the Pacific Asia*. New York: Morton Press.

Bermeo, Nancy (1990). "Rethinking Regime Change," *Comparative Politics* 23: 359–77.

——— (1992). "Democracy and the Lessons of Dictatorship," *Comparative Politics* 24: 273–91,

Bohrnstedt, George W. & David Knoke (1982). *Statistics for Social Data Analysis*. Itasca, IL.: F. E. Peacock Publishers.

Bollen, Kenneth (1993). "Liberal Democracy: Validity and Method Factors in Cross-National Measures," *American Journal of Political Science* 37: 1207–30.

Boyte, Harry (1990). *Commonwealth*. New York: Free Press.

Brady, David & Jongryn Mo (1992). "Electoral Systems and Institutional Choice: a Case of the 1988 Korean Elections," *Comparative Political Studies* 24: 405–29.

Brady, Henry E. & Cynthia S. Kaplan (1996). "Civil Society and Political Participation in Estonia and the United States," paper presented at the annual meeting of Midwest Political Science Association in Chicago, April 18–20.

Bratton, Michael & Nicolas van de Walle (1997). *Democratic Experiments in Africa*. Cambridge: Cambridge University Press.

Brull, Steven (1995). "Why Korea's Cleanup won't Catch on: Seoul's Neighbors Share its Corruption, but not its Political Will," *Business Week* (December 18): 52.

Bruszt, Laszlo & Janos Simon (1990–91). *The Codebook of the International Survey of Political Culture, Political and Economic Orientations in Central and Eastern Europe During the Transitions to Democracy* (unpublished document).

——— (1992). "The Great Transformation in Hungary and Eastern Europe: Theoretical Approaches and Public Opinion about Capitalism and Democracy," paper presented at the Georgetown University Workshop on Democratization and the European Public, Washington, DC.

Bunce, Valerie (1995). "Comparing East and South," *Journal of Democracy* 6 (3): 87–100.

Burkhart, Ross E. & Michael Lewis-Beck (1994). "Comparative Democracy: Economic Development Thesis," *American Political Science Review* 88: 903–10.

Burton, Michael, Richard Gunther & John Higley (1992). "Introduction: Elite Transformation and Democratic Regimes," in John Higley & Richard Gunther, eds., *Elites and Democratic Consolidation in Latin America and Southern Europe*. New York: Cambridge University Press, 1–32.

Butler, David & Austin Ranney, eds. (1992). *Electioneering*. Oxford: Clarendon Press.

Campbell, Angus (1981). *The Sense of Well-Being in America*. New York: McGraw-Hill.

Campbell, Angus & Philip Converse, eds. (1972). *The Human Meaning of Social Change*. New York: Russell Sage Foundation.

Campbell, Angus, Philip Converse & Willard Rodgers (1976). *The Quality of American Life*. New York: Russell Sage Foundation.

Caney, Simon (1992). "Liberalism and Communitarianism," *Political Studies* 40: 273–89.

Cantril, Hadley (1965). *The Patterns of Human Concerns*. New Brunswick, NJ.: Rutgers University Press.

Chan, Steve & Cal Clark (1992–93). "The Price of Economic Success," *Harvard International Review* 64: 24–26.

Cheng, Tun-jen & Lawrence Krause (1991). "Democracy and Development: With Special Attention to Korea," *Journal of North East Asian Studies* 10: 3–25.

Chey, Myung, Tai Whan Kwon & Doo Seung Hong (1989). *Sahoejosa Sibyeon (Ten Years of Social Surveys)*. Seoul: Institute of Social Sciences, Seoul National University.

Choe, Yonhyok (1997). *How To Manage Free and Fair Elections*. Goteborg, Sweden: Department of Political Science, Goteborg University.

Choi, Han Soo (1996). *Hankuk Sungojongchihak (The Study of Electoral Politics in Korea)*. Seoul: Daewangsa.

Choi, Jang Jip (1993a). *Hankuk Minjuijuui Iron (Theory of Korean Democracy)*. Seoul: Hangilsa.

———— (1993b). "Political Cleavages in South Korea," in Hagen Koo, ed., *State and Society in Contemporary Korea*. Ithaca: Cornell University Press, 13–50.

———— (1996). *Hunkuk Minjuui Jogungwa and Junmang (Conditions and Prospects of Korean Democracy)*. Seoul: Nanam.

———— (1997). "Hankuk Minjuui Teuksunggwa Jilnopen Minjuui Kunsulel Uihan Gwajai (Features of Korean Democracy and Tasks to Build a Democracy of High Quality)," paper presented at a conference "Korean Democratization, 10 years: Assessments and Prospects," Seoul, June 21.

Choi, Jang Jip & Hyun-Chin Im, eds. (1993). *Siminsahoeui Dojun* (Challenges of Civil Society). Seoul: Nanam.

Choi, Sang Yong, ed. (1997). *Democracy in Korea*. Seoul: Korean Political Science Association.

Chu, Yun-han (1992). *Crafting Democracy in Taiwan*. Taipei: Institute for National Policy Research.

———— (1996). "Taiwan's Unique Challenges," *Journal of Democracy* 7 (3): 69–82.

Chu, Yun-han, Hu Fu & Chung-In Moon (1997). "South Korea and Taiwan: the International Context," in Larry Diamond et al., eds., *Consolidating Third-Wave Democracies*. Baltimore: Johns Hopkins University Press, 267–94.

Clarke, Donald (1988). *The Kwangju Uprising: Shadows over the Regime Korea in South*. Boulder, CO.: Westview.

Clarke, Harold, Nitish Dutt & Allan Kornberg (1993). "The Political Economy of Politics and Society in Western European Democracies," *Journal of Politics* 55: 998–1021.

Close, David (1995). *Legislatures and the New Democracies in Latin America*. Boulder, CO.: Lynne Rienner.

Cohen, Joshua & Joel Rogers (1992). "Secondary Associations and Democracy," *Politics and Society* 20: 393–472.

Collier, David & Steven Levitsky (1997). "Democracy with Adjectives: Conceptual Innovations in Comparative Research," *World Politics* 49: 430–51.

Converse, Philip E. (1964). "The Nature of Belief Systems in Mass Publics," in Edward R. Tufte, ed., *The Quantitative Analysis of Social Problems*. Reading, MA.: Addison-Wesley, 168–89.

—— (1969). "Of Time and Partisan Stability," *Comparative Political Studies* 2: 139–71.

Copeland, Gary W. & Samuel C. Patterson, eds. (1994). *Parliaments in Modern World: Changing Institutions*. Ann Arbor, MI.: University of Michigan Press.

Cotton, James (1992). "Understanding the State in South Korea," *Comparative Political Studies* 24: 512–29.

Cotton, James ed. (1993). *Korea Under Roh Tae Woo*. London: Allen & Unwin.

—— (1994). *From Roh Tae Woo to Kim Young Sam: Politics and Policy in the New Korean State*. Melbourne: Longman.

—— (1995a). *Politics and Policy in the New Korean State: From Roh Tae Woo to Kim Young Sam*. New York: St. Martin's Press.

—— (1995b). "The Search for Political Opposition: The Next Challenge for Asian Democracy," in Sung Chul Yang, ed., *Democracy and Communism*. Seoul: Korean Association of International Studies, 141–57.

Crotty, William (1993). "Notes on the Study of Political Parties in the Third World," *American Review of Politics* 14: 659–94.

Cumings, Bruce (1989). "The Abortive Albetura: South Korea in the Light of Latin American Experience," *New Left Review* 173: 5–32.

—— (1997). *Korea's Place in the Sun*. New York: W. W. Norton.

Curtis, Gerald L. (1997). "A 'Recipe' for Democratic Development," *Journal of Democracy* 8 (3): 139–49.

Dahl, Robert A. (1971). *Polyarchy: Participation and Opposition*. New Haven: Yale University Press.

—— (1989). *Democracy and Its Critics*. New Haven: Yale University Press.

—— (1992). "The Problems of Civic Competence," *Journal of Democracy* 3 (4): 45–59.

Dahrendorf, Ralf (1990). *Reflections on the Revolution in Europe*. London: Chatto & Windus.

Dalton, Russell J. (1994). "Communists and Democrats: Democratic Attitudes in the Two Germanies," *British Journal of Political Science* 24: 469–93.

—— (1996). *Citizen Politics in Western Democracies*, 2nd edn., Chatham, NJ.: Chatham House.

—— (1997). "Citizen and Democracy: Political Support in Advanced Industrial Democracies," paper presented at the John F. Kennedy School of Government Workshop on Confidence in Democratic Institutions, Washington, DC.: August 25–27.

———— (1998). "Democracy and Its Citizens: Patterns of Political Change," (unpublished paper).

Desmond, Edward W. (1995). "The Legacy of Blood and Greed," *Time* (December 11): 17–21.

Diamond, Larry (1992). "The Globalization of Democracy: Trends, Types, Causes, and Prospects," in Robert Slater, ed., *Global Transformation and the Third World*. Boulder, CO.: Lynne Rienner, 31–69.

Diamond, Larry ed. (1994a). *Political Culture and Democracy in Developing Countries*. Boulder, CO.: Lynne Rienner Publishers.

———— (1994b). "Rethinking Civil Society: Toward Democratic Consolidation," *Journal of Democracy* 5 (3): 4–17.

———— (1996). "Is the Third Wave of Democracy Over?" (unpublished manuscript).

———— (1999). *Developing Democracy: Toward Consolidation*. Baltimore: Johns Hopkins University Press.

Diamond, Larry, Thomas Henriksen & Doh Chull Shin (1999). *Institutional Reform and Democratic Consolidation in Korea*. Stanford: Hoover Institution Press.

Diamond, Larry & Byung-Kook Kim (1998). *Consolidating Democracy in Korea*. Baltimore: Johns Hopkins University Press.

Diamond, Larry, Juan J. Linz & Seymour Martin Lipset, eds. (1990). *Politics in Developing Countries*. Boulder, CO.: Lynne Rienner.

Diamond, Larry, Marc Plattner, Yun-han Chu & Hung-Mao Tien, eds. (1997). *Consolidating Third-Wave Democracies*. Baltimore: Johns Hopkins University Press.

Dietz, Mary (1993). "In Search of Citizen Ethic," in George Marcus & Russell Hanson, eds., *Reconsidering the Democratic Public*. University Park, PA.: University of Pennsylvania Press, 173–85.

Di Palma, Giuseppe (1990a). *To Craft Democracies*. Berkeley: University of California Press.

———— (1990b). "Parliaments, Consolidation, Institutionalization: A Minimalist View," in U. Liebert & M. Cotta, eds., *Parliament and Democratic Consolidation in Southern Europe*. London: Pinter Publishers, 31–51.

———— (1993). "Why Democracy Can Work in Eastern Europe?" in Larry Diamond & Marc F. Plattner, eds., *The Global Resurgence of Democracy*. Baltimore: Johns Hopkins University, 31–51.

Dogan, Mattei (1997). "Erosion of Confidence in Advanced Democracies," *Studies in Comparative International Development* 32 (3): 3–29.

Dominguez, Jorge I., ed. (1994). *Authoritarian and Democratic Regimes in Latin America*. New York: Garland Publishing.

Dong, Wonmo (1997). "Civilian Democracy and the Politics of Leadership Change in Korea," in Christopher J. Sigur, ed., *Continuity and Change in Contemporary Korea*. New York: Carnegie Council on Ethics and International Affairs, 47–53.

Drakulic, Slavenka (1993). *How We Survived Communism and Even Laughed*. New York: Harper Perennial.

Dryzek, John S. & Jeffrey Berejikian (1993). "Reconstructive Democratic Theory," *American Political Science Review* 87: 48–60.

Duch, Raymond M. (1993). "Tolerating Economic Reform: Popular Support for Transition to a Free Market in the Former Soviet Union," *American Political Science Review* 87: 590–606.

———— (1995). "Economic Chaos and the Fragility of Democratic Transition in Former Communist Regimes," *Journal of Politics* 57: 121–58.

Easton, David (1975). "A Re-Assessment of the Concept of Political Support," *British Journal of Political Science* 5: 435–57.

Eberstadt, Nicholas (1992). "Taiwan and South Korea: The 'Democratization' of Outlier States," *World Affairs* 155: 80–89.

Eckstein, Harry (1998). "Lessons for the 'Third Wave' from the First: An Essay on Democratization," (unpublished paper).

Economist (1996). "Ex-Presidents on Trial," (March 23): 33.

———— (1997a). "The Trouble with South Korea," (January 18): 35–36.

———— (1997b). "Climbdown," (January 25, 1997): 34–35.

Ersson, Svante & Jan-Erik Lane (1996). "Democracy and Development: A Statistical Exploration," in Adrian Leftwich, ed., *Democracy and Development*. Cambridge: Polity Press, 45–73.

Evans, Geoffrey & Stephen Whitefield (1995). "The Politics and Economics of Democratic Commitment: Support for Democracy in Transitional Societies," *British Journal of Political Science* 25: 485–514.

Feng, Yi (1997). "Democracy, Political Stability, and Economic Growth," *British Journal of Political Science* 27: 391–418.

Finifter, Ada & Ellen Mickiewicz (1992). "Redefining the Political System of the USSR: Mass Support for Political Change," *American Political Science Review* 86: 857–74.

Fitzgibbon, Russell H. (1994). "Pathology of Democracy in Latin America," in Jorge I. Dominguez, ed., *Authoritarian and Democratic Regimes in Latin America*. New York: Garland Publishing, 2–13.

Flanagan, Scott & Aie-Rie Lee (1998). "Value Change and Democratic Reform in Japan and Korea," (unpublished paper).

Foley, Michael W. & Bob Edwards (1996). "The Paradox of Civil Society," *Journal of Democracy* 7 (3): 38–52.

Fox, Jonathan (1994). "The Difficult Transition from Clientelism to Citizenship," *World Politics* 46: 151–84.

Friedman, Edward (1994). "Generalizing the East Asian Experience," in Edward Friedman, ed., *The Politics of Democratization*. Boulder, CO.: Westview Press, 19–57.

Fu, Hu & Yun-han Chu (1996). "The Transformation of Civic Culture in Mainland China, Taiwan, and Hong Kong," paper presented at the annual meeting of the American Political Science Association, San Francisco, August 29–September 1.

Fuchs, Dieter, Giovanna Guidorossi & Palle Svensson (1995). "Support for the Democratic System," in Hans-Dieter Klingemann & Dieter Fuchs, eds., *Citizens and the State*. New York: Oxford University Press, 323–53.

Fukuyama, Francis (1992). *The End of History and the Last Man*. New York: Free Press.

———— (1995a). *Trust: The Social Virtues and the Creation of Prosperity*. New York: Free Press.

———— (1995b). "Confucianism and Democracy," *Journal of Democracy* 6 (2): 20–33.

———— (1997). "The Illusion of Exceptionalism," *Journal of Democracy* 8 (3): 146–49.

Gallup International Institute (1976). *Human Needs and Satisfactions*. Princeton: Gallup International Institute.

Gastil, John (1992). "Why We Believe in Democracy," *Journal of Applied Social Psychology* 22: 423–50.

Gibney, Frank (1992). *Korea's Quiet Revolution: From Garrison State to Democracy.* New York: Walker and Company.

Gibson, James L. (1995). "The Resilience of Mass Support for Democratic Institutions and Processes in the Nascent Russian and Ukrainian Democracies," in Bladimir Tismaneanu, ed., *Political Culture and Civil Society in Russia and the New States of Eurasia.* Armonk, NY.: M. E. Sharpe, 53–111.

––––––– (1996a). " 'A Mile Wide but an Inch Deep(?)': The Structure of Democratic Commitments in the Former USSR," *American Journal of Political Science* 40: 396–420.

––––––– (1996b). "Political and Economic Markets: Connecting Attitudes Toward Political Democracy and a Market Economy Within the Mass Culture of Russia and Ukraine," *Journal of Politics* 58: 954–84.

Gibson, James L. & Raymond M. Duch (1993). "Political Tolerance in the USSR," *Comparative Political Studies* 26: 286–329.

––––––– (1994). "Postmaterialism and the Emerging Soviet Democracy," *Political Science Researcher* 47: 5–39.

Gibson, James L., Raymond M. Duch & Kent L. Tedin (1992). "Democratic Values and the Transformation of the Soviet Union," *Journal of Politics* 54: 329–71.

Glain, Steve (1995). "South Koreans Say Bribes are Part of Life," *Wall Street Journal* (November 21): A15.

Glazer, Wolfgang & M. Mohr (1987). "Quality of Life: Concepts and Measurements," *Social Indicators Research* 19: 15–24.

Gould, Carole C. (1988). *Rethinking Democracy.* Cambridge: Cambridge University Press.

Gunther, Richard, Nikiforos Diamandouros & Hans-Jurgen Puhle, eds. (1995). *The Politics of Democratic Consolidation: Southern Europe in Comparative Perspective.* Baltimore: Johns Hopkins University Press, 1–32.

Gunther, Richard, P. Nikiforos Diamandouros & Hans-Jurgen Puhle (1996). "O'Donnell's 'Illusions': A Rejoinder," *Journal of Democracy* 7 (4): 151–59.

Gunther, Richard, Hans-Jurgen Puhle & P. Nikiforos Diamandouros (1995). "Introduction," in Richard Gunther, Nikiforos Diamandouros & Hans-Jurgen Puhle, eds., *The Politics of Democratic Consolidation: Southern Europe in Comparative Perspective.* Baltimore: Johns Hopkins University Press, 1–32.

Haberman, Clyde (1987). "Chun in Peace Offering to Student Protesters – U.S. Takes Role," *New York Times* (July 1): E1.

Hadenius, Axel (1992). *Democracy and Development.* Cambridge: Cambridge University Press.

Hadenius, Axel, ed. (1997). *Democracy's Victory and Crisis.* Cambridge: Cambridge University Press.

Haggard, Stephan & Robert R. Kaufman (1995). *The Political Economy of Democratic Transitions.* Princeton: Princeton University Press.

Hahm, Chaibong (1996). "Future of Korean Political Reform Drive," *Korean Focus* 4 (1): 5–11.

––––––– (1997). "The Confucian Political Discourse and the Politics of Reform in Korea," *Korea Journal* 37: 65–77.

Hahm, Chaibong & Sang Young Rhyu (1997). "Democratic Reform in Korea: Promise of Democracy," *Korea Focus* 5 (5): 38–49.

Hahn, Jeffrey W. (1991). "Changes in Contemporary Russian Political Culture," *British Journal of Political Science* 21: 393–421.

—— (1996). "Introduction: Analyzing Parliamentary Development in Russia," in Jeffrey Hahn, ed., *Democratization in Russia*. Armonk, NY.: M. E. Sharpe, 3–25.

Han, Bae Ho (1997). "Kim Young Sam Administration's First 4 Years," *Korea Focus* 5 (2): 1–17.

Han, Bae Ho & Soo Young Auh (1987). *Hankukui Jungchimoonhwa (Korean Political Culture)*. Seoul: Bummoonsa.

Han, Sung Joo (1974). *The Failure of Democracy in Korea*. Berkeley: University of California Press.

—— (1990). "South Korea: Politics in Transition," in Larry Diamond, Juan Linz & Seymour Martin Lipset, eds., *Politics in Developing Countries*. Boulder, CO.: Lynne Rienner Publishers, 313–50.

Held, David (1987). *Models of Democracy*. Cambridge: Polity Press.

Hermet, Guy (1991). "Introduction: the Age of Democracy," *International Social Science Journal* 128: 249–57.

Hibbing, John R. & Samuel C. Patterson (1994). "Public Trust in the New Parliaments of Central and Eastern Europe," *Political Studies* 62: 570–92.

Hibbing, John R. & Elizabeth Theiss-Morse (1995). *Congress as Public Enemy*. New York: Cambridge University Press.

Higley, John & Richard Gunther, eds. (1992). *Elites and Democratic Consolidation in Latin America and Southern Europe*. New York: Cambridge University Press.

Hirst, Paul (1994). *Associative Democracy*. Amherst, MA.: University of Massachusetts Press.

Horowitz, David (1990). "Comparing Democratic Systems," *Journal of Democracy* 1 (4): 73–9.

Hsiao, Hsin-Hung & Hagen Koo (1997). "The Middle Classes and Democratization," in Larry Diamond, Marc Plattner, Yun-han Chu & Hung-Mao Tien, eds., *Consolidating the Third Wave Democracies*. Baltimore: The Johns Hopkins University Press, 312–33.

Huang, The-fu (1997). "Party Systems in Taiwan and South Korea," in Larry Diamond, Marc Plattner, Yun-han Chu & Hung-Mao Tien, eds., *Consolidating Third-Wave Democracies*. Baltimore: Johns Hopkins University Press, 135–59.

Huber, Evelyn, Dietrich Rueschemeyer & John D. Stephens (1997). "The Paradoxes of Contemporary Democracy: Formal, Participatory, and Social Dimensions," *Comparative Politics* 29: 323–42.

Huntington, Samuel P. (1989). "The Modest Meaning of Democracy," in Robert Pastor, ed., *Democracy in the Americas: Stopping the Pendulum*. New York: Holmes and Meir, 11–28.

—— (1991). *The Third Wave: Democratization in the Late Twentieth Century*. Norman, OK.: University of Oklahoma Press.

—— (1996a). *The Clash of Civilizations and the Remaking of World Order*. New York: Simon & Schuster.

—— (1996b). "Democracy for the Long Haul," *Journal of Democracy* 7 (2): 3–13.

—— (1997). "After Twenty Years: The Future of the Third Wave," *Journal of Democracy* 8 (4): 3–12.

Hwang, Jong Sung (1997). "Analysis of the Structure of the Korean Political Elite," *Korea Journal* 37: 98–117.

Im, Hyon Jin & Ho Geun Song, eds. (1995). *Junhwanui jongchi Junhwanui Hankuksahoe (Politics of Transition and Korean Society in Transition)*. Seoul: Nanam.

Im, Hyug Baeg (1987). "The Rise of Bureaucratic Authoritarianism in South Korea," *World Politics* 39: 231–57.

—— (1994). "New Democracies and Structural Economic Adjustment," in Doh Chull Shin, Myeong Han Zoh & Myung Chey, eds., *Korea in the Global Wave of Democratization*. Seoul: Seoul National University, 123–36.

—— (1995). "Politics of Democratic Transition from Authoritarianism in South Korea," *Social Science Journal* 21: 133–51.

—— (1996). "Korean Democratic Consolidation in Comparative Perspective," paper presented at an international conference on "Consolidating Democracy in Korea," Seoul, June 19–20.

—— (1997a). "Jiyeondoegoitnun Minjujuui Gongowha (Delayed Democratic Consolidation and the Process and Problems of Political Democratization)," paper presented at a conference "Korean Democratization, 10 years: Assessments and Prospects," in Seoul, June 21.

—— (1997b). "The Compatibility of Confucianism and Democratic Civil Society," paper presented at the 17th World Congress of the International Political Science Association, Seoul, August 17–21.

—— (1997c). "The Critical Choice in 1997: Presidential Qualities," *Korea Focus* 5 (4): 1–15.

Inglehart, Ronald (1987). *Silent Revolution: Changing Values and Political Styles Among Western Publics*. Princeton: Princeton University Press.

—— (1988). "The Renaissance of Political Culture," *American Political Science Review* 82: 203–30.

—— (1990). *Culture Shifts in Advanced Industrial Society*. Princeton: Princeton University Press.

—— (1997). *Modernization and Postmodernization*. Princeton: Princeton University Press.

Inkeles, Alex, ed. (1991). *On Measuring Democracy: Its Consequences and Concomitants*. New Brunswick, NJ.: Transaction Publisher.

International Forum for Democratic Studies (1996). *Democracy in East Asia: Conference Report*. Washington, DC: International Forum for Democratic Studies.

Isaac, Jeffrey C. (1994). "Oases in the Desert: Hanna Arendt on Democratic Politics," *American Political Science Review* 88: 156–69.

Jackman, Robert & Ross Miller (1996). "The Poverty of Political Culture," *American Journal of Political Science* 40: 697–716.

Jacobs, Norman (1985). *The Korean Road to Modernization and Development*. Urbana, IL.: University of Illinois Press.

Jaung, Hoon (1997). "Korea: A New Democracy at a Crossroad," paper presented at a meeting on "Democratization, Party Systems, and Economic Growth" sponsored by the United Nations University, Kuala Lumpur, February 19–20.

—— (1998). "Institutional Reform and Democratic Consolidation in Korea," paper presented at the conference on "Institutional Reform and Democratic Consolidation in Korea," held at the Hoover Institution, Stanford University, January 8–9.

Jefferson, Thomas (1905). *The Writings of Thomas Jefferson*. (Memorial edition.) Washington DC.: The Thomas Jefferson Memorial Association of the United States.

Jordan, Mary (1995). "South Korea's Days of Reckoning," *Washington Post National Edition* (December 18–24): 16.

Jowitt, Kenneth (1992). *New World Disorder: the Leninist Extinction*. Berkeley: University of California Press.

Jung, Young-Dai (1993). "Kimyoungsam Datongryongui Gaihyok Inyomgwa Hankuk Minjuji (President Kim Young Sam's Reform Ideology and Korean Democracy)," *Korean Political Science Review* 27: 121–43.

Jung, Young-Tai (1997). "Yukgownghwakugwa Munminjongbuui Songgyuk (The Sixth Republic and the Character of Civilian Government)," paper presented at a conference "Korean Democratization, 10 years: Assessments and Prospects," Seoul, June 21.

Kaase, Max (1994). "Political Culture and Political Consolidation in Central and Eastern Europe," in Frederick D. Weil & Mary Gautier, eds., *Political Culture and Political Structure*. Research on Democracy and Society, Vol. 2. Greenwich, CT.: JAI Press, 233–74.

Karatnycky, Adrian (1997). "Freedom on the March," *Freedom Review* 28: 5–29.

Karl, Terry Lynn (1990). "Dilemmas of Democratization in Latin America," *Comparative Politics* 23: 1–21.

—— (1995). "The Hybrid Regimes of Central America," *Journal of Democracy* 6 (5): 77–86.

Karl, Terry Lynn & Philippe C. Schmitter (1994). "Democratization Around the Globe," in Michael T. Klare & Daniel C. Thomas, eds., *World Security: Challenges for a New Century*. New York: St. Martin's Press, 43–62.

Kellner, Douglas (1991). *Television and the Crisis of Democracy*. Boulder, CO.: Westview Press.

Kihl, Young Whan (1984). *Politics and Policy in Divided Korea*. Boulder, CO.: Westview Press.

—— (1994). "The Legacy of Confucian Culture and South Korean Politics," *Korea Journal* 34: 37–53.

—— (1995). "Political Democracy and Reform in South Korea: The Cultural Context of Democratization," in Sung Chul Yang, ed., *Democracy and Communism: Theory, Reality and the Future*. Seoul: Korean Association of International Studies, 455–91.

Kil, Soong-Hoom (1993). "Political Reforms of the Kim Young Sam Government," *Korea and World Affairs* 17: 419–31.

Kim, Byung-Kook (1994). "Politics of Democratic Consolidation in Korea," paper presented at the 16th World Congress of the International Political Science Association, Berlin, August 21–25.

—— (1996). "Parties, Elections, and the Party System Challenges of Democratic Consolidation in Korea," paper presented at an international conference "Consolidating Democracy in Korea," Seoul, June 19–20.

—— (1998). "Party Politics in Korea's Confucian Democracy: The Crisis of Success," in Larry Diamond & Byung-Kook Kim eds., *Consolidating Democracy in Korea*. Baltimore: Johns Hopkins University Press.

Kim, Byung-Kook & Jin Young Suh (1997). "Politics of Reform in Confucian Korea," *Korea Focus* (6) 5: 8–32.

Kim, Chong Lim (1984). *The Legislative Connection: The Politics of Representation in Kenya, Korea, and Turkey*. Durham, NC.: Duke University Press.

Kim, Chong Lim, ed. (1980). *Political Participation in Korea: Democracy, Mobilization, and Stability*. Santa Barbara: Clio Books.

Kim, Chong Lim & Yong-Gwan Kim (1995). "The Evolution of Obedience Norms in the National Assembly," *Asian Perspective* 19: 243–70.

Kim, Chong Lim & Seong Dong Pae (1981). *Legislative Process in Korea.* Seoul: Seoul National University Press.

Kim, Dae Jung (1998). "The Inaugural Address of the 15th President: Gooknangegbokgwa Jaedoyakei Sai Sidaerul Yeopsida (Let Us Open a New Era for the Nation to Overcome its Difficulties and Leap Again)." Seoul: the Office of the President.

Kim, Deog Ryong (1993). "Reform and National Development," *Korea and World Affairs* 17: 405–18.

Kim, Heemin (1995). "Building a New Party System: the Case of Korea," *Asian Perspective* 19: 195–219.

––––– (1997). "Rational Choice Theory and Third World Politics," *Comparative Politics* 30: 83–100.

Kim, Jae Yul (1993). "Democratization in Korea," in James Cotton, ed., *Korea under Roh Tae Woo.* Sydney: Australia: Allen & Unwin, 42–52.

Kim, Kwang Woong (1995). "Inherent Limits to Administrative Reform in Korea," paper presented at a conference organized by the Korean Association of Public Administration.

––––– (1996). "Structural Problems of the National Assembly," *Korea Focus* 4 (6): 36–46.

Kim, Kwang Woong & Sung Deuk Hahm (1997). "Democratization and Institutional Reform Under Kim Young Sam," paper presented at the 17th Congress of the International Political Science Association, Seoul, August 17–20.

Kim, Kwang Woong & Chan Wook Park (1992). "Public Attitudes Toward the National Legislature and Its Operation in the 6th Republic," *Korea Journal* 31 (2): 78–92.

Kim, Kyong-Dong (1997). "Confucianism, Economic Development, and Democracy," *Asian Perspective* 21: 77–97.

Kim, Myoung-Soo (1994). "Governmental Reform in the Republic of Korea," in Christopher J. Sigur, ed., *Continuity and Change in Contemporary Korea.* New York: Carnegie Council on Ethics and International Affairs, 33–46.

Kim, Sang Joon (1994). "Characteristic Features of Korean Democratization," *Asian Perspective* 18: 181–96.

Kim, Seong Wou (1997). "10th Anniversary of June 29 Declaration," *Korea Focus* 5 (4): 132–34.

Kim, Sunhyuk (1997). "State and Civil Society in South Korea's Democratic Consolidation," *Asian Survey* 37: 1135–44.

––––– (1996). "Civil Society in South Korea: Constraints and Ambiguities," *Journal of Northeast Asian Studies* 15: 81–97.

––––– (1998). "Civic Mobilization for Democratic Reform in South Korea," paper presented at the conference on "Institutional Reform and Democratic Consolidation in Korea," Hoover Institution, Stanford University, January 8–9.

Kim, Uchang (1993). "Cultural Construction: Politics and Culture in Modern Korea," in Hagen Koo, ed., *State and Society in Contemporary Korea.* Ithaca: Cornell University Press, 162–95.

Kim, Yong Ho (1994). "Party Politics and the Process of Democratization in Korea," in Doh Chull Shin, Myeong Han Zoh & Myung Chey, eds., *Korea in the Global Wave of Democratization.* Seoul: Seoul National University Press, 179–204.

Kim, Young Sam (1993). "Let's Join Forces for New Korea with Hope, Vision: His Inaugural Address," in Yonhap News Agency, ed., *Crusader for Democracy*. Seoul: Yonhap News Agency, 76–79

—— (1996), "1996 New Year's Address: Seigoeui Illeugoogga Geonsului Ggoomuil Nanoomio (Sharing the Dream to Build a First-Rate Nation in the World)," in the Secretariat of the President, ed., *Collections of President Kim Young Sam's Addresses*, vol. 3. Seoul: the Secretariat of the President.

Kinder, Donald R. & D. Roderick Kiewiet (1981). "Sociotropic Politics: The American Case," *British Journal of Political Science* 11: 129–61.

Kitschelt, Herbert (1995). *Party Systems in East Central Europe*, Studies in Public Policy No. 241. Glasgow: Center for the Study of Public Policy, University of Strathclyde.

Klingemann, Hans-Dieter (1997). "Mapping Political Support in the 1990s: A Global Analysis," paper presented at the John F. Kennedy School Workshop on Confidence in Democratic Institutions. Washington, DC, August 25–27.

Klingemann, Hans-Dieter & Dieter Fuchs, eds. (1995). *Citizens and the State*. New York: Oxford University Press.

Knight, Robin (1996). "A Global Moment of Truth," *U.S. News and World Report* (March 25): 49.

Knight, Robin & Victoria Pope (1994). "Back to the Future," *U.S. News and World Report* (May 23): 40–43.

Koh, B. C. (1997). "South Korea in 1996," *Asian Survey* 37: 1–9.

Koh, Byong-Ik (1996). "Confucianism in Contemporary Korea," in Wei-Ming Tu, ed., *Confucian Tradition in East Asian Modernity*. Cambridge, MA.: Harvard University Press.

Koo, Hagen (1993). "Strong State and Contentious Society," in Hagen Koo, ed., *State and Society in Contemporary Korea*. Ithaca, NY.: Cornell University Press, 231–48.

Korea-Gallup (1996). *Hankukinui Tupyohangtai (Korean People's Voting Behavior)*. Seoul: Korea-Gallup.

Korean Consortium of Academic Associations (1997). *Yoowolui Minjuhangjaenggwa Hankusahoe Sipyeon (June Mass Uprising and Korea Society in Ten Years)*. Seoul: Dangdae.

Korean Political Science Association (1995). *Korean Democracy Toward a New Horizon*. Seoul: Korean Political Science Association.

—— (1998). *Jaesibodae Daetongreongsungo Bunsukgwa Jungchigaehyok (Analysis of the 15th Presidential Election and Political Reform)*. Seoul: Korean Political Science Association.

Korean Political Science and Sociological Associations (1997). *Hankuk Minjuhwa Sibyon (Korean Democratization, 10 Years)*. Seoul: Korean Political Science and Sociological Associations.

Kornberg, Alan & Harold D. Clarke (1983). *Political Support in Canada*. Durham, NC.: Duke University Press.

Kristof, Nicholas (1995). "Ex-Seoul Chief Facing Verdict of Democracy," *New York Times* (December 4): A1, A4.

—— (1996a). "On Trial in South Korea, Ex-presidents Defend Coup," *New York Times* (March 21): A4.

—— (1996b). "At Crossroads of Democracy, South Korea Hesitates," *New York Times* (July 10): A3.

———— (1997a). "Seoul's Mighty, Once Immune, Now Feel the Arm of the Law," *New York Times* (October 14): A6.

———— (1997b). "Koreans Elect Longtime Dissident," *New York Times* (December 19): A1, A10.

———— (1997c). "Seoul's Departing President a Heroic Failure," *New York Times* (December 22): A6.

———— (1998). "Seoul Leader, Ex-Inmate Himself, is Slow to Free Political Prisoners," *New York Times* (March 10): A10.

Lagos, Marta (1997). "Latin America's Smiling Mask," *Journal of Democracy* 8 (3): 125–38.

Lakoff, Sanford (1996). *Democracy: History, Theory, and Practice.* Boulder, CO.: Westview Press.

Lane, Robert (1962). *Political Ideology.* New York: Free Press.

Lasswell, Harold (1951). *The Political Writings of Harold D. Lasswell.* New York: Free Press.

Lawson, Kay & Peter Merkl, eds. (1988). *When Parties Fail: Emerging Alternative Organizations.* Princeton: Princeton University Press.

Lawson, Stephanie (1993). "Conceptual Issues in the Comparative Study of Regime Change and Democratization," *Comparative Politics* 25: 183–206.

Leblang, David J. (1997). "Political Democracy and Economic Growth: Pooled Cross-Sectional and Time-Series Evidence," *British Journal of Political Science* 27: 453–72.

Lee, Aie-Rie (1993). "Culture Shift and Popular Protest in South Korea," *Comparative Political Studies* 26: 63–80.

———— (1994). "Culture Shift and Politicization in the Korean Public," *In Depth* 4: 63–80.

———— (1998). "Stability and Change in Korean Value," paper prepared for the 14th World Congress of the International Sociological Association, Montreal, July 26–August 1.

Lee, Aie-Rie & Sue Tolleson Rinehart (1995). "Korean Women's Politicization," *Women and Politics* 15: 53–83.

Lee, Aie-Rie & Yong U. Glasure (1995). "Party Identifiers in South Korea," *Asian Survey* 35: 367–76.

Lee, Gang Jo (1993). "KimYoungSamui Jidoryok Yoohyong (Types of Kim Young Sam Leadership)," *Korean Political Science Review* 27: 145–63.

Lee, Hyung (1995). "Local Elections Mark Return of Regionalism," *Korea Focus* 3 (4): 5–12.

Lee, Manwoo (1990). *The Odyssey of Korean Democracy.* New York: Praeger.

Lee, Nam Young, ed. (1993). *Hankukeui Sunko (Korea's Election).* Seoul: Nanam.

Lee, Yong Jo (1997). "Kimyongsamjongbu Gaehyokjongchi Dilemma (Dilemmas of The Kim Young Sam Government's Reform Politics)," paper presented at a conference "Korean Democratization, 10 Years: Assessments and Prospects," Seoul, June 21.

———— (1998). "Reforms Are Dead, Long Live Reforms: the Rise and Fall of Kim Young Sam's Embedded Reform," paper presented at the conference on "Institutional Reform and Democratic Consolidation in Korea," held at the Hoover Institution, Stanford University, January 8–9.

Leftwich, Adrian, ed. (1996). *Democracy and Development.* Cambridge: Polity Press.

Levine, Daniel (1990). "Paradigm Lost: Dependency to Democracy," *World Politics* 40: 377–394.

Lewis-Beck, Michael S. (1988). *Economics and Elections: The Major Western Democracies.* Ann Arbor: University of Michigan Press.

Liebert, Ulrike (1990). "Parliament as a Central Site in Democratic Consolidation," in U. Liebert & M. Cotta, eds., *Parliament and Democratic Consolidation in Southern Europe.* London: Pinter Publishers, 3–30.

Liebert, Ulrike & Maurizio Cotta, eds. (1990). *Parliament and Democratic Consolidation in Southern Europe: Greece, Italy, Portugal, Spain, and Turkey.* London: Pinter Publishers.

Lijphart, Arend (1991). "Double Checking the Evidence," *Journal of Democracy* 2 (3): 42–48.

Lindblom, Charles (1977). *Politics and Markets: The World's Political-Economic Systems.* New York: Basic Books.

Linz, Juan (1990a). "Perils of Presidentialism," *Journal of Democracy* 1 (1): 51–70.

——— (1990b). "Virtues of Parliamentarism," *Journal of Democracy* 1 (4): 84–91.

——— (1990c). "Transitions to Democracy," *Washington Quarterly* 13: 143–62.

Linz, Juan J. & Alfred Stepan (1996a). *Problems of Democratic Transition and Consolidation: Southern Europe, South America, and Post-Communist Europe.* Baltimore: Johns Hopkins University Press.

——— (1996b). "Toward Consolidated Democracies," *Journal of Democracy* 7 (2): 14–33.

Lipset, Seymour Martin (1994). "The Social Requisites of Democracy Revisited," *American Sociological Review* 59: 1–22.

Longley, Lawrence (1994). *Working Papers on Comparative Legislative Studies.* Appleton, WI.: Lawrence University.

MacDonald, Donald Stone (1990). *The Koreans: Contemporary Politics and Society.* Boulder, CO.: Westview Press.

MacKuen, Michael B., Robert S. Erikson & James A. Stimson (1992). "Peasants or Bankers?," *American Political Science Review* 86: 597–611.

Macpherson, C. B. (1977). *The Life and Times of Liberal Democracy.* New York: Oxford University Press.

Mainwaring, Scott (1993). "Presidentialism, Multipartism, and Democracy: The Most Difficult Combination," *Comparative Political Studies* 26: 198–227.

Mainwaring, Scott, Guillermo O'Donnell & J. Samuel Valenzuela, eds. (1992). *Issues in Democratic Consolidation: The New South American Democracies in Comparative Perspective.* Notre Dame, IN.: University of Notre Dame.

Mainwaring, Scott & Timothy R. Scully, eds. (1995a). *Building Democratic Institutions: Party Systems in Latin America.* Stanford: Stanford University Press.

Mainwaring, Scott & Timothy R. Scully (1995b). "Introduction: Party System in Latin America," in S. Mainwaring & T. Scully, eds., *Building Democratic Institutions.* Stanford: Stanford University Press, 1–34.

Mainwaring, Scott & Matthew J. Shugart (1997). "Juan Linz, Presidentialism, and Democracy," *Comparative Political Studies* 29: 449–71.

Manent, Pierre (1996). "On Modern Individualism," *Journal of Democracy* 7 (1): 3–10.

Mangahas, Mahar (1994). "Democracy and Economic Progress: The Filipino People's Perspective," paper presented at the XIII World Congress of Sociology in Bielefeld, Germany, July 18–23.

Manning, Robert A. (1995). "Korea: Culture of Retribution," *Los Angeles Times* (December 10): M1.

March, James G. & Johan P. Olsen (1995). *Democratic Governance.* New York: Free Press.

Marcus, George E. & Russell L. Hanson, eds. (1993). *Reconsidering the Democratic Public.* College Park, PA.: Pennsylvania State University.

McClosky, Herbert & John Zaller (1984). *The American Ethos.* Cambridge: Harvard University Press.

McDonough, Peter (1995). "Identities, Ideologies, and Interests: Democratization and the Culture of Mass Politics in Spain and Eastern Europe," *Journal of Politics* 57: 649–76.

McDonough, Peter, Samuel Barnes & Antonio Lopez Pina (1986). "The Growth of Democratic Legitimacy in Spain," *American Political Science Review* 80: 735–60.

———— (1994). "The Nature of Political Support and Legitimacy in Spain," *Comparative Political Studies* 27: 349–80.

———— (1998). *The Cultural Dynamics of Democratization in Spain.* Ithaca, NY.: Cornell University Press.

McDonough, Peter & Doh Chull Shin (1995). "Conservative Democratization and the Transition to Mass Politics in Korea," in Sung Chul Yang, ed., *Democracy and Communism.* Seoul: Korean Association of International Studies, 415–45.

McDonough, Peter, Doh Chull Shin & Jose Alvaro Moises (1998). "Democratization and Participation," *Journal of Politics* 60: 919–53.

McIntosh, Mary E. & Martha Abele Mac Iver (1992). "Coping with Freedom and Uncertainty: Public Opinion in Hungary, Poland, and Czechoslovakia, 1989–92," *International Journal of Public Opinion Research* 4: 375–93.

McIntosh, Mary & Martha Abele (1993). "The Meaning of Democracy in a Redefined Europe," paper presented at the Annual Meetings of the American Association for Public Opinion, St. Charles, Illinois, May 20–23.

McIntosh, Mary, Martha Abele Mac Iver, Daniel G. Abele & Diana Smelt (1994). "Politics Meet the Market in Central and Eastern Europe," *Slavic Review* 53: 483–512.

Mencius (1970). "Humane Government," in James Legge, ed., *The Works of Mencius.* New York: Dover Publications, Inc.

Mezey, Michael L. (1979). *Comparative Legislatures.* Durham, NC.: Duke University Press.

Miller, Arthur & Stephen Borrelli (1991). "Confidence in Government During the 1980s," *American Politics Quarterly* 19: 147–73.

Miller, Arthur H. & Gwyn Erb (1996) "Emerging Party Systems in Post-Soviet Societies: Fact or Fiction?", paper presented at the annual meeting of the International Society of Political Psychology, Vancouver, July 6–7.

Miller, Arthur H., William M. Reisinger & Vicki L. Hesli, eds. (1993). *Public Opinion and Regime Change: The New Politics of Post-Soviet Societies.* Boulder, CO.: Westview.

Miller, Arthur H., Vicki L. Hesli & William M. Reisinger (1994). "Reassessing Mass Support for Political and Economic Change in the Former USSR," *American Political Science Review* 88: 399–411.

———— (1995). "Comparing Citizen and Elite Belief System in Post-Soviet Russia and Ukraine," *Public Opinion Quarterly* 59: 1–40.

———— (1997). "Conceptions of Democracy Across Mass and Elite in Post-Soviet Societies," *British Journal of Political Science* 27: 157–90.

Mishler, William & Richard Rose (1994). "Support for Parliaments and Regimes in the Transition Toward Democracy in Eastern Europe," *Legislative Studies Quarterly* 19: 5–32.

———— (1996). "Trajectories of Fear and Hope," *Comparative Political Studies* 28: 553–81.

———— (1997). "Five Years after the Fall: The Trajectory and Dynamics of Support for Democracy in Post-Communist Europe," paper presented at the John F. Kennedy School Workshop on Confidence in Democratic Institutions, Washington DC.:, August 25–27.

Mo, Jongryn (1996). "Political Learning and Democratic Consolidation," *Comparative Political Studies* 29: 290–311.

Mo, Jongryn & Chung-in Moon (1998). "Democracy and Korean Economic Crisis," unpublished paper.

Moises, Jose Alvaro (1993). "Elections, Political Parties and Political Culture in Brazil: Changes and Continuities," *Journal of Latin American Studies* 25: 575–611.

Montero, Jose Ramon, Richard Gunther & Mariano Torcal (1997). "Democracy in Spain: Legitimacy, Discontent, and Disaffection," *Studies in Comparative International Development* 32: 124–60.

Moon, Bruce E. (1991). *The Political Economy of Basic Human Needs.* Ithaca, NY.: Cornell University Press.

Moon, Chung-In & Moon Ku Kang (1995). "Democratic Opening and Military Intervention in South Korea," in James Cotton, ed., *Politics and Policy in the New Korean State.* New York: St. Martin's Press, 170–91.

Moon, Chung-In and Yong-Cheol Kim (1996a). "A Circle of Paradox: Development, Politics, and Democracy," in Adrian Leftwich, ed., *Development and Democracy.* Cambridge: Polity Press, 139–67.

Moon, Chung-In & Song-Min Kim (1996b). "Democracy and Economic Performance in South Korea," paper presented at an international conference "Consolidating Democracy in Korea," Seoul, June 19–20.

Moon, Chung-in & Jongryn Mo, eds. (1998). *Democracy and the Korean Economy.* Stanford: Hoover Institution Press.

Morlino, Leonardo (1995a). "Democratic Consolidation: Definition and Models," in Geoffrey Pridham, ed., *Transition to Democracy.* Brookfield, VT.: Dartmouth Publishing Company, 571–90.

———— (1995b). "Political Parties and Democratic Consolidation," in Richard Gunther, Nikiforos Diamandouros & Hans-Jurgen Puhle, eds., *The Politics of Democratic Consolidation: Southern Europe in Comparative Perspective.* Baltimore: Johns Hopkins University Press, 315–88.

Morlino, Leonardo & Jose R. Montero (1995). "Legitimacy and Democracy in Southern Europe," in Richard Gunther, P. N. Diamandouros & Hans-Jurgen Puhle, eds., *The Politics of Democratic Consolidation.* Baltimore: Johns Hopkins University Press, 231–60.

Muller, Edward N. & Mitchell A. Seligson (1994). "Civic Culture and Democracy: The Question of Causal Relationships," *American Political Science Review* 88: 635–54.

Munck, Gerado L. (1994). "Democratic Transitions in Comparative Perspective: Review Article," *Comparative Politics* 26: 355–75.

Nathan, Andrew & Tiajin Shi (1993). "Cultural Requisites for Democracy in China," *Daedalus* 122: 95–124.

Nelson, Joan M. (1994) "Linkages Between Politics and Economics," *Journal of Democracy* 5: 49–62.

New York Times (1992). "Winning Ways in South Korea," (December 28): A10.

———— (1995). "The Upheaval in South Korea," (December 26): A14.

────── (1996). "Ghosts of Dictatorship in South Korea," (December 30): A10.
────── (1998), "Day of Hope in South Korea," (February 25): A22.
Nie, Norman H., Jane Junn & Kenneth Stehlik-Barry (1996). *Education and Democratic Citizenship in America.* Chicago: University of Chicago Press.
Nye, Joseph C., Philip D. Zelikow & David C. King, eds. (1997). *Why People Don't Trust Government.* Cambridge: Harvard University Press.
O'Donnell, Guillermo (1989). "Challenges to Democratization in Brazil," *World Policy Journal* 5: 281–300.
────── (1994). "Delegative Democracy," *Journal of Democracy* 5 (1): 55–69.
────── (1996). "Illusions about Consolidation," *Journal of Democracy* 7: 34–51.
O'Donnell, Guillermo & Philippe Schmitter (1986). *Transitions from Authoritarian Rule: Tentative Conclusions about Uncertain Democracies.* Baltimore: Johns Hopkins University Press.
Olson, David M. (1993). "Political Parties and Party System in Regime Transformation: Inner Transition in the New Democracies of Central Europe," *American Review of Politics* 14: 619–58.
────── (1994). *Democratic Legislative Institutions.* Armonk, NY.: M. E. Sharpe.
Olson, David M. & Michael L. Mezey, eds. (1991). *Legislatures in the Policy Process.* New York: Cambridge University Press.
Olson, David M. & Philip Norton, eds. (1996). *The New Parliaments of Central and Eastern Europe.* London: Frank Cass.
Pae, Sung Moon (1992). *Korea Leading Developing Nations.* Lanham, Maryland: University Press of America.
Paik, Young-Chul (1995). "Political Reform and Democratic Consolidation in Korea," *Korea and World Affairs* 18: 730–48.
Park, Chan Wook (1990). "Home Style in a Developing Polity," *Korea Journal* 30: 4–15.
────── (1993). "Partisan Conflict and *Immobilisme* in the Korean National Assembly," *Asian Perspective* 17: 5–37.
────── (1995). "Characteristics of Legislative Politics in Korea," *Korean Journal of Legislative Studies* 1: 14–38.
────── (1997). "The National Assembly in the Consolidation Process of Korean Democracy," *Asian Journal of Political Science* 5: 96–113.
────── (1998a). "Legislative-Executive Relations and Legislative Reform: Toward the Institutionalization of the Korean National Assembly," paper presented at the conference on "Institutional Reform and Democratic Consolidation in Korea," held at the Hoover Institution, Stanford University, January 8–9.
────── (1998b). "The Korean Presidential Election in December 1997: Kim Dae-Jung's Victory as a momentum for Democratic Consolidation," (unpublished paper).
Park, Chong-Min (1991). "Authoritarian Rule in South Korea: Political Support and Governmental Performance," *Asian Survey* 31: 743–761.
────── (1994). "Hankukeisuhui Bisungohjok Jongchichamyio (Non-electoral Participation in Korea)," *Korean Political Science Review* 28: 163–82.
────── (1997). "The Nature and Sources of Political Dissatisfaction in Democratizing Korea," paper presented at the 17th World Congress of the International Political Science Association, Seoul, August 17–21.
Park, Dong Suh & Kwang Woong Kim (1987). *Hunggugineh Minjujungchi Eishik (Democratic Consciousness among the Korean people).* Seoul: Seoul National University Press.

Park, Kil-Sung (1997). "Minjuwhawa Sahoejaedo Gaehyok (Democratization and Reform of Social Institutions)," paper presented at a conference "Korean Democratization, 10 Years: Assessments and Prospects," Seoul, June 21.

Park, Myung-Ho & Soo Chan Jang (1998). "Korean Voters as Rational Actors and their Political Learning Overtime," paper presented at the South Western Social Science Association convention, Corpus Christi, March 18–21.

Parry, Geriant, George Moyser & Neil Day (1992). *Political Participation and Democracy in Britain.* New York: Cambridge University Press.

Pasquino, Gianfranco (1990). "Party Elites and Democratic Consolidation: Cross-National Comparison of Southern European Experience," in Geoffrey Pridham, ed., *Securing Democracy.* London: Routledge, 42–65.

Pateman, Carole (1970). *Participation and Democratic Theory.* New York: Cambridge University Press.

―――― (1994). "Democracy at the Close of the Twentieth Century," keynote address presented at the International Political Science Association Round Table held in Kyoto, March 26–27.

―――― (1996). "Democracy and Democratization," *International Political Science Review* 17: 5–12.

Perlez, James (1994). "In Comeback, Communists in Hungary Win Majority," *New York Times* (May 30): 3.

Pinkney, Robert (1994). *Democracy in the Third World.* Boulder, CO.: Lynne Rienner.

Plasser, Fritz & Peter A. Ulram (1994). "Monitoring Democratic Consolidation: Political Trust and System Support in Central and Eastern Europe," paper presented at the 16th World Congress of the International Political Science Association, Berlin, August 21–25.

Pollack, Andrew (1996). "South Korean Ex-President, at Trial, Denies Taking Bribes," *New York Times* (February 27): A4.

―――― (1997). "Seoul Dusts Off an Old Law for a 'Familiar Threat'," *New York Times* (February 25): A3.

Powell, G. Bingham Jr. (1982). "Social Progress and Liberal Democracy," in G. Almond, M. Chodorow & R. Pearce, eds., *Progress and its Discontents.* Berkeley: University of California Press, 375–402.

Pridham, Geoffrey, ed. (1990a). *Securing Democracy: Political Parties and Democratic Consolidation in Southern Europe.* London: Routledge.

Pridham, Geoffrey (1990b). "Political Parties, Parliaments and Democratic Consolidation in Southern Europe: Empirical and Theoretical Perspectives," in U. Liebert & M. Cotta, eds., *Parliament and Democratic Consolidation in Southern Europe.* London: Pinter Publishers, 225–48.

―――― (1995). "The International Context of Democratic Consolidation: Southern Europe in Comparative Perspective," in Richard Gunther, Hans-Jurgen Puhle & P. Nikiforos Diamandouros, eds., *The Politics of Democratic Consolidation.* Baltimore: Johns Hopkins University Press, 166–203.

Prothro, James W. & Charles M. Grigg (1960). "Fundamental Principles of Democracy: Bases of Agreement and Disagreement," *Journal of Politics* 22: 276–94.

Przeworski, Adam (1991). *Democracy and the Market: Political and Economic Reforms in Eastern Europe and Latin America.* New York: Cambridge University Press.

―――― (1993). "Economic Reforms, Public Opinion, and Political Institutions in the Eastern European Perspective," in Luiz Pereira, Maria Maravall &

Adam Przeworski, eds., *Economic Reforms in New Democracies*. New York: Cambridge University Press, 132–98.

Przeworski, Adam, Michael Alvarez, Jose Antonio Cheibub & Fernando Limongi (1996). "What Makes Democracies Endure?," *Journal of Democracy* 7 (1): 39–55.

Przeworski, Adam & Fernando Limongi (1997). "Democracy and Development," in Axel Hadenius, ed., *Democracy's Victory and Crisis*. Cambridge: Cambridge University Press, 163–94.

Putnam, Robert D. (1993). *Making Democracy Work: Civic Traditions in Modern Italy*. Princeton: Princeton University Press.

Quade, Quentin L. (1991). "PR and Democratic Statecraft," *Journal of Democracy* 2 (3): 36–41.

Reisinger, William M., Arthur H. Miller & Vicki L. Hesli (1995). "Democracy and 'Democratic Values' among the Mass Publics in the Former Soviet Union," paper presented at the annual meeting of the Midwest Political Science Association, Chicago.

Reisinger, William M., Arthur H. Miller, Vicki L. Hesli & Kristen Hill Maher (1994). "Political Values in Russia, Ukraine and Lithuania: Sources and Implications for Democracy," *British Journal of Political Science* 45: 199–245.

Reisinger, William M. & Alexander E. Nitkin (1993). "Public Opinion and the Emergence of a Multi-Party System," in Arthur Miller, William M. Reisinger & Vicki L. Hesli, eds., *Public Opinion and Regime Change*. Boulder, CO.: Westview Press: 168–96.

Remmer, Karen (1993). "The Political Economy of Elections in Latin America, 1980–91," *American Political Science Review* 87: 393–407.

––––––– (1995). "New Theoretical Perspectives on Democratization," *Comparative Politics* 28: 103–22.

Republic of Korea Ministry of Finance and Economy & Korea Development Institute (1998). The *DJnomics*. Seoul: The Republic of Korea Government Printing Office.

Revel, Jean-François (1993). *Democracy Against Itself: The Future of the Democratic Impulse*. New York: Free Press.

Robinson, Pearl (1994). "Understanding Regime Change and the Culture of Politics," *African Studies Review* 37: 39–67.

Rohrschneider, Robert (1994). "Report from the Laboratory: The Influence of Institutions on Political Elites' Democratic Values in Germany," *American Political Science Review* 88: 927–41.

––––––– (1996). "Institutional Learning Versus Value Diffusion," *Journal of Politics* 58: 442–66.

Roniger, Luis & Ayse Gunes-Ayata, eds. (1994). *Democracy, Clientelism, and Civil Society*. Boulder, CO.: Lynne Rienner.

Rose, Richard (1992). "Escaping from Absolute Dissatisfaction: A Trial-and-Error Model of Change in Eastern Europe," *Journal of Theoretical Politics* 4: 329–71.

––––––– (1994). *What is the Chance for Democracy in Central and Eastern Europe?* Studies in Public Policy No. 236. Glasgow: Center for the Study of Public Policy, University of Strathclyde.

––––––– (1995). "Freedom as a Fundamental Value," *International Social Science Journal* 145: 457–71.

––––––– (1997). "Where are Postcommunist Countries Going?," *Journal of Democracy* 8 (3): 92–108.

Rose, Richard & Christian Haerpfer (1994). *New Democracies Barometer III: Learning from What is Happening,* Studies in Public Policy No. 230. Glasgow: Center for the Study of Public Policy, University of Strathclyde.

―――― (1996). *New Democracies Barometer IV: A 10-Nation Study,* Studies in Public Policy No. 262. Glasgow: Center for the Study of Public Policy, University of Strathclyde.

Rose, Richard & William Mishler (1994). "Mass Reaction to Regime Change in Eastern Europe: Polarization or Leaders and Laggards?," *British Journal of Political Science* 24:159–82.

―――― (1996). "Representation and Leadership in Post-Communist Political Systems," *Journal of Communist Studies and Transition Politics* 12: 224–46.

Rose, Richard, William Mishler & Christian Haerpfer (1997). "Social Capital in Civic and Stressful Societies," *Studies in Comparative International Development* 32 (3): 85–111.

―――― (1998). *Democracy and its Alternatives.* Baltimore: Johns Hopkins University Press.

Rose, Richard & Doh Chull Shin (1997). "Discerning Qualities of Democracy in Korea and Post-Communist Countries," paper presented at the 17th World Congress of the International Political Science Association, Seoul, August 17–20.

Rose, Richard, Doh Chull Shin & Neil Munro (1999). "Tension Between Democratic Ideal and Democratic Reality: the Korean Example," in Pippa Norris, ed., *Critical Citizens: Global Support for Governance.* Oxford: Oxford University Press.

Rosenberg, Tina (1995). *The Haunted Land: Facing Europe's Ghosts after Communism.* New York: Random House.

Rosenstone, Steven J. & John Mark Hansen (1993). *Mobilization, Participation, and Democracy in America.* New York: Macmillan.

Rueschemeyer, Dietrich, Evelyn Huber Stephens & John D. Stephens (1992). *Capitalist Development and Democracy.* Chicago: University of Chicago Press.

Rummel, R. J. (1995). "Are Democracies less likely warlike than other Regimes?," *European Journal of International Relations* 1: 447–79.

Russett, Bruce (1993). *Grasping the Democratic Peace: Principles for a Post-Cold War World.* Princeton: Princeton University Press.

Rustow, A. Dankwart (1994). "Dictatorship to Democracy," in Uner Kirdar & Leonard Silk, eds., *A World Fit for People.* New York: New York University Press, 54–66.

Sakong, Il (1993). *Korea in the World Economy.* Washington, DC.: Institute for International Economics.

Sanger, David (1997). "The Stock of 'Asian Values' Drops," *New York Times* (November 23): 4–1.

Sartori, Giovanni (1987). *The Theory of Democracy Revisited.* Chatham, NJ.: Chatham House.

―――― (1991). "Rethinking Democracy: Bad Polity and Bad Politics," *International Social Science Journal* 129: 437–50.

―――― (1995). "How Far Can Free Government Travel?," *Journal of Democracy* 6 (3): 101–11.

Scalapino, Robert A. (1993). "Democratizing Dragons: South Korea and Taiwan," *Journal of Democracy* 4 (3): 70–83.

―――― (1997). "A Tale of Three Systems," *Journal of Democracy* 8 (3): 150–55.

Schlesinger, Arthur (1997). "Has Democracy a Future?," *Foreign Affairs* 76: 2–12.

Schmitter, Philippe C. (1988). "The Consolidation of Political Democracy in Southern Europe," (unpublished manuscript).

——— (1992). "The Consolidation of Democracy and Representation of Social Groups," *American Behavioral Scientist* 35: 422–49.

——— (1994). "Dangers and Dilemmas of Democracy," *Journal of Democracy* 5 (2): 57–74.

——— (1995a). "More Liberal, Preliberal, or Postliberal?," *Journal of Democracy* 6 (1): 13–22.

——— (1995b). "The Consolidation of Political Democracies: Processes, Rhythmes, Sequences, and Type," in Geoffrey Pridham, ed., *Democratic Transitions*. Brookfield, VT.: Dartmouth Publishing Company, 535–69.

Schmitter, Philippe C. & Terry Lynn Karl (1991). "What Democracy Is and Is Not," *Journal of Democracy* 2 (3): 75–88.

Schmitter, Philippe C. & Javier Santiso (1998). "Three Temporal Dimensions to the Consolidation of Democracy," *International Political Science Review* 19: 69–92.

Schneider, Ben Ross (1995). "Democratic Consolidations: Some Broad Comparisons and Sweeping Arguments," *Latin American Research Review* 30: 215–34.

Schumpeter, Joseph (1976). *Capitalism, Socialism, and Democracy*. London: Allen & Unwin.

Schwartz, Barry (1987). *The Battle for Human Nature*. New York: Norton.

Seligson, Mitchell A. & John A. Booth (1993). "Political Culture and Regime Type: Evidence From Nicaragua and Costa Rica," *Journal of Politics* 55: 777–92.

Sen, Amartya (1993). "The Economics of Life and Death," *Scientific American* 268: 75–88.

Seong, Kyoung-Ryung (1996a). *Cheijei Byondonui Sahoehak (Political Sociology of Regime Transformation)*. Seoul: Haneul.

——— (1996b). "Civil Society and Democratic Consolidation in Korea, 1987–1996: Achievements and Unresolved Problems," paper presented at an international conference "Consolidating Democracy in Korea," Seoul, June 19–20.

——— (1998). "Delayed Decentralization and Incomplete Consolidation," paper presented at a conference "Institutional Reform and Democratic Consolidation" held at the Hoover Institution, Stanford University, January 8–9.

Seoul National University Institute of Social Development (1996). *Seigeiui Gahyok Hankukui Gaehyok (Global Reform and Korean Reform)*. Seoul: Institute of Social Development, Seoul National University.

Shim, Jae Hoon (1997a). "Here to Zero: In Just Four Years, President Kim Has Fallen Dramatically From Grace," *Far Eastern Economic Review* (March 13): 16–17.

——— (1997b). "South Korea: Rose-Tinted Glasses," *Far Eastern Economic Review* (July 17): 23.

——— (1997c). "Shall He Last?," *Far Eastern Economic Review* (May 15): 22.

Shim, Jae Hoon & Charles S. Lee (1997). "Blue House Blues," *Far Eastern Economic Review* (February 20): 16–17.

Shin, Doh Chull (1989). "Political Democracy and the Quality of Citizens' Lives: A Cross-National Study," *Journal of Developing Societies* 5: 30–41.

——— (1994). "On the Third Wave of Democratization: A Synthesis and Evaluation of Recent Theory and Research," *World Politics* 47: 135–70.

——— (1995). "The Quality of Mass Support for Democratization," *Social Indicators Research* 34: 1–15.

Shin, Doh Chull, Myung Chey & Kwang Woong Kim (1988). "Cultural Origins of Public Support for Democracy in Korea: an Empirical Test of the Douglas-Wildavsky Theory of Culture," *Comparative Political Studies* 22: 217–38.

Shin, Doh Chull, Kwang Woong Kim, Myung Chey & Chan Wook Park (1990). *Hankuk Minjujongchiui Mirae (The Future of Korean Democracy)*. Seoul: Seoul National University Press.

Shin, Doh Chull & Richard Rose (1997). *Koreans Evaluate Democracy: A New Korea Barometer Survey*, Studies in Public Policy No. 292. Glasgow: Center for the Study of Public Policy, University of Strathclyde.

Shin, Doh Chull & Huoyan Shyu (1997). "Political Ambivalence in South Korea and Taiwan," *Journal of Democracy* 8 (3): 109–24.

Shin, Doh Chull, Myeong-Han Zho & Myung Chey (1994). *Korea in the Global Wave of Democratization*. Seoul: Seoul National University Press.

Shin, Myungsoon (1993). "Hankuk Jongdanjaedoui Gaehyokui Pilyosung (The Need to Reform the Korean Party System)," paper presented at a seminar on "Party Reform and Political Funds," Seoul.

——— (1997). "Change and Continuity in South Korean Electoral Politics," paper presented at the 17th World Congress of the International Political Science Association, Seoul, August 17–21.

——— (1998). "An End to Costly Election Campaigning," *Korea Focus* 6 (1): 8–14.

Sigur, Christopher J., ed. (1993). *Korea's New Challenges and Kim Young Sam*. New York: Carnegie Council on Ethics and International Affairs.

——— ed. (1994). *Continuity and Change in Contemporary Korea*. New York: Carnegie Council on Ethics and International Affairs.

Simon, Janos (1994). "What Democracy Means for Hungarians," paper presented at the World Congress of the International Political Science Association, Berlin, August 21–25.

Sklar, Richard L. (1996). "Towards a Theory of Developmental Democracy," in Adrian Leftwich, ed., *Democracy and Development*. Cambridge: Polity Press, 24–44.

Sniderman, Paul (1975). *Personality and Democratic Politics*. Berkeley: University of California Press.

——— (1981). *A Question of Loyalty*. Berkeley: University of California Press.

Sohn, Hak-Kyu (1989). *Authoritarianism and Oppression in South Korea*. London: Routledge.

Sohn, Ho Chul (1993). "Hankukui Jongchigaehyok Model (The Korean Model of Political Reform)," paper presented at a seminar organized by the Korean Political Science Association.

——— (1995). *Haebanghu Osipyeonui Hankuk Jongchi (Fifty Years of Korean Politics Since Liberation)*. Seoul: Saegil.

Song, Ho Geun (1997). "Baejeidein Minjuhwawa Iubodein Ijungjonwhan (Exclusive Democratization and Stalled Double Transition)," paper presented at a conference "Ten Years of Korean Democratization: Assessments and Prospects," Seoul, June 21.

Soong, James (1992). "Political Development in the Republic of China on Taiwan," *World Affairs* 155: 62–66.

Sorensen, Georg (1993). *Democracy and Democratization*. Boulder, CO.: Westview Press.

Stanley, Alessandra (1995). "Anger at the Status Quo," *New York Times* (December 15): A10.

Steinberg, David (1995). "The Republic of Korea: Pluralizing Politics," in Larry Diamond, Seymour Martin Lipset & Juan Linz, eds., *Politics in Developing Countries*, 2nd edn., Boulder, CO.: Lynne Rienner, 369–416.

――― (1996). "Consolidating Democracy in South Korea," paper presented at an international conference "Consolidating Democracy in Korea," Seoul, June 19–20.

――― (1997). "Civil Society and Human Rights in Korea: on Contemporary and Classical Orthodoxy and Ideology," *Korea Journal* 37: 145–65.

――― (1998). "Korea: Triumph and Turmoil," *Journal of Democracy* 9 (2): 76–90.

Stepan, Alfred & Cindy Skach (1993). "Constitutional Frameworks and Democratic Consolidation: Parliamentarism versus Presidentialism," *World Politics* 46: 1–22.

Sullivan, John L., J. Piereson & G. E. Marcus (1982). *Political Tolerance and American Democracy.* Chicago: University of Chicago Press.

Sullivan, John L., Michael Shamir, Patrick Walsh & Nigel S. Roberts (1985). *Political Tolerance in Context.* Boulder, CO.: Westview.

Sullivan, Kevin (1995). "Culture of Corruption Bound Korean Companies, Officials," *Washington Post* (November 19): A21.

Szalai, Alexander & Frank Andrews, eds. (1980). *The Quality of Life.* Beverly Hills, CA.: Sage Publications.

Sztompka, Piotr (1991). "The Intangibles and Imponderables of the Transition to Democracy," *Studies in Comparative Communism* 24: 295–331.

Tarrow, Sidney (1994). *Power in Movement.* New York: Cambridge University Press.

Tedin, Kent L. (1994). "Popular Support for Competitive Elections in the Soviet Union," *Comparative Political Studies* 27: 241–71.

Thomassen, Jacques (1995). "Support for Democratic Values," in Hans-Dieter Klingemann & Dieter Fuchs, eds., *Citizens and the State.* New York: Oxford University Press, 383–416.

Thompson, Dennis (1970). *The Democratic Citizen.* New York: Cambridge University Press.

de Tocqueville, Alexis (1956). *Democracy in America.* Richard D. Heffner, ed. New York: Mentor.

Toka, Gabor (1995). "Political Support In East-Central Europe," in Hans-Dieter Klingemann & Dieter Fuchs, eds., *Citizens and the State.* New York: Oxford University Press, 354–82.

――― (1997). "Political Parties in East and Central Europe," in Larry Diamond, Marc Plattner, Yun-han Chu & Hung-Mao Tien, eds., *Consolidating Third Wave Democracies.* Baltimore: Johns Hopkins University Press, 93–134.

Tu, Wei-Ming, ed. (1996). *Confucian Tradition in East Asian Modernity.* Cambridge, MA.: Harvard University Press.

Vanhanen, Tatu (1997). *Prospects of Democracy: A study of 172 Countries.* London: Routledge.

Verba, Sidney, Norman Nie & Jae-On Kim (1978). *Participation and Political Equality.* New York: Cambridge University Press.

Verba, Sidney, Kay L. Schlozman & Henry E. Brady (1995). *Voice and Equality: Civic Voluntarism in America.* Cambridge, MA.: Harvard University Press.

Wade, Larry L. & Sung Jin Kang (1993). "The Democratic Breakout in South Korea," *Asian Perspective* 17: 39–70.

Wall Street Journal (1992). "Democracy Wins One," (December 22): A12.

Ward, Ian (1993). "Media Intrusion and the Changing Nature of the Established Parties in Australia and Canada," *Canadian Journal of Political Science* 26: 477–506.

Warren, Mark (1992). "Democratic Theory and Self-Transformation," *American Political Science Review* 86: 8–23.

Weffort, Francisco (1989). "Why Democracy?," in Alfred Stepan, ed., *Democratizing Brazil.* New York: Oxford University Press, 327–50.

———— (1993). "What is a New Democracy?", *International Social Science Journal* 136: 245–56.

Weil, Frederick D. (1989). "The Sources and Structure of Legitimation in Western Democracies," *American Sociological Review* 54: 682–706.

———— (1993). "The Development of Democratic Attitudes in Eastern and Western Germany in a Comparative Perspective," in Frederik D. Weil, Jeffrey Huffman & Mary Gautier, eds., *Democratization in Eastern and Western Europe.* Research on Democracy and Society, Vol. 1. Greenwich, CT.: JAI Press, 195–225.

———— (1994). "Political Culture, Political Structure, and Democracy," in Frederick D. Weil, Jeffrey Huffman & Mary Gautier, *Political Culture and Structure.* Research on Democracy and Society, Vol. 2. Greenwich, CT.: JAI Press, 65–115.

Weil, Frederick D., Jeffrey Huffman & Mary Gautier, eds. (1993). *Democratization in Eastern and Western Europe.* Research on Democracy and Society, Vol. 1. Greenwich, CT.: JAI Press.

———— (1994). *Political Culture and Structure.* Research on Democracy and Society, Vol. 2. Greenwich, CT.: JAI.

Wells, Kenneth M., ed. (1995). *South Korea's Minjung Movement: The Culture and Politics of Dissidence.* Honolulu: University of Hawaii Press.

Weyland, Kurt (1995). "Latin America's Four Political Models," *Journal of Democracy* 6 (4): 125–38.

Whitehead, Laurence (1989). "The Consolidation of Fragile Democracies: a Discussion with Illustrations," in Robert A. Pastor, ed., *Democracy in the Americas: Stopping the Pendulum.* New York: Holmes and Meier, 76–95.

Wong, Jan (1996). *China Blues: My Long Journey from Mao to Now.* New York: Doubleday.

Yang, Ho Min (1996). "Pathology of Political Parties," *Korea Focus* 4 (2): 20–3.

Yang, Sung Chul (1995). "An Analysis of South Korea's Political Process and Party Politics," in James Cotton, ed., *Politics and Policy in the New Korean State.* New York: St. Martin's Press, 6–34.

———— ed. (1995). *Democracy and Communism.* Seoul: Korean Association of International Studies.

Yoon, Dae Kyu (1990). *Law and Political Authority in South Korea.* London: Routledge.

Zakaria, Fareed (1997). "The Rise of Illiberal Democracy," *Foreign Affairs* 76: 22–43.

Ziegler, Charles E. (1997). "Transitional Paths of Delegative Democracies: Russia and South Korea," (unpublished manuscript).

Index

DATE DUE

| GAYLORD | | | PRINTED IN U.S.A. |